GOODNIGHT
CHILDREN
EVERYWHERE

AND OTHER PLAYS

GOODNIGHT CHILDREN EVERYWHERE

AND OTHER PLAYS

RICHARD NELSON

THEATRE COMMUNICATIONS GROUP
NEW YORK
2004

Goodnight Children Everywhere and Other Plays is published by
Theatre Communications Group, Inc., 520 8th Avenue, 24th Floor,
New York, NY 10018–4156

This publication is made possible in part with public funds from the New York State Council on the Arts, a State Agency.

Lyrics from "Goodnight Children Everywhere," written by Harry Phillips and Gaby Rogers, published by Cecil Lennox Ltd., a Kassner Group Company, Exmouth House, 11 Pine Street, London ECIR OJH. Lyrics from "The Bells of St. Mary's," written by A. Emmett Adams and Douglas Furber, published by Chappell & Co. Inc., c/o Warner Chappell Music Inc., 10585 Santa Monica Boulevard, Los Angeles, CA 90025. Lyrics from "Hernando's Hideaway," from *The Pajama Game*, written by Richard Adler and Jerry Ross, Lakshmi Puja Music Ltd. and The Songwriters Guild, 1500 Harbor Boulevard, Weehawken, NJ 07087. All rights reserved.

TCG books are exclusively distributed to the book trade by Consortium Book Sales and Distribution, 1045 Westgate Dr., St. Paul, MN 55114.

LIBRARY OF CONGRESS CATALOGING-IN-PUBLICATION DATA
Nelson, Richard, 1950-
Goodnight children everywhere and other plays / by Richard Nelson.
p. cm.
ISBN-13: 978-1-55936-244-3
ISBN-10: 1-55936-244-8 (pbk. : alk. paper)
I. Title.
PS3564.E4747G663 2004
812'.54—dc22
2004023864

Cover photo by Leslie Williamson
Cover design by Carol Devine Carson
Text design and composition by Lisa Govan

First Edition, December 2004

CONTENTS

Introduction
by Janice Paran
vii

SOME AMERICANS ABROAD

1

TWO SHAKESPEAREAN ACTORS

81

NEW ENGLAND

199

GOODNIGHT CHILDREN EVERYWHERE

275

FRANNY'S WAY

357

INTRODUCTION

There's a character in a Steven Dietz play, a Vietnam vet still retailing anecdotes from the sixties, who travels the world in pursuit of the Rolling Stones. He shows up at every concert venue with a hand-lettered sign and a mission: to make his way to the edge of the stage and hold up his sign, which bears the following legend: Just Stop.

Richard Nelson, it should be hoped, has received no such injunction. For more than twenty-five years he has written conscientiously, prolifically and importantly for the American theatre and, when his own country's stages have proved inhospitable, for British ones. With more than two dozen titles (comprising original plays, libretti and adaptations) to his credit, and new ones appearing at regular intervals, he has become a kind of cottage industry within the profession, a reliable purveyor of quality theatrical goods. Nowadays that sounds suspect; most contemporary playwrights are lucky to claim half a dozen really good plays, and many fizzle out, or move on, after two or three. Nelson has managed to stay in the game with distinction, and though talent, luck and perseverance have contributed to his longevity, they don't explain it. He has lasted because he takes the theatre seriously; he treats it as a complex, reflective and illuminating art that enriches the discourse of a healthy culture, and he writes for it accordingly. That is his vocation. Never one to tailor his subject matter or style to prevailing theatrical fashions or industry norms, he has consistently put craft over career. A good move, as it turns out.

His first professionally produced plays, dubbed his "reporter plays" because journalists feature prominently in them, introduced him as a writer singularly engaged by the moral and political failings of a post-Watergate era, and eager to frame those failings from a variety of perspectives. In *Yablonski* at the Mark Taper Forum in 1975, and again in *Jungle Coup* and *Conjuring an Event* (first seen in New York in the late 1970s), he raised tantalizing questions about how a story is told and who is telling it, musings that characterize much of his subsequent work in one way or another.

Over the course of the next decade, Nelson served a kind of extended apprenticeship in the American not-for-profit theatre, filling artistic posts at various regional theatres, immersing himself in the classical repertoire, and exploring new directions in his writing through a bevy of new plays (*The Vienna Notes, Bal, The Return of Pinocchio*, to name just three) and adaptations (including *Don Juan, The Suicide, The Marriage of Figaro, Three Sisters* and *Accidental Death of an Anarchist*). Those catch-as-catch-can years were a valuable prelude to what came later; they trained him to move with ease between the past and the present, the epic and the familiar in his writing, and they intimated a major talent in the making, but wide-scale recognition eluded him, and his itinerant professional life took its toll.

Principia Scriptoriae, produced at Manhattan Theatre Club in 1986, was a turning point. The play, a coolly provocative tale of two writers imprisoned in Latin America, caught the eye of the British director David Jones, who lobbied hard to stage it at England's Royal Shakespeare Company. Nelson was soon embraced by the RSC, which provided him the one thing he had not yet found: a theatrical home. He spent the better part of the next ten years as an Honorary Artistic Associate there, soaking up the contradictions of cultural identity and drawing inspiration from them. With the exception of *Franny's Way*, all the plays in this volume were commissioned and first produced by the RSC.

Some Americans Abroad, Nelson's first RSC commission, tackles a subject that a "foreigner" writing for an English company might safely undertake: the behavior of a group of American academics on an English theatre tour. Nelson had gone on one such trip himself as an undergraduate and had spent a year in Manchester after graduation, so presumably he had some personal experience to draw from, but his chosen theme was a shrewd one, nonetheless, since it allowed him—an upstart American playwright—to write for an English audience without writing about the English.

Exploiting his insider/outsider status to wicked effect, Nelson depicts an egregiously self-deluded crowd of penny-pinching Anglophiles as they dash from play to play, showcasing their cultural sophistication and congratulating themselves on their superiority to garden-variety American tourists, all the while turning a blind eye to their own craven conduct. While English audiences surely appreciated Nelson's ability to skewer American pretensions in the play's original outing, Americans may have the last rueful laugh, caught as we are in the play's mischievous double bind, guilty of the squirm-inducing behavior we readily denigrate. Still, Nelson's purpose is ironic, not satiric; he is less interested in sending up American affectation (though he does so with deadly and hilarious accuracy) than he is in examining its roots.

For the principal characters in *Some Americans Abroad*, most of whom are approaching middle age, England is sustenance, if more in fancy than in practice; it opens up horizons that have begun to shrink. Rather than face their diminishing prospects, the limits of their imaginations or their own pusillanimity, Nelson's tourists busy themselves with petty academic rivalries and political perorations, resurrect tales of their youthful rebellion, and cling to their notion of England as a cultural restorative, badly managed, to be sure, and spoiled by commercialism, but rich in provenance. England is the vessel into which they pour their sublimated yearnings, and when they gather at dawn on Westminster Bridge to recite from Wordsworth and sing "God Save the Queen," it's hard to miss the desolation, and the envy, in their bathos.

In 1849, the English actor William Charles Macready brought his touring production of *Macbeth* to New York's Astor Place Opera House. The American actor Edwin Forrest, meanwhile, staged a rival production at the Broadway Theatre. Tensions between the two companies escalated, and on May 9th of that year, thousands of

Forrest supporters amassed outside the Opera House to disrupt Macready's performance. A violent scuffle broke out between stone-wielding hotheads and the unarmed policemen on patrol. The militia, called in to restore order, fired into the crowd, and twenty-three people were killed. The Astor Place Riot, as it became known, was the springboard for Nelson's next play, *Two Shakespearean Actors*, which imagines the events that led up to that fateful evening.

Nelson frequently sets plays against a backdrop of social and political upheaval, and he could hardly have chosen a more combustible scenario in which to consider the relation between the artist and the larger world. It is a matter of historical record that Forrest, a fiercely patriotic performer and the first American actor to gain international acclaim, provoked Macready on more than one occasion; that Macready's choice of venue, the upscale Astor Place Opera House, was viewed as elitist by Forrest's mostly working-class supporters, and that a chauvinistic New York press further inflamed anti-British sentiment. But *Two Shakespearean Actors* is, more than anything else, a rough-and-tumble backstage drama about the egos, anxieties and aesthetics of two charismatic nineteenth-century actors—differently gifted—caught in the crossfire of a class and culture skirmish for which they're only partly to blame. Nelson, who knows and loves his theatre history, treats us to tasty chunks of their dueling Macbeths, their antithetical approaches to acting (a nineteenth-century version of the form vs. feeling debate), their backbiting and their brio. Theirs is a worthy contest, for all of their boorishness and bad manners, and they circle each other like pros, wary and grudging in their mutual curiosity. In the play's great final scene, where Nelson does history one better, Forrest gives temporary sanctuary to his rival, and as the world outside collapses into chaos, they talk shop, movingly, not in denial of their circumstances, but in tacit acknowledgment of them.

It is the drama *around* the drama that frequently captures Nelson's attention, which explains why the Astor Place Riot itself gets second billing in *Two Shakespearean Actors* and why *New England* begins, rather than ends, with a suicide. It makes for a stunning coup de théâtre—barely five minutes into the action, an onstage character puts a bullet through his brain—but it's almost as if, having dispensed with that grand gesture, Nelson can settle down to his real business, which is to observe the fallout. He writes about effects, not causes.

On the surface, *New England* might be seen as the inverse of *Some Americans Abroad*. A beautifully modulated drama about expatriate Brits living at loose ends in the United States, it turns the tables on the English/American cultural divide that gave Nelson his conceit for the earlier play. This time it's the English who find themselves alternately seduced and dismayed by their surroundings, and they're just as quick to disassociate themselves from their embarrassing countrymen as their counterparts in *Some Americans Abroad* are. ("The funny thing about living in America as a foreigner is the way you see other foreigners act," says one of them.) But for the characters in *New England* (the irony of the title speaks for itself), displacement is a condition, not a circumstance, and it defines them in complicated, often unspoken, ways.

The soon-to-be dead man is a music professor who moved to the U.S. twenty years earlier. He shares his comfortable Connecticut home with his girlfriend of two years, and it is she, along with a hapless weekend houseguest, who must play host to her dead lover's grown children and his twin brother when they all descend upon the house—a house that is home to none of them—in the hours after the suicide. The gathering is manic-depressive in the extreme, as reunions occasioned by sudden death tend to be, enlivened by trivial turf warfare, untempered eruptions of the id, ever-shifting familial alliances and periodic displays of America-bashing. Nelson astutely maps the underlying psychic territory, nudging us toward an awareness of how the father's life, of which we learn very little, has in fact cast its unhappy shadow on his children's fates. Their family diaspora, propelled by a certain self-destructive streak, has yielded scant comfort, and nobody seems to belong anywhere.

Nelson made several trips to Russia in the two years before writing the play, and it seems reasonable to suppose that it is a deliberate homage to Chekhov, and to *Three Sisters* in particular. So many echoes of the Prozorovs—a dead father, siblings who have lost their way, a sense of entitlement gone awry—can be heard in the hush and hubbub of *New England*. There are notable variations as well, including not one but two interlopers (the much-resented girlfriend and a diabolical French daughter-in-law who out-Natashas Natasha), along with the presence of the houseguest who—like similar "outsider" characters in other Nelson plays—

serves as adjudicator and onlooker. Nevertheless, the two plays share an essentially existentialist outlook; both create an experience of life lived while waiting for deliverance. If *Three Sisters* is, as the critic Richard Gilman has argued, a play about characters who do not go to Moscow, *New England* is a play about characters who already went. Except that Moscow is called America, and once they got there, they discovered that nothing had really changed.

It should be clear by now that the idea of home is central to Nelson, and nowhere is it more poignant than in *Goodnight Children Everywhere*. The time is 1945, the setting is a flat in South London, and the occasion is the homecoming of a seventeen-year-old boy, who was evacuated to Canada at the beginning of World War II. His parents have since died, and his three doting sisters—barely older than he is, though one is pregnant and married to a man more than twice her age—are on hand for his arrival, eager to resume their interrupted family life.

The play takes its title from a 1940 Vera Lynn recording whose nursery reassurances provided wartime comfort to a generation of Brits and whose sentimentality gave shape to emotional need. For the siblings in *Goodnight Children Everywhere*, the song has a private significance, one they invented as means of connecting to the memory of their parents, and Nelson's repetition of the tune underscores their vulnerability. Deprived of the solace that shared trauma can supply, they are children still, headstrong and homesick, learning all over again how the world works. Left to navigate the passage into adulthood without proper guidance, they wear their grown-up roles like dress-up clothes, and their long-awaited reunion, with its confusing reminders of long-ago rhythms and the heedless passage of time, discombobulates them all.

Goodnight Children Everywhere marked Nelson's transition to a newly invigorated American career. The play won London's Olivier Award for Best New Play in 2000, but by that time Nelson was already turning his attention homeward, and, increasingly, to his own directing. He mounted the play's American premiere at New York's Playwrights' Horizons in 1999, and at the same theatre later that year, he took over the direction of *James Joyce's The Dead*, his ravishing musical meditation (co-written with Shaun Davey) on Joyce's masterful short story. The musical moved to Broadway and to theatres around the country, winning Nelson new admirers and a new level of visibility on American stages.

Nelson wrote *Franny's Way* knowing he would direct it. Like all of his work, it has a specific milieu, and the incidents it touches upon are intimately related to time and place—in this case, Greenwich Village in the summer of 1957. Two teenage girls and their grandmother have made a trip from upstate New York to visit a young relative and her husband, who are still mourning the recent death of their infant daughter. The visit lasts a couple of days, during which time quietly momentous truths in their respective personal lives, agitated, it seems, by the sweet hot syncopation of New York City streets, burble to the surface in life-defining ways. Or so it seems to Franny. Not the teenaged Franny of 1957, who has shortened her given name in earnest homage to J. D. Salinger and who suffers her first heartbreak during that New York stay, but the Franny she will become decades later, the one who remembers thinking that Sullivan Street was "the very soul and center of the goddamn universe" the one Nelson has inserted as a narrator. He uses her sparingly; she neither opens the play nor closes it, and though she recounts a few details of what happens to the characters later, she in no way provides an epilogue. There is nothing conclusive about her; she is an intermediary between the fiction of the play and the fact of the audience, an agreed-upon convention, creating a context that gives texture and consequence to events as they unfold and reminds us of the mitigating hand of time.

She also reminds us, obliquely, of Nelson's hand. It is no accident that *James Joyce's The Dead* and the works that have followed it (*Madame Melville*, *Franny's Way*, *My Life with Albertine* and *Rodney's Wife*) all make use of narrators. Nelson's writing of late demonstrates his growing attentiveness to the myriad perplexities of everyday living and his shift to a style of dramaturgy that is more glancing in its reference to them; that leaves more and more to the imagination and to the actor's craft. His decision to direct his own work has probably contributed to an increased reticence on the page—he can fill in the blanks in the rehearsal hall, if necessary—but beyond that, there is a sense that he is impatient, at this point in his career, to find new forms for the impulses, perceptions and discoveries that make up his created worlds. Those worlds aren't abstract; they are character-based renderings of recognizable human experience, but they are distillations, refractions, as he is careful to suggest. It's hard to imagine him moving in a symbolist direction—he's too much of a humanist and an empiricist for that—but in these most recent works, realism, in the conventional sense, has given way to a more self-conscious theatricality. Franny, as narrator, makes explicit the questions posed by his earliest work: What is a story? How is it told? Who is telling it? She is there for her reasons, which are also his, persistently: to orient us to a view of the world, to locate—or devise—a path through its uncertainties. That is his vocation.

Janice Paran
DRAMATURG/DIRECTOR OF PLAY DEVELOPMENT
THE MCCARTER THEATRE CENTER
PRINCETON, NEW JERSEY
NOVEMBER 2004

SOME
AMERICANS
ABROAD

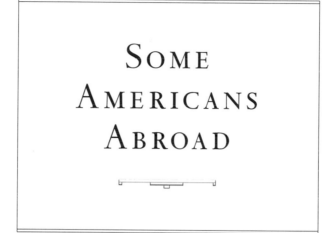

For Colin Chambers and Frank Pike

PRODUCTION HISTORY

Some Americans Abroad was commissioned by the Royal Shakespeare Company. It was first performed at The Pit in London on July 19, 1989. It was directed by Roger Michell; the design was by Alexandra Byrne, the lighting design was by Rick Fisher, the music was composed by Jeremy Sams; stage management was by Eric Lumsden, Sheonagh Darby and Sarah West Stevens and the musicians were Pip Hinton, Christopher Nightingale and Sandy Burnett. The cast was as follows:

JOE TAYLOR	Anton Lesser
KATIE TAYLOR	Kate Byers
PHILIP BROWN	Oliver Cotton
FRANKIE LEWIS	Diane Fletcher
ORSON BALDWIN	John Bott
HARRIET BALDWIN	Patricia Lawrence
HENRY MCNEIL	Simon Russell Beale
BETTY MCNEIL	Amanda Root
DONNA SILLIMAN	Caroline Harding
JOANNE SMITH	Candida Gubbins
AN AMERICAN	Joe Melia

Some Americans Abroad was subsequently produced by Lincoln Center Theater (Gregory Mosher, Director; Bernard Gersten, Executive Producer) at The Mitzi E. Newhouse Theater in New York on February 11, 1990. It was directed by Roger Michell; the design was by Alexandra Byrne, the lighting design was by Rick Fisher, the music was composed by Jeremy Sams; the stage managers were Michael F. Ritchie and Sarah Manley and the musicians were Michelle Johnson, Joshua Rosenblum and Michael Goetz.

The cast was as follows:

JOE TAYLOR	Colin Stinton
KATIE TAYLOR	Cara Buono
PHILIP BROWN	John Bedford Lloyd
FRANKIE LEWIS	Frances Conroy
ORSON BALDWIN	Henderson Forsythe
HARRIET BALDWIN	Jane Hoffman
HENRY MCNEIL	Bob Balaban
BETTY MCNEIL	Kate Burton
DONNA SILLIMAN	Elisabeth Shue
JOANNE SMITH	Ann Talman
AN AMERICAN	John Rothman

Characters

JOE TAYLOR, recently appointed Chairman of
the English Department, thirty-eight

KATIE TAYLOR, his daughter, attends the college, eighteen

PHILIP BROWN, Professor of English, thirty-seven

FRANKIE LEWIS, Associate Professor of English, forty-one

ORSON BALDWIN, retired Chairman of
the English Department, late sixties

HARRIET BALDWIN, his wife, sixties

HENRY MCNEIL, Assistant Professor of English, thirty-five

BETTY MCNEIL, his wife, thirty-six

DONNA SILLIMAN, a student at the college, twenty

JOANNE SMITH, a graduate of the college, twenty-six

AN AMERICAN, forties

All the characters are American.

Setting

1989, various locations in England

Each scene has a title—the location of the scene—which should
be projected moments before the scene begins.

ACT ONE

SCENE I

LUIGI'S RESTAURANT IN COVENT GARDEN

Joe Taylor, Henry and Betty McNeil, Frankie Lewis, Philip Brown and Katie Taylor around a table, toward the end of their meal.

JOE *(To Philip)*: First, that does not mean I am in favor of a nuclear war—

PHILIP: You are arguing for a situation that will make such a war more—

JOE: Let me finish!

(The rest of the table only halfheartedly listens to this conversation as they finish their meals, sip their coffee, finish their wine, etc.)

(To the others) He twists everything. Anyone else want to jump in, go right ahead. Put me out of my misery. *(Laughs)*

PHILIP *(To the others)*: I'm waiting for him to get to Gorbachev—

JOE: Gorbachev supports me! The whole idea of Gorbachev supports my argument! *(To the others)* We got Gorbachev, didn't we? *(Turns to Philip)* Philip, what could be clearer? Please.

7

What I have been saying, the point to be made here is—to go
out and protest— To— What? Chain yourself to some gate of
some plant or some boat or whatever—

PHILIP: Frankie, pass me the last of that wine, please. That's if no one—

HENRY: No, no. It's yours. *(Turns to his wife)* Betty?

BETTY: I'm fine.

(Frankie passes the wine. Philip pours into his glass.)

JOE: If you don't want to—

PHILIP: Go ahead.

(Beat.)

JOE: I want to know what's the purpose in all that? In the protesting. What? *(Beat)* Disarmament??? *(Beat)* Come on, what
does that mean?

FRANKIE: What does dis—?

JOE: When one says one is quote unquote for disarmament, what
does one mean? Peace???? *(Beat)* Who the hell isn't interested
in peace?

PHILIP: It's about creating a pressure . . .

JOE: A unilateral pressure? What the hell is that? Is anyone really
suggesting—seriously suggesting—that we should just junk
our bombs? *(Beat)* Of course they're not. They are suggesting—demanding that we keep negotiating. Well—I agree!
(Beat) If that is the purpose of these adventures, then I agree
with them. I agree with the purpose.

PHILIP: But now you'll argue that such actions as these protests,
they only make the country weaker which only makes real
negotiations less—

JOE: I'm not saying that. Don't paint me into that corner, OK? *(Beat)*
Jesus Christ, I am a goddamn liberal, Philip. *(Beat)* Listen to me.
You are not listening. *(Beat. To the others)* Am I that hard to
understand? *(To Philip)* If the point of protesting is simply to
pressure negotiations. Fine. I understand this. This is not what
I'm criticizing. *(Finishes his wine)* My point is the intellectual
dishonesty involved in saying one is for disarmament when
everyone is for disarmament. It's like saying you're *for* love!

PHILIP *(To the others)*: There was a time actually not too many years
ago— *(Laughs)*

JOE: I know. And we learned something from that, didn't we? *(Beat)* I did. Let's not delude ourselves that we are actually changing things. Or changing much. It is truth, honesty that I'm after. *Say* what you're doing! *Say* what you mean! For Christ's sake is it so hard to be honest? *(Beat)* I know things are complicated these days but you know what I think—I think things have always been complicated. *(Beat)* The man who wrote *Hamlet* understood that the world was complicated.

(Short pause.)

PHILIP: This is true. Good point.

HENRY: Are we off political science and on to literature now?

PHILIP: If we are, then the perfect example which refutes you, Joe, is that piece of intellectual mush we sat through this afternoon. Talk about idiotic debates.

JOE *(To the others)*: I knew he was getting to this. *(Smiles)* Look, it's a beautiful play. And that's not just my opinion.

HENRY: It's anthologized—

PHILIP: Straw men—set up to be knocked down. That's how Shaw works. The world presented in that play was *tricky*, not complicated. Shaw enjoyed trickiness, not real thinking.

JOE: And that is one opinion. *(To the others)* Shaw's reputation this half-century has gone up and down, up and down. *(Laughs)*

PHILIP: The world today makes such a play ridiculous.

JOE: Come on, it was funny. You laughed.

PHILIP: I laughed. At a play. I didn't appreciate the effort at political argument. Or rather the trivialization of political argument. *(Beat)* Look, in the end I think we're saying the same thing. The world is complicated. Too complicated for a George Bernard Shaw to express—

JOE: I think that play is very profound.

HENRY: You teach it in your Modern Brit class, don't you?

JOE: Yes, I do, Henry, thank you. *(Beat. To Philip)* It may be a little schematic—

PHILIP: You mean a little watered down.

JOE: But a schematic argument sometimes is the best way to present a complex moral position. Breaking the argument apart piece by piece, it illuminates the position. Or the conundrum. If

that's what it is. Often in surprising ways. If you'd like I'll
show you what I mean.

PHILIP: Look everyone, I'm sorry for getting him started.

FRANKIE: I doubt if you could have stopped him.

JOE: That's not funny.

HENRY: It's interesting, really.

BETTY: Very interesting.

JOE: Thank you. *(To Philip and Frankie)* You want me to show you
or not? *(Beat)* So—capital punishment. I'll make my point
with that. Let me ask Frankie. A woman we all know who has
strong moral opinions.

FRANKIE: Since when? *(Laughs)* He must have got me confused
with someone else. How much wine *are* we drinking?

(Laughter.)

JOE: Capital punishment, Frankie. Good or bad? *(Beat)* Come on,
good or bad?

FRANKIE: Bad. Of course. Morally indefensible.

JOE: You are sure of that?

FRANKIE: Yes. Yes I am sure, Joe.

JOE: But if I were to present an argument—

FRANKIE: For vengeance? If you believe in vengeance then of
course—

JOE: Not vengeance. *(To the others)* Here now is our complicated
world at work. *(Beat)* While I was in grad school, I was moon-
lighting for a small paper. I interviewed a guy in prison. A
killer. Sentenced to *life* imprisonment. He was first sentenced
to death, but now it was life imprisonment.

PHILIP: After the Supreme Court knocked down—

JOE: Yeah. Whatever. Well, Buddy—that's the guy's name; I went
to see Buddy. And he started to tell me that *he* favored the death
penalty. A killer in prison!

FRANKIE: Well—a death wish. Like that man in— Where was it?
Utah? Nevada?

JOE: No. No, there's no death wish, Frankie. When his sentence was
changed to life, he was very very happy about that. He did not
want to die. *(Beat)* Here's what he said: because he was under
a life sentence—actually three, he'd murdered three people and
he'd no possibility for parole—the guards in the prison, they

knew there was nothing, no recourse left for them if Buddy tried to do something. I mean, he was there for good, for*ever*. There was *no* deterrent. Get it? *(Beat)* So they treated Buddy like an animal. *(Beat)* Why wouldn't they, right? *(Beat)* And this—as you can imagine—dehumanized our Buddy. So—he told me—he thought there should be a death penalty for people who were in prison for life but who *then* kill a prison guard. This would be his one case when the death penalty would apply.

(Short pause.)

PHILIP: Interesting.

JOE: Isn't it?

FRANKIE: I'd never heard—

JOE: Buddy's argument is in favor of treating people like human beings. In this case the threat of death *helps* the prisoner.

HENRY: You should write an article, Joe; you've got something that's publishable.

JOE: Thank you. *(To Frankie)* Now you see the problem. As any philosopher knows—you find *one* case that is acceptable, in this case where *killing* is acceptable; then the *moral* argument falls by the wayside. It's all case by case then, instead of a debate about *morality*.

FRANKIE: Which is what we're always trying to achieve with abortion.

JOE: Exactly. *(Short Pause)* Don't get me wrong, I think the death penalty is inhuman. I'm just saying, see how tricky things can get? *(Beat)* Not to wax pretentious, but I do think the mind is really quite extraordinary. *(Beat)* The pursuit of truth is a bumpy road. But one we all have chosen to follow. Or we wouldn't be teachers.

HENRY: Beautifully said, Joe.

PHILIP: But what the hell does any of that have to do with a hack playwright like Shaw?

(He laughs; the others laugh.)

JOE *(Laughing)*: Nothing. Nothing at all, Phil!

(Pause. They sip their coffee.)

HENRY: What a provocative discussion.

FRANKIE: Katie, this must be very boring for you.

JOE: Nah, she's used to it. She can take it.

KATIE: You should see him at home. Dinner's like a senior seminar.

(Some light laughter.)

PHILIP: Lunch with Joe in the canteen is like a senior seminar.

FRANKIE: Mary says being married to him is like living in a senior seminar!

(Laughter.)

JOE: OK. OK. It's not all that funny. *(Beat. To Katie)* I hope, young lady, you do not treat all of your teachers with such disrespect.

KATIE: I promise I save all of my disrespect for my father.

(Laughter.)

BETTY: Very good!

HENRY *(Shushing her, under his breath)*: Betty!

FRANKIE *(Over this exchange)*: As any child should!

(Laughter.)

PHILIP: Or does, you mean!

(Laughter. Pause. Philip picks up the bill and looks at it.)

HENRY: Is that the check?

PHILIP: Yes.

(He hands Henry the bill.)

BETTY: Katie, your father was telling me this afternoon that you've not been to England before.

KATIE: No I haven't.

BETTY: How exciting it all must be for you.

KATIE: I'm having a good time. *(Beat)* The plays are great.

HENRY: Aren't they. *(Puts the bill back down)* When do we go to Stratford?

JOE: Next Thursday. *(To Frankie)* Next Thursday?

(She nods.)

BETTY *(To Katie)*: You'll love Stratford.
HENRY *(To Katie)*: You'll come back to England in maybe ten years, Katie, and it'll all still be here. That's what I love about England. *(Beat)* We first came ten years ago.

(Short pause.)

FRANKIE: Last year's plays were better, I think.
BETTY: Do you? Then they must have been really marvelous because so far— *(Stops herself)*
FRANKIE: I wasn't saying that this year's—
BETTY: No, no. I know you weren't.

(Short pause.)

KATIE: The play today wasn't bad.
JOE: Hear that, Phil? That's one for me. *(To Katie)* Good for you.
KATIE: The woman who played Barbara, she was great, I thought.
FRANKIE: She *was* good.
HENRY: Excellent.

(Short pause.)

KATIE: The Undershaft, wasn't he in *Jewel in the Crown?*
HENRY: Was he?
KATIE: I think so.
PHILIP: Hmmmmmm. *(To Henry)* You saw *Jewel in the Crown*, didn't you?
HENRY: Not all of it.
PHILIP: Treat yourself. When it comes back on—
BETTY: We will.

(Short pause.)

JOE: Mary sends her best.
FRANKIE: You talked to her?

JOE: Katie and I did. *(Beat)* It's her birthday.
PHILIP: Really? What a shame not to have you—
JOE: She understands. *(Beat)* It was important to her that Katie could come. So she's happy.

(Short pause.)

PHILIP: Well—happy birthday, Mary!
THE OTHERS: Yes, happy birthday.

(Pause.)

JOE: Maybe we should pay this. *(He takes the bill. Short pause. He turns to Frankie)* What did you have Frankie?
FRANKIE: The veal.
JOE: Right. So should I be banker? *(Beat)* Let's see that's . . .
FRANKIE *(Taking out money)*: Will this cover it?
JOE: One second.
BETTY *(To Henry)*: What did we have?
HENRY: I had the lasagna. That was six pounds ten pence.
PHILIP: Plus tax and tip.
FRANKIE: I forgot about the tip. *(Reaches into her purse for more money)*
BETTY *(Putting money down)*: This I'm sure will be plenty. *(Beat)* Won't it?
JOE: And the wine? Do we all put in for the wine?
PHILIP: I certainly do. I must have had—
HENRY: I only had one glass. How much is one glass?
JOE: I'll figure it out. A bottle was— How many glasses in a bottle?
BETTY: Five. No more than five. They're big glasses.
KATIE: Dad—
JOE: Put your money away, I'll pay for you.
KATIE: But I have money.
JOE: Save it. In this town, you'll need it, trust me.
FRANKIE: Did the salad come with the entrée?
KATIE: I had ice cream.
JOE: I have that.
KATIE: And a coffee.
PHILIP: So did I.
BETTY: Wasn't that an espresso?
PHILIP: Yes, yes, I'm sorry. Is that more?

JOE: One at a time. I have to do one at a time. This is getting too complicated.

SCENE 2

A garden behind a small cottage. A few tables, chairs. A path leads off in one direction. Harriet Baldwin, with a tray of tea, cups, etc., and Katie.

HARRIET: They must have gone down the path. He must be showing them Lamb House. If you want to catch up—
KATIE: No, thanks.

(Short pause. Katie rubs her shoulders as Harriet begins to set a table for tea.)

HARRIET: You're not chilled, are you? We could sit inside. I suppose it may seem a little nippy.
KATIE: I'm fine. I have the sweater. And my coat is just—
HARRIET *(Not listening)*: I find it— Such weather. I don't know. Just bloody invigorating. One learns after all these years what the British see in their gardens. *(Almost drops a teacup)*
KATIE: Mrs. Baldwin, you're sure I can't—
HARRIET: Lamb House is where Henry James lived.
KATIE: I know. Dad read all about it to me on the train.
HARRIET: It's much bigger than this house. He got the gout there. *(Short pause)* I suppose it's half the reason Professor Baldwin and I have retired to here, if the truth be told.
KATIE: So Dad says.
HARRIET: Jamesian Sussex. *(Beat)* Just the name is quite seductive. Though we very seriously considered Dickensian London. At first I favored this. We even checked out a flat near the East End. *(Beat)* The Barbican Towers. Lovely. *(Beat)* Beautiful fountain. *(Beat)* Daniel Defoe Tower it was in. We both feel Defoe a very underrated writer. But they gave him a nice tower though. Your father, of course, Katie, kept suggesting Liverpool because of Hawthorne having been consul there. *(Beat)*

We took the train up. *(Beat)* I don't think your father's ever really been to Liverpool.

KATIE: I don't know.

HARRIET: There's Wordsworth country, of course. We thought of this. *(Beat)* Stratford obviously was out of the question. One might as well be living in Connecticut. *(Beat. She blows on her hands)* It's not that much warmer in there. The central heating is being put in. If we had known how much that would cost— But we did get all this for a very modest price. Something like this in the States— Something historic like this— *(Beat)* You couldn't touch it. We couldn't have touched it. *(Beat)* We consider ourselves very lucky, Katie. Very lucky. *(Finishes setting the table)* English, isn't it?

KATIE: I'm sorry?

HARRIET: Joe's hooked you for the department, I understand.

KATIE: Oh. Yes. I'm an English major now.

HARRIET: Excellent. A great department. Professor Baldwin knew how to pick teachers. So even though we're retired . . . *(Beat)* You will not be sorry. Our English department is one of the best departments in the whole college.

(Orson Balwin, Joe and Philip enter from the path.)

PHILIP *(To Orson)*: I stood right up and said—remember, I was only a sophomore. But I stood there and said to Professor Wilson— *(To Joe)* Did I ever tell you this?

JOE: What story are you telling now?

PHILIP: About quoting Gandhi to Professor Wilson.

JOE: Oh, that one.

PHILIP: I said to Professor Wilson—something like: let the judges be judged by the laws they enforce. I don't remember the exact quote. *(Beat)* But what I meant was: if this faculty disciplinary committee was going to kick me out of school for stopping an army recruiter, then they were going to be judged by the war that recruiter was working for.

JOE: Wasn't he clever, Orson?

ORSON: Who was going to judge them? I don't get it.

PHILIP: I was talking—morally. I was after their consciences.

JOE: Wilson, I'm sure, would have been very upset.

PHILIP: The most liberal professor on the campus at the time. Half of my philosophy class with him was on pacifism.

JOE: I took the class. That's why Gandhi's just a brilliant idea.
PHILIP: Let's say I made my point.
JOE: It must have blown his mind.
PHILIP: He hated the war as much as—
ORSON: I'll find the sherry.

(Beat.)

JOE: Orson, I'm sorry, we're—
ORSON: Please. Every generation needs its war stories. Sherry, Katie?
JOE: I don't think she's ever even had sherry, have you?
KATIE: I'll pass. But thanks for asking, Professor Baldwin.

(Orson leaves in the direction of the house. Short pause.)

HARRIET: I'm also making tea.
PHILIP: You're spoiling us.

(Short pause.)

JOE: Now, if I'd tried Gandhi on the town judge . . . *(Beat)* When
   we stopped our recruiter.
PHILIP *(To Katie)*: This is a different recruiter. *(To Joe)* He'd either
   have tarred and feathered you—
JOE: Dumb as a brick, that man. Hated anyone from the college.
   You know he gave me a suspended sentence. It's still on my
   record. In some people's eyes even today I'm a criminal, a rad-
   ical criminal.
HARRIET: In whose eyes? I'm sorry, but I don't understand what
   you're—
KATIE: They stopped a soldier from recruiting students for the war.
PHILIP: We each did. At different times.
JOE: I had already graduated. But I was still in Middlebury because
   Mary was still a student. *(Beat)* Phil was also still as student.
HARRIET: When was this? I haven't heard anything about this.
JOE: Years and years ago, Harriet. The Dark Ages. *(Beat. To Katie
   and Philip.)* And I didn't get any faculty committee, I was arrest-
   ed. By the police. *(Beat)* Mary was pregnant with Katie. Fifty
   dollars for bail. That's what I made in a week at the bookshop.
HARRIET: I'm sorry—which bookshop?

JOE: At the Grange. Before it was a movie theatre.

HARRIET: I loved that bookshop. *(To Katie)* It had a fireplace.

JOE: It was a gas. There wasn't a chimney.

HARRIET: And big chairs. And a cat.

JOE: That was our cat. Before we had Katie, Mary and I had a cat.

PHILIP: I remember that cat. What was its name? Che?

JOE: I don't remember.

KATIE: I think Mom said it was Che.

JOE: Who can remember? *(To Philip)* You had a dog named Fidel.

PHILIP: It wasn't my dog. I didn't feed it.

JOE: You named it.

(Short pause.)

PHILIP: How did we get on to . . . ?

JOE: I don't know. *(Beat)* Orson's Henry James class. And to that from Lamb House.

PHILIP: That's right.

JOE: Philip was saying how he had to cut Orson's class so he could go and stop the recruiter.

PHILIP: I didn't ask. I just did it. I was a sophomore.

HARRIET: You had to have been a good student to get into his James seminar as a sophomore.

PHILIP: This was second semester.

HARRIET: Still . . .

KATIE: And Professor Baldwin, he was understanding . . . about your cutting the class.

(Orson enters with the sherry and glasses.)

PHILIP: No, he tried to flunk me. He didn't even stop there, he tried to get me kicked out of school. I thought he was a fascist. To this day, I can't help tying Henry James to fascism. *(Laughs)*

JOE: Not completely off the mark.

HARRIET: *(To Orson)*: Dear, I think these young men are calling you a fascist.

(Orson shrugs and sets down the drinks.)

JOE: Orson, you really tried to kick Philip out of school?

ORSON: I tried to kick them all out. *(Beat)* As for you, maybe I even talked to the town judge. I thought you should get at least six months. In a prison. *(Short pause)* You weren't a student anymore so of course I was speaking only as a concerned citizen. *(Beat)* I think I talked to him. I wanted to at least.

(Pause.)

JOE *(Suddenly laughs)*: You're joking.
ORSON: No.

(Pause.)

PHILIP *(To Joe)*: He tried to get you thrown into—?
JOE: But you hired me—both of us—right out of grad school. You brought us into the department.
ORSON: In life, you take one thing at a time. *(Downs his sherry)* My understanding was that my students were in college to study. Those who wished not to or had better, more relevant things to do, were welcome to go do them.

(Pause.)

PHILIP. *(Changing the subject)*: Lamb House is quite beautiful, Katie. If you feel like it you really should go and take a look. *(To Orson)* James spent what? Maybe twenty years there.
ORSON: Didn't you read the plaque?

(Frankie comes out of the house; she puts on her coat.)

FRANKIE: No one's been murdered by terrorists today. Though Donna Silliman has left her passport on a bus.
ORSON: Silliman? Is that Jewish?
JOE: No. *(Beat. Confused, he looks at the others)* I think her background's Greek. But what does that have to do with anything?

(Orson shrugs.)

FRANKIE: Henry's taking her to the embassy.
ORSON: Henry?
PHILIP: Henry McNeil. He and his wife are with us as well.

ORSON: Really? The department is that affluent now? *(Laughs to himself and shakes his head)*

(Short pause.)

PHILIP *(To Frankie)*: If you feel like it, Lamb House is just—
HARRIET: No one ever lost their passport when we ran the trip. *(Beat)* What sort of girl is this one?
ORSON: She's not Jewish.
HARRIET: I heard this, Orson.

(Beat.)

JOE: Well— She's— *(Beat)* She's smart. *(Beat)* She's fine. Isn't she, Katie? Katie knows her.
KATIE: I don't *know* her. I've talked to her a few times. She's OK. She's really OK. *(Beat)* I like her.

(Short pause.)

JOE *(To Orson)*: Katie likes her.

(Orson nods and pours himself another sherry.)

(Looks at Frankie and Philip) Orson, since Henry McNeil's name has come up on its own. Would you have a minute or two for business?

(Short pause.)

ORSON *(Nodding toward Katie)*: What about . . . ?
JOE: Katie, maybe you should go take a look at Lamb House now.
HARRIET: Or come inside with me. I was just about to make the salad.
KATIE: I'd be happy to help, Mrs. Baldwin. *(To the others, as they go)* I understand. Department business.

(They go into the house.)

JOE: It was easier, Orson, when she wasn't going to the college. She wasn't interested in anything we talked about then. Anyway, about Henry.

ORSON: I know what you—
JOE: You probably do, but let me say it anyway.
ORSON: And I told you—
JOE: I know you did, but please, Orson, I'm the chairman of the department now, not you. *(Short pause)* Sorry.
ORSON: Never be sorry for saying the truth.

(Short pause.)

JOE: The dean says— *(To Philip and Frankie)* Correct me if I mis-state. *(To Orson)* He says that we either release Henry after this term or offer him tenure track. It's no more one-year contracts for him. *(Beat)* Of course he's right. It isn't fair to anyone.
ORSON: No. It isn't. *(Beat)* But I gather, Mr. Chairman, that you don't wish to offer him—
JOE: His degree, Orson, it's from Case Western Reserve. That's not exactly Harvard.
ORSON: No.
JOE: That is not our standard.
ORSON: No.
PHILIP: He's been great to have, though. Really filled the gaps. Who else was going to teach Milton?
FRANKIE: He's a dear, lovely man.
PHILIP: And Betty— Everyone adores her.
JOE: They paid their own way here. He wanted that much to come. *(Beat)* I guess he felt if he came then—
ORSON: He's here to kiss ass, is that what you want to say?
JOE: No, I'm not— I wouldn't put it that way. *(Beat)* He's not official. His being here. That's all I meant to say.

(Pause.)

PHILIP *(Finally)*: Any advice, Orson?
ORSON *(Turning to them)*: If you're talking about next year—
JOE: We are.
ORSON: Then you'd better start interviewing, it's already—
JOE: We have.

(Beat.)

ORSON: Then McNeil already knows.

JOE: No. *(Beat)* No, he doesn't.

PHILIP: He's hoping for one more year. He's been applying all over the place. But he's set his sights a little too high, we think.

ORSON: Of course! We've spoiled him!

FRANKIE: He's had a couple of close calls.

JOE: Henry getting something, that would be the answer. That's the hope.

ORSON: Yes, that would let you off the hook. *(Laughs to himself. Short pause)* I don't see what choice you have but to tell him. Especially as you've begun to interview.

JOE: We've offered someone his job actually.

ORSON: Then—

JOE *(Turning to Philip and Frankie)*: Young woman out of Yale. Very bright, isn't she? She'll teach Milton as well. Seems to be he's even a hobby of hers, if you can believe that. *(Laughs. No one else does. To Orson)* She hasn't *signed* the contract. I guess we could lose her. I had thought that maybe we shouldn't tell Henry until we were absolutely sure we had this new person. I didn't want to get the department in a hole.

ORSON: No. You don't want to do that. Never do that. *(Beat)* The problem then is—what to tell Henry now.

JOE: I know you've had to deal with things like this before.

PHILIP: He's spent a lot of money, just the airfares for him and Betty—

ORSON: Have you thought about telling McNeil the truth?

(Joe looks to Frankie and Philip.)

JOE: We've been telling him the truth, Orson. You don't think that we've been lying—?

ORSON: I mean all the truth. Everything. Tell him he's out. Come next year that is the fact, isn't it?

JOE: Yes, but— *(He looks at Philip and Frankie)* Yes. That is the fact. Even if this woman from Yale doesn't— I have a file of at least ten others.

ORSON: I'm thinking of the department now. *(Turns and points his finger at Joe)* As you should be, Joe. *(Beat)* The longer you wait the more resentful he's going to be. This sort of situation, it can cause a lot of shit. Suddenly you have a teacher who isn't bothering to teach anymore. This has happened, Joe.

JOE: I know the case you're talking about.

PHILIP: If that's the thinking, why not just tell Henry the last day of classes when he can't do any harm? *(Beat)* I'm not suggesting this.

ORSON: It wouldn't work. He'd have forced the issue weeks before with the dean. *(Beat)* You tell him now, you also tell him he's got a recommendation from you whenever he needs it. Whether he's resentful or not *there's* his reason for behaving himself.

(Pause.)

JOE: Then the right thing seems to be to tell him. *(Beat)* The truth.

ORSON: If I were you.

(Short pause.)

PHILIP: I agree with Orson. We should tell him.

FRANKIE: We have to, Joe. *(Beat. To Philip)* I love Henry, don't you?

(Short pause.)

JOE: Then— OK. *(To Frankie and Philip)* I'll do it. While we're here, I'll do it. *(Beat)* This week I'll— *(Beat)* Tomorrow I will do it. *(Beat)* Thanks, Orson. Thanks for your wisdom.

(Orson nods and pours himself more sherry.)

ORSON *(Pouring)*: Too bad Henry's not black. He'd get a job like that. *(Snaps his fingers)*

PHILIP: Orson, that's— *(Stops himself)*

ORSON: How are the children, Frankie?

FRANKIE: Great. *(Beat)* And Howard's great, too. Sends his best.

JOE: Howard was given the Stirling Biology Chair, you know.

ORSON: I read this in the *Alumni Review*. Congratulations.

(Harriet and Katie come out.)

HARRIET: Can we come out now? You looked from the window like you were winding down.

ORSON: I'm sorry, we didn't mean to—

HARRIET: Dinner will be ready in ten minutes.

(They sit. Pause.)

ORSON: Anyone want more sherry?

(They shake their heads.)

HARRIET: So how many students do you have with you this year?
JOE: It's twenty-two, isn't it? Counting Katie.
KATIE: Why wouldn't you count me, I'm a student.
JOE: And we've seen what? Fifteen plays so far, in the first two and a half weeks. Another, I think—
PHILIP: Twelve or thirteen to go.
FRANKIE: We've seen some wonderful things. We'll be in Stratford later this week.
ORSON: The students will love that. When I ran this course Stratford was always the high point. *(Short pause. Laughs to himself)* I remember a *Much Ado* we saw—
JOE: I think I was with you that year.
FRANKIE: We saw a *Misanthrope* that was very funny, Orson.
ORSON: I don't like French plays. I don't know why.
PHILIP: There was the Shaw. Katie just loved the Shaw.
KATIE *(Smiling)*: I didn't say I loved it that much!
JOE: Don't back down now!

(He laughs. All except the Baldwins laugh.)

ORSON: Shaw is very underestimated today. Very. You know they've discovered some letters between James and Shaw. Very interesting.
HARRIET: You've been to the National, I suppose.
FRANKIE: A few times already. It's like nothing else, is it?

(Short pause.)

PHILIP: At one of the buffets we had a main course and wine and it cost what?
FRANKIE: Five pounds at the most.
JOE: Not even that much.
PHILIP: It was under three. I mean, it was cheap.

SCENE 3

FOYLE'S BOOKSHOP, STREET LEVEL

A large table full of books with only their spines showing (the sale table). Joe, Philip and Henry browse through the books on the table. Pause. Philip picks up a book.

PHILIP *(To Joe)*: Have you read this?
JOE: Oh God.
PHILIP: I know what you mean.

(He puts the book back. Pause.)

HENRY *(With a book)*: This I found pretty interesting.
JOE: Did you?

(Pause. They browse.)

PHILIP *(With another book)*: I think he really missed the boat on Whitman.
JOE: He's good on Irving though.
PHILIP: I didn't realize anyone even read him on Irving anymore. *(Beat)* I didn't realize anyone read Irving anymore. *(Looks to Henry)*
HENRY: I don't.

(Joe picks up a book.)

PHILIP: What's that?
JOE *(Putting it back)*: Second printing. *(Picks up another)* Ever met him?
PHILIP: Booth? No.
JOE: You should, it's an experience.
HENRY: I question some of the things he has to say about Conrad.
PHILIP: You do?

(Beat.)

HENRY: You know I did my thesis on Conrad.

25

PHILIP: Then you should know. *(Short pause. He looks at the picture of Booth on the book)* We shared a table at the MLA one day. If you'd had to watch him eat, you'd never read a word he wrote again. *(Philip has taken the book and now puts it back)* At least not on art.

JOE *(Without looking up)*: In Chicago? *(Beat)* Was the MLA that year in Chicago?

PHILIP *(Browsing)*: Atlanta.

(Beat.)

HENRY: I was at the one in Chicago.

(Pause.)

JOE: Philip was there, too, weren't you? You brought that Native American Indian woman to dinner with us. To this day, Mary thinks he's interested in Native American literature.

PHILIP: I've done some research! *(Laughs)* She was beautiful. Made Chicago almost bearable. Though I do remember being tired all the time. *(Laughs)*

JOE *(To Henry)*: And Mary keeps saying he needs to be fixed up. That's how little she understands men.

(They browse.)

Jesus Christ. *(Picks up a book)* This is the sort of thing that should be burned. *(Opens it)* I know for a fact that he spent just two years on Hawthorne at the Princeton Library. In and out of Hawthorne scholarship in two years! And he writes a book. *(Beat)* Junk. Nothing's digested. This is the sort of thing that drives me crazy. *(Beat. He puts the book back, continues to browse. Without looking up)* I reviewed it for the *Hawthorne Quarterly*. You'd think I'd raped his daughter, the letter he wrote me. *(Laughs)*

PHILIP: I don't see anything I want here. I'm going upstairs to drama.

JOE: I'll stay down here with Henry.

HENRY: I was thinking of going—

JOE: Stay with me. Come on.

(Henry looks to Philip.)

I'd like the company.

(Beat.)

PHILIP: We'll meet here in an hour and then go to Dillons.
JOE: Fine.
PHILIP *(To Henry)*: OK?
HENRY: Sure. Yeah. I didn't know we were—
PHILIP: Where's Betty?
HENRY: She's probably in fiction.
PHILIP: Good for her. That's where I'd be if I only had the time. *(As he leaves)* She can come to Dillons as well of course.

(He goes. Short pause.)

JOE: I thought that went without saying. About Betty coming with us.
HENRY: It does. Of course it does.
JOE: Show me what you're getting?
HENRY *(Picking up the pile of paperbacks at his feet)*: I'll probably put a few back.
JOE: Huh. *(Beat)* Nice. The Penguins though you probably can get half off. There are a million places that— Just down the street, at the Penguin shop, in the basement. They're used, but . . .
HENRY: I wouldn't care about that. I happen to even prefer used paperbacks. It's sort of a thing of mine . . .
JOE: I'd look there first.
HENRY: Thanks. I'll put these back.
JOE: Henry? *(Beat)* Also, on the corner—
HENRY: The used shop. I've been—
JOE: With the green front.
HENRY: Right. I know, when you go in—
JOE: Also in the cellar. There's a whole room of Penguins.
HENRY: There are? *(Beat)* Terrific.

(Long pause. Joe slowly checks out Henry's pile of books. Henry pretends to browse.)

JOE: Just wanted to save you some money.
HENRY: I appreciate it. I do. *(Beat)* So I guess now I can buy a few more books. *(Laughs)* It's a disease, it really is, isn't it? That's what Betty calls it. She says that if I were given the choice between a last meal or a last book, I'd—

JOE *(Not listening; looking through one of his books)*: I hadn't realized . . .

HENRY: What? *(Beat)* Looks interesting, doesn't it? I figure if I'm teaching Milton I might as well— You know.

JOE: That's quite admirable.

(Pause.)

HENRY: I love teaching Milton actually.

JOE: That's—lucky.

(Joe laughs, then Henry joins in, a little nervously. Short pause.)

(Going back to browsing) No luck with the job hunt, I suppose.

HENRY: You'd be the first to hear, Joe. After Betty. Of course.

JOE: Right, I didn't think— *(Stops himself)* She's incredibly well liked, you know. One hears that all the time.

(Henry nods.)

HENRY: Joe. I know it'd make life a lot easier for you, if I got—

JOE: That is so like you, Henry! *(Beat)* Here you are, with a problem, and what do you do? You worry about me? *(Pats him on the back)* You are something.

HENRY: It's a tight market out there.

JOE: Tell me about it. The number of applications I get . . . You wouldn't want to know. *(Beat)* But I've got to think, you— Henry, you!

(Pause. Joe pretends to browse again.)

HENRY: Joe, if I ask you something, you'll be honest with me won't you?

JOE: You have to ask that??

HENRY: I mean it. The truth, OK? *(Beat)* Not just for me, but for Betty and the kids. I just need to know.

JOE: Henry, what are you talking about?

HENRY: I know maybe I should have waited for you to bring it up. But it's why you wanted to talk to me, isn't it? Why you didn't want me to go with—?

JOE: Henry, you're not making any sense.

(Pause.)

HENRY: Joe, is there any chance of my keeping my job past June? *(Beat)* Look, I've accepted that tenure track is out of the question. I've put that out of my mind.

JOE: That—was a good thing to do. *(Beat)* I would not count on getting tenure track.

HENRY: No. *(Laughs to himself)* I don't anymore. But still with one more year under my belt. One more year and, Joe, I'd be pretty damn attractive to a lot of colleges.

JOE: You're attractive to a lot of colleges already, Henry. You just need to get a little lucky.

HENRY: I do have two interviews lined up.

JOE *(Big smile)*: Now that's good to hear! Great for you, Henry. I told everyone it would only be a matter of time.

HENRY: They're both with high schools, Joe.

(Short pause.)

JOE: Oh shit.

HENRY: Is there *any* chance at all of my staying on for one more year? I'm not asking for a definite yes, just is there a chance? *(Beat)* You know I'd teach anything.

JOE: That's never been an issue.

HENRY: If I had a whole year more. You see what I'm saying. There's hardly anything out there now. Whereas next year, I know for sure of three positions, because of retirements . . .

(Joe is looking back at the table of books.)

I'm sorry, if this isn't the right time. You want to look at—

JOE *(Looking up)*: No. No.

(Short pause.)

HENRY: Have you already hired someone to replace me? *(Beat)* You have, haven't you?

JOE: Who told you that? Henry, with you still thinking that you could be hired back?

HENRY: Then you haven't?

JOE: We've interviewed. Of course.

HENRY: I've heard this. This does not surprise me. That's OK.

JOE: I wouldn't want to give you a lot of hope.

HENRY: I'm not asking for a lot. *(Short pause)* Joe. Look at me and tell me.

JOE *(Looking at him)*: No one's been hired yet. No.

HENRY: OK. Good. *(Breathes deeply)* Excellent. Thank you. Just to have this talk has made this trip worthwhile. I'll go find Betty and tell her we're going to Dillons.

JOE: And put those Penguins back and save yourself some money.

HENRY: I will. I'll do that. Thanks. Thanks a lot, Joe. *(He turns to go and sees Betty who has just entered)* There you are.

BETTY: The system they have in this store, it drives me crazy. First you have to find the book. Then you stand in one line to get a bill, you take the bill to the cash line, you pay the cash person, then you go back—

HENRY: Buy it at Dillons. We're going there next.

BETTY: Are we?

JOE: Actually I'm set to go anytime. We just have to find Philip.

HENRY: I'll find him. I have to put these books back anyway.

JOE: He's up in drama.

HENRY: That's what he said. *(Turns to go, then back to Betty)* You don't mind? About Dillons?

BETTY: No.

HENRY: Good. Thanks. *(Hurries off)*

(Joe goes back to looking through the books. Pause.)

BETTY: You didn't tell him, did you, Joe?

(Joe looks up.)

JOE: About?

BETTY: You've hired his replacement. *(Beat)* Frankie told me last night after all of you got back from the Baldwins'.

JOE: She did, did she.

BETTY: I asked her and she told me. I knew you'd have been talking about Henry's situation. And Frankie had the guts to tell me the truth.

JOE: Betty, how do you know what I've told Henry and what I haven't told—

BETTY: He won't even go to his interviews, Joe! He's dreaming. And what are we supposed to do? I don't even know where we'll live. Do you know how much this trip cost? Do you know why he insisted we come? *(Beat)* He was hoping if we hung around with—

JOE: I know!!! *(Short pause)* It's going to break his heart to teach high school.

BETTY: True enough.

JOE *(Turning to her)*: You want to break his heart?!!!

BETTY: That doesn't make sense, Joe.

(Pause.)

JOE: I only want to be kind. I think there is a place for kindness in this world! A place for caring! For decency! *(Short pause. He rubs his eyes, then leans on the table, sighs)* Look. I talked to him, OK? Two minutes ago.

BETTY: You told him? You actually told him you'd hired—?

JOE: You saw how he looked. You can thank me for being so gentle with him.

BETTY: And he understood you? *(Beat)* And he understood you?!

JOE: I was as clear as I could be, Betty. I can't do any more than that.

BETTY: I suppose not.

(Short pause.)

JOE: You know Henry. He dreams. He hears what he wants to hear sometimes.

BETTY: OK.

JOE: But if you're saying what I should have done was shove the fact in his face, well—

BETTY: No, Joe, no.

JOE: I did the best I could. And it was one of the hardest things I've ever had to do to a friend. And Henry is my friend, Betty.

(Beat. She nods.)

So it is done. It's done. Now enough is enough. *(He starts to browse again)* I even saved him some money on some books.

BETTY: Thank you.
JOE *(Picking up a book)*: Catch!

(He throws her the book. She catches it.)

I understand you like fiction. I hear that's good. I don't have much time for fiction myself ... *(Beat)* Let me buy that for you. I think it's only fifty pence.

SCENE 4

LYTTELTON BUFFET

Joe and Joanne Smith sit at a table; pastry and tea in front of them. Joanne has a small shoebox beside her.

JOANNE: No, I didn't mean that! I love Stratford. I really do. And the Royal Shakespeare Company, it's— It's world famous, isn't it? What more could you want? *(Beat)* It's just—
JOE: Joanne, I know what you're going to say.
JOANNE: I don't think you can—
JOE: You're going to say, the problem with Stratford is— Well, to be brutally blunt, it's all the Americans. Right?
JOANNE: How did you—?
JOE: Look, I feel the same way. Every time I go there it drives me crazy.
JOANNE: You, too? Professor Taylor, I can't tell you how—
JOE: I don't know what it is about the place. Attracts them like flies.
JOANNE: London's not nearly so bad.
JOE: They at least hesitate in London.
JOANNE: By and large they do.
JOE: But in Stratford! Last year I think six different people came up to me. I hadn't said anything. I had even avoided eye contact. But if they sniff you out as an American—
JOANNE: Which in Stratford does not take a bloodhound.
JOE: I tried once wearing a nice tweed cap. I loved this cap. Some guy from Louisiana nearly knocks me down, he was so excited to tell me he'd bought the same sort of cap in Edinburgh. *(Pronounces the "gh" as a strong "g")*
JOANNE: I know they come right at you.

JOE: Why do I care where they're from, this is what I don't understand. So they happen to be American and so am I. So big deal.

JOANNE: Right.

JOE: We have nothing in common. I don't know— They make the
whole thing feel cheap.

JOANNE: By "the whole thing" you mean being here.

JOE: Absolutely.

JOANNE: I get the same feeling.

JOE: For you it must be— Because you're actually living here. You're
a resident and everything. *(Beat)* Then to be taken for a tourist.

JOANNE: It drives me crazy. So I hardly go to Stratford anymore.
And never. Never in the summer.

JOE: *That* must be a nightmare. The summer.

JOANNE: Imagine your worst nightmare and then double it.

(Pause. They sip their tea.)

JOE *(Taking a bite of a pastry)*: Delicious. Would you like to try—?

(She shakes her head no.)

JOANNE: I used to feel a little funny about it. They are after all from
my country. But— *(Beat)* Then you hear them shout.

JOE *(Eating)*: If they just acted like they were guests.

JOANNE: My husband doesn't mind. He finds them sort of—

JOE: But he's not American. So he's not the one being embarrassed.

JOANNE: That's true. Well put. *(Beat)* I'll explain it that way to him.
(Short pause) Sometimes when I'm in a shop I try not to say
anything. I just point. Maybe they'll think I'm English or
something. Maybe that I don't even speak English. That I'm
foreign. So I point.

JOE: The accents some people have.

JOANNE: They don't hear themselves. *(Beat)* Sometimes it's funny,
but sometimes— *(Short pause)* Anyway.

JOE: Right. Anyway.

(She starts to open the box.)

JOANNE: It's good to talk to someone who— Well— You know.

JOE: I know. *(Offering her the last bit of pastry)* Are you sure?

JOANNE: No, thanks. *(She starts to take out piles of tickets with rubber bands around them)*

JOE *(Eating the last bite)*: Incredible, the caliber of food sold in a theatre.

JOANNE: Here's the last lot.

JOE *(Eating)*: Everyone—by the way—has been raving about the seats we've had.

JOANNE: Good, I'm pleased to hear that. You never really know what you'll get.

JOE: I don't think we've had one bad seat.

JOANNE: Knock wood. So—here's for this afternoon, the Lyttelton. It's wonderful by the way. You'll have a great time.

JOE: Terrific.

JOANNE *(Handing over bunches of tickets)*: The Simon Gray is tonight. *(Beat)* It's short. *(Beat)* Tomorrow's Stratford. Friday's Stratford again. Then the day off. That's correct, isn't it?

JOE *(Going over his list that he has taken out)*: That's correct.

JOANNE: Good. *(Beat)* Then there's Saturday night back at the Barbican. I finally got *Les Mis* on Monday.

JOE: Thank you. Mary and I saw it in New York. The kids'll love it.

JOANNE: Tuesday, the Royal Court.

JOE: What's there?

JOANNE: I forget. It's in previews.

JOE: Oh really. That could be fun.

JOANNE: Something very Royal Courtish to be sure.

JOE: I know what you mean. *(Laughs to himself)*

JOANNE: Something at Wyndham's on Wednesday afternoon, then a free evening and you're gone on Thursday. So there you have the rest of it. *(Pushes the tickets toward him)* James, I'm afraid, is working late these days in the city. He sends his regrets about Wednesday night.

JOE *(Looking at the tickets)*: I'm sorry to hear—

JOANNE: But if you wouldn't mind my coming alone . . .

JOE *(Looking up)*: Alone? Of course not! Why would we mind? *(Beat)* James must be doing very well.

JOANNE: He is. He is. *(Beat)* We're going to buy a boat.

(Beat.)

JOE: We haven't decided on the restaurant. But I'll—

JOANNE: There's no rush. I'm home most nights. *(Beat)* And there's a machine.

JOE: I'll call. When we've decided.

JOANNE: Good.

(Philip has entered with a tray.)

PHILIP: Joe, would you excuse me for a second? *(To Joanne)* Sorry to interrupt.

JOE: Philip, you haven't met Joanne Smith.

PHILIP: I don't believe I—

JOE: Joanne, Philip Brown.

JOANNE: How do you do?

PHILIP: How do you do? *(To Joe)* I don't mean to—

JOE: Joanne's the one who bought us the theatre tickets.

PHILIP: Oh right! Joe's former student. Wonderful seats. Every show's been great.

JOE *(To Joanne)*: See what I mean? *(To Philip)* Come and sit with us.

PHILIP: Frankie's in line—

JOE: She can join us, too. Sit down. Come on, there's room.

(Philip puts his tray down.)

And now—tell us what's the news on the Rialto? *(Laughs. No one else does)*

PHILIP: Donna Silliman's still missing

JOE *(Looking at his watch)*: She's going to miss another play. What do some of these kids think they're here for?!

JOANNE: What's this?—

PHILIP: One of our students, she wasn't in her room last night, and— Well, you heard.

JOE: I just do not understand this kind of thing!

JOANNE: But I guess it's got to happen all the time.

PHILIP: Every year. Something happens every year.

JOE: This one's already lost her passport once.

JOANNE: There's always one.

PHILIP: We got from one of the students that she's been seeing some boy. From Amherst, if you can believe it. He's with another school group. We're trying to find out what hotel they're staying in.

JOE: You've called Amherst?

PHILIP: Frankie did. She charged it to your room. It didn't seem fair to have it on her expenses.

JOE: That's fair.

PHILIP: It seems that yesterday and today—Frankie should tell you herself—but these are their free days and the students have been encouraged to travel around a little bit. So Donna probably went with the guy somewhere.

JOE: So she'll be back tomorrow. When we're in Stratford. *(Beat)* Great.

PHILIP: She probably hasn't thought to look at the schedule.

JOANNE: I am sure it will all work out.

JOE *(To Philip)*: Speaking of Frankie, where was she last night?

PHILIP: Last night? We were all at the theatre. What was the name of that play? After a while they begin to blur, don't they?

JOANNE: I can check the— *(Takes out her schedule)*

JOE: I mean later. After Katie told me about Donna, I knocked on Frankie's door.

PHILIP: And she didn't answer?

(Joe shakes his head.)

That's funny. *(Shrugs)* I don't know. Maybe she's a sound sleeper, Joe. *(Beat)* Why are you asking me?

JOANNE: It was *Les Liaisons Dangereuses.*

PHILIP: What was?

JOANNE: The play we saw last night.

PHILIP: That's right. With the girl with the naked back. I remember that one.

(Frankie enters with a tray.)

FRANKIE: Is there room for—

JOE: Of course there is. Philip, move over.

FRANKIE: I could sit—

JOE: No. No. *(To Joanne)* Frankie Lewis, Joanne Smith.

PHILIP: Joanne's the woman who—

FRANKIE: Yes, we met the other day. Katie introduced us.

JOANNE: Yes, that's right.

FRANKIE: Each day the seats get even better. *(Nods to Philip)* Philip.

PHILIP: Frankie.

FRANKIE: Phil's told you, I gather.

PHILIP: Told what?

JOE: That we have a runaway.

PHILIP: That. Yes, he knows.

FRANKIE: I wouldn't say "runaway." That's a little melodramatic, wouldn't you say? She'll be back.

JOE: When we're in Stratford.

FRANKIE: They're not children, Joe. *(To Joanne)* You were a student of Joe's

JOE: My first year teaching.

JOANNE: I even babysat for Katie. *(To Joe)* I didn't tell you we had tea one afternoon last week. She's really— She's grown up.

FRANKIE *(To Joe)*: That's where we ran into each other. At the Tate.

JOANNE: Right. And Katie introduced us.

FRANKIE *(Picking up the Hamleys bag she brought with her)*: This is in your way.

JOANNE: No, it's—

FRANKIE: I'll set it over here. *(She does)* Something for the boys from Hamleys.

JOE: Frankie has two beautiful boys.

JOANNE: Congratulations.

(Short pause. Suddenly Philip laughs to himself.)

PHILIP: It's funny—but when I first came in and saw Joe talking with a strange attractive young woman—

JOE: Joanne Smith.

PHILIP: I know. But I didn't know then. I didn't know you knew her, Joe. *(Shakes his head and laughs)* So my first thought, seeing these two, was—now that is so unlike Joe Taylor. *(Laughs)* But then it turns out you do know her. She even used to babysit . . . *(Laughs. The others are confused about what he is saying)* Never mind.

(Pause.)

FRANKIE *(To Joe)*: Donna Silliman will come back to the hotel, find we're gone, we'll leave a message and she can take a train and join us or wait for us. *(Beat)* What else can we do?

PHILIP: Oh Joe, you wanted to ask Frankie about last night?

JOE: I knocked—

PHILIP: He knocked on your door. What time was that?

JOE: About—four.

PHILIP: About four, he knocked. *I* told him you must be a very sound sleeper.

FRANKIE: Well I am, Joe. *(Beat)* I am a very sound sleeper. Everyone knows that.

PHILIP: Hopefully, not everyone.

(He laughs. Then the others laugh. Finally Frankie joins in.)

FRANKIE: I don't know about anyone else, but I'm still getting over my jet lag. *(Beat)* But at least I don't go dozing off in the middle of a show.

JOE: Once! The second night we're here!

FRANKIE *(To Joanne)*: He refused to take a nap.

PHILIP: He kept saying he'd taken this trip so many times, he didn't need a—

JOE: OK! OK! *(Beat)* Christ, will you ever let me forget it?

(Short pause.)

FRANKIE: I'm sorry I didn't hear you knock.

(Joe nods. Beat.)

JOE: Joanne's been to the play we're seeing this afternoon. She loved it.

JOANNE: It's very funny. I love those old Aldwych farces. They're so English.

JOE: They really are.

JOANNE: I don't think they'd work at all in America today, do you?

JOE: I can't see how. It takes a special . . .

JOANNE: I know what you mean. *(Beat)* James's family is right out of one of those plays actually. *(Laughs to herself)* The first time I met them— They don't live posh or anything like that, but there is a cook. She used to be James's nanny. *(Beat)* One of the family, she is. And everyone is always saying that. Helen from Glasgow. *(Beat)* They could not have been kinder to me. James's father, Freddy—he insists I call him Freddy—and once he gets into a chair you begin to wonder if he'll ever move out of it. *(Beat)* Or so his mother says. James's sister made us all watch the telly. James tried to argue but I said I'd love to. I'd only been here a month and I'd hardly got used to English telly so I thought here was my chance to ask questions. *(Beat)* So this man comes on; he tries to make some jokes which are not funny, I think to myself. Then he says something like: "The girl went up to the boy and put her hand into his—" He paused and a middle-aged woman completes the sentence with: "—her hand into his *golf bag.*" And everyone laughs. *(Beat)* Even James laughed I noticed. This is peculiar I think to myself. *(Beat)* "Into his golf bag." She continues now: "—and pulls out a club which she used to wiggle his—" She pauses and a middle-aged man now completes the sentence with: "Wiggle his tee out of the ground." *(Short pause. She sips her tea)*

JOE: Huh.

JOANNE: This goes on and on. And when it ends the man who started it all drops his trousers to reveal that his underpants look like the British flag. *(Short pause)* What's amazing about England is that in time you begin to find this sort of thing funny as well. *(Beat)* Or so I'm told. James says it's the weather. *(Beat)* In any event, I don't think a good old Aldwych farce would work in America.

JOE: No.

PHILIP: No.

(Pause.)

FRANKIE: Have you lived in London long, Joanne?

JOANNE: About sixteen and a half months.

(Short pause.)

PHILIP: It must have been a lot of work getting us the tickets.

JOANNE: It was fun. I love it. *(Beat)* I love going to the theatre. Even going to the box office. It's something to do. *(Beat)* Professor Taylor, I'd love to do it again next year.

JOE *(Hardly before she's finished)*: Consider yourself hired! *(To the others)* Right?

FRANKIE: Absolutely.

PHILIP: You're the chairman!

JOANNE: Thanks. Thank you. *(Beat. She begins to stand up)* I should be going. You all probably have a million things to do.

JOE: Us? No. We have nothing to do. What time's the show?

FRANKIE: 2:30.

JOE: 2:30. We've got another hour.

(Joanne sits back down. Pause.)

(Finally) Frankie, I'm sure I don't need to say this, but I do think we should try to keep it to ourselves.

FRANKIE: Keep what to ourselves??

JOE: That Katie was the one who told us about Donna Silliman not being in her room. *(Beat)* Last night. Before I knocked on your door. And you were asleep. *(Beat)* I don't want the kids to start thinking she's a . . .

PHILIP: Spy?

JOE: Yeah. I guess. Yeah.

JOANNE: That must be hard for Katie.

JOE: She handles it well.

JOANNE: Oh, I'm sure she—

JOE: There's Henry and Betty.

(Henry and Betty enter with trays.)

Over here! There's room over here! *(To the others)* Let's squish together a little more.

(They do.)

BETTY: You're too crowded. We'll sit outside.

JOE: It's raining.

BETTY: It stopped.

JOE: It's wet then.

HENRY: If you think there's room.

JOE: Of course there's room.

(Everyone starts to squeeze together; Joanne stands.)

JOANNE: Actually, look at the time. I should be off.

HENRY: I hope we're not—
JOE: There's plenty of—
JOANNE: Really. I just noticed the time. Thanks.

(She goes. They sit.)

PHILIP: She's the one who bought the tickets.
HENRY: Oh. *(Stands and shouts)* Beautiful seats!!!
JOE: Don't shout.
HENRY: What?
JOE: Never mind.

(Long pause.)

(To Philip) What if she gets pregnant?

(Philip quickly turns to Frankie then back to Joe.)

PHILIP: What?
JOE: Donna Silliman. On this trip. What if she got pregnant? She could you know.
PHILIP: Perhaps even as we speak.
FRANKIE: Philip!
PHILIP: But really is that our problem? *(Beat)* You're not leading up to a discussion of abortion rights, are you?
JOE: No. *(Laughs)* No. *(Beat)* I could if you want.
FRANKIE: That's OK.

(Pause. Betty and Henry eat.)

JOE: Look, while I have you all together like this.
FRANKIE: Like what?
PHILIP: He means— so uncomfortable.
BETTY: If we're in the way—
JOE: I just want you all to know that *I* know I'm the chairman of the department. So you can relax. *(Beat)* For better or worse that is the case. And as the chairman I personally will accept full responsibility for what happens to any of the students. OK? Do you hear me—I accept full responsibility. So the rest of you can relax.

PHILIP: Good for you.

FRANKIE: Thanks.

(Short pause.)

HENRY: Baldwin, when he was chairman, would never have had the guts to say that.

(Betty sighs and turns away.)

What? What did I say?

(Awkward pause as they try to eat and drink their tea crammed together like this.)

JOE *(Who has been hiding his face in the box full of tickets)*: Who's going to keep the tickets? If they're left with me they're sure to end up lost.

(Laughs. No one else does.)

SCENE 5

WATERLOO BRIDGE

Joe and Henry walk back across the bridge from the National Theatre. Late afternoon.

JOE: Let's stop here. Wait for them to catch up. *(Beat)* It's just drizzling.

HENRY: I didn't even notice.

(Short pause. Joe looks back. Henry looks back.)

They're taking pictures.

(Beat.)

JOE: It was a wonderful performance, didn't you think? *(Laughs to himself)* The English have such a delicious sense of humor.

HENRY: Very well put. *(Beat)* When he hid under the table—
JOE: You heard me laughing?
HENRY: I think I was laughing even louder.
JOE: That I very much doubt. *(Laughs. Short pause)* The butler was
    excellent. He never changed his expression.
HENRY: A very good actor.

(Short pause.)

JOE: We could keep . . . *(He nods ahead)* If you want.
HENRY: I don't mind waiting.

(Short pause.)

JOE: Quite the view.

(Henry nods. Beat.)

HENRY: Though I think it's even more impressive from the Nation-
    al's side.

(Short pause.)

JOE *(Suddenly turning to Henry)*: While I have you like—
HENRY *(Who has turned at the same time, and speaks at the same
    time)*: Joe, I just want to—

(They both stop. They laugh.)

Go ahead.
JOE: No, no. Please.

(Beat.)

HENRY: I only wanted to say that— I want to apologize for the way
    Betty's been acting.
JOE: Why? How has she been—?
HENRY: I don't know what's gotten into her. I've told her I think
    she's being quite a drag on the whole—
JOE: Henry, she's—

HENRY: Why, I don't know. Maybe it's the pressure about the job. I try to tell her things do work out. *(Laughs)* But— *(Smiles and shrugs)* Maybe she's just a little homesick.

JOE: Maybe.

(Beat.)

HENRY: When this whole trip is over I'm sure she'll realize what a good time she had.

JOE: Of course she will. *(Short pause)* Quite the view. *(Beat)* Sometimes I think it all looks like a postcard. That I'm inside a postcard. You ever feel that way? *(He turns and faces Henry, putting his hand on his shoulders)*

HENRY: A lot.

(Joe smiles and nods and begins to turn back.)

So what were you—? You were going to say something. *(Beat)* You started—

JOE: Henry . . . *(Beat)* Look, I have no right to ask you for a favor.

HENRY: What are you talking about? You can say this with all the favors you have done me?

JOE: I've done nothing. *(Beat)* You paid your own way here. What you do with your time—

HENRY: Ask me the favor, Joe. Ask me!

JOE: Promise me, if you don't want to—

HENRY: Ask, for Christ's sake.

(Short pause.)

JOE *(Turning and looking over the Thames)*: Philip is staying behind tomorrow. To wait for Donna Silliman. *(Beat)* The Amherst class is due to check back into their hotel by two tomorrow. We think it's a fair guess that Donna will be at ours around the same time.

HENRY: So Phil's going to be waiting at the hotel. I think that is a very good idea. I support this, Joe.

JOE: Good. *(Beat)* I'm pleased you agree. I am. I need your support.

HENRY: You can always count on that.

JOE: I know. I do. *(Short pause)* But that wasn't the favor, Henry. *(Beat)* Phil, I think, should have some company while he's waiting.

HENRY: And that's what you want me to do.

JOE: I have no right to ask this.

HENRY: You have every right. Donna's been one of my students. I have a responsibility here as well.

JOE: That's very very generous, Henry.

HENRY: Bull. It's what anyone would do. So—it's settled. I'll stay behind. Have you talked to Phil about this?

JOE: He suggested it.

HENRY: I'm flattered.

JOE: He wanted company. *(Beat)* He wanted your company.

HENRY: Who likes to be alone? Should we keep out hotel rooms for the day?

JOE: No. I don't want this costing you anything. You can wait in the lobby. And the second she shows up, you and Phil bring Donna to Stratford.

HENRY: By train?

JOE: I suppose so. I leave that up to you. Maybe there's a bus. I don't know. *(Beat)* Henry, you do this and I think the department will owe you at least a dinner.

HENRY: I don't expect anything.

JOE: And we'll make sure Betty's—

HENRY: She won't give you any trouble.

JOE: I meant, we'll look after her. *(Short pause)* Beautiful night. The rain makes it very impressionistic. *(Beat)* I wonder how much a sign like that cost.

HENRY: Just the electricity. The number of flashing bulbs.

JOE: The National Theatre really must have money.

HENRY *(Looking back)*: They're coming now.

JOE *(Ignoring him, recites)*:

> This City now doth, like a garment, wear
> The beauty of the morning; silent, bare,
> Ships, towers, domes, theatres, and temples lie
> Open unto the fields, and to the sky . . .

(Beat.)

HENRY: Wrong bridge.

JOE: Yes. I know.

HENRY: I didn't mean to—

JOE *(Ignoring him)*: The last time I was on this trip, I tried to get Baldwin to get a group, students, some of the teachers, whoever wanted to, nothing formal, and we'd all get up very early and go to Westminster Bridge, and just as the sun began to rise, we'd read—

HENRY: That poem.

JOE *(Turning to Henry)*: Just how Wordsworth wrote it. But Baldwin said who the hell would get up at dawn.

HENRY: He's wrong. I would. *(Beat)* Maybe when we get back to London—

JOE: You think others would come?

(Betty and Frankie enter, both under umbrellas.)

BETTY *(To Henry)*: Others would come where? And how much does it cost?

FRANKIE *(To Joe)*: Aren't you soaked? Here, get under the umbrella.

(He does.)

HENRY: It's a surprise. Right, Joe? For when we all get back.

(Philip enters with his camera.)

PHILIP: Wait a minute. Let me get one of the four of you.

(They stop and turn to him.)

FRANKIE: When we get back from where?

JOE: From Stratford.

FRANKIE: Right, now we go to Stratford.

(As she finishes her line, flash from camera.)

JOE: Another one.

(Awkward pause as they wait for Philip to take the photo.)

ACT TWO

SCENE 6

IN FRONT OF THE ROYAL SHAKESPEARE THEATRE,
STRATFORD-UPON-AVON

Joe and an American man, during the interval of the matinee. Joe has a rolled-up poster under his arm and eats ice cream from a cup; the American smokes a cigarette and looks through a program.

AMERICAN: They don't have any pictures of the actors in their costumes. *(Beat)* Did you notice?

(Joe shakes his head.)

A shame. The costumes are terrific.
JOE: Please. *(Beat)* Please, don't shout.
AMERICAN: He's good. *(Points to a picture)* Don't you think he's good?

(Joe eats and nods.)

What a costume he's got. *(Beat)* You got a poster. I was thinking of getting one. Which one did you get?

47

(Joe hesitates, then shows him.)

Maybe I'll get that one, too.

JOE: There are plenty of other—

AMERICAN: Look here. *(Shows him an advertisement in the program)* They seem to have all kinds of shit. *(Reads)* "RSC Merchandise." *(Beat)* Posters. T-shirts. Records. Here's an RSC shopping bag. RSC address book. The Game of Shakespeare. What do you think that's about?

(Joe shrugs, looks away.)

Maybe my niece would like that, she loves Monopoly. She kills me at it. *(Laughs)* She's ruthless. I wonder what kind of skills this game teaches. *(Beat)* So what part of the States do you come from?

JOE: I'm British. I'm a naturalized British citizen. *(Beat)* I tutor at Oxford.

AMERICAN: No kidding. I'm in insurance. *(Beat)* So for someone like you all this must be pretty old hat.

(Joe nods without looking at him.)

Would you believe this was my first time? It is. Every year for years I've been promising myself . . . *(Beat)* Finally— Here I am. *(Laughs to himself)* The thrill of a lifetime. *(Turns to Joe)* Doesn't eating that stuff make you even colder?

JOE: Not if you're English.

(American nods, shrugs, looks at the program, then up.)

AMERICAN: Theatre's my hobby, you know. We've got a very successful little theatre back home. The high school lets us use the auditorium. I've seen some so-called professionals that weren't any better, really. *(Laughs to himself)* Last summer we did Thornton Wilder's *Our Town*. You want to know whose arm they twisted to play the Stage Manager? *(Laughs)* I wasn't half bad either! *(Beat)* Nothing like these guys, of course. *(Nods toward the theatre)* These guys are real pros. I'm not even in their league, let me tell you. I don't even deserve to wipe the sweat off these guys' faces. You know what I mean? *(Laughs to himself)*

(Frankie hurries in.)

FRANKIE *(As she enters)*: It's just the intermission? How long *is* the play?

JOE: They're saying all the words. Every now and then they have to do that. So have they called?

FRANKIE: They're here.

JOE: Here? When? They were supposed to call first.

FRANKIE: They rented a car.

JOE: A car?! I told them to take a train or a bus. I'm not sure we have it in the department budget to rent a—

FRANKIE: Joe, Donna Silliman wants to talk to you.

JOE: Sure. And I want to talk to her. As soon as this is over, I'll—

FRANKIE: Now.

(Short pause.)

JOE: Now?? *(Looks toward the theatre)* But there's still—

FRANKIE: I think you should go.

JOE: In my whole life I've only seen one professional production of—

FRANKIE: I think it's important.

(He hesitates.)

JOE: Why? What happened?

FRANKIE: She's in my room. Come and talk to her.

JOE: And Phil and Henry?

FRANKIE: They went off sight-seeing. Since they missed the start of the play.

(Joe hesitates, then goes back to the American.)

JOE: My program, could I have it back, please? I have to leave.

AMERICAN: Sneaking out?

JOE: No, I am not "sneaking out."

AMERICAN: They do go on and on—

JOE: I am not sneaking out!

AMERICAN *(Handing the program to him)*: I'm not sure I would have paid a pound for that.

JOE: And now there is no need, is there? *(He turns and goes off with Frankie)*

ANNOUNCEMENT: Ladies and gentlemen, will you please take your seats. The performance is about to begin.

(The American puts out his cigarette and goes off toward the theatre.)

SCENE 7

TRINITY CHURCH GARDEN, STRATFORD-UPON-AVON

A garden bench. Henry and Philip sit. Philip holds a piece of paper; a large book is next to Henry.

PHILIP *(Referring to the paper)*: I tell you they cheated us. And I'm not saying that because we only had the car for a few hours. I knew we had to pay for the full day.

HENRY: I can't believe they would—

PHILIP: Why not? *(Beat)* Because William Shakespeare lived here? Wise up, Henry. *(Beat)* What insurance did you agree to?

HENRY: I don't know. Whatever—

PHILIP: You don't know. So first, without even asking, they stick us for the maximum insurance.

HENRY: How do you know that's the maximum?

PHILIP: Because why wouldn't they?

(Beat.)

HENRY: If it was up to me to ask for less insurance then it's our fault.

PHILIP: He saw we were in a hurry. So he took advantage. Did you add this up? *(Beat)* I just did. Add it up. *(Hands the paper to Henry)* Are you adding it up?

HENRY: Yeah. *(Short pause)* OK. *(Hands the paper back)*

PHILIP: Now what excuses are you going to make for them?

HENRY: So they overcharged us by five pounds, big deal.

PHILIP: Five pounds *is* a big deal to a lot of people, Henry.

HENRY: They made a mistake. I doubt if they'd bother to cheat someone for five pounds.

PHILIP: Five pounds is five pounds! Five pounds adds up! First thing in the morning I'm going down there and get that five pounds back.

HENRY: Do what you want. If it'll make you happy.

PHILIP: It's not my five pounds. It's the department's five pounds. *(Beat)* And you're coming with me.

HENRY: I'm not going to act like that for five pounds.

PHILIP: You mean like you've been cheated? You have been cheated, Henry.

HENRY: Spend half a day to get back five pounds? Who's being foolish now?

PHILIP: It's the principle, Henry!

HENRY: You'll embarrass yourself!!

PHILIP: Have some guts, will you?!!!

(Henry turns away. Pause.)

OK. Sorry. *(He pats Henry on the leg)* Sorry. I didn't mean . . . Hey, I guess we're just different people, that's all.

(Henry turns back to him, nods and then smiles.)

(Folding up the bill) Forty-nine pounds for three hours. Fuck. *(Puts the bill in his pocket. Short pause)*

HENRY: You should have been the one to choose the insurance.

PHILIP: You did fine. You did.

(Short pause. Henry picks up the large book—it is The Collected Works of William Shakespeare—*and begins to thumb through it.)*

HENRY *(Without looking up)*: Joe got the message, I hope.

PHILIP: He must have.

HENRY *(Looking at his watch)*: We said 5:30. It's almost six.

PHILIP *(Shrugging)*: Maybe the idea didn't interest him.

HENRY: It was his idea. In London he was the one who suggested we do this. *(Beat)* This kind of thing. *(Beat)*

PHILIP: Well, I think we should have started with just the three of us.

(Betty enters from the direction of the church, carrying a small bag.)

BETTY: No Joe or Frankie?

(They shake their heads.)

PHILIP *(Standing)*: Sit down. I dried the bench with my handkerchief.
BETTY: No, Phil, don't—
PHILIP: Please, I've been sitting and driving all afternoon.
HENRY *(Suddenly standing)*: So have I. *(Offers his seat)* Please—
BETTY: I don't want to sit.

(They are all standing now.)

HENRY *(Nodding toward her bag)*: What'd you get?

(Betty opens the bag and takes out some postcards.)

BETTY: They were thirty pence each. But I figure since it's going to
     a church.
PHILIP: Thirty pence?! *(Shakes his head in disgust. Short pause)* It's
     the same in the States though. Ever been to the gift shop at say
     the Statue of Liberty? They rip you off there, too.

(Pause.)

HENRY *(Having looked at the cards, now hands them back)*: They're
     nice. You should have bought more.

(Short pause.)

BETTY: I thought this idea to read the poem was Joe's.
PHILIP: We were just commenting on that. *(Short pause)* So how was
     the play this afternoon? It broke my heart to miss it, you know.
BETTY: I think two Shakespeares in one day is asking for trouble. But
     the kids seemed to follow this one. But we'll see what they're
     like after tonight. *(Beat)* It was three and a half hours long.
PHILIP: But I'll bet it seemed like an hour, right?

(Philip turns to Henry and laughs. Henry laughs lightly.)

BETTY: Why is that funny?

(Frankie hurries in.)

FRANKIE: Joe said to go on without him.

PHILIP: What's the matter?

HENRY: What's going on?

FRANKIE: Donna Silliman is . . . She's pretty hysterical actually.
I have to go back.

PHILIP: Wait a minute. *(To Henry)* She was fine in the car, wasn't she?

HENRY: Fine.

PHILIP: What's she saying?

FRANKIE: Henry, Joe would like you to drop by the hotel before the
play. Just for a second.

HENRY: Sure. I can go now if—

PHILIP: Hey, if you're going then—

FRANKIE: Stay. He just needs a minute. There's plenty of time.
(Beat) He's trying not to make this into a big thing.

HENRY: Make what into a big thing?—

BETTY: What happened?

PHILIP *(Trying to take Frankie's hand)*: Frankie, are you OK? You
look

FRANKIE *(Pulling her hand away)*: I'm great. I'm feeling just great,
Philip. *(Beat)* How are you feeling? *(Beat. She turns to go)*
Please just read the poem

(She hesitates, then hurries off. Pause. They look at each other.)

PHILIP: And I thought we were finished with Donna Silliman for
the day, but I guess not. *(Short pause)* I wonder what Joe wants
to see us about.

BETTY: Henry. He wants to see Henry.

(Short pause.)

HENRY: We better start if I'm going to see Joe before the show. *(Beat)*
Who wants to begin? *(Beat)* How about Betty? *(No response)*
Betty?

*(He holds out the book to her; after a moment she takes it, and
begins to read:)*

BETTY: "To the memory of My Beloved, the Author, Mr. William Shakespeare, and what he hath left us":

> To draw no envy (Shakespeare) on thy name,
> Am I thus ample to thy Booke, and Fame;
> While I confesse thy writings to be such,
> As neither Man, nor Muse, can praise too much.
> 'Tis true, and all men's suffrage. But these wayes
> Were not the paths I meant unto thy praise:
> For seeliest Ignorance on these may light,
> Which, when it sounds at best, but eccho's right . . .

(Betty hands the book to Henry.)

HENRY *(Reading)*:

> Or blinde Affection, which doth ne're advance
> The truth, but gropes, and urgeth all by chance;
> Or crafty Malice, might pretend this praise,
> And thinke to ruine, where it seem'd to raise.
> These are, as some infamous Baud, or Whore,
> Should praise a Matron. What could hurt her more?
> But thou art proofe against them, and indeed
> Above th'ill fortune of them, or the need . . .

(Henry hands the book to Philip.)

PHILIP *(Reading)*:

> I, therefore will begin. Soule of the Age!
> The applause! delight! the wonder of our Stage!
> My Shakespeare, rise; I will not lodge thee by
> Chaucer, or Spenser, or bid Beaumont lye
> A little further, to make thee a roome:
> Thou art a Moniment, without a tombe . . .

SCENE 8

BAR OF THE ARDEN HOTEL, STRATFORD-UPON-AVON

Night. The bar is closed. Joe sits at a table with Katie and Donna Silliman. They are laughing.

JOE *(To Donna)*: Sounds like his theatre class was studying Harrods a lot more closely than they were the Royal Shakespeare Company. *(Laughs)*

DONNA: I think they were. *(Beat)* Looking at the kids, some of the kids and the clothes they were wearing, I think a basic knowledge of Harrods may have been a prerequisite for the class.

JOE: Yeah. *(Laughs)* What a waste of money. I don't know, maybe I'm old-fashioned but here is this opportunity— It's like a living education. That's what England could be. I think that's what our course tries to realize. *(Beat)* I don't know if we succeed. *(No response)* We try. *(Beat)* I think we come quite close to succeeding. *(Beat)*

DONNA: Sure. You mind if I—?

(She takes out a packet of cigarettes from her purse. Joe shakes his head.)

Katie? *(Offers her one)*

KATIE: Thanks.

(She takes one. Joe looks at her.)

For Christ's sake, it's a cigarette!

DONNA: Every week they had three days off to do what they wanted. No classes or anything.

KATIE: For travel?

DONNA: For farting around. That's how I met Chip. *(Beat)* He was bored. He'd *bought* a ticket to one of the plays we were seeing. *(Beat)* Do you believe that?

(Katie shakes her head.)

JOE: Why is that so—?

DONNA: On his own he bought a ticket!

JOE: I don't find that—

DONNA: He could have done anything. But he went to see this play. *(Beat)* You'd really like him, Professor Taylor. He's a very good student. Reads a lot. Likes to go to bookstores. *(Beat)* He wants to teach. *(Beat)* We were walking out of the theatre and he sort of tapped me on the shoulder and asked for a light.

(Smokes) I asked where he was from. He asked where I was from. You're in a foreign country, it's nice to see someone from home. *(Beat)* It makes you feel relaxed.

KATIE: I feel the same way. I've met two, three Americans on this trip.

DONNA: They're not— I don't know, critical.

KATIE: They see the same things you see.

DONNA: That's it. Exactly. *(Beat)* Though there's always . . . *(Laughs)* One afternoon last week I went with Chip and his class on a quote unquote walking tour of Kensington. The teacher got everyone to count Rolls-Royces. Unbelievable.

KATIE: You're kidding!

JOE: I'm sure there was—

DONNA: I'll bet I know more about the English theatre than his teachers do.

JOE: Donna, you—

DONNA: OK, I missed a few plays. OK, I missed a few classes. *(Beat)* OK, I missed a lot of plays and a lot of classes, but I'll tell you what, I'm going to see everything we see for the rest of the time we're here.

JOE: We go home in six days, Donna.

DONNA: In those six days, then. *(Short pause. She smokes)* Chip's now gone to Paris. *(Beat)* His girlfriend made him go. It was either me or Paris. So I was really upset. That's why that stuff in the car— *(Beat)* I didn't need that.

JOE: No.

KATIE: No one does.

DONNA: I was vulnerable.

JOE: We understand.

DONNA: He scared me. Professor Brown scared the hell out of me.

(Beat.)

JOE: Talk about it as much as you want.

(Long pause. Donna rubs her eyes and almost cries.)

DONNA *(Suddenly turning)*: You're not going to get Chip into trouble? It wasn't his fault. I forgot about Stratford. *(Beat)* Chip's not his real name, you know.

JOE: As we said at dinner, if you're willing to forget about it, Donna, we're willing to. *(Beat)* At dinner you seemed to be willing to.

DONNA: I am. *(Beat)* But what Professor Brown did—nothing like that ever happened to me—

JOE: A misunderstanding.

DONNA: How do you misunderstand—?

JOE *(Turning to Katie)*: I thought this was over. We had dinner. We talked about this.

DONNA: And my parents? You'll talk to my parents?!

JOE: Why do you assume that? *(Beat)* We have six more days. They can be lovely days, Donna. But that will be mostly up to you. *(Short pause)* I'm not trying to treat this lightly. I don't want you saying that's what I did. If there's more you want to say? *(Beat)* We can stay up all night if you like. I don't want to be unhappy with the way I have handled what's happened. *(Beat)* What you say has happened.

DONNA: Do you think I'm lying—

JOE: I don't want you to get home and start complaining! I don't want you saying— Look, Katie's been here. She's heard everything.

KATIE: Is that why you wanted me here?

(Pause.)

JOE: We know his name isn't Chip. We know his name. *(Short pause. Looks at his watch)* The play's over. Maybe you and Katie would like to—

KATIE: The rest of the class was going to a pub. I know which one.

(Katie hesitates, then gets up. Philip and Henry enter.)

HENRY: Joe, you missed the whole play, I thought *Anthony and*—

JOE: We got talking. *(To Donna)* We finished, right? *(Beat)* Right?

DONNA *(Standing)*: I think we should go.

JOE: Donna, before you do. *(Beat)* I think if for no other reason than for my sake, you should say what you recall happened in the car. To Professor Brown. *(Beat)* To his face. *(To Philip)* I don't want you saying I put words in her mouth.

PHILIP: What's this about?

JOE: Phil, please. *(Beat)* Donna.

DONNA *(After a long sigh)*: I told Professor Taylor what you tried to do to me in the car on our way up here.

(Short pause.)

PHILIP: Which was??
DONNA: You tried to touch me. In fact, he did touch my breast.
Actually he grabbed it. I had to push him away.
PHILIP: Joe, this is—
JOE: Wait. *(Beat)* Donna. Is there anything else you wish to tell me?
Anything at all?

(She shakes her head.)

You're satisfied that you've had an honest hearing? *(Beat)*
Then you can go.

(Katie and Donna start to go.)

Katie?
KATIE: What, Dad?
JOE: You have money?
KATIE: Yes.
JOE: Buy her what she wants.

(Katie and Donna leave. Pause.)

Sorry that the bar's closed.
PHILIP *(Stunned)*: You don't believe that girl.
HENRY: She's lying, isn't she?
PHILIP: Of course. *(Laughs to himself)* Why would I—? How
could I—? *(Beat)* Henry was in the car the whole time.
HENRY: Except for about three minutes when I went into a gas sta-
tion for directions. I already told Joe this.
PHILIP: You already . . . ? You knew about this? When did Donna—?
JOE: As soon as you got here. I talked to Henry before the show.
PHILIP *(To Henry)*: So throughout the play—
HENRY: Joe made me promise not to say anything. He wanted to get
to the truth first. *(Beat)* And I think that was the right decision,
Joe.
PHILIP: But you told Betty?
HENRY: I've always made it clear, you tell me something, you are
telling her something. I do not keep secrets from her.

PHILIP *(To Joe)*: He tells Betty. *(Beat)* And it wasn't three minutes in that gas station! It was more like thirty, forty seconds, Henry. *(Short pause)* Anyway, I didn't do anything. Why would I do something like that? What am I crazy, Joe?

(Long pause.)

JOE: I don't think she's going to make a fuss. She was as scared about being yelled at for staying out and missing the bus here . . . *(Beat)* Katie and I took her out for dinner this evening. That's why I missed the play. I figured something had to be done.
PHILIP: To bribe her you mean?
JOE: She's quite relaxed about it all now, I think. You saw her. *(Beat)* A few hours ago . . . Sit down, Phil.

(Philip hesitates, then sits.)

HENRY: Betty's waiting in the lobby. She wants to take a walk. After sitting all day in the theatre— *(Beat)* It's hardly even drizzling anymore.
JOE: Good.

(Henry hesitates, then leaves.)

God, what an evening!
PHILIP: What I do not understand is: are you saying you believe this girl.
JOE: No. *(Beat)* Of course not.
PHILIP: Thank you. Thank you.
JOE: Frankie called the dean—
PHILIP: The dean? Frankie? She also knew?
JOE: She's the one who got me. As a woman I think Donna—
PHILIP: Bullshit!!
JOE: As a woman I think Donna found it easier to talk to her. Initially. Then I came into the picture. As the chairman of the department.
PHILIP: What did the dean say?
JOE: Donna's been having a lot of trouble of late. She's close to failing. This course—if we decided to flunk her . . . *(Beat)* I promised her we wouldn't by the way.

PHILIP: Another bribe?

JOE: I just didn't think it was right. A whole academic career should not come down to a course like— I mean, you can't force someone to go to the theatre. *(Laughs. Beat)* The dean respects you, Phil. *(Beat)* Not once did he suggest anything but respect for you. He said that if you denied trying to molest—

PHILIP *(Standing up)*: Of course I deny it! What am I now, a rapist?!!

(Short pause; he hesitates then sits down.)

JOE: Then when you have this sort of thing, where it's one person's word against another's. And there's no proof. And there isn't, Phil. She couldn't show Frankie one scratch or anything. Then it's the dean's policy to not get involved if he can help it. *(Beat)* I respect him for that. He said basically that I should ignore the matter as best I could. *(Beat)* He even said we shouldn't have called. This sort of thing, it's best to keep it— You know. You see I'm learning my job. *(Smiles)* Things get so damn complicated. And then there's the fact that we're friends. I wouldn't want people to have accused me of—

PHILIP: You're not the one being accused!! *(Short pause)* Henry's wrong about the three minutes.

JOE: He just wanted to be safe. He didn't want to underestimate.

PHILIP: Fuck. *(Beat)* One messed-up girl accuses me of pawing her and you, Henry, Frankie, the dean, Betty— Who else did you call? Baldwin?

JOE: Yes.

PHILIP: You called Baldwin? *(Beat)* You called Baldwin? I don't believe it.

JOE: He said he remembers warning you once about—

PHILIP: About what?!

JOE: Something about a girl, he couldn't remember.

PHILIP: When I was a student!

JOE: Ah. He didn't say that.

PHILIP: I was fucked-up over this girl. Another student! I wasn't fucking molesting anyone!!!

JOE: I just had to be sure. *(Beat)* I didn't know what to do. Baldwin suggested I call the dean. That's where that came from. So blame him, Phil. He said I should protect myself. *(Beat)* I talked it over with Frankie. She agreed to make the call.

I think hearing about it from a woman . . . We didn't want to scare the dean. *(Beat)* We thought this was a great idea. I was happy to have her the one who called. *(Beat)* The dean could have said—get her on the next plane. Get you on the next plane. He could have said a million things. We didn't know. But now—it's over. There will be no report, nothing. This I have learned. *(Beat)* Katie, by the way, was here the whole time tonight. Donna can't change her story. Or add to it now. Katie heard everything. That was my idea.

PHILIP *(Quietly)*: But you thought that I could—

JOE: Let's go to a restaurant. I think we can still get a drink in a restaurant. Let me buy you a drink. *(Beat. Not looking at him)* How was the play? You know I felt awful letting my ticket just waste like that. I wish I could have found somebody. There must have been somebody. If I had known I'd have given it to our maid. She'd have been thrilled. A free ticket to *Antony and Cleopatra*. *(Beat)* I feel bad. You're hurt. I don't want you to be hurt.

PHILIP: You know, Henry probably said three minutes hoping it'd get me into trouble. He's going to need a job soon after all.

JOE: Phil, Henry wouldn't—

PHILIP: I'm joking.

JOE: Don't even joke like that. People don't act that way. *(Short pause)* So—should we go?

PHILIP: I did touch her shoulder. I remember this. She was staring out of the car. I asked her if she needed to go to the bathroom. She said nothing. So I touched her shoulder.

JOE: There's nothing wrong with that. You were trying to get her attention, right? *(Short pause)* Frankie said she'd leave a note at the desk about where she'd be eating. So if we felt like joining her . . . *(Beat)* Do you feel like joining her? She was a great help with Donna. You should know this. She never let up for a minute. Even more than me she never believed Donna Silliman for a second. She was right there—demanding to know which breast. Everything. She even yelled at her. Right from the beginning, she— *(Beat)* She cared, Phil. *(Beat)* But that shouldn't come as a surprise, because she—

PHILIP: Sleeps with me? Is that what you're going to say? That it took a woman I sleep with to defend me from attempted rape?!! *(Beat)* Thanks. Thanks a lot. That makes me feel a whole lot better.

(Pause.)

JOE: No. *(Beat)* I wasn't going to say . . .

(Short pause.)

PHILIP *(Looking up at Joe)*: You knew about us, didn't you? You assume everyone knows that sort of thing. We haven't exactly been subtle about it. I think even Howard knows.

JOE: Of course I knew. *(Laughs)* Sure.

(He didn't know and now Philip knows this.)

But what I was *going* to say was . . . Well, she's a friend. *(Beat)* That's what I wanted to say. The other— That has nothing to do with this, I'm sure. *(Pause)* How was the play? I can't tell you how much I wanted to see it. Of all the plays to miss. You know I'm working on an article on *Antony and Cleopatra*. How often do you get the chance . . .

PHILIP *(Without looking at him)*: There's a matinee tomorrow. I could take over the class.

JOE: No, no. It's my turn. *(Beat)* Let me think about it. *(Beat)* Anyway, this morning I was working on it. Amazing what you can still discover. Things hidden everywhere! *(Beat)* You read and read and read and still you find things. *(Beat)* In the fourth act there's a scene. Eros is putting armor on Antony and Cleopatra's there? *(He turns to Philip who nods)* Well this is— iconographically speaking—*The Arming of Mars*, Phil. It's the painting brought to life! Eros is Cupid, see. Antony is Mars, of course. And Cleopatra, she's even referred to as Venus in the play, isn't she? *(Beat)* She is. So what I've discovered is: Shakespeare has gone and written a scene and based it on a painting! *(Shakes his head)* Structurally then, here is a representation not of life, but of another representation!!

(Short pause.)

PHILIP: That's—publishable.

(Short pause.)

JOE: Maybe I should clean up this mess.

(He begins to pick up the glasses off the table, dumps the ashes from the ashtray into a glass, crumples up little bits of garbage, etc.)

SCENE 9

PIZZA HUT, UNION STREET, STRATFORD-UPON-AVON

Later that night. Frankie at a table; Joe is taking off his coat and sitting down. Frankie has a pizza and a pitcher of beer in front of her.

FRANKIE: I think it's supposed to close in—
JOE: He's just taking a short walk. But if you want to go, we—
FRANKIE: No, I was just— When I ordered they said they close in—
(She looks at her watch)
JOE: I don't want anything anyway.

(He starts to stand up.)

FRANKIE *(Looking around)*: But I guess they'll tell us.
JOE: True enough.

(He sits back down. Frankie eats.)

Take your time. *(Short pause)* He said he'd only be a minute or so. *(Beat)* He wanted a few minutes by himself.
FRANKIE: How's he doing? How did he take it?
JOE: What was there to take? Everything was settled. Wasn't it?
FRANKIE: Still just to be accused of something like . . . *(Shrugs, eats)*
That's got to make you . . . I don't know. *(Beat)* A little bitch tries to save her butt and almost ruins your career? I mean, in different hands, Joe, something like this— His heart must have stopped for a few beats. Mine would have. *(Beat)* The world can start to look pretty scary if you let it.
JOE: Yeah. *(Beat)* But he must have known that you and I would never . . .
FRANKIE: Once he caught his breath, but before that . . . What a nightmare for him. *(She pours some beer)* You're sure you don't want—

(Joe shakes his head.)

JOE: Save it for Phil. *(Short pause)* I think taking her out to dinner helped out a lot. Good idea.
FRANKIE: Thanks.
JOE: Once she relaxed.
FRANKIE: Once you said we weren't going to flunk her.

(He shrugs.)

The department I think should pay for— And not just hers, but your dinner as well, Joe.

(He shrugs.)

I'm serious. Did Katie go with you, too?
JOE: She was a big help.
FRANKIE: I told you she would be. So then the department should pay for her dinner as well. It was business, Joe, remember that. *(Beat)* Keep the receipt. *(Short pause)* How much was dinner?
JOE: We ate at a pub.

(Short pause.)

FRANKIE: Henry says they got cheated on the car rental.
JOE: Shit.
FRANKIE: They were in a hurry, so— He and Phil are going to argue with them tomorrow.
JOE: Good luck.
FRANKIE: They should have kept it until tomorrow. We could have all gone for a drive. Wouldn't have cost any more, except for mileage.
JOE: They weren't thinking.
FRANKIE: Henry didn't want to park it on the street.
JOE: Oh.
FRANKIE: Makes sense.

(He nods. Short pause.)

JOE: How was the play tonight?
FRANKIE: That's right, of all the plays for you to have missed—

JOE: I'm thinking of seeing the matinee. Phil offered to—

FRANKIE: Do it, you won't regret it.

JOE: What with the article I'm writing—

FRANKIE: You told me. That's why I said of all the plays . . .

JOE: Oh right.

(Pause.)

FRANKIE: Joe. I want to say that I think you handled this whole— problem—perfectly. I thought you should hear someone say that.

JOE: Thank you. I appreciate it. *(Beat)* We try. *(Laughs)* Thanks, Frankie.

FRANKIE: The worst-case scenario would have been to try and keep it from the school. Better have the dean think you're too cautious than— No one likes surprises. You can't be too careful.

JOE: No.

FRANKIE: You've really got to protect yourself, don't you? Even when it's a silly obvious lie like this; it still could have snowballed. That little bitch . . . *(Beat)* I couldn't have had dinner with her, Joe. I lied when I said since you weren't, then I should be at the play. I couldn't have even sat and looked at her. *(Beat)* To accuse Phil. A man I—

JOE *(Interrupting)*: Respect.

FRANKIE: I think we both do. Why not one of us next?

JOE: You can't be too careful, you're right.

FRANKIE: It's frightening.

JOE: Absolutely. *(Short pause. Without looking at her)* We're sure he didn't do what she said he did?

FRANKIE: Joe?? How can you—?

JOE: We're positive?

FRANKIE: He's our friend! He's your best friend!

JOE: Who knows anything about their friends?

FRANKIE: That's a sad admission. *(Looks at him)* What don't you think you know?

(Finally he turns away and shrugs.)

JOE: I will have a little of that. *(Pours some beer into a glass)* What's important is that we have been fair to all sides.

FRANKIE: I can agree with that.

JOE: I'm sure Phil understood what I had to do.

FRANKIE: If he doesn't, he will. Come on, you're already a ten times better chairman than Baldwin ever was.

JOE: I agree. *(Laughs to himself)* He was an asshole. *(Beat)* He is an asshole.

(He laughs. She laughs.)

FRANKIE: It's going to be a pleasure serving under you, sir.

(She smiles and salutes. He smiles, shrugs, then nods. Pause.)

By the way, Joe, the other day when you asked why I hadn't answered the door when you had knocked? Late at night. *(Beat)* Remember that?

JOE: I remember.

FRANKIE: I realized later— *(Beat)* I'm not that sound a sleeper to sleep through a guy knocking for— I'll bet you knocked for a while.

JOE: I did.

FRANKIE: Anyway, I realized that I hadn't been in my room at that time. What time was it?

JOE: About four.

FRANKIE: I'd had trouble sleeping. Jet lag. I guess. And so I'd gone out walking. Imagine a woman going out walking say in New York. *(Laughs)*

JOE: She wouldn't.

FRANKIE: No. *(Beat)* So if it ever comes up, why it would I don't know—I was out walking. *(Beat)* Howard knows I'm not a sound sleeper.

(Joe looks down.)

I called Howard today. There's two feet of snow.

JOE: There's always two feet of snow.

FRANKIE: So—nothing's changed. I told him we were having a wonderful time.

JOE: Except for all the girls claiming Phil's trying to rape them.

(She hesitates, then laughs. He does not laugh.)

FRANKIE *(Laughing)*: At least we can laugh about it now. *(Short pause)* I also told Howard how you and I had been palling around a lot together. Spending a lot of time— He liked to hear that.

(Frankie looks at Joe, who looks back. Philip enters.)

PHILIP: You're still here.

JOE: They're about to close.

FRANKIE: Sit down. We have a few minutes yet. Here, finish my beer. I'm sure you can use it.

(Philip sits.)

JOE: How was the walk?

(Philip nods.)

FRANKIE: Must have been a traumatic night.

PHILIP: I'm fine.

FRANKIE: Joe was saying how well you took—

PHILIP: I just wish to God someone would have just asked me. That's all.

JOE: Come on, I did ask—

PHILIP: To be the last person on the goddamn earth to know! You know what that feels like?!

FRANKIE: Joe did what he thought was best.

PHILIP: For Joe!

JOE: That's not fair.

FRANKIE: He's just learning his job.

JOE: Don't apologize for me. A minute ago—

PHILIP: He still has a lot to learn about how to treat people.

FRANKIE: He's sorry, Phil.

JOE: I'm not! *(Beat)* How the hell did I know you didn't try to fuck her?!! *(Short pause)* I know now of course. *(Beat. He whispers)* I wished to avoid accusing you. I was trying to do what was right.

FRANKIE: He was, Phil. That's what Joe was trying to do.

(Short pause. Philip takes the crust left from Frankie's pizza and eats.)

JOE: Frankie called Howard today.

(Philip looks at Frankie.)

There's two feet of snow.

FRANKIE: He sends his best to everyone.

(Beat.)

PHILIP: Nice guy, Howard.

JOE: Phil, Frankie was saying that the other night—when I knocked on her door, she *wasn't* asleep. She was out—walking.

PHILIP: Frankie, he knows about—

JOE: I don't know anything!

(Frankie looks to Philip, then to Joe. Pause.)

FRANKIE: I don't know about you two but I'm exhausted. How long was that play? *(Beat)* To be honest, I think it was about a week ago that I suddenly started to feel that if I had to see one more play— *(Beat)* One more three-and-a-half-hour play. *(Beat)* The fannies the English must have. Tough as leather. *(Short pause)* But that passed. Once I saw the light at the end of the tunnel. Once I had that feeling of being over the hump. *(Laughs)* Come on, they're closing.

PHILIP: We can finish our beers. *(Beat)* The play we're seeing on Tuesday is supposed to be very interesting. I was reading about it.

FRANKIE: Which one is that?

PHILIP: I forget the title. But it's a new play. Very political they say.

JOE: That'll be fascinating. That's very English.

FRANKIE: True.

(Beat.)

JOE: In the tradition of Shaw.

PHILIP: Please God, don't let it be that!

(Philip laughs; Frankie laughs; then Joe laughs lightly.)

JOE *(After a big yawn)*: I don't know about you but I'm ready to go home.

Scene 10

WESTMINSTER BRIDGE

Early morning. It is raining, cold and windy. Henry, Frankie, Betty, Philip, and Katie have come with Joe to Westminster Bridge. They all hold a single piece of paper. Joe reads from a book of poetry by Wordsworth.

JOE *(Reading)*:
>This City now doth, like a garment, wear
>The beauty of the morning; silent, bare,
>Ships, towers, domes, theatres, and temples lie
>Open unto the fields, and to the sky;
>All bright and glittering in the smokeless air.
>Never did sun more beautifully steep
>In his first splendor, valley, rock, or hill;
>Ne'er saw I, never felt, a calm so deep!
>The river glideth at his own sweet will:
>Dear God! The very houses seem asleep,
>And all that mighty heart is lying still!

(Joe slowly closes the book. In the near distance, Big Ben begins to strike six. No one looks at anyone else; six people alone in their own thoughts. One wipes the rain off his face, one puts up an umbrella but then takes it down because it is too windy—a portrait of loneliness. When the clock finishes, Joe opens his single piece of paper, and everyone, following Joe's lead, begins to sing quietly, so as not to embarrass themselves—and of course in their American accents.)

EVERYONE *(Singing)*:
>God save our gracious Queen
>Long live our noble Queen,
>God save the Queen!
>Send her victorious,
>Happy and glorious,
>Long to reign over us,
>God save the Queen!

(Joe starts the second stanza, others follow, though with a little more difficulty.)

O Lord our God, arise
Scatter her enemies,
And make them fall.
Confound their politics,
Frustrate their knavish tricks,
On Thee our hearts we fix,
God save us all!

(Pause.)

JOE: Third stanza. *(He looks down at the paper)*

SCENE II

LUIGI'S RESTAURANT, COVENT GARDEN

The same restaurant as in the first scene, though a larger table. Toward the end of their meal: Joe, Henry, Betty, Frankie, Philip, Katie, Orson, Harriet and Joanne.

FRANKIE: It will be nice to get home.
JOE: Back to the real world. Back to work! *(Laughs to himself)*
PHILIP: Don't remind me. Now we have all those journals to read.
    (Beat) Orson, not only do we have to see the plays, but then
    we have to read what our students thought about them.
ORSON: I know the system.
HENRY: Phil, I enjoy reading what my students—
PHILIP: I'm kidding, Henry.

(He looks at Henry who looks away.)

FRANKIE: It has been a great time.
JOE: I think we've all enjoyed ourselves.

(Pause. They eat.)

HARRIET: Has everyone tried to pack? I remember—when was that,
    dear?
ORSON: I don't know what the hell you're talking about.

HARRIET: Yes you do. *(Beat)* I don't remember the year, but our things didn't fit. We had to buy a whole new suitcase at the very last minute. *(Laughs)*

ORSON: The suitcase broke. We bought a new one because it had broken.

HARRIET: That was another year.

ORSON *(Shaking his head)*: Oh forget it. What does it matter? So we bought a suitcase. Who cares? *(He drinks from his wineglass. Short pause)*

HARRIET *(To the others)*: It's those martinis.

ORSON: It is not those martinis!

(Short pause.)

FRANKIE *(To Henry and Betty)*: You never did get down to their home in East Sussex, did you? *(Beat)* It's very beautiful. Historic, I should say.

JOANNE *(To Orson)*: You must be very pleased.

BETTY *(To Frankie)*: We were never invited.

(Beat.)

HARRIET: You weren't— Oh I'm terribly — You weren't waiting for a formal—?

(Beat.)

BETTY: No. We weren't waiting for anything formal. *(Beat)* I suppose there was just so much we wanted to do. And the time just vanished.

(Short pause.)

HENRY: Well *we've* packed everything. Except what we'll use tonight. *(Beat)* Everything fits. We tried to restrain ourselves— *(Laughs)*

BETTY: The trip cost us enough as it was.

(Pause.)

JOE: I suspect tomorrow morning will be a real madhouse. How did *you* handle it, Orson? Some of the students say they'll take the tube to the airport.

FRANKIE: But the luggage some of them now have.

JOE: That's what I'm saying. And half of them I'm sure are down to their last fifty pence.

ORSON: That's their problem.

(Beat.)

PHILIP: Orson's right. Let them find their own way. It's good training.

(Short pause.)

FRANKIE: What time are we supposed to meet?

JOE: In the lobby at eight. No later than eight.

PHILIP: We better say 7:30.

(Pause.)

FRANKIE *(To Joanne)*: We're really sorry we didn't get the chance to meet your husband, Joanne. It's funny, in the beginning it seemed like there was going to be so much time—

PHILIP: Where did the time go?

(Joe looks at Philip, then at Frankie. Philip turns away.)

JOANNE: He's hoping maybe next year.

(No one seems to understand.)

My husband. He's—

ORSON: What does your husband do?

JOANNE: He works in the financial city. *(Beat)* Near St. Paul's.

ORSON: Good for him.

FRANKIE: I love St. Paul's.

JOE *(To Joanne)*: Of course, whenever you're back in the States—

JOANNE: We're talking about a trip—

FRANKIE: We'd love to see you. Both of you.

JOE: Katie would even let her old babysitter have her room, I suppose.

KATIE: I'm never there. I'm in a dorm.

JOE: And why I don't know. *(To Joanne)* Do you know how much housing is now? Everything's gone crazy. *(Beat)* But Mary said Katie should have the whole experience of college. I mean, how's she going to have bull sessions with her friends until three in the morning if her parents are right next door? *(Laughs)* That sort of thing. Right, Katie?

ORSON *(Eating)*: Or how's she going to have boys in her bed when her parents are in the next room?

(Short awkward pause.)

KATIE *(To Orson)*: That didn't stop me in high school.

(Beat, then laughter.)

HARRIET: Good for you. Give it back to him.

JOE: By the way, I was reading through Katie's journal this morning—

KATIE: Dad!—

JOE: You let me. I wasn't doing anything you didn't know about. She's got some real interesting things to say about the RSC's *As You Like It*. Very interesting.

PHILIP: Really? . . .

JOE: You'll have to read it.

HENRY: I'd like to.

JOE *(To Katie)*: *The Tempest* I think you missed the point of though.

FRANKIE: That's easy enough to do.

HARRIET: Especially at her age.

(The others nod. Pause. They eat.)

JOE: What did anyone think of the play last night?

PHILIP: There's a loaded question.

JOE: No. Really. I haven't heard anyone say a word.

ORSON: What was the play last night?

JOE: What was the title? I don't remember. That says something. *(Laughs)* Some new play, Orson. I wouldn't rush out.

PHILIP: I liked it.

73

(Beat.)

JOE: Good. *(Shrugs, then laughs)*
PHILIP: Look, your problem is that you don't think politics belongs in the theatre.
JOE: First, I've never said that. In fact, I have often argued the opposite. Who defends Shaw?
FRANKIE: Please, keep Shaw out of this.
JOE: And second, I happen to believe there is a difference between politics and sentimental whining. *(Beat)* I would kill to see real political thinking on the stage. Where real problems are really addressed, Phil. Where I can be engaged! I am not a dumb person. We should not be treated like we were. This is all I'm saying.
PHILIP: And last night—
JOE: If someone is going to start preaching to me then he—or she— better have something very very interesting to say. That's all. But to be a captive audience, forced to listen either to what I already know or what I know to be a very simplistic, you know, explanation, then—well, I want to run screaming into the night. Period.
PHILIP: Bullshit. I repeat, your problem is that you don't think politics, today's politics, even belong in a play.
ORSON: Why is that a problem?!!

(Pause.)

KATIE *(Standing)*: Excuse me. Before you get started again, I promised some of the women I'd join up with them. It's our last night as well.
JOE: Yes. You told me you'd have to leave early.
HENRY: It was our pleasure to have you, even if for a short time.
HARRIET: She's our godchild, you know.
BETTY: I didn't know.

(Katie has opened her purse.)

JOE: No, no, no! Please, Katie. I'm not that poor. I'm not rich, God knows, but I'm not so poor as that.
KATIE: Thanks, Dad. *(She turns to leave)* Don't stay up too late.
HARRIET *(Laughing)*: Listen to her.
JOE: Katie, wait a minute. You still have your camera?

KATIE: Yes.

JOE: Come on, all of us. Come on. *(Starts moving people together)*

KATIE: I don't know if there's enough—

JOE: Try. What's to lose? A little closer. *(Beat)* Of our last night.

KATIE: OK.

(Everyone is posed.)

Ready? One. Two. Three.

JOE: Everyone smile. Are we smiling?

(Click. Everyone moves.)

Another one.

ORSON: No, no. One's enough.

PHILIP: Please, Joe. We're still eating.

JOE: It's probably too dark anyway.

(He waves Katie off. She leaves)

FRANKIE: Thanks, Katie!

HENRY: Thanks!

(Short pause.)

JOE: So in this play, we're meant to feel sympathy for miners. Good.
Fine. Who doesn't like miners?

ORSON: In my day—

PHILIP: Anyone with a political view you tried to arrest, Orson.

ORSON: Only when it got in the way of—

HARRIET: Please.

JOE: And it gave me goose bumps. This play. Why?

PHILIP: Because it touched—

JOE: Because it pushed obvious buttons! Things in this world are
complicated. Not simplistic. You don't help yourself or anyone
else by not recognizing that. By not using the mind you've got.
(Beat) Isn't that what we teach? Isn't that why we have our students read what we do—so that they can learn to think? *(Beat)*
A mind is not a reflex, it is a living thing.

HENRY: The president of the college said that at last year's graduation.

JOE: I know. And I liked it.

(Short pause.)

PHILIP: And I liked the play. So that's that.

FRANKIE: I liked it, too.

JOE: Who doesn't like a good cry?

FRANKIE: I learned something about miners.

JOE: You learned what you already believed, Frankie. Period. *(Beat)* Trust me, this sort of theatre is old-fashioned. We went through that twenty years ago. *(Beat)* You certainly don't find it in the States anymore. *(Beat)* And in another five, ten years you won't find it here either. *(Beat)* I don't want to see it. Americans don't want to see it. *(Pause)* Sorry, I'm dominating the—

PHILIP: We argue like this all the time.

FRANKIE *(To Orson and Harriet)*: They do. This I can swear to.

ORSON: Nice to see ideas still being discussed in the department. *(Beat)* I was afraid after I'd left . . .

(Beat.)

JOE *(Nodding toward Philip)*: He's fun to argue with. He really is. advocate. Five kids with armbands walking around telling the college to disinvest in South Africa, and you'd think from listening to Phil that it's the sixties all over again. *(Laughs)*

PHILIP: Disinvestment has a point.

JOE: Of course it has a point. I don't argue with that. It's your Pollyannaish hope that is so irritating! It's like he never learns! *(Beat)* Of course South Africa's bad! Of course!!!

(Long pause. They eat.)

BETTY: Professor Baldwin, how is your book coming? Frankie was telling me a little about it.

JOANNE: What is the book about?

HARRIET: Orson is editing the collected letters of Harold Frederic for Cornell University Press.

ORSON: I'm writing the introduction as well.

FRANKIE: That I didn't know.

(Short pause.)

JOANNE: I'll be ignorant, who's Harold Frederic?
HENRY *(Before anyone else can answer)*: Nineteenth-century American novelist. Very interesting. Very important.
JOANNE: Never heard of him.
PHILIP: Edmund Wilson liked him.

(Pause.)

HARRIET: We've gotten the proofs.
FRANKIE: You're that close?
ORSON: Mmmmmmmmmmmmm. *(Short pause)* Harriet's been helping, haven't you? *(Beat)* We read them out loud to each other, as we proof. Every night from six to nine. We do about fourteen pages an evening that way. *(Beat)* Harriet has a lovely voice. *(Pause)* Henry James helped raise money for Frederic's family when he died.
HARRIET: He died drunk. *(Beat)* He had a drinking problem.

(Short pause.)

ORSON: He was a good friend of James. He lived quite a long time in England.
HARRIET: He is said to have called Henry James an effeminate old donkey who lives with a herd of other donkeys around him and insists on being treated as if he were the Pope. *(Beat. To Orson)* I think I got that right.
ORSON: I doubt if Frederic either said it or felt that way. It is part of the Frederic myth though. *(Beat)* He had two wives, though only one officially. Two sets of children. One in America, one here. He liked women. They liked him.
HARRIET: Though both families he stuck in the country while he himself went off to carouse in the city. *(She shakes her head)*
JOANNE: Sounds very—
ORSON: He wrote *The Damnation of Theron Ware*. Do you know it?

(Joanne shakes her head.)

A very sexy book. *(Beat)* I reread it all the time.

(Pause.)

JOANNE: While I have all of you here, I was wondering if there was anything different or whatever that I could do for next year. If you don't mind I'd like to pick your brains.

PHILIP: I don't know.

HENRY: We had great seats.

JOANNE: I'm sorry I couldn't get any speakers.

FRANKIE: I think it worked out just fine like it did.

JOE: Sometimes a speaker, well, if they don't know the class . . .

JOANNE: I wanted to get an actor.

BETTY: That would have been interesting.

JOANNE: There's a friend of a friend who knows someone who is with the Royal Shakespeare Company.

PHILIP: Really? The students would have loved that.

JOANNE: But he wanted fifty pounds.

PHILIP: For one class? Forget it.

JOANNE: That's what I said. I had thought that they'd do this sort of thing for free.

FRANKIE: I would, too.

PHILIP: You'd think they'd want to meet their audience.

JOE: Or just for the publicity.

JOANNE: But if you are interested for next year . . .

JOE: We'd have to put it in the budget.

PHILIP: Absolutely.

JOANNE: Then I guess it was a good thing I didn't tell the guy it was OK.

PHILIP: For next year? He needs to know now?

JOANNE: For this time. He said he needed an answer right then and there.

JOE: That would have been a disaster, really. I think we're what? Quite a lot in the red already. What with the car rental.

FRANKIE: Oh and I said the department should pay for Joe's dinner in Stratford.

HENRY: With Donna Silliman?

ORSON: Who's Donna Silliman?

BETTY: That girl who said Phil—

ORSON: Oh yes. The department should pay for that sort of thing. *(Beat)* Got caught with your pants down, did you, Philip? *(Laughs)*

PHILIP: She made it up, Orson.

ORSON *(Laughing)*: I'm sure she did! I'm sure! *(Short pause)* Henry, I hear you have to move on. All I can say is you shall be missed, dear boy.

HENRY: I don't think that is totally settled as yet. For next year, I mean. *(He looks around. No one looks at him)*

ORSON: Too bad you're not black.

JOE: I don't know about anyone else, but I'm beginning to feel the wine.

ORSON: Yes, we should get another bottle!

FRANKIE: No, no! *(Beat)* I think I wouldn't mind getting back. I haven't even started to pack.

JOE: I thought you were going to pack this afternoon. What did you do all day if you didn't pack? *(He suddenly turns to Philip)*

PHILIP: We should get the check.

JOE *(Staring at him)*: We already have.

HENRY: Let me see. *(Takes the bill)*

PHILIP: I think we should treat Joanne.

FRANKIE: Yes, for all her tireless work.

JOANNE: No, really.

JOE: Out of the department?

PHILIP: We should split hers.

JOANNE: No, no please, it's I who—

PHILIP: We insist.

JOE: If she wants to pay, Phil.

(Short pause.)

JOANNE: I'm serious. Let me pay for myself.

(Philip hesitates, then nods.)

ORSON *(To Betty)*: Within twenty-four hours of Henry James having two strokes, he was calling for a thesaurus; the doctor had called his condition paralytic and he thought there was a more accurate word. *(Laughs)* He loved words. I suppose you have to.

HARRIET: Orson.

(He is quite drunk now.)

I'll pay ours. What did you have, the beef spaghetti?

(He shrugs.)

At least one of these four bottles is yours. We'll pay for one whole bottle.

BETTY: Actually, I think he drank—

PHILIP: I'll buy your drinks, Joe. You bought me drinks at the Barbican.

JOE: But only because you bought me drinks at the National. No, no, you don't owe me.

PHILIP: Still, that's OK.

JOE: No. *(Beat)* Katie didn't have anything to drink, did she? Did anyone notice?

BETTY: She must have. Her glass has been used.

HENRY: Put in something. Don't put in much.

JOE: Let's say seven pounds twenty. What's the VAT on that?

PHILIP: Just estimate, Joe.

BETTY *(To Henry)*: Here's some money.

JOE: Let me look at that. *(Takes the bill)* I say we leave no more than ten percent. I mean we're leaving tomorrow, right? We're not coming back for a year.

END OF PLAY

Two
Shakespearean
Actors

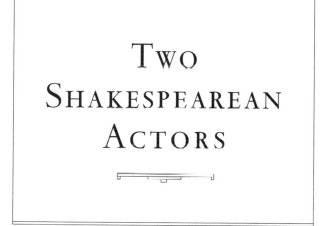

For Anton Lesser and Roger Michell

PRODUCTION HISTORY

Two Shakespearean Actors was commissioned by the Royal Shakespeare Company. It opened at the Swan Theatre, Stratford-upon-Avon, on August 29, 1990. It was directed by Roger Michell, with assistant direction by Clarissa Brown; the set design was by Alexandra Byrne, the lighting design was by Rick Fisher, the music was composed by Jeremy Sams and the stage managers were Jondon Gourkan, David Mann and Liz Lawrence. The cast was as follows:

EDWIN FORREST	Anton Lesser
MISS JANE BASS	Polly Kemp
MISS HELEN BURTON	Catherine White
MISS ANNE HOLLAND	Georgiana Dacombe
TILTON	George Raistrick
THOMAS FISHER	George Anton
ROBERT JONES	Ken Shorter
MR. BLAKELY	Arnold Yarrow
SCOTT	Trevor Martin
JOHN RYDER	Paul Jesson
WILLIAM CHARLES MACREADY	John Carlisle
CHARLES CLARK	Michael Gardiner
MRS. POPE	Penny Jones
GEORGE BRADSHAW	John Warnaby
FREDERICK WEMYSS	Alfred Burke
JAMES BRIDGES	Vincent Regan
JOHN SEFTON	Michael Bott
MR. CHIPPINDALE	Bill McGuirk
PETER ARNOLD	Andrew Havill
CATHERINE FORREST	Mary Chater
MISS WEMYSS	Rowena King
DION BOUCICAULT	Ciaran Hinds

AGNES ROBERTSON	Yolanda Vazquez
WASHINGTON IRVING	John Bott

Two Shakespearean Actors was subsequently produced by Lincoln Center Theatre (Gregory Mosher, Director; Bernard Gersten, Executive Producer) at The Cort Theatre on December 17, 1991. It was directed by Jack O'Brien; the set design was by David Jenkins, the costume design was by Jane Greenwood, the lighting design was by Jules Fisher, the sound design was by Jeff Ladman, the original score was by Bob James; the fight director was Steve Rankin, the production stage manager was Alan Hall and the stage manager was Deborah Clelland. The cast was as follows:

EDWIN FORREST	Victor Garber
MISS JANE BASS	Jennifer Van Dyck
MISS HELEN BURTON	Judy Kuhn
MISS ANNE HOLLAND	Hope Davis
TILTON	Tom Lacy
THOMAS FISHER	Graham Winton
ROBERT JONES	John Wojda
MR. BLAKELY	Richard Clarke
SCOTT	Jeffrey Allan Chandler
JOHN RYDER	Zeljko Ivanek
WILLIAM CHARLES MACREADY	Brian Bedford
CHARLES CLARK	Alan Brasington
MRS. POPE	Le Clanché Du Rand
GEORGE BRADSHAW	Michael Butler
FREDERICK WEMYSS	Bill Moor
JAMES BRIDGES	Tim MacDonald
JOHN SEFTON	James Murtaugh
MR. CHIPPINDALE	Mitchell Edmonds
PETER ARNOLD	Ben Bodé
CATHERINE FORREST	Frances Conroy
MISS WEMYSS	Katie Finneran
DION BOUCICAULT	Eric Stoltz
AGNES ROBERTSON	Laura Innes
WASHINGTON IRVING	Tom Aldredge

Other actors and servants were played by: David Andrew MacDonald, Katie MacNichol, Susan Pellegrino and Thomas Schall.

CHARACTERS

Actors at the Broadway Theatre
(in parentheses, the parts they play)

EDWIN FORREST (Macbeth; Metamora), early forties

MISS JANE BASS (1st Witch), twenties

MISS HELEN BURTON (2nd Witch; Goodenough), twenties

MISS ANNE HOLLAND (3rd Witch; Nahmeokee), twenties

TILTON (Porter; Church), sixties

THOMAS FISHER (Young Siward; Kaneshine), late twenties

FANNY WALLACK (Lady Macbeth); forties

ROBERT JONES (Banquo, Malcolm; Annawandah), early thirties

MR. BLAKELY (Duncan; Errington), fifties

SCOTT (normally plays Macduff, but is injured), thirties

JOHN RYDER (fills in as Macduff), English and
the traveling companion of Macready, thirties

Actors at the Astor Place Opera House
(in parentheses, the parts they play)

WILLIAM CHARLES MACREADY (Macbeth), English, late fifties

CHARLES CLARK (Macduff), forties

MRS. POPE (Lady Macbeth), thirties

GEORGE BRADSHAW (Banquo), forties

FREDERICK WEMYSS (Siward, Old Man), sixties

JAMES BRIDGES (Young Siward, 3rd Witch, Ross), early twenties

JOHN SEFTON (1st Witch, Donalbain), forties

MR. CHIPPINDALE (2nd Witch), forties

PETER ARNOLD (Malcolm), twenties

Others

CATHERINE FORREST, wife of Edwin, English, thirties

MISS WEMYSS, an aspiring actress,
daughter of Frederick Wemyss, late teens

DION BOUCICAULT, playwright and actor, English/Irish, thirties

AGNES ROBERTSON, actress and Boucicault's wife, late twenties

WASHINGTON IRVING, writer and amateur actor, sixties

OTHER ACTORS AND SERVANTS

SETTING

The play concerns imagined events surrounding the following
true incident: on Thursday May 10, 1849, while the English actor
William Charles Macready was performing *Macbeth* at
the Astor Place Opera House in New York City, a riot erupted
which resulted in the death of thirty-four people and the injury
of more than a hundred more.

Each scene has a title—the location of the scene—which should
be projected moments before the scene begins.

ACT ONE

SCENE I

THURSDAY MAY 3, 1849. 11 P.M.

A tavern, New York. Two large tables.

At one table, six men and two women: William Charles Macready, John Ryder, Charles Clark, George Bradshaw, James Bridges, Frederick Wemyss, Mrs. Pope and Miss Wemyss. With the exceptions of Miss Wemyss and John Ryder, all are members of Macready's acting company, which is now rehearsing a production of Macbeth at the Astor Place Opera House.

At another table: Tilton, an older actor, who is a member of the acting company with which Edwin Forrest is now performing at the Broadway Theatre.

The Macready group has been here for some time; beer, wine, etc., on the table. Tilton has only just arrived.

CLARK *(To Tilton as he sits down)*: How did it happen?
BRADSHAW: Before you answer that, who was he playing?
TILTON: Cassio.

(Beat.)

BRADSHAW: Scott as Cassio? I thought he was Forrest's Iago?

MRS. POPE: Not this season. *(Beat)* Earlier in the season.

TILTON: Who told you that?

MRS. POPE: In Baltimore wasn't he Iago?

TILTON: Scott told you that.

MRS. POPE: Didn't he sit here, at this very table, and say he was born to play Iago? *(Beat)* I heard him say this. Did anyone else hear him say this? *(Beat)* He said this is what he learned from playing the part in Baltimore. Or maybe it was Philadelphia.

TILTON: He's never played Iago in his life. *(Beat)* Once he played it. Something like five people had to get sick at the same time. It took that sort of luck. And then he knew about every third line. That's not playing Iago. *(Beat)* He's never actually played the part.

MRS. POPE: You played Iago, did you, Tilton?

TILTON: For years and years. *(Short pause)* Anyway, he slipped. Playing Cassio he slipped. And . . . *(Beat)* I wasn't on stage. This is what everyone was telling me.

CLARK: How much of the finger did he cut off?

TILTON: All of it! *(Beat)* I don't know. There was blood everywhere, though. I saw his shirt. After he left, it was there lying across a chair. *(Beat)* Blood all over it. *(Beat)* Someone said the dagger cut it all off and it was still on stage. *(Beat)* But I didn't see it. So . . . *(Shrugs)*

(Short pause.)

BRADSHAW: What else was Scott playing, Tilton?

TILTON: Let me think. In *Jack Cade*—what? What does he play? *(Beat)* I'm not in *Jack Cade*. I don't remember. *(Beat)* He's very good in it, they say. *(Beat)* But we don't do *Jack Cade* for—two weeks? I don't remember. I think that. And then there's his Macduff. He does play Macduff. I don't know what Ned'll do about losing a Macduff. There's a part I also used to play.

MRS. POPE: I can see how that would have been a very good role for you.

TILTON: My wife always said that same thing. She loved my Macduff. *(Beat)* I always thought that odd—for a wife to like such a part—what with all that happens to his family in the play.

MRS. POPE: I doubt if she was thinking about it that way.
TILTON: She was a smart woman, Mrs. Pope.
MRS. POPE: I remember her well.

(Beat.)

RYDER *(Suddenly standing and calling)*: If you need a Macduff! If
   this— If he—

(Others look at him.)

I know the part. I've played . . . I'm not doing anything at
this— Now. *(Turns to Macready)* Unless you think—

(Beat.)

CLARK *(Introducing)*: Mr. John Ryder.

(Tilton nods.)

And Mr. Macready, I'm sure you—
TILTON: I have seen you on stage many many times, sir.

(Macready smiles, then turns to Ryder.)

MACREADY *(Nodding toward Tilton)*: What's his—?

(Ryder shrugs.)

MRS. POPE: Tilton.

(Macready shakes his head, not knowing who he is. Short pause.)

TILTON: I shall pass this information along to Mr. Forrest.
RYDER: Thank you. I would appreciate it. *(Sits. Beat. Suddenly he
   stands again)* Would you care to join us? If that's all—
TILTON: I am supposed to save— *(Gestures "this table")*

(Ryder nods and sits. Pause.)

BRADSHAW: I wonder how long he'll be out.

(Beat. Mrs. Pope looks at him.)

Scott.

WEMYSS: I wonder if he was drinking. Scott drinks.

MRS. POPE: Not anymore. Not like when he did drink.

WEMYSS: He was drinking like that last week.

MACREADY *(Interrupting, not having listened to what anyone has been saying)*: I only want to say—to all of you—that I am having a wonderful time. So thank you.

(Others nod at him.)

MRS. POPE *(To Wemyss)*: When did you see him last week?

MACREADY *(Interrupting again)*: I think our rehearsals . . . I want you to know I could not be more pleased. And I am not speaking as an Englishman to— *(Beat)* No, I happen to love American— Everyone here is so— It's rich. It's—I was telling John just the other day, wasn't it? I was saying that *I* think American accents, they are so much closer to what Shakespeare himself spoke. You are so much closer. I think this has almost been proven. I mean, you—as American actors— I appreciate the way you have taken me in. The warmth. I feel this. I— *(Beat)* Thank you. *(Beat. Stares at Clark)* Much closer to what Shakespeare himself spoke. You! Without even— Just instinctively. All one's sophistication, it really can get in the way, can't it?! *(Laughs)* We poor English actors—right, John? Well, it's so much hard work and practice and study, and then one comes here and sees you— How you— The energy it comes so easy for you. *(Short pause. He looks at each actor at his table, one by one)* Anyway, I salute you. I have wanted to say this all week. Every night I tell John, I meant to say this. Here I have found in New York, an American group of— Which is almost like a group of English actors. I can't say more. *(Short pause)* Let me get some more to drink. *(He reaches for money)* I won't stay long, I promise you. Don't worry. *(Laughs to himself)* I want to buy— I want to pay— *(Takes out some money and turns to Ryder)* John, would you . . . ?

(He hands money to Ryder, who hesitates. Macready drinks. Ryder goes off to the bar. Pause.)

WEMYSS *(To Mrs. Pope)*: Last week. Maybe Tuesday. He was in here drinking like he used to.

MRS. POPE: I'm sorry to hear that.

BRADSHAW: And after he slipped and cut himself –

TILTON: Cut it off. The whole finger's off.

BRADSHAW: He then what? What happened to the—

TILTON: They finished the scene. Everyone. Scott, too. Like nothing happened. Blood was spurting and he stays.

MRS. POPE: Incredible.

MACREADY: Good for him! Good for him!

MRS. POPE *(To herself, shaking her head)*: For two dollars a performance.

CLARK: Something like that happens, you don't think, you act instinctively.

MRS. POPE: Stupidly.

MACREADY *(Banging the table, ignoring everyone)*: Good for him! *(Laughs)* John's like that, too. My good friend John. *(Gestures toward Ryder, then laughs)* He was in *Spartacus*. With me. This was with me in Leeds. *(Coughs, getting everyone's attention)* Listen to this. He needs to come on with his arm on fire. And we have worked this out. Carefully. *(Beat)* His arm on fire. *(Beat)* A metal band is put around his arm. And he carries a blanket—so if anything does happen . . . Which it shouldn't, but you want to be safe. This is an actor that I employ. I must be safe. The blanket he is to take and pat out the flame if— Whatever. If he needs to, has to. Anyway, he lights the flame just before his entrance. And he comes on now. *(Beat)* Fire blazing. Great effect. But someone this time has missed a cue. So we wait a moment. This happens even in the English theatre, let me tell you. Someone misses an entrance. *(Beat)* So the fire blazes for a little longer than it is supposed to. But John, he— He does nothing. Then he leaves. And so on. But then later we hear that his whole arm is quite badly burned. *(Beat)* He had let it burn! And why? Because he said— *(Beat)* The line he is to speak—he has a line which normally comes only a few seconds after he enters, but—and now this line, because of the mistake, it's coming a bit later, he says it—the line—I forget the line, but he says it. And it gets a nice little laugh. It always gets a nice little laugh. *(Beat)* And he says, that's why he didn't want to pat out the fire. Because he needed the blaze, he thought, to get that nice laugh. *(Beat)* So he let his arm burn! *(Laughs. Short pause)* Just to get the laugh!

MRS. POPE: We understood.

(No one else is laughing.)

MACREADY *(Laughing)*: I love John. From that day, I have loved him. That's the sort of—I don't know. *(Beat)* Nothing deceptive about him. Very rare for an actor. *(Beat)* A good friend. *(Smiles)* A good man to have around. *(Drinks)*

(Long pause.)

TILTON *(Finally)*: Scott's wife was nearly hysterical. *(Beat)* She's pregnant.

BRADSHAW *(To Mrs. Pope)*: You know his wife.

(She nods.)

MACREADY *(Suddenly hitting the table again)*: In England, acting is a noble profession, gentlemen! *(Beat)* And ladies.

(Ryder enters with more to drink. No one says anything as he sets the drinks down. Awkward pause.)

I won't ask you to show your scar, John. *(Laughs)*

MRS. POPE *(Quickly changing the subject)*: Anyone else seen Hackett?

WEMYSS: Why would we—?

MRS. POPE: He's offering seasons. He offered me a season.

WEMYSS: I wouldn't take a season.

MRS. POPE: He's doubled what he's paying. At least for me. *(Beat)* I may take a season.

BRADSHAW: He never asks me. We socialize. My wife sees his wife. Two three times a month, I think. But he never . . .

TILTON: He came around last week after *Richelieu.*

MRS. POPE: I heard this.

TILTON: He made offers. *(Beat)* To Jack. To Mary. To Florence.

BRADSHAW: Why does he need both Mary *and* Florence?

WEMYSS: Which Jack? Wheatley?

TILTON: Hooper. Jack Hooper.

MRS. POPE: Jack Wheatley's ill. Didn't you know?
WEMYSS: No. No, I didn't.

(Beat.)

BRADSHAW: I thought you'd worked a lot with Wheatley.
WEMYSS: No.
BRADSHAW: Weren't you together in—
WEMYSS: Wheatley wasn't in it then. When I was. *(Beat)* I took over his role. I saw him play the role. We've met. We've been out together. Many times. In groups. Nice man. *(Beat)* He's not that old.
CLARK: He is a nice man.
BRIDGES: He has children everywhere.
MRS. POPE: I've heard this.
WEMYSS: Where is he?
TILTON: At home. Went back to his wife.

(Short pause.)

WEMYSS *(To his daughter)*: We're about the same age. Wheatley and me.
MACREADY *(Grabbing Clark's shoulder)*: Mr. Clark, it was a very good rehearsal today. Very good.

(Beat.)

CLARK: Thank you.

(Short pause.)

MRS. POPE: Mr. Macready, as you've brought up the rehearsals . . . *(Looks at the others for a second)* Do you happen to know if I'll be needed tomorrow in the afternoon?
MACREADY: I don't know. *(Short pause)* You have something else to do.
MRS. POPE: If I'm needed I will be there. *(Short pause)* If I'm not my sister has planned a tea— She would like me to— She needs some help. *(Beat. Turns to the others)* But I wouldn't want to— If it's a bother. I can work all morning. Right through lunch if you wish. If that would help.

MACREADY: I'll do what I can, Mrs. Pope.

MRS. POPE: I don't want to be a problem, so if— *(Turns to the others)* If it's going to cause anyone any . . . *(Beat)* Is it? *(Beat)* I guess it isn't, Mr. Macready. No one said—

MACREADY: I'll do what I can, Mrs. Pope.

(Long pause. Only now does it become clear just how drunk Macready is. He holds his head, breathes heavily, then finally, and suddenly, stands up.)

And now I will go. *(Beat)* Before I drink too much. I do not want to drink too much. John, will you see me to a cab?

(Ryder stands and takes Macready's arm. Macready turns to the others and points.)

A good day! A very good day it has been! Do not be disheartened!

WEMYSS *(Standing)*: Actually we can help. We're leaving as well. *(To his daughter)* Let's go, Catherine.

MISS WEMYSS *(To the others)*: Thank you for letting me join you. I have enjoyed myself very much.

(Wemyss takes Macready's arm from Ryder and helps him out. Catherine follows. Ryder watches them go.)

CLARK: Why should we be disheartened? He said he thought rehearsals were going well. I think rehearsals are going well.

MRS. POPE: Please sit and stay, Mr. Ryder. Unless you have to . . .

(Beat.)

RYDER: No. *(Looks around the table)* I don't have to . . . Thank you. I'd like to very much. *(Sits back down. Pause)* Any idea who Mr. Forrest will get to play Macduff?

TILTON *(Before anyone can answer)*: Ever seen Macready act?

MRS. POPE: We're rehearsing with—

TILTON: I mean from the audience. I have seen him many many times. *(Beat)* Each time—it gets even worse.

MRS. POPE *(To Ryder)*: Sorry, he's—

RYDER *(Holding up his hand)*: No, no, please, don't—not for my sake. Just—

CLARK: He's been fine to work with. *(Beat)* I've worked with worse.

MRS. POPE: He actually spent some time with me on a scene he isn't even in.

BRIDGES: I saw his Richard in Philadelphia on his last tour. *(Beat)* I don't much like that sort of acting. It's not why I go to the theatre.

CLARK: People like it.

TILTON: English people like it.

BRADSHAW: Not just English people. He's performed all around the—

TILTON: Then people who want to be English people. They like it.

BRADSHAW: Maybe.

BRIDGES: Rich people like it.

TILTON: I agree with that too.

MRS. POPE: The Astor Place Opera House people will like it. So he'll do fine. We'll do fine.

BRIDGES: As long as there's an audience.

MRS. POPE: I say take what you can get.

(Short pause.)

BRIDGES: On my own, I never go to the Astor Place.

MRS. POPE: It's expensive.

BRADSHAW: The dressing rooms are rather nice though.

MRS. POPE: They are, aren't they?

(Short pause.)

RYDER: I've— *(Beat)* I have played Macduff.

BRADSHAW: English actors I'll wager are very different from American actors.

MRS. POPE: I hear when they go out—like this, as a group—they only speak in verse to each other.

RYDER *(Quickly)*: No, that's not true. We don't.

(The others laugh.)

We really don't. *(Realizes that it is a joke and laughs with the others)*

TILTON: I've worked with English actors. The first thing you learn is never leave out your money.

MRS. POPE: When someone's passing through—when anyone is—
and you know you can't find him again, you do not leave out
your money. It has nothing to do with being—
BRIDGES: Are you enjoying America, Mr. Ryder?
CLARK: You've been before?
RYDER: No, I haven't. *(Beat)* That's why Mr. Macready, well,
besides wanting the company, he thought I should see for
myself. He said, "John, you are not going to believe this. I want
to be there to see your face."

*(Beat. Thomas Fisher, Jane Bass, Helen Burton, and Anne
Holland—all actors working with Edwin Forrest at the Broadway
Theatre—enter, on their way to Tilton's table, which he has been
saving for them.)*

FISHER *(While entering)*: This one? Is this our table? How many—?
(Starts to count chairs)
MISS BASS *(To Mrs. Pope at a distance)*: Hello. How are you?

(Mrs. Pope smiles and nods.)

FISHER: We'll need another chair.
TILTON: Who's—?
FISHER: Ned and Robert are at the bar getting the drinks.
CLARK: You can use these chairs.
FISHER *(Going to the table for the chairs)*: Nice to see you.
CLARK: And you. *(Beat)* You know—
FISHER: Of course I do. Why don't you— If you want.
MRS. POPE: We're leaving. I'm leaving. We've been here how long?
FISHER *(Taking the chairs back to the other table)*: Another time then.
BRADSHAW: Absolutely.

(The Macready table now watches the other table.)

TILTON *(To Miss Bass)*: How's Scott? Anyone seen Scott?
MISS BASS: Ned spoke to him. *(Beat)* The doctor wants him to sleep.
MISS BURTON: He wanted to come out with us. *(Smiles and shakes her
head)*
MISS HOLLAND: He's going to be fine.
TILTON: Someone was saying they'd seen him drinking.

MISS BASS: Tonight?

TILTON: They said this tonight, yes.

FISHER: He didn't seem himself, did he? Even in the dressing room. *(Beat)* And he never dries.

MISS HOLLAND: He dried tonight?

FISHER: I think so. *(Beat)* I'm not sure, but I think so. Sometimes with Scott it's hard to tell.

MISS HOLLAND *(To Miss Burton)*: Save a place for Robert.

(Miss Burton looks at her and moves over a chair.
Edwin Forrest and Robert Jones, also an actor with Forrest's Broadway Theatre company, enter carrying drinks.)

FORREST *(While entering)*: I'm spilling. *(To Jones, who is behind him)* Watch your step, don't slip. *(Beat)* Someone should get a cloth and I don't want anyone to slip.

MISS BASS *(Getting up)*: I'll ask at the bar.

CLARK: We have a cloth. *(To Bridges)* Give me that. Give me the cloth.

(Bridges does.)

(Holding up the cloth) We have one.

FORREST: Thank you.

MISS BASS: I'll take it.

(She takes the cloth. Forrest looks at Jones.)

JONES: Clark. Charlie Clark.

FORREST: Thank you, Mr. Clark. *(Starts to turn, stops, looks back at Clark)* Have we worked together?

CLARK: No. No, sir. *(Beat)* Not yet. *(Laughs)* Hopefully some day.

(Forrest nods.)

JONES: Charlie is—in fact, you all are, aren't you? Working with Mr. Macready on his *Macbeth*.

MRS. POPE: We are. That's right.

FORREST: And it's going well?

(They nod.)

Good. *(Winks at them and goes to the other table)*
JONES *(To the Macready table)*: If you'd like to join—
RYDER: I'd love to. Thanks. *(Gets up. Introducing himself)* Ryder. John Ryder.
JONES: How do you do? English?
RYDER: That's right.
CLARK *(To others)*: Why don't we . . . He's asked us. I'm going to. *(Gets up)*
MRS. POPE *(Getting up)*: I can just stay a minute more.
BRADSHAW: Me, too. One minute.

(They move toward the other table, carrying their drinks. Forrest is beginning to serve.)

FORREST: Who doesn't have a glass? Who wants wine? Who wants beer? *(Beat)* Why don't I just pass it around.
RYDER: I heard you had a problem during the performance tonight.

(Short pause.)

FORREST: We did, yes. *(Beat)* Poor Mr. Scott, he—
TILTON: I told them, Ned.
FORREST *(Turning to Tilton, then back to Ryder)*: Then you know. *(To the others)* Please, help yourselves. *(Beat. To Ryder)* Have we worked together?
RYDER: I've never performed in America. Not that I have anything against it. *(Beat)* I'm a friend of Mr. Macready's. I help him.
FORREST: I've been to England.
RYDER: Of course I know that. I've seen you—
FORREST: Perhaps I saw you do something there.
RYDER: Perhaps.
FORREST: I'm sure I have. *(Stares at Ryder then turns to Fisher)* Mr. Fisher, I've a few notes about tonight that I'd like to give before I forget them. That's if you have a moment.
FISHER: Of course, Ned.
FORREST: Bring your chair.

(Fisher brings his chair and sits next to Forrest. Others have sat as well, except for Ryder.)

RYDER *(A little too loud)*: What role was the poor man who hurt himself playing?

(Short pause. Others choose to consciously ignore Ryder's question.)

FORREST *(Barely audible, to Fisher)*: First let me say, what I thought you were doing in our first scene was quite laudable . . .

TILTON *(To the others)*: You just missed Macready himself.

BRIDGES: He was with us. He bought us . . .

(Conversations begin. Small groups of two or three, with only Ryder excluded.)

CLARK: I've got work in Cincinnati whenever I want it.

MISS BURTON: They all say that. Then you get to Cincinnati.

CLARK: Not this time. I believe these people. *(Beat)* These people are different.

MISS BURTON: Go to Cincinnati then.

(Many overlapping conversations now so no one is understandable. This goes on for a few moments. Then blackout.)

SCENE 2

1 A.M.

Parlor, Edwin Forrest's house. A few chairs, a bookcase, etc. Forrest and Miss Bass sit in chairs, fairly near each other, and occasionally glance at each other. They also have glasses in their hands. Bradshaw stands at the bookcase browsing through the books. Ryder stands looking through a scrapbook. Long pause. Ryder closes the scrapbook, sets it on a table, notices a silver snuffbox and picks it up.

RYDER: This is beautiful.

FORREST *(Turning to Ryder)*: Read what it says. *(Beat)* Read it out loud so Mr. Bradshaw can hear.

(Bradshaw stops browsing.)

RYDER *(Reading from the snuffbox)*: "Presented to Edwin Forrest, Esq., by the members of the Sheffield Theatrical Company, as a mark of their esteem for him as an actor and a man."

(Beat.)

FORREST: Something to cherish.
RYDER: Certainly . . .
FORREST: Coming as it does from actors.

(Short pause.)

BRADSHAW: This was when you were in England . . .
FORREST: The last time. Let me see it. I haven't noticed it for a long time.

(Ryder hands him the box. Miss Bass gets up and goes to Forrest to look at the box. Short pause.)

(To Miss Bass) They had a nice little ceremony. The man who made the speech was a very lousy actor.

(He smiles, the others laugh lightly.)

Brooke, I think his name was. Do you know him, Mr. Ryder?
RYDER: I don't know. I—I don't think so.
FORREST: I thought being English . . .
RYDER: Maybe I do. I don't know. *(Beat)* Brooke? I don't know.

(Forrest hands the box back to Ryder.)

It is a beautiful box. *(Puts it back on the table)*
FORREST *(Holding up a decanter)*: Would anyone—?
RYDER: I'm fine, thank you.

(Forrest turns to Bradshaw, who shakes his head and goes back to browsing. He turns to Miss Bass, who now sits on the arm of his chair.)

MISS BASS *(Holding up her glass)*: I haven't touched what I have.

(Forrest puts the decanter down without pouring a drink.)

FORREST *(Without looking at Ryder)*: Have you already gone through both scrapbooks, Mr. Ryder?
RYDER: I— Both? No. I didn't know there were two. I've only seen this—
FORREST: Miss Bass knows where the other one is kept.
MISS BASS: I'll get it. *(Goes to a table, opens a drawer, takes out a book)*
FORREST: I call that section the Shakespeare Corner, Mr. Bradshaw.
BRADSHAW: I can see why. *(Laughs)*
FORREST: Warburton's edition is certainly worth a look.
BRADSHAW: Which is?. . .
FORREST: To your left. *(Beat)* Up one. Two over. There. That's right.

(Bradshaw takes out a book.)

I have nearly all the editions of Shakespeare's work. Even—
(Stops himself and smiles) But we'll get to that. *(Turns to Miss Bass, who has the scrapbook)* I'll take that, please. *(Turns back to Bradshaw)* The actor's work—I don't have to tell you—is much more than what is on the stage. These are but some necessary tools for one's investigations. *(Takes the scrapbook and opens it)* Come here, Mr. Ryder. I plan to exhaust all of your enthusiasm as well as your patience.
RYDER: I'm the one who asked to see—
FORREST *(Pointing out things in the scrapbook)*: Here I am as Richard III. *(Smiles)* This was in Dublin, you'll be interested to know.

(Forrest stares at the picture. Pause. Ryder looks at Miss Bass and then at Bradshaw, who has come to look over Forrest's shoulder. Finally, Forrest turns the page.)

Romeo.

(Forrest stares at the picture, then sniffles, takes out a handkerchief and wipes a tearing eye. Ryder watches this, aware that he has no idea what is going on and uncomfortable because of this.)

I also played Mercutio. First I played Mercutio. I was only a boy then.

(He smiles at Miss Bass, who smiles and takes his hand.)

Mr. Wallack was the Romeo. He was much too old. Much. He should have known better. *(Beat)* Someone should have told him. Been honest with him. *(Sighs and stands)* I promised to show you something, didn't I, Mr. Bradshaw. Excuse me. *(Goes off)*

BRADSHAW *(To Ryder)*: What's he? . . .

(Ryder shrugs.)

I think I will have a little of that.

(He pours himself a drink. The atmosphere in the room has suddenly relaxed.)

RYDER *(To Miss Bass)*: Have you worked with Mr. Forrest before? *(Beat)* I mean before this season.

(She looks at Bradshaw, then back at Ryder.)

MISS BASS: Yes. Yes. I have.

RYDER: Then maybe you can help me. Do you think he was being serious when he said he wanted me for Macduff?

MISS BASS: Yes, I'm sure he was being serious, Mr. Ryder. *(Beat)* He needs a—

RYDER: Sometimes you don't know. People say all sorts of things. *(Beat)* Especially late at night.

MISS BASS: Rehearsals are tomorrow. I'm sure he expects you there.

BRADSHAW: You know the part.

RYDER: In England I've played it a hundred—

(He stops himself as Mrs. Catherine Forrest enters. She is in her dressing gown. Awkward pause.)

MRS. FORREST: I thought I heard voices. *(Beat)* Is my husband here or do you just come on your own now, Miss Bass?

BRADSHAW: He went to get something.

(Mrs. Forrest begins to go off in that direction.)

MISS BASS: How are you, Mrs. Forrest?

(She ignores this and goes off. Beat.)

RYDER: I hadn't realized he had a wife.

(From off the sound of an argument. Forrest and his wife shouting at each other, though exactly what they are shouting about cannot be heard. Ryder, Bradshaw and Miss Bass try to ignore them. Ryder pours himself a drink.)

BRADSHAW *(To Ryder)*: Have you seen the——? *(Nods toward the bookcase)*
RYDER: I haven't had the chance yet. But I'd love to. *(Goes to the bookcase)*
BRADSHAW: An extraordinary collection.

(They pretend to browse, as the argument continues off. Finally Forrest enters alone carrying a large book.)

FORREST *(While entering)*: Pope's edition is also worth looking through. But before that . . . *(Beat. Holds up the book)* Here is what I wanted to show you. *(Sits)* The most precious thing I own.

(Ryder and Bradshaw come closer.)

I dare say, I believe it to be the only First Folio in the New World.
RYDER: First Folio——? *(Instinctively reaches for it)*
FORREST: Gentle. Gentle, Mr. Ryder. *(Beat)* She breathes. This book. She lives. *(Opens it and reads)* "Mr. William Shakespeare's Comedies, Histories & Tragedies. Published according to the True original copies. London. Printed by Issac Jaggard and Ed. Blout, 1623."

(Pause. Forrest has heard something.)

Now she's crying.

(Mrs. Forrest can be heard crying in the next room.)

(To Ryder) Feel the cover.

(He does.)

As smooth as a child's face. As smooth as a face. *(Rubs his hand across Miss Bass's face)* What one needs to study to be a Shakespearean actor. *(Gently pats the book)* The truth lies in our hands. *(Beat)* The ignorance of the world knows no bounds, Mr. Ryder. I have twice been criticized for reading "dead vast" instead of saying "dead waste." Some quartos have it even as "wast"—what ever that is supposed to mean— and also as "waist"—W-A-I-S-T. *(Laughs)* But in here, Mr. Ryder, our true authority, it is "vast." *(Beat)* "Vast" for the vacancy and void of night. For the deserted emptiness. Not "waste." Not for what has been thrown away. "Vast"! For the hole, the H-O-L-E! The loss of what is, what was, a loss that shall always remain a loss! *(Beat)* You study. You learn. *(Beat)* Like a face. That smooth. Rub your face against the book and feel it. Against your flesh.

(Ryder takes the book and rubs it against his face, then hands it to Bradshaw, who does the same. Pause.)

(Without looking at Ryder) Some of Macduff's lines we cut, Mr. Ryder. I shall give you such cuts tomorrow. *(Pause)* Poor Scott, cut his finger off from here. *(Holds up his finger)* Blood was everywhere. Somehow it even got on the sheets. *(Beat)* Big stain on Desdemona's sheets. I noticed that as I— I was holding the pillow. *(Looks up at them)* Sometimes you lose yourself so much in a role. *(Beat)* Sometimes you— *(Beat)* Sometimes you are lost.

(Mrs. Forrest's crying is louder for a moment.)

RYDER: Maybe we'd better . . . *(Beat)* If I'm going to be ready for rehearsal. *(Tries to smile)*
FORREST: I was good as Othello tonight. They got their money's worth.

(Short pause. Ryder doesn't know whether to leave or not. Black-out.)

SCENE 3

2 A.M.

Parlor of Macready's rooms at the New York Hotel. Miss Wemyss sits alone. Ryder has just entered.

RYDER: I'm sorry, I— Is Mr. Macready . . . ?
MISS WEMYSS: He'll be right out. He's just in there.

(Ryder nods. Pause. He paces, not knowing whether to stay or go; she watches him, smiling when she catches his eye.)

RYDER: He left me a note. *(Beat)* Downstairs. When I came in they gave me the note. *(Beat)* It said he wanted to see me as soon as I . . . *(Beat)* I just got in. It's probably too late.
MISS WEMYSS: I don't know.

(Short pause.)

RYDER *(Putting on his hat)*: Tell him I—

(Macready enters in his dressing gown.)

MACREADY: Come in, John, please come in.
RYDER: It's very late.
MACREADY: Thank you for coming. Sit down. I'll fix us a drink.
RYDER: I've had plenty tonight.
MACREADY: A nightcap never hurts. *(Pause. Pours them drinks)* You've met Miss Wemyss?
RYDER: Tonight. At the tavern. With her father—
MACREADY: Of course you have! Of course! Where is my head? *(Laughs to himself. To Miss Wemyss)* And what about you, my dear, what may I get you?
MISS WEMYSS: I don't wish anything, Mr. Macready. I am content as I am.

(He suddenly bursts out laughing.)

MACREADY: I don't know what it is about her, John, but everything she says makes me laugh.

(Miss Wemyss smiles at Ryder.)

RYDER: I think we should talk in the morning.

(Wemyss enters carrying a teapot.)

WEMYSS *(While entering)*: This is all I could—from the kitchen.
They insisted they put it in a teapot though. I don't understand
this thinking. *(Beat)* I had to stand down there and watch them
pour a whole bottle into a teapot. *(He shakes his head)*
MACREADY *(Holding up the decanter)*: Now pour it into here, Mr.
Wemyss. *(Turns to Ryder)* We were beginning to get a little
low.

*(Wemyss pours the liquor out of the pot and into the bottle. He is a
bit drunk.)*

Your daughter just said something very funny. Very funny.

(Wemyss turns to his daughter and smiles. He continues to pour.)

(To Ryder) What did she say?
RYDER: I don't know. Why is Mr. Wemyss—? What's he doing
here?
MACREADY *(To Miss Wemyss)*: What is it you said?
MISS WEMYSS: I don't remember anymore.

*(Macready bursts out laughing, then turns to Ryder patting
Wemyss on the shoulder.)*

MACREADY: Frederick here wanted a little advice, didn't you?
WEMYSS: You've been very helpful, William.
MACREADY: His daughter— This is his daughter. She wishes to
become an actress. Isn't this true, my dear?

(She smiles.)

WEMYSS: She has the looks for it, I think. Look at her.

(She smiles again at Ryder.)

MACREADY: And— *(Beat)* You— What? You wondered, correct? If there might be some place in London—to learn. He thinks she should learn in London. That says something, does it not? *(Beat)* Someone to learn from.

WEMYSS: Someone to even befriend . . . *(Turns to his daughter)* You don't know what can happen when a young woman is that far away from her family. *(Turns to Macready)* She has a lovely family. Five daughters. They take care of each other.

MACREADY *(To Ryder)*: I am going to look into matters for her. I shall see what there might be for— I don't know. *(Beat)* Perhaps an apprenticeship? *(Beat)* Perhaps at Drury Lane? How would that strike you, my dear? *(Smiles)*

WEMYSS: Drury Lane would be excellent.

MACREADY: I cannot promise of course.

WEMYSS: No one is asking for a promise, William. No one. Are we?

MISS WEMYSS: I'm not.

(Macready looks at her, smiles and finally sighs a drunk sigh. Pause.)

RYDER: What did you want to see me about?

MACREADY: Drink, John. We have a whole new teapot full of drink.

(He gestures for Ryder to take his drink. Ryder doesn't move.)

Oh yes. That. *(Turns to Miss Wemyss)* What would you do, Miss Wemyss? Would you ignore the threats?

RYDER: What threats? What are you talking about?

(Macready laughs and nods at Ryder.)

MACREADY *(To Miss Wemyss)*: Now everyone is getting worried. Don't panic, Mr. Ryder, please. *(Laughs. Pause. Stops laughing and turns to Ryder)* Mr. Wemyss has been telling me that we are under threat. Or do I exaggerate?

WEMYSS: No. *(Beat)* Mr. Macready's life is, I believe, in some danger.

RYDER: For what? Who—?

WEMYSS: There have been letters. I have one here. *(Takes out a letter and hands it to Ryder)* I didn't want to mention it at the tavern, with—

(Ryder holds out the letter to Macready.)

MACREADY: I've seen it, John. You read it. See what you think.

WEMYSS: Though most in the company have been—*are* aware at least that something . . . You feel it in the air, I suppose. And we've all heard I guess that there are persons who are upset—

RYDER: For what reason?!

MACREADY: Because I dare to perform the noble Thane on the same night in the same city as does the sainted American, Mr. Edwin Forrest! *(Turns to Wemyss)* Is that not the true reason?

WEMYSS: I don't know. *(Beat)* Maybe. I know it's what you think.

MACREADY: Of course it's the reason for these attacks! A perceived competition with their idol, their native idol! *(Beat)* Ridiculous. *(Beat)* Sheer effrontery—on my part. This is how they see it. Pure gall. And of course it would be upsetting. On the same night! For all to compare! Of course they are worried! *(Laughs)* And an Englishman, no less! Look at the spelling. The illiterate bastards. Probably Irish.

RYDER: I don't understand what they're demanding.

MACREADY: Short of a complete surrender and my going home immediately, you mean. *(Laughs to himself)* All in good time. All in good time.

(Beat.)

WEMYSS: The letters are meant to frighten—

RYDER *(To Macready)*: And you take the threats seriously?

MACREADY: I don't. *(Laughs)* I don't. But others may. *(Beat)* So I am suggesting that we contact Mr. Forrest, present him with this irksome situation we, as guests, now confront in his homeland, and no doubt he shall do the honorable thing and see fit to perform some other of his multitude of roles that evening. *(Beat)* Let's say *Metamora*. *(Beat)* I understand he is especially convincing as an Indian. Americans can be, you know. An Englishman would be hopeless as a savage. A pity I will not be able to see this performance myself. *(Beat)* John, I think I am asking you to do this.

RYDER: I doubt if Mr. Forrest will change his repertoire at this late—

MACREADY: He has to! *(Short pause)* He has many plays—they are cast—they can be mounted. I have scheduled only *Macbeth*. I have only a company for *Macbeth*. It would be impossible for me to do anything else. *(Beat)* Besides, I understand after the accident tonight he doesn't even have a Macduff. So if he needs to explain to the public—

RYDER: He has a new Macduff. *(Pause)* He asked me. *(Beat)* You have Clark. You wanted Clark. I didn't have anything to do. I know I'm here to help you, but I can do both. I know the role for Christ's sake! *(Beat)* I told Forrest I would have to speak with you first. And if you objected . . . *(Beat)* He was desperate. But . . . Do you object?

MACREADY *(Without looking at him)*. We are a fraternity, John—the acting fraternity. We know no borders. Have no flags. *(Beat)* So how can I object to helping out Mr. Forrest. Wouldn't he do the same for me? I'll get someone else to speak with him. Someone with less to lose.

RYDER: That's not fair.

WEMYSS: I'd be happy to.

RYDER: Forrest's performance is sold out. It would be nearly impossible at this point to change the schedule.

MACREADY *(Suddenly turning on him)*: Men and women are being threatened with violence, John, and you talk about an inconvenience?!! *(Beat)* I do not say this for myself. Do you understand? *(Beat)* But these actors work under my protection. I have their safety as my responsibility. *(Sips his drink)* We have not yet sold out. *(Beat)* Two *Macbeths* in one evening may be too much for New York to bear. *(Beat)* I cannot change. I have told you why. If he does not, these scoundrels, these ignorant hooligans have the guts, I'm afraid, to attempt what they have threatened. Does Mr. Forrest realize what he will be instigating? Consciously or not. Will he alone accept the responsibility for our well being? *(Short pause)* I'm sure we'll be fine. *(Shrugs)* I'm pleased you found work. I truly am.

RYDER: He asked me. I didn't seek it. I must have said no ten times. *(Laughs)*

MACREADY: So—what else could you do? *(Reaches for the letter, takes it from Ryder, and looks at it again)* I knew nothing of any problems. Any such—tensions. Where did they come from? I should have been warned. To hate one simply because one is accomplished. *(Beat)* Had I known . . . *(Shakes his head)*

RYDER: You knew—I knew that there's some resentment when any English actor—

MACREADY: I am not any English actor! *(Beat)* And I knew of no such resentment, John!! *(Sits and sighs)* Such incidents make one long for home even more.

(Miss Wemyss begins to stand.)

Please everyone, there is no need to hurry off.

(She sits. Short pause.)

RYDER: It's very late.

MACREADY: Yes it is. Yes. *(Pause)* I wrote Mrs. Macready. *(To Ryder)* This was where I was when you came in. *(To Miss Wemyss)* You didn't mind, did you? Being left on your own? *(Short pause)* I spoke of this loneliness. Being away from home. *(Beat)* She must be getting tired of such letters. *(Laughs to himself)* But it is like being suspended upon the edge of a cliff. This is how much of your country feels to me, Mr. Wemyss. As a cliff.

(Wemyss nods.)

I try to go to sleep and a hundred devils attack me. *(Beat)* And tie me up. *(Beat)* Little devils. *(Yawns)* If I did not know how important what I bring is. *(Beat)* The need. When one is hearing Shakespeare spoken correctly for the first time. *(Smiles)* It is an honor. And it is a burden. One I shall gladly pass on to younger men. *(Beat)* When they emerge. *(Beat)* I'm tired. Don't go yet.

(Pause.)

WEMYSS: I have been to Drury Lane myself once. This was years ago when I was a much younger man. *(Beat)* I think my daughter could be very comfortable there. I have told all my children—there is nothing like England. Nothing in the world.

MISS WEMYSS: Mr. Macready has not offered to . . .

(Beat.)

MACREADY *(Looking at her and smiling)*: I shall. I do. *(Beat)* But will I remember I've offered in the morning? *(Laughs)* Let me think about it.

(Pause. Macready sits, staring at nothing. Miss Wemyss smiles. Wemyss stands behind Macready's chair and sips his drink. Ryder doesn't know whether to leave or not. Blackout.)

SCENE 4

THE NEXT DAY, THE AFTERNOON

A bare stage, representing the stage of the Astor Place Opera House (Macready's company) and the Broadway Theatre (Forrest's company), during rehearsals of the two Macbeths.

Broadway Theatre, Act I.iii

Drums. Then thunder. The Three Witches (Misses Bass, Burton and Holland) are on.

1ST WITCH:
> . . . nine times nine,
> Shall he dwindle, peak and pine.
> Though his bark cannot be lost.
> Yet it shall be tempest-tost.

2ND WITCH: Show me, show me.

3RD WITCH:
> Here I have a pilot's thumb,
> Wrecked as homeward he did come.

(Drum within.)

ALL:
> A drum! A drum!
> Macbeth doth come.

(Macbeth [Forrest] and Banquo [Jones] enter.)

MACBETH:

So foul and fair a day I have not seen.

BANQUO:

How far is't called to Forres?—What are these,
That look not like th'inhabitants o'th' earth
And yet are on't?

MACBETH:

Speak, if you can. What are you?

1ST WITCH:

All hail, Macbeth! Hail to thee, Thane of Glamis.

2ND WITCH:

All hail, Macbeth! Hail to thee, Thane of Cawdor.

3RD WITCH:

All hail, Macbeth, that shalt be King hereafter!

BANQUO:

Good sir, why do you start, and seem to fear
Things that do sound so fair? To me you speak not.
Speak then to me, who neither beg nor fear
Your favors nor your hate.

1ST WITCH: Hail!
2ND WITCH: Hail!
3RD WITCH: Hail!

1ST WITCH:

Lesser than Macbeth, and greater.

2ND WITCH:

Not so happy, yet much happier.

3RD WITCH:

Thou shalt get kings, though thou be none.
So all hail, Macbeth and Banquo!

MACBETH:

> Stay, you imperfect speakers, say from whence
> You owe this strange intelligence, or why
> Upon this blasted heath you stop our way
> With such prophetic greeting. Speak, I charge you.

(Witches run off, Macbeth and Banquo give chase.)

Astor Place Opera House, Act I.iii

The Three Witches, all male (Bridges and two older men: John Sefton and Chippindale), Macbeth (Macready) and Banquo (Bradshaw).

1ST WITCH: Hail!
2ND WITCH: Hail!
3RD WITCH: Hail!

1ST WITCH:

> Lesser than Macbeth, and greater.

2ND WITCH:

> Not so happy, yet much happier.

3RD WITCH:

> Thou shalt get kings, though thou be none.
> So all hail, Macbeth and Banquo!

MACBETH:

> By Sinel's death I know I am Thane of Glamis,
> But how of Cawdor? The Thane of Cawdor lives,
> A prosperous gentleman, and to be king
> Stands not within the prospect of belief,
> No more than to be Cawdor.

(Witches run off, Macbeth and Banquo give chase.)

Broadway Theatre, Act I.vii

Out of the shadows enters Macbeth (Forrest).

MACBETH:

> If it were done when 'tis done, then 'twere well
> It were done quickly. If th'assassination
> Could trammel up the consequence, and catch
> With his surcease success: that but this blow
> Might be the be-all and the end-all, here,
> But here upon this band and shoal of time,
> We'd jump the life to come. But in these cases
> We still have judgment here, that we but teach
> Bloody instructions which, being taught, return
> To plague th'inventor. This even-handed justice
> Commends . . .

Astor Place Opera House, Act I.vii

Macbeth (Macready) alone.

MACBETH:

> . . . Will plead like angels, trumpet-tongued against
> The deep damnation of his taking-off,
> And pity, like a naked new-born babe,
> Striding the blast, or heaven's cherubim, horsed
> Upon the sightless couriers of the air,
> Shall blow the horrid deed in every eye
> That tears shall drown the wind. I have no spur
> To prick the sides of my intent, but only
> Vaulting ambition, which o'erleaps itself
> And falls on th'other.

(Pause. Finally Macbeth [Macready] turns toward the wings and gives a small nod. Lady Macbeth [Mrs. Pope] enters.)

How now? What news?

MACREADY *(To Mrs. Pope)*: Closer. Closer. There. Now look at me. *(Beat)* I look at them and you look at me. Thank you.

(Beat.)

MACBETH:

> How now? What news?

Broadway Theatre, Act II.i

Macbeth (Forrest) enters with a torch.

MACBETH:

> Is this a dagger which I see before me,
> The handle toward my hand? Come, let me clutch thee.
> I have thee not, and yet I see thee still.
> Art thou not, fatal vision, sensible
> To feeling as to sight? Or art thou but
> A dagger of the mind, a false creation
> Proceeding from the heat-oppressed brain?
> I see thee yet, in form as palpable
> As this which now I draw.
> Thou marshall'st me the way . . .

The Broadway Theatre and Astor Place Opera House, Act II.i (continued)

Both Macbeths (Macready and Forrest) now continue the speech together, though not necessarily in sync.

BOTH MACBETHS:

> . . . that I was going,
> Mine eyes are made the fools o'th'other senses,
> Or else worth all the rest. I see thee still,
> And on thy blade and dudgeon gouts of blood,
> Which was not so before. There's no such thing.
> It is the bloody business which informs
> This to mine eyes.

(Lights begin to fade on Forrest at the Broadway Theatre.)

Now o'er the one half-world
Nature seems dead, and wicked dreams abuse
The curtained sleep.

*(Macready is alone now, the stage representing only the Astor
Place Opera House.)*

MACBETH:
Thou sure and firm-set earth,
Hear not my steps which way they walk, for fear
The very stones prate of my whereabout,
And take the present horror from the time,
Which now suits with it. Whiles I threat, he lives.
Words to the heat of deeds too cold breath gives.

Broadway Theatre, Act II.iii

Very loud pounding or knocking is suddenly heard. Porter (Tilton) hurries on.

PORTER: Here's a knocking indeed! If a man were porter of hell
gate, he should have old turning the key.

(Another knock.)

Knock, knock, knock. Who's there, in th'other devil's name?

(Beat.)

TILTON: Wait, I think I jumped. It's what? Is it: "Knock, knock"?
Or "Knock, knock, knock"? Which is the first, the two or the
three knocks? *(Beat)* Please, which is the first?!
PROMPTER *(Off)*: It's the three "knocks" first.
TILTON: Really? *(Beat)* Thank you. *(Beat)* Sorry. *(Goes back to his
position, then suddenly breaks it)* Now let me get this straight.
It's the three "knocks," then the two "knocks," right? And then
it's the three again, am I correct? And then it's the two again?
PROMPTER: That is correct.

TILTON: So it's three "knocks" and the "devil's name" line. Then two "knocks" and the "Beelzebub."

PROMPTER *(Off)*: The three "knocks" are with the "Beelzebub" and the two are with the "devil's name."

TILTON: What?

PROMPTER *(Off)*: And it's the "devil's name" line that comes first. *(Beat)* After the *three* "knocks."

(Tilton stares in disbelief.)

Then the third one—also after three "knocks"—is the "English tailor" bit. Then comes "too cold for hell." *(Beat)* After three more "knocks." *(Beat)* I'm sorry, after *two* more "knocks." *(Beat)* Yes, that's right, it is two more "knocks" for the last one. Is that clear?

(Short pause. Tilton tries to shake off confusion.)

TILTON *(Rubbing his eyes)*: Let me start again. *(As he exits)* I'm sorry to hold everyone up.

(He leaves. Pounding. He hurries on.)

PORTER: Here's a knocking indeed! *(Stops himself)*

TILTON: I don't have the slightest idea what I'm saying now. All I'm thinking about is how many goddamn "knocks" I have!

(Short pause. Forrest enters with others in the company.)

Sorry, Ned.

FORREST: Take your time.

TILTON: I'm fine. I knew it. Ask anyone and they'll tell you I knew it perfect. *(Beat)* I was just a little uncertain of the "knocks." *(Awkward pause)* Would you mind if I . . . just for now, if I said as many "knocks" as I want. As come out. That's what's . . .

FORREST: Say what you want. I mean it. *(To others)* Ready? Let's continue. *(Leaves with the others)*

TILTON *(As he exits, to the Prompter, off)*: Hear that? I can say as many "knocks" as I damn well want! *(Exits)*

Astor Place Opera House, Act II.ii

Mrs. Pope (Lady Macbeth) stands to one side as Macready (Macbeth) plays both Macbeth and Lady Macbeth.

MACREADY *(Knocking with his foot, as Macbeth):*
>Whence is that knocking?—
>How is't with me when every noise appals me?
>What hands are here! Ha, They pluck out mine eyes.
>Will all great Neptune's ocean wash this blood
>Clean from my hand? No, this my hand will rather
>The multitudinous seas incarnadine,
>Making the green one red.

(He hurries to a side and enters now as Lady Macbeth. As Lady Macbeth:)

>My hands are of your color.

And blah-blah-blah. Whatever the lines. More knocking. *(Knocks with his foot)* Something about retiring to the bedroom. I take you by the hand. Like this. Come here.

(Mrs. Pope goes to him, he takes her hand.)

MACBETH:
>To know my deed, 'twere best not know myself.

(He knocks with his foot.)

>Wake Duncan with thy knocking! I would thou couldst.

MACREADY: Head on my shoulder. And look down. Down.

(Beat. As they exit.)

And I look out as we leave.

(They exit.)

Broadway Theatre, Act II.iii

Porter (Tilton) is alone on stage. Pause.

TILTON: I've dried. I've never dried.

FORREST *(Entering)*: What's the line? Give him the line.

TILTON: I don't remember anything. What's my character? What's the name of the play? *(Laughs)* I'm kidding. *(Laughs)* I'm sorry everyone. My apologies to all of you. It's one of those days. *(Laughs)*

FORREST: Just say your last line and we'll keep going. *(Turns to go)*

TILTON: What's my last line?

PROMPTER *(Off)*: "I pray you remember the porter."

(Pause. Tilton is alone on stage.)

TILTON: Ready?

(He sighs, then:)

PORTER *(Unaware of the mistake he is making)*: I pray the porter remember.

(Macduff [Ryder] enters.)

MACDUFF:
>Was it so late, friend, ere you went to bed
>That you do lie so late?

TILTON: I don't know those lines. We cut those lines. I wasn't supposed to know them.

FORREST *(Entering)*: You enter with me, Mr. Ryder. Each from different sides. *(Calls off)* What's the line?

PROMPTER *(Off)*: "Our knocking has awaken."

FORREST: "Our knocking has awaken." *(Beat)* From different sides.

RYDER: The rest is cut.

FORREST: I thought someone was giving Mr. Ryder the cuts?!

(They go. Tilton is alone.)

TILTON: From my last line? *(Beat)* What was my last line again?

PROMPTER *(Off)*: It's "I pray you remember the porter." It's not
  "I pray the porter remember."
TILTON: "I pray the . . ."
PROMPTER: Which is what you said the last time.
TILTON: I said—? *(Beat)* I couldn't have said . . . *(Beat)* I did?
  I heard—
FORREST *(Off)*: Please, Tilton, begin!

(Short pause.)

TILTON *(Does not know what to say)*: I . . . Uh.

Astor Place Opera House, Act IV.i

*Thunder and lightning. Macbeth (Macready) and the Three Witches
(Sefton, Bridges and Chippindale). The Witches sit on the ground.*

MACBETH:
  I conjure you, but that which you profess,
  Howe'er you come to know it, answer me.

1ST WITCH: Speak.
2ND WITCH: Demand.
3RD WITCH: We'll answer.

1ST WITCH:
  Say if thou'dst rather hear it from our mouths
  Or from our masters.

MACBETH: Call 'em—

*(Macready stops himself. He goes to one of the Witches and pulls
his dress down a little so less of his leg can be seen, then continues:)*

  Call 'em, let me see 'em.

(Thunder and an explosion.)

Broadway Theatre, Act IV.i

*Macbeth (Forrest), the Three Witches (Misses Bass, Burton and Holland)
and 1st Apparition.*

1ST APPARITION:
>Macbeth, Macbeth, Macbeth, beware Macduff!
>Beware the Thane of Fife. Dismiss me. Enough.

(1st Apparition leaves.)

MACBETH:
>Whate'er thou art, for thy good caution thanks.
>Thou hast harped my—

*(Forrest stops himself. He goes to 1st Witch and pulls her dress up
a little, so more of her attractive leg can be seen, then continues:)*

>Thou has harped my fear aright.

1ST WITCH:
>Here's another,
>More potent than the first.

(Thunder and an explosion.)

Broadway Theatre, Act IV.iii

Macduff (Ryder) and Malcolm (Jonas).

MACDUFF *(With great passion)*: Fit to govern?
>No, not to live! O nation miserable,
>With an untitled tyrant bloody-sceptered,
>When shalt thou see thy wholesome days again,
>Since that the truest issue of thy throne
>By his own interdiction stands accursed.
>And does blaspheme his breed? O, my breast—
>Thy hope ends here!

(Beat. They begin to walk off.)

JONES: Calm down, calm down. You've got the part.

(They exit.)

Astor Place Opera House, Act V.vii

Macbeth (Macready) enters.

MACBETH:
>They have tied me to a stake. I cannot fly,
>But bear-like I must fight the course. What's he
>That was not born of woman? Such a one
>Am I to fear, or none.

(Enter Young Siward [Bridges].)

YOUNG SIWARD: What is thy name?
MACBETH: Thou'lt be afraid to hear it . . . My name's Macbeth.

YOUNG SIWARD:
>The devil himself could not pronounce a title
>more hateful to mine ear.

(They fight. This should be a much stiffer battle than Forrest will fight. Young Siward is slain. Macbeth drags him off.)

Broadway Theatre, Act V.vii

Macbeth (Forrest) and Young Siward (Fisher) enter fighting. This should be a quite thrilling sword fight. Then Young Siward is slain.

MACBETH: Thou wast born of woman,
>But swords I smile at, weapons laugh to scorn,
>Brandished by man that's of a woman born.

(He drags off the body.)

Astor Place Opera House, Act V.x

Continuation of previous scene. Macduff (Clark) enters, then Macbeth (Macready).

MACBETH:

> Why should I play the Roman fool, and die
> On mine own sword? Whiles I see lives, the gashes
> Do better upon them.

MACDUFF: Turn, hell-hound, turn.

MACBETH:

> Of all men else I have avoided thee.
> But get thee back. My soul is too much charged
> With blood of thine already.

MACDUFF:

>   I have no words;
> My voice is in my sword, thou bloodier villain
> Than terms can give thee out!

(They fight.)

MACBETH:

> . . . I bear a charmèd life, which must not yield
> To one of woman born.

MACDUFF: Despair thy charm,
> And let the angel whom thou still hast served,
> Tell thee, Macduff was from his mother's womb
> Untimely ripped.

MACBETH:

> Accursèd be that tongue that tells me so,
> For it hath cowed my better part of man!

MACDUFF:

> "Here may you see the tyrant."

MACBETH:

Before my body
I throw my warlike shield. Lay on, Macduff,
And damned be him that first cries, "Hold, enough!"

(They exit, fighting.
Act V.xi. Malcolm [Arnold], Siward [Wemyss] and others enter.
Macduff enters with the bloody head of Macbeth.)

MACDUFF:
. . . Hail, King of Scotland!

ALL: Hail, King of Scotland!

MALCOLM:

We shall not spend a large expense of time
Before we reckon with your several loves
And make us even with you. What's more to do
Which could be planted newly with the time,
As calling home our exiled friends abroad,
That fled the snares of watchful tyranny,
Producing forth the cruel ministers
Of this dead butcher and his fiend-like queen—
So thanks to all at once, and to each one,
Whom we invite to see us crowned at Scone.

(Flourish. They exit. Then immediately some of the actors cross
the stage, taking off costumes, etc., all a bit tired. As they exit:)

Broadway Theatre, Act V.vii

Macbeth (Forrest) and Macduff (Ryder) enter fighting.

FORREST: Watch it. There. That's right. There.

(Then as Macbeth:)

MACBETH: Before my body
I throw my warlike shield. Lay on, Macduff,
And damned be him that first cries, "Hold, enough!"

(They fight on stage. Finally Macbeth is stabbed and falls. Mac-duff, with some hesitation, raises his sword and appears to cut off Macbeth's head. A head falls on the ground. Macduff picks it up. Others enter.)

MACDUFF *(With the head)*:
    Hail, King of Scotland!

ALL: Hail, King of Scotland!

(Tableau. Blackout.)

SCENE 5

5 P.M.

The Broadway Theatre. Forrest's dressing room. Table, a couple of chairs. Forrest sits, taking off his makeup. Throughout the scene he changes from his Macbeth costume to his normal clothes. Ryder, still in costume, stands.

FORREST: I don't know how this is any of my business.
RYDER: I think— The basis for the threats—or so Mr. Macready believes—seems to be the fact that you are both performing the same play on the same—
FORREST: So are you, Mr. Ryder. *(Beat)* So are you.

(Beat.)

RYDER: On the same night. It's a competition that these people— whoever they are—are trying to . . . I don't know. Build up?
FORREST: According to Mr. Macready.
RYDER: According to Mr.—
FORREST: This is what he has concluded.
RYDER: That's right. *(Beat) I'm* only passing it along. I'm the mes-senger. That's all I am.
FORREST: I understand.

(Short pause.)

RYDER: Anyway, a competition. English version—

FORREST: You're English.

RYDER: I'm not saying that it's logical. *(Beat)* English versus American. There is still, I suppose, a certain lingering—passion? It's uncorking this—these tempers that has Mr. Macready truly worried and why he believes there might be truth to the—

FORREST: Do the threats mention me?

(Beat.)

RYDER: No. Not the letter I saw.

FORREST: So the basis for the threats actually remains in some doubt.

RYDER: They do criticize him for being foreign.

FORREST: I have been criticized in England for being foreign! *(Short pause)* So they do not mention me. They do not mention that Mr. Forrest happens, by coincidence, to be performing the same—

RYDER: Mr. Macready believes—

FORREST: He has an opinion! *(Beat)* And if I were Macready and I held such an opinion, the obvious action to take would be to change my schedule and perform something else.

RYDER: *He* can't.

FORREST: Too bad. *(Short pause)* Then cancel.

(Knock at the door. Door opens, Tilton peeks in.)

TILTON: Sorry about this afternoon, I . . .

FORREST *(Continuing to Ryder)*: But this is Mr. Macready's business and it has nothing to do with me. *(Beat. To Tilton)* Sorry about what? What happened? Did something happen?

TILTON: I don't know where my mind was. It suddenly went . . .

FORREST: I don't know what you're talking about, Tilton. Please. *(Continues to undress. Beat)*

TILTON: Thanks, Ned. Thank you. *(Turns to go, bumping into Fisher on his way out)* Sorry. *(Leaves)*

FISHER: You wanted to see me, Ned?

FORREST: Come in, Thomas, come in.

RYDER: Would you like me to—

FORREST: Sit down, please. Both of you. *(Beat)* I was just about to compliment Mr. Ryder on his performance. After our little misfortune last night, we seem to have landed on our feet. *(Beat)* Thanks to Mr. Ryder.

FISHER: Nice work.

FORREST *(Turning to Ryder)*: You know I *have* seen you act before. In fact, I do believe I have seen you play this part before. Now where was it? *(Beat)* Could it have been in Edinburgh?

RYDER: I have played in—

FORREST: I recall sneaking in one wet night to catch Mr. Macready—

RYDER: Yes, I did play Macduff to Mr. Macready's—

FORREST: But it was you whom I remember, Mr. Ryder. *(Beat)* I thought you were magnificent. The best Macduff I have ever seen.

RYDER *(Smiling at Fisher; to Forrest)*: Thank you.

FORREST: You see, most Macduffs don't realize that it is revenge that is driving the man. Passionate revenge. They don't show this. *(Beat)* The part is not about Good triumphing. Who the hell knows if the man's good or not? It is hate that drives him. *(Beat)* Ugly, sweaty hate. *(Beat)* I hardly even remember the performance of the Macbeth.

RYDER: Mr. Macready—

FORREST: For that one night, the play should have been called *Macduff.*

(Beat.)

RYDER *(Smiling)*: Mr. Forrest, I think you're putting me on. To call the play—

FORREST: It would have been justified. By your performance. *(Beat)* By your energertic and dominating performance. *(Short pause. To himself)* Macduff! *(Beat)* Macbeth need hardly even appear. *(Beat)* What about a drink? The three of us? *(Takes out a bottle and a few glasses)*

RYDER: I don't really think—

FORREST: I insist. Please. *(Pause. Pours and hands out glasses)* To you. And to our wonderful production which unfortunately we must call—*Macbeth. (He drinks)*

(Fisher laughs at the way Forrest is making his point with Ryder.)

(Turning quickly to Fisher) Mr. Fisher, you know we are scheduled to play here for the next five weeks.

FISHER: Of course I do, yes. Why do you—?

FORREST: I ran into Mr. Hackett the other day. Actually I believe it was just this morning. He said something about having engaged actors already for a tour. Do you know anything about this?

FISHER: I've met Hackett maybe two or three times in my whole life.

FORREST: I thought you worked for him once. I thought this is what you told me when I hired you for here.

FISHER: I worked for him. I did. *(Beat)* But he wasn't around much.

FORREST *(To Ryder, smiling)*: It appears this tour is to be in— What was the exact date? I forget. But I do remember it was about three and a half weeks from today. *(Beat)* Or a week and a half before we finish our season here. *(Beat)* You haven't talked to Mr. Hackett about joining this tour, have you?

FISHER: That wouldn't be right, Ned.

(Pause.)

FORREST: I hear your brother hasn't been well.

FISHER: What do you mean? I don't have a—

FORREST: So I'm sure there are a few unanticipated expenses. *(Beat)* For the remainder of our season, I have decided to raise your pay by five dollars a performance. *(Beat)* Rather, let's call it a bonus—to be collected at the end of our run.

(Short pause.)

FISHER: Thank you. I can use it. *(Beat)* Is there anything else, you . . . ?

FORREST: No.

(Fisher nods, puts down his glass and goes. After he has closed the door:)

You son of a bitch! *(To Ryder)* He's been in rehearsal for a week with Hackett. *(Beat)* He's good though. Good with the sword.

(Miss Bass enters, still in costume. She does not knock. Throughout the rest of the scene, she undresses and changes into her normal

clothes. Ryder takes notice of this, though for Forrest and Miss Bass it seems to be quite normal.)

MISS BASS *(While entering)*: Can Helen come with us to the party? *(Beat. She turns to Forrest)* Mr. Robert Jones is taking Miss Anne Holland to dinner tonight. So you can imagine how Helen is feeling.

FORREST: I don't know how large the party's supposed to be.

MISS BASS: I can't leave her alone. I just got her to stop crying.

FORREST: Fine. *(Beat)* Of course she can come. Maybe you, Mr. Ryder, would like to join . . .

RYDER: I'm having dinner with Mr. Macready tonight. Otherwise . . . *(Short pause)* I'll tell him I passed along his message. I should go. *(Goes to the door)* By the way, thank you for last night. It was a pleasure to— And I am pleased you like my Macduff. I'm a bit more critical of it than you though. *(Beat)* I think I should try to, I don't know. I just think I could be subtler. After all, the play Shakespeare wrote isn't called *Macduff*, is it?

(He forces himself to laugh, then leaves. Long pause. Forrest begins to get dressed.)

MISS BASS: I've heard that there are quite a few unsold tickets for Mr. Macready's *Macbeth*.

FORREST *(Without looking up)*: Is that true? *(Laughs to himself)*

MISS BASS: Why is that . . . ?

(He looks up, shakes his head, suddenly sits and sighs. She looks at him.)

(Trying to be bright) So where's the party?

FORREST: New York Hotel.

MISS BASS: You're sure they won't mind us bringing Helen . . . ?

FORREST: I'm sure it's a big party. That's what I remember my wife saying at least.

MISS BASS: The bigger the better. For us.

(Pause. Forrest slowly turns to her.)

What? What?

FORREST: My wife doesn't want you in our house anymore. She has made this clear to me. This morning. *(Beat)* Do you mind?

MISS BASS: Then—she's not welcome in mine either. *(Beat. Smiles)*

FORREST *(Sigh of relief)*: Thank you. You make this much easier. *(Smiles, then nearly begins to cry)*

MISS BASS: Ned? . . .

FORREST: I don't know what it is, Jane. *(Beat)* For no reason my eyes start to well up. *(Wipes his tears, breathes deeply, sighs)* Life's not half as much fun as theatre. *(Continues to get dressed)*

(Blackout.)

SCENE 6

8 P.M.

A private drawing room, New York Hotel.
    Macready, Ryder, Mrs. Forrest, Dion Boucicault and his wife, Agnes Robertson, in the middle of conversation.

MACREADY: He said she was fifty if she was anything, and when she finished, she told Johnstone that her parts include not only Desdemona but also Juliet.

(He smiles and shakes his head, sips his drink. The others smile as well.)

Then in Pittsburgh—a town he said one should be lucky enough to avoid—he's to play Lear with a Goneril who never was sober (for four days, he swears), a Cordelia who not only talked nonsense, as if she had concluded that nonsense was Shakespeare's intention, and she was only clarifying this point, but who also was a good three to four years older than him, and John Johnstone, well you've seen him.

MRS. FORREST: Not for years, has he . . . ?

MACREADY *(Turning back to Boucicault)*: He's— What? How would you describe . . . ?

BOUCICAULT: No one would say he was too young for the part. Of Lear.

MACREADY: It happened rather quickly as well.

AGNES: His son died.

MACREADY: Is that it? I didn't know.

(Short pause.)

BOUCICAULT: So his Cordelia was even older than—

MACREADY: Which he said actually made the relationship rather interesting.

BOUCICAULT: It's different.

MACREADY: Anyway, he finally just felt that the performance he was giving was just too good for them. They cheered, of course, but he was convinced they didn't know what in the world they were cheering for.

(Short pause.)

BOUCICAULT: Hmmmm. *(Looks at Agnes for a moment, then turns to Ryder)* Mr. Ryder, has this been your experience of—?

RYDER: No. *(Beat)* Actually it hasn't. I think Americans—

MACREADY *(Interrupting)*: Nor has it been mine, Mr. Boucicault. American people are really rather charming and decent as well as intelligent in an instinctive sort of way. The actors I am working with, they may not know certain things, things you or I or your wife might take for granted, but that doesn't mean they aren't quick to learn.

AGNES: Being married to an American, Mrs. Forrest, you must have had experiences.

MRS. FORREST: Oh yes. Very many.

(Pause. They look to her to continue.)

MACREADY *(Finally)*: Not only are they quick to learn, they are eager. They're more like children than us old jaded English actors. *(Laughs lightly, as do others)* It's a fascinating country, it truly is!

AGNES: Whatever it is, it at least sounds somewhat refreshing after the London theatre.

RYDER: Absolutely nothing was happening there when we left.

BOUCICAULT: And it's got worse, hasn't it?

(He turns to Agnes, who nods.)

Kean's made a complete mess of the Princess.

AGNES *(To the others)*: Not a complete—

BOUCICAULT: He has, it's true. *(Beat)* I gave him *The Corsican Brothers*—for nothing—for nearly nothing he has the play of the century. What is clearly my best play; what is going to be my most successful play that will make *London Assurance* seem like . . . Whatever. *(Beat)* Crowds fight to get into my play. This play cannot lose money. *(Turns to Agnes)* He ran it for what—?

AGNES: Not long enough.

BOUCICAULT: I try to tell him. *(Shakes his head)* What is in it for me? I don't get a pound more if he plays the play or not. Not there. At the Princess he can play it forever and I don't get a farthing more. *(Beat)* It's going to be done here. *(Beat)* Last night Hackett agreed to take it.

MACREADY: When did he say—?

BOUCICAULT: Sometime after the new year. He didn't give me dates. *(Beat)* But it's definite. *(Beat)* We're going to work out a deal. *(Beat. Laughs)* We're here one week and—! I love America.

(Short Pause.)

AGNES *(Smiling)*: Hopefully we're saying the same thing next week. *(Beat)* At first we were very happy with Kean.

BOUCICAULT: I never was, Agnes. It was the Princess Theatre that I loved. A beautiful theatre.

MACREADY: This is true.

BOUCICAULT: What does Kean replace my play with? *Twelfth Night.* He insists on doing this play. *(Beat)* It's not a bad play. *(Beat)* But I tell him just run the goddamn *Corsican Brothers* until no one comes anymore. Does this sound mad?!

AGNES: Dion—

BOUCICAULT: Let me finish! *(Beat)* It's as if they don't want to make money. *(Beat)* It is exactly as if they don't want to make money!

(Pause.)

RYDER: That is very good news about Hackett.
AGNES: He's going to tell us for sure next week.

(Short pause.)

BOUCICAULT: Have any of you been to Cincinnati?
MRS. FORREST: Cincinnati? *(Looks at the others)* No I haven't.
MACREADY: No. *(Beat)* Why? Is there something . . . ?
BOUCICAULT: It's just that I always have loved that name: Cincinnati.

(Pause. They sip their drinks.)

MACREADY: Five Brits all in one room. In America. That doesn't
happen very often.
MRS. FORREST: Yes it does.

(Pause.)

AGNES: We've reserved a small table in the dining room. As soon as
Mr. Forrest . . .
MRS. FORREST: I think it might be dangerous to wait for my husband.

(Short pause.)

BOUCICAULT: Perhaps then we should go right to our table. We can
bring our drinks.

(They hesitate.)

AGNES: We should leave a message at the front desk.
RYDER: He may have forgotten. Maybe there was something else.
MRS. FORREST: Do you know if Mr. Forrest has gone somewhere
else?
RYDER: No. *(Beat)* I don't know anything.
MRS. FORREST: I'll leave the note.
BOUCICAULT: We'll just be—
MRS. FORREST: Yes.

(As the others move off toward the dining room:)

BOUCICAULT: So you're staying here as well?

MACREADY: It's near the theatre.

AGNES: They've been very nice to us.

MACREADY *(To Agnes)*: Here, let me carry your drink.

AGNES: Thank you.

(They are gone. Having watched them go, Mrs. Forrest sighs and sits. After a moment she stands again and turns to go off toward the front desk just as Forrest enters with Miss Bass and Miss Burton. Forrest stops. Short pause.)

FORREST: Where's the party?

MRS. FORREST: What party are you talking about? And where have you been?

FORREST: Boucicault's party. You told me tonight was Boucicault's party. We've been looking all over the hotel . . .

MRS. FORREST: It's not a party. It's a dinner, Mr. Forrest. A small dinner.

(Short pause.)

FORREST: Then I made a mistake.

MISS BASS: If you want us to go, Ned . . .

FORREST: Where's the dinner?

MRS. FORREST *(Nodding)*: Through there.

(Beat.)

FORREST: What's a few more places? *(Tries to laugh)* They're through there?

(She does not respond. He hesitates, then leads the women in the direction of the dining room.)

MRS. FORREST: Edwin.

(He stops.)

FORREST *(To Misses Bass and Burton)*: I'll join you in a minute. Just introduce yourselves. It'll be fine. *(Beat)* It's fine.

(They go. Short pause.)

MRS. FORREST: What have you been doing?
FORREST: Rehearsing.
MRS. FORREST: What have you been doing?
FORREST: One of the girls, Miss Burton, she's upset because her boyfriend—the boy she thinks is her boyfriend . . . *(Beat)* You know who I mean. *(Beat)* My Banquo. Well, tonight he's taken another actress, Miss—
MRS. FORREST: Why do I care? How could you invite them?
FORREST: They're actresses in my—! *(Stops himself. Short pause)* I made a mistake. I am sorry. *(Beat)* I invited them to what I thought was— I can't tell them to leave. *(Beat)* It would be profoundly embarrassing to just . . . *(Beat)* Let's just get through this, Catherine.

(The others all return from the dining room.)

AGNES: No, it's my fault really for not reserving a larger table.
MRS. FORREST: What's—?
MACREADY: We don't all fit around the table.
BOUCICAULT: And they said they can't add on— The space in there, there's no—

(Beat.)

AGNES: They're seeing what they can do. They asked us to wait.

(Awkward pause.)

FORREST: I'm sorry if I caused any trouble.
AGNES: Of course not. We're very pleased and honored you could come. And your guests. We're very anxious to get to know all sorts of Americans.
FORREST: Thank you.
AGNES: Aren't we?
BOUCICAULT: We are. *(Beat)* We certainly are.

(Another awkward pause.)

AGNES: I'll see if anything's been figured out yet.

(She goes. Short pause.)

FORREST: Mr. Boucicault, it is very nice to see you again. I hope your voyage was comfortable.

(They shake hands.)

BOUCICAULT: Very. Thank you. You of course know Mr. Macready.
FORREST: We've met before. How do you do?
MACREADY: How do you do?
BOUCICAULT: And Mr. Ryder.
FORREST: Mr. Ryder is my Macduff at the moment actually.
BOUCICAULT: Really? I didn't— You didn't say anything.
MACREADY: I have an American Macduff for New York. I thought it a good thing. *(Beat)* He's very good as well.

(Short pause.)

RYDER: Funny, Mr. Forrest, you asked me what I was doing this evening— I guess you were going to invite me here. And here I am already. *(Laughs lightly)* With Mr. Macready. *(Beat)* I told you I was having dinner with Mr. Macready.
MRS. FORREST: My husband invited you as well?

(Pause.)

FORREST *(To Miss Bass)*: You've been introduced, I—
MISS BASS: Actually . . . *(Shakes her head)*
MISS BURTON: No, we—
BOUCICAULT: I'm terribly sorry.
FORREST: Miss Burton. Miss Bass.

(An exchange of polite greetings. Short pause.)

They are two of my witches.

(The others nod as if this explains something.)

MISS BURTON: I'm the second.

MISS BASS: I'm the first.

(Agnes enters, followed by a maid and a servant carrying tables.)

AGNES: They think we'll actually be more comfortable in here. We'll set up to eat in here. And we can add on as many tables as we wish. *(Beat)* In case others should drop in. *(Beat)* I do love it when people feel they can just drop in. *(Beat)* For dinner.

(During much of the scene, the tables are set up, then set with tablecloths, plates, glasses, etc.)

BOUCICAULT: I hear wonderful things about your *Macbeth*, Mr. Forrest. *(Beat)* Or should I say, all of your *Macbeth*, as it seems half of your cast is with us tonight.
FORREST: Thank you. *(Short pause)* And let's not leave Mr. Macready out. *His Macbeth* I have seen! Where was it? I was just today telling Mr. Ryder. Baltimore? Cincinnati?
BOUCICAULT: Agnes—Cincinnati?

(She nods and smiles.)

RYDER: It was Edinburgh.
MACREADY: I hadn't known. Had I known—
FORREST: You were ... Unforgettable. Even now I can close my eyes and see you there. *(Beat)* As Macbeth. *(Beat)* Unforgettable.
BOUCICAULT: Yes. And yours, it's on everyone's lips.
FORREST: What brings you to New York, Mr. Boucicault?
MACREADY: He's sold his *Corsican Brothers* to Hackett. They're doing it next year.
FORREST: I hope you got the money in your hand. He'll promise anything.

(Boucicault looks at Agnes.)

AGNES: My husband has a new play.
FORREST: What's the title?—
BOUCICAULT: I don't want to bother you two— *(Beat)* Actually, now that I think of it you both could be of some help to me.

That's if you don't mind. I wouldn't want you to think you had to work for your dinner.

(He laughs. No one else does.)

AGNES: I think we can sit down.

BOUCICAULT: Please, let's— *(Gestures for all to go to the table)* The play is called *Shakespeare in Love.*

RYDER: Who's sitting there?

AGNES: Dion should be at the head. Then Miss—

MISS BURTON: Burton.

AGNES: Burton to his left. And who—? Mr. Forrest? Or would you rather sit by your wife?

FORREST: I don't care where I sit.

BOUCICAULT: And it's about Shakespeare.

AGNES: I'll sit at the other end. Mr. Ryder, then . . . *(Points to where he should sit)*

MRS. FORREST: Then I'll sit there. *(Goes to her seat)*

BOUCICAULT: And he is in love. Shakespeare.

AGNES: Then Mr. Macready.

MACREADY: Where?

AGNES: Right here, next to Dion and Mrs. Forrest.

BOUCICAULT: He's in love with a neighbor.

MACREADY: How old is he?

BOUCICAULT: He's in his late thirties I would say. Though that could be changed. *(Beat)* He can be older. He can be younger.

AGNES: And that leaves Miss Bass. Miss Bass on the other side of Mr. Forrest. Who has Miss Burton on one side and Miss Bass on the other.

MRS. FORREST: My husband will be in heaven.

AGNES: Shall we sit?

(They do.)

BOUCICAULT: It's a comedy. A rather fantastical comedy. Because, you see, various characters from his plays come back to him— to try to help him or they are just plain jealous of this love affair and are feeling neglected. They are very unhappy that this affair is upsetting their lives. *(Beat)* It's a very good idea, isn't it?

AGNES: Dion, they aren't serving the food. Maybe they've forgotten about us.

BOUCICAULT: Why would they? *(Gets up)* I'll go and see. Excuse me. Remind me where I was.

(He goes. Short pause.)

AGNES: It's nice in here. *(Beat)* To have a whole room by yourself. *(Beat)* Things do work out.

FORREST: Mr. Macready, Mr. Ryder was telling me about some threats against . . . *(Turns to Ryder)* Who exactly were they against?

MACREADY: Threats?

RYDER: About Monday. About the two *Macbeth*s.

MACREADY: Threats??

RYDER: About being foreign. The letters you received.

MACREADY: Threats???

RYDER: You asked me to talk to Mr. Forrest and—

MACREADY: Oh those. Silly ridiculous rumors. I'm sure the same must happen to you, Mr. Forrest. Jealous people.

FORREST: In England it happens to me all the time.

(Beat.)

MACREADY: One learns to ignore such things.

(Short pause.)

FORREST: You're selling very well, I hear.

(Short pause.)

MRS. FORREST: They don't like English people.

FORREST: Who are they?

(She shrugs.)

You don't know what you're talking about.

(She looks down, puts her head in her hands.)

AGNES: Do you like English people, Miss . . .

MISS BURTON: Burton. Sure. *(Smiles)* What's there not to like? *(Beat)* What's *to* like? People are people. *(Shrugs)* There are good and there are bad.

(Miss Bass smiles.)

What's funny?
MISS BASS: Nothing.
MISS BURTON: You're laughing at me.
MISS BASS: I'm not, Helen.
AGNES: What you say is true.
RYDER: Very true.

(Beat.)

AGNES: Dion doesn't like English people, but then he's Irish.
MACREADY: By the way, except for the accent, you'd hardly notice. He's very well groomed.
AGNES: I don't think I will tell him that.
MISS BASS: Why wouldn't I like you, Mrs. Forrest? *(Beat)* Just because you're English?

(Pause.)

MRS. FORREST: I wasn't talking about you. I wasn't talking to you. *(Turns to Agnes)* The women, you'll find, it will shock you, Agnes. No—subtlety. No—charm, that I can see. So of course they will do anything. Anything. *(Shakes her head)* Sometimes for nothing, sometimes they want to be paid for it. *(Turns to Forrest)* Isn't that right?
FORREST: Catherine.
MRS. FORREST: The men are much more subtle. No, perhaps subtle is the wrong word. *(Beat)* Tricky. This is the word. They can be very very . . . *(Short pause. Without looking at anyone)* My apologies. To all of you. Including Miss Burton and Miss Bass. *(Beat)* I promise you I do not normally act in this manner.

(Beat. Boucicault comes back in, followed by a servant with some food.)

BOUCICAULT: I don't know what they were waiting for. Anyway, I was talking about my play. *(Beat)* A very nice idea, isn't it?

Shakespeare in love. So who should play Shakespeare? *(Sits back down)* That seems to be the question. *(Beat)* You both know actors. On both sides of the ocean. Who would be good to play our greatest dramatist? *(Beat. To Miss Burton)* I'm having a reading next week. In the afternoon so all of you busy theatre actors can come. *(Beat)* The reading isn't completely cast yet. *(Beat)* Any ideas about who could play Shakespeare? Not in the reading. I'll play him in the reading. *(Beat)* He'd have to be a major actor. Think about it. *(Suddenly laughs)* But as I said—I don't want you to think you have to work for your dinner. *(Laughs, stops, looks at the food)* This looks good.

(Blackout.)

SCENE 7

I A.M.

The same. The dinner is long over, though the dishes remain on the table, as well as wine bottles, glasses, etc.

Mrs. Forrest and Agnes have left some time earlier. Forrest, with Miss Bass at his side, sits at the table and talks to Macready, who has his head on the table, and occasionally to Boucicault, who sits next to Miss Burton, and at times turns and stares at her and smiles. Ryder is out for a pee.

FORREST: I'm serious. I think what one must do—what the battle finally is about. For us. You need to— With your hands out—keeping it all away—all out of the way. *(Beat)* Everything that is coming at you. The distractions and everything. Everything like that. Out there. The moment you go off the stage it is like—to me, I feel this—it is like they are trying to take it all away from you. *(Beat)* Tell you it never happened. What you felt out there on stage! What you knew you had done out there on the stage!

(Short pause.)

MISS BURTON *(To Boucicault)*: Will you stop smiling at me!

(He smiles and takes a sip of wine.)

FORREST: They may mean well. These people. Well-wishers mean
well, but— *(Beat)* Sometimes I think it's all just interference.
And the test we are putting ourselves through . . . Have been
put through— By whom? Where does it come from? God?
I don't know. But it's to push all that away. Not let it break into
the art of what we do.

(Short pause.)

MACREADY *(Lifting up his head for a moment)*: The world should be
left behind. In the dressing room.
FORREST: It certainly should not be brought onto the stage. *(Beat.
To Miss Bass)* You don't agree.
MISS BASS: I didn't say any—
FORREST: Take an argument you might have. With—? Anyone. A
friend. *(Beat)* A wife. You have this argument. You're boiling
over. Then you must play Hamlet. If you try to bring that
argument into—onto— *(Beat)* You have to push it all away.
Become someone who has not had an argument. In this case
who does not have a wife.
MACREADY *(Lifting head)*: And into someone whose father just died.
FORREST: Exactly.

(Beat.)

MACREADY: Now if my father *had* just died and I *had* to play Hamlet
that night—
FORREST: This I would love to see.
MACREADY: That would be— *(Beat)* Yes. *(Smiles)*
FORREST *(Smiling)*: But fathers don't die every time we play Hamlet. *(Beat)* Instead, bills are sent that day which can be wrong.
You step in horseshit on the street. Wives don't listen when
you talk to them. You lose your favorite pen. Or hat. Or your
right shoe. Or other stocking. *(Beat)* Or you fall in love that
day. Or hear a joke that you cannot forget and cannot stop
smiling about. Your brother writes and says he's going to visit.
The breakfast wasn't at all what you wanted. *(Beat)* And then
you play Hamlet. Then you become someone else. *(Beat)* To

do this you must learn to forget. *(Takes a sip of wine)* Sometimes I think this is my favorite part of being an actor.

(Pause. Ryder enters and sits.)

RYDER: What did I miss?

(Macready, without picking up his head, just shakes his head.)

BOUCICAULT *(Standing up, to Ryder)*: Good idea. I have to go, too.

*(He leans over and tries to kiss Miss Burton, who slaps him hard
across the head. Others turn and see this. Boucicault smiles and
leaves.)*

MACREADY *(With head down)*: For me I think I like being able to—
It's not forget. But I know what you mean.
MISS BURTON *(Standing)*: I think I should be leaving, it's—
MISS BASS: Helen, it's only—
MISS BURTON: He's climbing all over me. That's not what I came for!
FORREST: Sit over here with us. We'll make room.
MISS BASS: I'll move over.
FORREST: Come on. Come on. We won't stay much longer.

*(Forrest and Ryder move a chair for her. She sits next to Miss Bass,
protected from Boucicault by both Forrest and Ryder.)*

MACREADY *(Finally)*: As I was saying—
FORREST *(To Miss Burton)*: We're talking about why we act. What
we— Why do you act?
MISS BURTON: I don't know.

(He looks at her and nods. He turns back to Macready.)

MACREADY: It's hard to explain really. Where shall I begin? *(Beat)*
You see—as Descartes has said—inside us all are these— He
called them animal spirits. *(Beat)* Which are really, what other
people call *passions*.

(Short pause. Forrest nods.)

And they're all—these spirits—they're bordered, they're all
sort of fenced in. *(Suddenly remembering)* You could also call
them *emotions. (Beat)* Anyway, they're fenced in. But when
one of them escapes from the others—and is not quickly
caught by—I don't know, spirits who do the catching, like
sheepdogs catch—

(Beat.)

FORREST: Sheep.
MACREADY: That's right. Like sheepdogs catch sheep. Anyway, when
one escapes and is not caught, then it becomes a very deep, a
very—a very passionate— *(Beat)* What?! *(Beat. He remembers)* Feeling! Feeling. *(Short pause)* So what an actor does,
I believe, is this: philosophically speaking—I haven't studied
enough philosophy, I'd like to study much more, but . . .
well— People like us who are busy doing!— But, as I was saying, the art of the actor— *(Beat)* What was I going to say?
I was about to say something that was very clear. I remember.
The art of the actor is like ripping down the fences. *(Beat)* And
tying up the sheepdogs. *(Beat)* And letting the spirits loose. A
few at a time. Or more! Depending on the part. Letting them
roam for a while. *(Short pause)* So, that's what I love about acting. *(Pause)* I don't know how clear I've been.
FORREST: No, no, you've been . . . *(Nods and shrugs)*

*(During this, Boucicault enters, noticing that Miss Burton has
moved. He hesitates, not knowing where he should now sit. He
brings a chair, trying to squeeze in next to Miss Burton.)*

MISS BURTON: There's no room here.
MACREADY: Dion, stay over there.
BOUCICAULT: There's no one over there.

(He stands behind Miss Burton, making her very uncomfortable.)

FORREST *(To Macready)*: That was very interesting.
MACREADY: I've only tried to explain it to one other person, and he
laughed so— *(Shrugs)* You can see how I might be a little—
about talking about . . .

FORREST: Please! *(Beat)* Please, we are all actors here.

MISS BASS *(Standing up)*: I'll sit over there.

(She moves to where Miss Burton had been sitting. Boucicault follows, going back to his seat.)

FORREST *(To Macready)*: No one would make fun . . .

RYDER *(To Macready)*: What's that on your sleeve? Don't move, I'll kill it. *(Goes to get something off Macready's jacket)* I got it! Oh my God, it's an escaped animal spirit! Quick, kill it! Kill it! Kill it!

(He laughs at his joke, Macready and Forrest ignore him.)

MACREADY: It's a theory. A way of talking about something that is not easy to talk about.

(Forrest nods.)

BOUCICAULT: In my play, *Shakespeare in Love,* Shakespeare, by falling in love, can't write. Or doesn't want to write. *(Beat)* His talent dies. This is why the characters from his plays—

MACREADY: I thought we finished talking about your play, Dion.

BOUCICAULT: Had we? I'm sorry, I didn't know. *(Short pause. He turns to Miss Bass)* Which witch? *(Through his drunkenness he has trouble saying this)* Which witch do you play? May I ask? *(Beat)* In *Macbeth.*

MISS BASS: I'm the first witch.

BOUCICAULT: Ah, the first one. Mmmmmmmmm. Not the one I would have chosen for you, but a good one just the same.

MACREADY *(Standing with difficulty)*: I have no more to say. So I am going to bed.

(Ryder stands, then Forrest.)

FORREST *(To the women)*: I shall take you two home.

BOUCICAULT: Wait a minute! What about my problem? How shall I choose between you on Monday night? Whose *Macbeth* do I attend?

FORREST: It doesn't matter to—

BOUCICAULT: Perhaps I shall have to flip a coin. Who has a coin? I have a coin. *(Beat)* Ready? Heads and I go to Mr.—Forrest's.

And tails to Mr. Macready's. *(He flips. The coin falls under the table)* I will get it. No one move. I am getting it.

(The others stand and watch as Boucicault crawls under the table.)

I can't—did anyone see which way it rolled? *(Bumps his head)* Ow!

(He grabs Miss Burton's ankle.)

MISS BURTON: Stop that!

(She kicks him, he laughs.)

Get me out of here.
MISS BASS: We're going. Ned?
FORREST: It is late.
BOUCICAULT: I have it! I found it! *(Comes out from under the table)* Here it is. *(Looks at the coin)* I forget. Who had tails and who had heads?

(The others immediately move to leave, ignoring Boucicault.)

FORREST: Mr. Ryder, I shall see you on Monday.
RYDER: I'll be there.
MISS BASS: Can we drop you off somewhere?
RYDER: I have rooms here in the hotel.
MISS BASS: So you don't have far—
RYDER: No.
MISS BASS: They're comfortable rooms I hope.
FORREST: Do you want him to show you them?
MISS BASS: Ned!
FORREST: I didn't mean— *(Turns to Boucicault)* Mr. Boucicault, I thank you for this evening.
MACREADY: Yes, a lovely affair.
BOUCICAULT: Is everyone leaving?
MISS BURTON: We are.
FORREST: Mr. Macready, we have a cab.
MACREADY: I'm staying in the hotel as well.
FORREST: Ah. *(Leaving)* Helen. Jane.

MACREADY *(Leaving)*: So—I'm home.

BOUCICAULT *(Leaving)*: Thank you for coming. *(To Miss Burton)* It was charming to meet you.

(In the distance, we hear them say goodnight and they are gone. Blackout.)

SCENE 8

THREE DAYS LATER, MONDAY, MAY 7. 7:30 P.M.

The Astor Place Opera House, backstage.

A curtain upstage represents the stage and audience for production of Macbeth, *Act I.iii. Through the curtain, in silhouette, we see the three Witches (Sefton, Chippindale and Bridges). Someone makes a thunder sound.*

Downstage of this curtain, in the backstage area, actors in and out of costume listen, wait and mill around. After a moment, one actor with a drum bangs on it, and from "the stage," one vaguely hears:

3RD WITCH:
> A drum! A drum!
> Macbeth doth come.

ALL:
> The Weird Sisters, hand in hand,
> Posters of the sea and land,
> Thus do go about, about:
> Thrice to thine, and thrice to mine,
> And thrice again, to make up nine.
> Peace!— The charm's wound up.

(Dressed in costume, Macready enters the backstage. He slaps Bradshaw [Banquo] on the back. Bradshaw enters "the stage." From the audience, one hears cheers and yells. Macready smiles.)

MACREADY *(To the actor with the drum)*: They think he's me.

(He makes his entrance on "the stage.")

147

So foul and fair a day I have not seen.

(Before he can even get the sentence out, boos and cries ring out from the audience, then screaming and yells and violent insults. The other actors look at each other. From "the stage," Banquo is heard trying to go on, as do the Witches, but all is chaos. Finally, Macready can be heard screaming:)

Stay, you imperfect speakers, tell me more!

(But he is drowned out. Suddenly someone rips down the curtain, and Macready's face is seen to be completely bloodied; he staggers back, ducking the things being thrown at him. Other actors run for cover. Macready stumbles and turns to an actor:)

Who are they? What do they want?!

(The Witches hurry in [Sefton, Chippindale and Bridges].)

MRS. POPE *(Taking Macready)*: Sit down. Over here. Let me get you a cloth.

(She takes him to a chair.)

BRIDGES: He's bleeding.
MACREADY: They tried to kill me! *(Grabs Chippindale)* They want to kill me!
CHIPPINDALE *(Taking the cloth from Mrs. Pope)*: Give me that. Let me wipe your face.

(Macready screams.)

MACREADY: I haven't done anything to them. They have interrupted my performance! *(Stands)*
MRS. POPE: Sit down.

(The yelling and screaming continue from the audience.)

BRADSHAW *(Entering from the stage)*: They're breaking the seats.
CHIPPINDALE: Get them to stop!

BRADSHAW: And how am I supposed to do that?!

MACREADY: Shoot them!

BRIDGES *(Who has been listening to the crowd)*: They're calling for Mr. Macready.

SEFTON: Tell them he's left! Tell them he's gone!

(He pushes Bridges to go on stage.)

MACREADY: I haven't left.

BRIDGES *(Stopping and hesitating)*: They'll tear down the theatre!

MACREADY: I'm here.

SEFTON: Somebody tell them!

(No one moves, then Sefton goes to the stage.)

MACREADY: I have a performance to give. People have paid to see me perform.

BRIDGES *(To Chippindale)*: What are they screaming now?

SEFTON *(Repeating)*: "Kill the English Bastard. We have our own actors now. Long live Ned Forrest."

MACREADY: I have to finish!

SEFTON *(Off, to the audience, yelling)*: Mr. Macready has left the theatre!

MACREADY: I need to finish!

SEFTON *(Off, to the audience, yelling)*: Mr. Macready has left the theatre!

(Yelling and screaming continue. The others watch Macready.)

MACREADY: I wish to continue my . . .

SEFTON *(Off, to the audience, yelling)*: Macready has left the theatre!!!

(Beat. Screaming dies down. Suddenly there is a deafening cheer from the audience. Blackout.)

ACT TWO

SCENE I

The stage of the Broadway Theatre during a performance of Meta-
*mora. Forrest as the title character and Miss Holland as Metamora's
wife, Nahmeokee. The last few minutes of the play.*

METAMORA: Nahmeokee, I look up through the long path of thin air,
and I think I see our infant borne onward to the land of the
happy, where the fair hunting grounds know no storms or
snows, and where the immortal brave feast in the eyes of the
giver of good. Look upwards, Nahmeokee, the spirit of thy
murdered father beckons thee.

NAHMEOKEE: I will go to him.

METAMORA: Embrace me, Nahmeokee—'twas like the first you gave
me in the days of our strength and joy—they are gone. *(Places
his ear to the ground)* Hark! In the distant wood I faintly hear
the cautious tread of men! They are upon us, Nahmeokee—
the home of the happy is made ready for thee.

(He stabs her, she dies.)

151

She felt no white man's bondage—free as the air she lived—
pure as the snow she died! In smiles she died! Let me taste it,
ere her lips are cold as the ice.

*(Loud shouts. Roll of drums. Kaneshine [Fisher] leads Church
[Tilton] and soldiers.)*

CHURCH: He is found! Metamora is our prisoner.

METAMORA: No! He lives—last of his race—but still your enemy
lives to defy you still. Though numbers overpower me and
treachery surround me, though friends desert me, I defy you
still! Come to me—come singly to me! And this true knife that
has tasted the foul blood of your nation and now is red with the
purest of mine, will feel a grasp as strong as when it flashed in
the blaze of your burning dwellings, or was lifted terribly over
the fallen in battle.

CHURCH: Fire upon him!

METAMORA: Do so, I am weary of the world for ye are dwellers in it;
I would not turn upon my heel to save my life.

CHURCH: Your duty, soldiers.

(They fire. Metamora falls.)

METAMORA: My curses on you, white men! May the Great Spirit
curse you when he speaks in his war voice from the clouds!
Murderers! The last of the Wampanoags' curse be on you! May
your graves and the graves of your children be in the path the
red man shall trace! And may the wolf and panther howl o'er
your fleshless bones, fit banquet for the destroyers! Spirits of
the grave, I come! But the curse of Metamora stays with the
white man! I die! My wife! My queen! My Nahmeokee!

*(He falls and dies. A tableau is formed. Drums and trumpet sound
a retreat. Slow curtain. Blackout.)*

Scene 2

While at the same time

Macready's rooms, New York Hotel.

The actors from the Astor Place Opera House production of Macbeth, *including Clark, Mrs. Pope, Wemyss, Bridges, Bradshaw, Sefton, Chippindale and Arnold, are all shouting for explanations about what has happened. They are shouting at an elderly Washington Irving, who stands next to Macready, who now wears a bandage on his head, and looks weary.*

IRVING *(Over the shouts)*: Quiet, please! Please, let me finish!
MACREADY: Listen to him!

(The actors quiet down.)

IRVING: Mr. Macready has been persuaded—to give tomorrow night a second performance of his glorious *Macbeth*.

(This upsets the actors again and all speak at once: "Who's going to perform it?" "Isn't once enough?" "You have to be joking!" etc.)

(Over the shouts) We believe there is no significant risk! For him. And for those of you who wish to join him on the stage.

(In shock they quiet down again.)

MACREADY *(As if this makes everything clear)*: Mr. Forrest has been spoken to—
IRVING: Mr. Forrest has agreed to perform only *Metamora* for some time.
MACREADY: So there'll be no more of this—
IRVING *(Over him)*: Not that he had anything to do with last night. But we can thank him for his consideration.

(Macready bites his tongue.)

CLARK *(To others)*: It seems like a big risk to—

IRVING (*With sudden vehemence*): Of course it's a risk! There's a risk in any important endeavor. And this is important!!!

(*Works to get a grip on himself*) Or maybe, sir, you wish to let these hooligans determine what can and cannot be presented on our stages? In our books? By our speakers. Is that what you want, sir?

CLARK: Of course, I don't want—

IRVING: Then take some responsibility!!! That is what I am saying. What I've been asked to say—by a delegation of citizens. (*Beat*) All leading citizens I hasten to add, who met together this morning. One conclusion of this meeting was the designation of a person to express for all a deep apology to Mr. Macready.

(*He bows to Macready, who accepts the apology.*)

And to you other actors as well.

(*A shorter bow to them. Then he laughs to himself and explains:*)

I told them I was probably the worst person for this job. I told them—you probably had never even heard of me. (*Laughs. No one else does*) Of Washington Irving.

ARNOLD: I didn't realize that's who he—

MRS. POPE: Shh.

IRVING: But I was assured. (*Takes out a letter*) Together we signed a letter—with not only our apologies but also our word that should you agree to another performance, you shall be protected. You shall be safe. (*Hands the letter to an actor*) Police will be stationed throughout the theatre and outside.

(*This concerns the actors. They look at each other: "Police???"*)

The mayor has put the militia on notice.

(*The actors begin to panic again: "The Militia?!" "Soldiers? Why do we need soldiers?!"*)

MACREADY: Quiet. Please.

(They turn to Macready.)

Not that it will affect any one of you in making a decision. *(Beat)* But you might like to know that our producers have offered us seventy-five percent of the house. Fifty to me. Twenty-five to be split by you. *(Beat)* It's generous. But I doubt if money alone would be enough to . . . to . . . But it's generous. *(Short pause)* So think it over. Mr. Irving has kindly arranged for food in the dining room. So please—join us if you wish.

(Silence as they put their hats and gloves on, etc., preparing to leave. After a moment:)

MRS. POPE *(To Wemyss, under her breath):* An angel just passed.
IRVING: Mrs. Pope?

(She nervously turns to him.)

Can Mr. Macready count on you to attend rehearsal in the morning?

(She hesitates, looks at the others, who watch her, then:)

MRS. POPE: In the morning? If it isn't an inconvenience—the afternoon would be a lot better for me. My sister's staying with me with her two children—

(Everyone starts smiling, trying not to laugh, which only makes her explain more.)

—and she works in the mornings. But maybe I could ask Mrs. Seymour, she lives just below—

(All the actors are laughing.)

MACREADY: Come when you can, Mrs. Pope.
MRS. POPE: I don't understand why you're laughing.

(The mood is suddenly lightened.)

WEMYSS *(To Bradshaw)*: Bradshaw, maybe Banquo should enter with Macbeth—as it says, I think, in the text.
MACREADY: It says that? I should read the text more carefully.

(Laughter.)

ARNOLD: Perhaps Banquo should enter downstage of Macbeth!

(Laughter.)

SEFTON *(Kidding him)*: Or even in front of him!

(Big laugh.)

BRADSHAW: Oh I don't think my character would ever do that.
MACREADY: We should rehearse it and see.

(Laughter. Nearly everyone slowly starts to head off to the dining room and the promised food.)

(To Wemyss as he passes) And how is your lovely daughter, Mr. Wemyss, does she still wish to become an actress?
WEMYSS: She's a thick one.
MRS. POPE *(Behind him)*: We never learn.

(Irving is in a conversation with Bradshaw, etc.)

IRVING: You actors are so full of—life.
BRADSHAW *(To Bridges)*: I'm glad he said "life."

(Irving suddenly stops them from leaving.)

IRVING: A story! During one of our amateur theatricals. There were these soldiers running through a—"wood." The trees about so far apart. And one actor with his gun like this. *(Horizontal)* And he gets caught on the trees and he flips over and the whole army—all five or six of us—we flip over, too. *(Laughs and laughs. Then leading them off)* Every one of you must have stories like that.

(All are gone except for Clark and Macready. Short pause.)

MACREADY: You're not joining us, Mr. Clark? You're not hungry?

(Clark looks at Macready, then:)

CLARK: Who ever heard of an actor who wasn't hungry, sir.
MACREADY: Good for you, Mr. Clark.

(Macready slaps him on the back as they go.)

Good for you.

(Blackout.)

SCENE 3

11 P.M.

The tavern.
 Boucicault, Agnes and Fisher at one smallish table. Fisher is reading Boucicault's play. At a nearby table, Tilton and Scott, who has a bandaged hand, sit and drink.
 Ryder has just entered, and has been stopped at Tilton's table to be introduced to Scott.

TILTON: Mr. Ryder played Macduff, when you—the other night—
SCOTT: Oh yes. How do you do?
TILTON: He was quite good.
SCOTT: Oh how nice.
RYDER: There wasn't much time to . . . *(Smiles)* You understand.
SCOTT: That's how the theatre often works. If one doesn't like it then one gets out. *(Turns to Tilton and laughs)*
RYDER: How is the finger? *(Beat)* I hope . . . everyone was hoping . . .
SCOTT: The finger is gone, Mr.— *(Turns to Tilton)*
TILTON: Ryder.
SCOTT: And at the moment I can't move my hand at all. *(Beat)* They say that will change. Some time.

(Beat.)

RYDER: I heard you were a wonderful Macduff. That you are a—
I'm sure I didn't do justice . . . *(Beat)* No doubt your public was
profoundly disappointed with me last night.
SCOTT: My public? *(Laughs and pours himself a drink)*
RYDER: Excuse me, I have friends . . .

(He nods toward Boucicault's table. Scott does not look at him.)

SCOTT *(To Tilton)*: Who's buying by the way? I don't have any
money.

(Ryder goes to Boucicault's table.)

TILTON: Don't worry about that.
SCOTT: I wasn't worrying.
RYDER *(Sitting at Boucicault's table)*: Sorry. I dropped by backstage.
I asked Ned to join us, but— I don't know.

(They nod. Beat.)

Mind if I—?
BOUCICAULT: No, no, of course not.

(Ryder pours himself a drink.)

RYDER *(Nodding toward Scott)*: I took over for him in—as Macduff.
He— There had been an accident with—
AGNES: We heard about that, didn't we?
BOUCICAULT: The finger?
RYDER: That's right.

(Short pause. Boucicault watches Fisher for a reaction as he reads.)

AGNES *(Turning to Tilton)*: The performance tonight was terribly
exciting. Thank you. I didn't know this play.
TILTON: Which play are you—?
AGNES: We were at *Metamora*. The three of us. *(Beat)* Actually we
were hoping that the rest of the company . . .

TILTON: I don't think they're coming. Sometimes no one goes out. Sometimes it's only me.

SCOTT: But if you're going out—

TILTON: It's the closest tavern. *(Short pause)* Some of them have to go home. *(Beat)* Scott here always had to go home. His wife made him.

SCOTT: Now she's sick of me. *(Turns to Tilton)* Still she doesn't give me any money. *(Shakes his head in disgust)*

TILTON: You saw it tonight? It was good tonight. I liked everything I did.

RYDER: Forrest was extraordinary.

AGNES: Wasn't he? There was a rawness, like some powerful animal—

RYDER: The nobleness of the character. That's what I was taken—

SCOTT: I play the Indian who betrays him.

RYDER: That's a very interesting role.

SCOTT *(To Tilton)*: Who played him tonight?

TILTON: Jones.

SCOTT: Jones? *(Smiles and shakes his head)* I knew he wanted to play my character.

(Short pause.)

AGNES: Everyone was very good. Thank you. *(Turns back to her table. To Ryder)* It is a pity Mr. Macready did not feel—

RYDER: I don't blame him. I wouldn't want to sit in a theatre of all places, not after last—

AGNES: He would have a good time. He could have forgotten, at least for a short while—

RYDER: I only asked him once, I knew there was no—

BOUCICAULT: But to see Mr. Forrest in a native role. This is what he missed. *(Beat)* Tonight you could really see his talent. Couldn't you Agnes?

(Before she can answer.)

The effect upon the women especially, this was most noticeable. I don't think an Englishman could ever play such an Indian. They wouldn't be able to create the effect—upon the women. An Irishman wouldn't have a problem, of course, but an English actor—

RYDER: I—I don't know.

BOUCICAULT: With English actors, there's always a . . . *(Turns to Agnes)* What am I trying to say, Agnes?

(She doesn't respond. He smiles, she does not.)

TILTON *(From the other table)*: Shame about Mr. Macready.

BOUCICAULT: I was there, you know. *(Shakes his head)* Extraordinary. The look on Macready's face. He—I'm sure—thought they were going to kill him. *(Smiles)*

RYDER: I don't think it's funny.

BOUCICAULT: Of course it's not funny. I didn't say it was. *(Beat)* Anyway, I thought he could have kept performing.

AGNES: Dion—

BOUCICAULT: It wasn't that many people for Christ's sake. But . . . *(Beat)* Whatever, it's all part of a day for an actor. *(Laughs)* Sometimes they love us, sometimes they—

SCOTT: I think they should have shot him. That's what I would have liked to see.

(Fisher stops reading and looks up.)

TILTON: Come on, that's—

SCOTT: I mean it. *(Beat)* He has no right to be here. People like him have no right. So he gets what he deserves. This is my opinion. *(Beat)* I mean, why the hell did we fight a war? Why did we fight two wars?! They invade us! We threw them off! We don't need the goddamn English telling us—

FISHER: Stop it, Scott.

SCOTT: American actors for America! I don't see what is so wrong with that?!

RYDER: I doubt if the point of those hooligans was to support American actors.

SCOTT: What hooligans? Who are you calling hooligans? You don't even know why they did what they did.

RYDER: And you do?

SCOTT: If they're like me, they're just fed up. You fight war after war—

TILTON: When did you fight a war? You didn't fight, Scott.

SCOTT: I wanted to. But I had a job. I would have if I hadn't had the job.

FISHER: Tilton is the only one of us who fought . . .

TILTON: I fought and I didn't die. That's all that's worth remembering.

(Beat.)

SCOTT *(Suddenly standing and pointing to Ryder)*: He took my job!

FISHER: *You* cut off your finger!

SCOTT: I slipped!

FISHER: Blame Jones too then! He's got your role too!

SCOTT: I do blame him! He was a friend. I was nice to him.

FISHER: But he's not English.

SCOTT: He's from Maryland. I've learned in my life never to trust someone from Maryland. I should have listened to myself.

FISHER: So it's people from Maryland, people from England. You're talking nonsense.

SCOTT: Is it nonsense that when we go to their country, they spit in our face?!

TILTON: Are you talking Maryland or England now?

SCOTT *(Pointing to Ryder)*: Ask him, he knows what I'm talking about!

RYDER: We have never spat in your—

TILTON *(To Scott)*: When have you ever been to England?

SCOTT *(Pointing to Boucicault and Ryder)*: You make fun of us! *(Turns to Tilton)* Don't be an idiot, Tilton, you know they do! We don't need them, that's all I want to say. *(Beat)* Go home! Leave us alone! We don't want you! We don't need you taking our jobs!

RYDER *(To Agnes)*: All this is about is my playing Macduff—

TILTON: It's his accident. Excuse him.

SCOTT: Don't apologize—

TILTON: You're grouchy, Scott. *(Beat)* He's grouchy. *(Beat)* Ask his wife. Why do you think she let him out? Because he's been so grouchy. *(Tries to laugh. To Scott)* If your wife heard you talk like that . . .

SCOTT: Shut up.

FISHER: Don't embarrass yourself!

(Pause.)

TILTON: Just a few months ago he was saying how much he wanted to visit England. *(To Scott)* Weren't you? *(Beat)* To visit London. *(Beat)* It must be very nice.

(Awkward pause.)

FISHER *(Starting a new conversation, he slaps the manuscript he has been reading)* I like this play. I think I could be very interested in appearing in this play.

(Boucicault smiles at Agnes, then:)

BOUCICAULT: We're just talking about the reading at this point. There's no pay of course. For a reading. I understand this is the practice.

FISHER: But Hackett you say is interested. Has he mentioned dates?

BOUCICAULT *(Shrugging and looking at Agnes)*: November?

FISHER: I might have a problem with that. I might be doing a play in Philadelphia in November. Nothing's set. But they want me, I know they want me.

BOUCICAULT: But you're available for the reading.

FISHER: The part is Hamlet, am I right?

BOUCICAULT: None other than—Hamlet. Who doesn't want to play Hamlet?

FISHER: Right. *(Beat)* But it appears that in your play—Hamlet, as far as I can tell, has only about five lines.

BOUCICAULT: This is true. He comes into Shakespeare's study and tries to help him figure out what he should do about being in love with his neighbor.

FISHER: And he does this in five lines.

BOUCICAULT: The part is Hamlet for God's sake. *(To Agnes)* I don't think I've ever met an actor who didn't want to play Hamlet. *(Moves to take the manuscript away)* Maybe you'd rather play Romeo.

FISHER *(Taking the script back)*: How big is Romeo?

BOUCICAULT: Five, six lines, same as Hamlet.

FISHER: Maybe I can play them both.

BOUCICAULT: It's an interesting thought, but they appear in the same scene. *(Opens the script)* Here. Romeo arrives in Stratford while Hamlet is still there and tries to find out why Shakespeare isn't writing anymore. Hamlet of course already knows but he can't make up his mind whether to tell someone.

RYDER *(Holding up a pitcher of beer, to Scott and Tilton)*: We have some beer.

(Scott turns away, ignoring him.)

TILTON: No, thank you.

FISHER *(Continuing)*: Who played Hamlet in the London production?

BOUCICAULT: What was his name? A very good actor. The next Kean everyone was saying. He found a lot to do with the part. There's a lot there.

FISHER: The next Kean? And he just played Hamlet?

BOUCICAULT: Just Hamlet. He seemed satisfied.

FISHER: And Hackett's definitely interested?

BOUCICAULT: I'm just talking about a reading.

FISHER *(No longer listening)*: I like Hackett. And he likes me. *(Beat)* Still I never thought he'd ever hire me for Hamlet.

(He starts to look through the script again. Boucicault looks at Agnes and rolls his eyes—all this to cast a small role in a reading. Forrest enters.)

RYDER: There he is! It's Ned.

AGNES *(To Boucicault)*: He came.

FORREST: Forgive me, I forgot where John said you were going to go.

BOUCICAULT: Sit down, sit down. Here's a glass.

(Forrest sits; Boucicault pours him a glass.)

AGNES: I can't tell you how much we loved the performance—

SCOTT *(Calling out)*: Ned!

(Forrest turns.)

Ned? *(Forrest suddenly gets up)*

FORREST: Mr. Scott, what a surprise! You weren't in the audience tonight—

SCOTT: No, no. I wasn't.

TILTON: I dragged him out of the house—

SCOTT: My wife threw me out— *(Beat)* For the night.

TILTON: He'd been driving her—

FORREST: How's the finger?

SCOTT: I'm getting better. They say in a few days, I'll . . .

FORREST: That's good to hear. *(Beat)* You'd be proud of young Jones. He's doing his best.

SCOTT: Good. *That's* very good to hear. *(Beat)* They really say that in a few days—

FORREST: Let me buy you a drink.

SCOTT: No, no, please, it's I who should—

FORREST: What are you drinking? Here. *(Puts money on the table)* You're looking great. *(Smiles and goes back to his table. Short pause)*

BOUCICAULT: I enjoyed tonight a great deal.

(Forrest nods.)

It made me think perhaps I should try my hand at an American theme. *(Turns to Ryder)* Maybe an Indian play as well.

AGNES: It seemed very authentic.

(Forrest turns and looks at Fisher, who looks up.)

FISHER: Mr. Boucicault's play. He wants me to play Hamlet.

BOUCICAULT *(Quickly)*: In the reading. This Saturday. You'll be there, I hope.

FISHER: I don't know yet if I'm available for the full production.

BOUCICAULT *(To Forrest)*: So we'll have to hold our breath for a while.

(Short pause.)

FORREST *(Distracted, pointing to a glass)*: Is this mine?

AGNES: That one there. Yes.

(Forrest drinks.)

FORREST: The house was full tonight I gather. It felt that way.

BOUCICAULT: Packed.

AGNES: Thank you for the seats.

RYDER: The couple next to us was sobbing at the end.

(Beat.)

AGNES: I was sobbing at the end.

(Beat.)

BOUCICAULT: If I *were* to attempt an Indian play, Mr. Forrest, I don't imagine you'd be interested in seeing—

FORREST *(Not listening)*: Sometimes you can feel an audience giving back as much as you are trying to give them. *(Beat)* It felt like that. You were a good audience.

BOUCICAULT: I know exactly what you mean.

FORREST: And sometimes— *(Turns to Ryder)* How is Mr. Macready? I meant to write him today.

RYDER: He's— In shock? *(Shrugs)* How should he be?

BOUCICAULT: I was there, you know. We were. It was unbelievable.

FORREST *(To Ryder)*: What about his wounds? I heard—he was cut?

BOUCICAULT: There was blood all over the stage. When he walked off, Macready's face was covered. You couldn't see his—

RYDER: It was cut. On his forehead. *(Turns to Boucicault.)* It looked worse than it was.

(Short pause.)

FORREST *(Without looking at anyone)*: I've heard someone—someone was saying, I forget who it was—they were saying that people think I'm somehow . . . *(Beat)* That I bear a responsibility.

BOUCICAULT: For last night?

FORREST: This is what I've heard.

FISHER: People are nervous, all kinds of things are being said.

RYDER: I have heard this as well, Mr. Forrest. You try to tell people that—

AGNES: No one can—

FORREST: As if attacking Macready's *Macbeth* was somehow praising mine. This is thinking I do not grasp myself. *(Smiles)* It's ridiculous. It's unfair. If they knew—if only someone had come to me and said there could be trouble. I now understand there were threats made days ago.

RYDER: Mr. Forrest—

FORREST: Let me finish. Where was Mr. Macready? Why did he not confide in me? We had dinner only the other day. He said nothing, isn't that right, Mr. Ryder? You were there.

RYDER: That's correct.

FORREST: Just the other day, we had dinner. My wife and I did. *(Beat. He sighs)* As if I don't have enough to worry about. *(Beat)* We don't know who these thugs were, do we? Or even what they wanted. *(Shakes his head)* It seems so unnecessary. *(Beat)* How many were there? I've heard at least ten different accounts.

BOUCICAULT: They were in the balcony. Most of them were in the balcony, weren't they?

FORREST: I've even heard . . . *(Beat)* I'm sure this is not true. You were there. I'm sure he did the right thing. *(Beat)* But someone was saying—who was it? *(Shrugs)* They were saying that if Macready had only stayed on the stage and shouted back at them.

AGNES: He tried this. *(Turns to Boucicault)* Have you—

FORREST: Oh. Then he tried.

BOUCICAULT: Not for that long though.

FORREST: Really? *(Beat)* I mean we've all had audiences that—I don't know. Can't be pleased, I suppose. Nothing will please them. *(Beat)* We get such audiences here. Maybe not in England, but—

BOUCICAULT: You get them in England. You really get them in Scotland.

AGNES: Scotland can be bad, this is true.

FORREST: Then you know what I'm talking about. How sometimes one needs to fight back. To assert oneself. You let a crowd have their way . . . *(Shrugs)* If you don't lead . . . *(Beat)* I'm sure it's not true, but it is possible that Mr. Macready—for whatever reason—was simply unable to lead. Unable to do his job. *(Beat)* And so—he ran away.

RYDER: I don't think that's fair.

FORREST: Is it fair to blame me?

(Short pause.)

RYDER: No. That isn't fair either.

FORREST: Because some unhappy people decide to rip up some seats while shouting out my name?

RYDER: They shouted your name? That I hadn't heard. *(To Boucicault)* Did you—?

BOUCICAULT: They did. That's true.

FORREST: I'm an actor. What can I do? *(Beat)* People sit in their seats and dream about you, until what they dream isn't you. *(Beat)*

What people shout . . . *(Shrugs)* I have enough things . . .
(Pause. Looks to Agnes and Boucicault) My wife, Catherine—
she left me today. This morning.

AGNES: Oh God, I'm sorry—

FORREST: She'd—had enough, she said. So she walked out. *(Beat)*
I don't need this other— I did nothing wrong!! He should have
just yelled them down. Had the guts to yell them down. And
then all of . . .

(Macready has entered with Clark and Bradshaw.)

MACREADY: Mr. Forrest.

(Forrest turns and stands.)

FORREST: You don't look any worse for wear. Please, won't you—

MACREADY: We just took a table in the next room. I heard you were
here and . . . *(Beat)* I want to thank you for changing to
Metamora.

(Forrest nods.)

It will help to— This so-called rivalry.

FORREST: What rivalry? *(Beat)* I heard that in some quarters we are
both being blamed for what happened last night.

MACREADY: I had not heard that we both were being blamed.

RYDER: Mr. Forrest was just saying that they were shouting out his
name.

MACREADY: I remember hearing it very distinctly.

FORREST: It will all calm down.

MACREADY: Of course it will. *(Beat)* It has nothing to do with us,
does it?

FORREST: No. Nothing.

(Beat.)

MACREADY *(Suddenly turning to Ryder)*: Where have you been,
John? I expected to see you this evening.

RYDER: I went to Mr. Forrest's *Metamora.* I told you I was going.
I asked you to go.

MACREADY: Did you? *(Beat)* I suppose it is all very—original. My loss, no doubt. Get us some liquor, will you? Different kinds. You choose. *(Turns to go, stops, goes back)* Oh, I forgot. You need my money, don't you? *(Puts money on the table)* Don't be too long.

(Macready, Clark and Bradshaw, both who have stayed at some distance, now leave. Pause.)

RYDER: I better . . . *(Stands)* Perhaps, first I'll finish my wine. *(Sits)* I just have a sip left. *(Drinks it)*
FORREST: Let me fill up your glass.

(After some hesitation, Ryder hands him his glass. Forrest pours him another drink.)

On tour, a few years ago, in a small southern town, I happened to cast as my Ophelia the daughter of a preacher. *(Beat)* I had not known this. And the true extent of his rage had been kept from me. *(Beat)* But as I made my first entrance, I heard the clicks of many revolvers being cocked. *(Beat)* You know, it never occurred to me to leave that stage.

(Pause. Then blackout.)

SCENE 4

2 A.M.

A small attic apartment.
 Forrest and Ryder come up the stairs (up through a trap); they carry lanterns.

FORREST: I'm surprised you're even interested. Watch your step.
RYDER: I'm interested in talking about anything. And everything.
FORREST *(Holding up the lantern and looking around the room)*: I told you it was small. But it is convenient. Put it over there.

(Ryder sets down his lantern.)

Sit down, sit down. *(Beat)* One block from the theatre. *(Lights another lantern)* It is a place to get away.

RYDER: I'm sure—

FORREST: Sit down, please, Mr. Ryder. And when they throw you out of the tavern, it is a place to get a drink. Let me get you that drink. *(Goes to a cabinet and takes out a bottle, glasses, etc. Pause)* It's cold tonight. Cold for May. *(Beat)* Feels like it's going to rain. But that I am sure is something you are used to.

RYDER: Rain? *(Smiles)* I don't miss it.

FORREST: Do you miss anything? *(Beat)* Won't you miss—?

RYDER: I haven't agreed to anything, Mr.— Ned. I thought we were just . . . *(Beat)* I'd probably be interested in a season. *(Beat)* A four- or five-month season. Depending on where it is. Where you are going. There's much more of this country I'd like to see. I'm not homesick yet. *(Looks at him)* I admired your performance tonight enormously.

(The door opens and Miss Bass enters, a blanket around her shoulders. Underneath she is naked, having just been woken up.)

MISS BASS: What time is it ? *(Sees Ryder)* Oh, I'll . . . I didn't know you'd . . .

FORREST: Have a drink with us, Jane. You know John, of course

MISS BASS: Yes, of course. Let me get some clothes on

(She goes. Pause.)

FORREST: She lives here. *(Beat)* She looks after it for me. *(Beat)* I'm pleased you enjoyed *Metamora* tonight. I paid for that play, you know. Had a contest. The best play on an American topic *(Beat)* That came in. It was a mess. Wrote three-quarters of it myself. *(Beat)* Fits like a glove now. Could play some of it in my sleep. And they can't get enough of it. Anywhere I go. *(Beat)* You'll see yourself. *(Beat)* I don't need anyone for *Metamora*.

RYDER: I wasn't suggesting— That's not why I—

FORREST: I need a Buckingham. *(Beat)* A Mercutio. An Edgar, son of Gloucester. As well as Macduff of course.

RYDER: That's very generous.

FORREST: Between you and me . . . We can talk about Iago another time.

RYDER: I've played Iago.

FORREST: That's good to know. *(Short pause)* In my production he's very subtle. The man who plays him now is very good.

RYDER: I'll come and see—

FORREST: We do New Orleans, St. Louis, Cincinnati, then to Baltimore and Philadelphia. Then back here for a month for Hackett. *(Beat)* This is November.

RYDER: I thought Boucicault's play was to be done by Hackett in—

FORREST: The problem of course is can I afford you. *(Beat)* You are probably very expensive.

RYDER: You know what you paid for one Macduff.

FORREST: You are very expensive.

(Miss Bass enters, having quickly dressed.)

(Getting up) Let me get you a—

MISS BASS: I can get a drink myself.

(Forrest sits back down. Short pause.)

RYDER: I should probably be— *(Starts to stand)*

FORREST: Don't be silly. Sit down. We don't have that many guests, do we?

(Ryder sits. Short pause.)

MISS BASS: I'm sorry I couldn't join you at the tavern tonight. I was exhausted. *(Beat)* Did I miss anything?

FORREST: Did you miss—? Did she, John?

RYDER: I . . . *(Shrugs. He has been fiddling with a manuscript that is in front of him)*

FORREST: Boucicault's play. Take a look if you want. *(Beat)* I'm supposed to be reading it. *(Beat)* He asked me to— *(Turns to Miss Bass)* I've read most of it. I've read some of it. He says Macready's interested if you can believe that.

RYDER: I doubt if— *(Beat)* I don't know.

MISS BASS: I've tried to read it tonight. *(Rolls her eyes and laughs. Short pause)*

FORREST: John loved *Metamora*.

MISS BASS: Ned wrote most of that.

(Pause.)

RYDER: It's a lovely apartment. *(To Miss Bass)* It's yours?

(She turns to Forrest, then back.)

MISS BASS: Yeah. *(Beat)* It's mine.
RYDER: It's very convenient.
MISS BASS: Isn't it?
FORREST: John has asked to join us for a season.
RYDER: I haven't actually— *(Stops himself and smiles)* If Ned can find a place for me. *(Short pause. Suddenly stands)* Really, it is late. I must go.

(No one else gets up.)

Thank you for the drink.
FORREST *(Gesturing that he could stand)*: Let me.
RYDER: I think I can let myself out. *(Takes the lantern)* Miss Bass. *(Beat)* Ned.

(He goes. Long pause.)

MISS BASS *(Finally)*: Do you want to go to bed?

(Forrest doesn't respond.)

It was nice having company. It was nice to—entertain. This way. *(Beat)* He's a nice man. Why he wants to work in America when—
FORREST: He liked my performance. He wants to work with me.
MISS BASS: I didn't mean . . . *(Beat)* He must have many reasons. Maybe things in England weren't working out so . . . I don't know, Ned. I'm sorry I brought it up.

(He sips his drink. Short pause.)

I ran into our landlord this morning. *(Beat)* The rent's due. *(Beat)* I know I reminded you already, but—I didn't know if you'd forgotten. *(Beat)* Sometimes you do forget. *(Laughs. He doesn't seem to hear her)* Ned? *(Beat)* My— *(Opens her mouth widely)* I broke a tooth.

(He looks at her.)

I'm sorry to bring it up now. I know you're tired but— *(Beat)* This is the only chance we seem to have, so . . .

(He takes out some money and sets it down.)

I don't like to beg.

FORREST: You're not begging.

(Short pause.)

MISS BASS: My mother wrote. She's finally coming to visit. I don't believe it, I've asked her a hundred times. *(Beat)* I guess she finally accepts my being an actress. *(Laughs to herself)* She wants to stay here. She thinks it's—mine. *(Beat)* She'll stay for three weeks.

(Short pause. Forrest just sits there.)

Do you mind? *(Beat)* Do you mind? *(Short pause)*

(Blackout.)

SCENE 5

LATER THAT NIGHT

Macready's room, New York Hotel.
Macready asleep, drunk, in a chair. Ryder sits in another chair, reading Boucicault's manuscript. Pause. Suddenly Macready screams—he's having a nightmare.

RYDER: It's all right. Calm down. It's me. It's me.

(Macready opens his eyes, he breathes heavily; looks around him.)

You had a dream.

(Pause. Heavy breathing; rubs his eyes.)

MACREADY: How long have I— When did you . . . ?
RYDER: You asked me in, remember? We were talking. You were
telling me about the meeting. *(Beat)* With Irving. *(Beat)* You
fell asleep.
MACREADY: What time is it?
RYDER: Nearly half past four.
MACREADY: I can't sleep in my bed.
RYDER: That's what you'd been saying . . . That's why— *(Gestures
"I am here")* Let me get you a drink. It helped before.
MACREADY: I'm going to smell for days. *(Smiles)* My spit will intox-
icate at least the first three rows.

(Even bigger smile. Ryder brings him a drink. He sips.)

It was an actor's dream, John.
RYDER: Not surprising.
MACREADY: The actor's dream. *(Beat)* Do cobblers and coat makers
have their dreams? One wonders. Though mine was an interesting variation. It wasn't that I could not remember my lines
or what part I was playing or which play I was in, rather—it
was the reverse. *(Beat)* In my dream, I was speaking all the
parts. One second I was— Whatever. I can't remember. Then
the next, I was speaking back to me. Then entering to tell me
something. Then telling me to leave so I could be alone and
have my soliloquy. *(Beat)* Rather exhausting this was. And
rather unnerving to the other actors whose parts I was obviously usurping. Thus one by one they—my fellow actors—
retreated from the stage and allowed me to be alone with various other me's. *(Beat)* One or two left quite angrily too. This
I could not understand. After all I was much better than they
could ever hope to be. They should have appreciated this.
(Short pause) When it came time for Macduff to kill Macbeth—so obviously this was *Macbeth*—I found myself in a
quandary, of course. *(Laughs to himself)* The audience was
cheering. They screamed. Were they praising my performing?
Were they after my death? I did not understand the effect I was

having. *(Beat)* And then—as the script calls for it—I killed myself, or rather my Macduff killed my Macbeth. And the pain, it was horrific. *(Short pause. Looks at Ryder)* I knew every part, and was good. *(Laughs. Beat)* I shall be afraid now to go to sleep again. The sun should be up when?

(Ryder shrugs.)

What time did you come here?
RYDER: It was a little after two.
MACREADY: And I was up then?
RYDER: I think you had been asleep, but . . .

(Short pause.)

MACREADY *(Suddenly starts)*: Had I written to my wife?! I always write to my wife!
RYDER: Yes. You had. It's . . . *(Nods to the table. Short pause.)*
MACREADY *(Suddenly starts again)*: And when you came, there were crowds in the streets. Angry crowds!
RYDER: No. *(Beat)* The streets were . . . A few carts. A few people. *(Beat)* That must have been another dream.

(Macready notices the manuscript in Ryder's hands.)

Boucicault's play. I see he gave you a copy. *(Beat)* Did you read it?
MACREADY: I looked at it. *(Beat)* Forrest is interested. That's what one hears.
RYDER: I wouldn't know. I don't— *(Beat)* Maybe.

(Pause.)

MACREADY: They say I will be safe. Besides the police they may even circle the entire theatre with soldiers. Nothing can happen. *(Beat)* Soldiers. *(Beat)* What a country. And now you want to stay here. This is what you were telling me, wasn't it? *(Beat)* See, I was awake.
RYDER: I didn't think—
MACREADY: I was even listening.

(Beat.)

RYDER: Then you know, and that is that.

MACREADY: Is it? *(Beat)* I paid your way here *and* back, Mr. Ryder.

RYDER: I have done everything you've asked.

MACREADY: You were brought here to work for me, not for Mr. Forrest!

RYDER: I shall make sure you are safely on a ship and very comfortable. That's where my responsibility ends!

(Pause.)

MACREADY *(To himself)*: Alone on the stage. The actors are deserting me. Dreams and life. Life and dreams. How can you stomach such a country where soldiers stand around theatres?! *(Beat)* When audiences— But of course you didn't see this. You were busy playing for Mr. Forrest.

RYDER: You agreed that I could.

MACREADY: How could I say no? *(Beat)* This does not mean I approved, John. I had hoped you'd have recognized your own responsibility. Your own duty. But . . . *(Beat)* This is how one learns about one's friends. *(Short pause)* I will never employ you again. *(Beat)* Never.

(Pause. Ryder says nothing.)

I may change my mind, but that is how I feel at this time, John. *(Beat)* I'm planning a season at the Drury Lane. Nothing has been cast. Except the leads, of course. We can talk about anything you wish. *(Beat)* We can talk now.

RYDER: I will be back in few months. It's only for a few months.

MACREADY: Oh. You didn't say that. *(Beat)* Then we will talk in those few months. *(Beat)* How many is a "few"?

RYDER: Three.

(Short pause.)

MACREADY: In two months, I begin to cast. *(Pause)* Forrest has parts for you?

RYDER: If he didn't, he wouldn't be asking—

MACREADY: Make him give you excellent parts, John! In America you deserve excellent parts, remember that.

RYDER: I saw his *Metamora* tonight.

MACREADY: I have seen this performance. *(Beat)* Years ago. Seven years or so ago. *(Beat)* Somewhere. He has power. In this role.

RYDER: Absolutely. When he kills his wife—

MACREADY: Ah. Yes. True. *(Beat)* And that must have been quite heartfelt tonight.

(Ryder looks at Macready.)

His wife has left him, you know. Just today. Everyone was talking about it. *(Beat)* She's staying with a friend. Just left him a note. *(Pause)* Metamora is a very good role for him. I would never attempt it myself. *(Beat)* Audiences love it. *(Shakes his head)* He's made a fortune from it. *(Beat)* I understand he's building a castle of some sort just up the Hudson. All from the money he's made from . . . *(Beat)* Lucky him. *(Beat)* Every actor is staying. I don't have to replace anyone. I take my hat off to all of them. Not one is deserting. *(Beat. To himself)* Actors. By and large we are good and decent people. *(Beat)* So they left the stage and there I am trying to kill myself! *(Laughs)* I can see myself as Macduff. I'd be a very good Macduff. If the part were larger. Mmmmmmmmm. *(Smiles to himself)* Mmmmmmmmm. I'm waking up. *(Beat)* Let's wait for the sun to rise. Which, like stage light, will keep us out of the dark. *(Takes a sip of his drink)*

(Short pause. Blackout.)

SCENE 6

MAY 10, 1849. 8:30 P.M.

The wings of a stage, first representing the wings of the Broadway Theatre, later the wings of the Astor Place Opera House. The "stage" is just off, where the end of Act Two of Metamora *is in progress.*

A number of actors in soldier and Indian costumes wait and watch; they include Fisher and Miss Holland.

From the stage: the council chamber scene. Errington (Blakely), Metamora (Forrest), Goodenough (Miss Burton) and Annawandah (Jones).

Tilton enters the wings from the dressing rooms.

In the wings:

On stage:

TILTON: How's it going?

MISS HOLLAND: Fine. It's going fine.

TILTON: Either of you been outside tonight? I just stepped out. It's crazy out tonight. A bunch of drunks nearly knocked me down.

FISHER: It's fine in here. It's a good house.

TILTON: Is it? *(Checks out the audience)* I was thinking I might even skip the tavern tonight . . .

(They listen to the silence from the stage.)

FISHER: Ned's dried. He's dried.

MISS BASS *(Entering from the stage)*: Do something! Help him!

TILTON: Get a script!

MISS HOLLAND *(At the same time)*: Give him a line!

MISS BASS *(To Fisher)*: Bang the——!

METAMORA: You believe his words.

GOODENOUGH: We do, and will reward his honesty.

METAMORA: Red man, say unto these people they have bought thy tongue, and thou hast uttered a lie!

ERRINGTON: He does not answer.

METAMORA: I am Metamora, thy father and thy king.

ERRINGTON: Metamora o'erawes him—send the witness home.

METAMORA: I will do that! Slave of the white man, go follow Sasamond.

ERRINGTON: Seize and bind him.

METAMORA: Come! My knife has drunk the blood of the false one, yet it is not satisfied!

(Silence from the stage.)

MISS BURTON *(From the stage)*: Prompt! Prompt!

(They listen.)

TILTON: He never dries.

MISS BASS *(To Miss Holland)*: Every time Ned comes off stage he says he sees his wife out there. She's not. I checked.

(Metamora/Forrest runs into the wings. Fisher gives a drum-roll. Huge applause is heard coming from the theatre. Forrest gets a hold of himself and returns to the stage for a bow. Others follow.)

TILTON *(The last to go)*: It is a good house tonight.

METAMORA: From the east to the west, in the north and in the south shall cry of vengeance burst, till the lands you have stolen groan under your feet no more!

ERRINGTON: Secure him!

METAMORA: Thus do I smite your nation and defy your power.

ERRINGTON: Fire on him.

(Soldiers fire on stage.)

(The applause fades away. From the stage one hears Macbeth and we are in the wings of The Astor Place Opera House, II.iii. Numerous actors in costumes wait and watch. From the stage:)

MACBETH:
　　. . . there, the murderers,
　　Steeped in the colors of their trade, their daggers
　　Unmannerly breeched with gore. Who could refrain
　　That had a heart to love, and in that heart
　　Courage to make's love known?

LADY MACBETH:　　　　　　Help me hence, ho!

MACDUFF: Look to the lady.

(Scene continues "on stage." Lady Macbeth [Mrs. Pope] is carried from the stage. As she enters the wings:)

BRIDGES: How is it out there?

MRS. POPE: A couple of people in the balcony. A couple of boos nothing else.

BRIDGES: Then that's not too bad, is it?
MRS. POPE: No. It'll all be fine.

(On stage, continuing:)

MACDUFF: And so do I.
ALL: So all.

MACBETH:
> Let's briefly put on manly readiness
> And meet i'th' hall together.

ALL: Well contented.

(Macbeth [Macready], Macduff [Clark] and Banquo [Bradshaw] enter from the stage. Scene between Malcolm and Donalbain continues off.)

MACREADY *(Entering)*: I've played to better houses.
BRADSHAW: They're nervous.
CLARK: That is true.
MACREADY: The soldiers still outside?
BRIDGES: There seem to be even more.
MACREADY: Don't complain.
BRIDGES: I wasn't—

(Malcolm [Arnold] and Donalbain [Sefton] enter from the stage and Bridges [Ross] and Wemyss [Old Man] leave the wings and enter on the stage for Act II. iv—a heavily cut version.)

SEFTON *(To Macready, as a joke)*: As soon as you get off they settle down and listen.
MACREADY: Very funny, Mr. Sefton.

(He smiles. Suddenly from above, the sound of a window being smashed by a rock. Everyone stops. The scene on stage has stopped as well.)

BRIDGES *(From the stage)*: What was that?!
MACREADY: Keep playing, Mr. Bridges! Everyone, do not stop, please!

(The scene continues on stage.)

MRS. POPE: They're putting in a new sewer across the street. Did you notice? They've got stones piles all over the place.
ARNOLD: I guess some boy couldn't resist.
MRS. POPE: That's just what I was thinking.

(Clark [Macduff] leaves the wings and joins the scene on stage. From the stage:)

ROSS: How goes the world, sir, now?
MACDUFF: Why, see you not?

(The scene continues.)

MACREADY *(To Mrs. Pope)*: How's your sister?
MRS. POPE: Who?
MACREADY: Didn't the other day you say something about your sister visiting?
MRS. POPE: Did I? She's good. Very good.

(Bradshaw [Banquo] leaves the wings for the stage as Clark, Wemyss and Bridges come into the wings.)

BRIDGES *(Entering, to Macready)*: I'm sorry, it's just when I heard—
ARNOLD: Some boys—with stones.
BRIDGES: Oh. Oh that's what it was.
CLARK: What is it about that audience? There's something—
MACREADY: As someone was saying—they're nervous. *(Turns to Bridges and smiles)* As some of us are.

(He smiles, laughs. The others laugh.)

CLARK: There's something else. I can't put my finger on it.
MACREADY *(To Mrs. Pope)*: We're on.
CLARK: Wait a minute! I got it. They're all men! The audience! There aren't any women!
ACTOR: Let me see. *(Goes to look)*
MACREADY: We're on!

(Macready and Mrs. Pope enter the stage, followed by Bridges and others. Trumpet fanfare.)

ARNOLD: Maybe we should have a few police back here with— I'll go see if . . . *(Moves toward off)*

(At the same time, from the stage:)

MACBETH: Here's our chief guest—

LADY MACBETH:
> If he had been forgotten,
> It had been a gap in our great feast—

(A scream from the audience. Arnold stops. The acting on stage stops. Clark turns back to Arnold.)

ARNOLD: What's—?
CLARK: Someone's tried to jump—from the balcony. Police are trying to—
CHIPPINDALE *(Entering from the dressing rooms)*: They're bolting the doors!
MACREADY *(On stage, at the same time, to his actors)*: Do not stop! Keep speaking!!
CHIPPINDALE: They are bolting the doors! We're being locked in!

(Arnold goes off to see.)

CLARK: They caught the man. The police have him.

(A cheer from the audience.)

LADY MACBETH: . . . in our great feast,
> And all-thing unbecoming.

MACBETH:
> Tonight we hold a solemn supper, sir,
> And I'll request your presence.

BANQUO: Let Your Highness
> Command upon me, to the which my duties—

(Suddenly a number of windows are broken, large rocks crash against the door of the theatre. On stage the play tries to continue but is hardly audible.)

CHIPPINDALE: Jesus Christ.

(Then there is a single gunshot from outside the theatre.)

CLARK: What was that?
SEFTON: I heard it.
CLARK: Who's firing?

(Bridges hurries in from the stage.)

BRIDGES: What was that? We heard a gunshot.
CLARK: It was from—

(Suddenly many gunshots ring out, and screams. Then the full-fledged sounds of riot from outside.)

BRIDGES: They're storming the doors. They want to kill us.

(Panic from the house and stage, Macready and the other actors hurry into the wings.)

MACREADY: What's going on? Where are the police? Why aren't the police back here?!
MRS. POPE: They're setting fires in the balcony.
CHIPPINDALE *(Yelling)*: The balcony's on fire!!
BRADSHAW: Open the doors and get the soldiers in here.

(Panic. No one knows where to go. The battles being waged in the house get closer; Arnold appears from above and hoists a ladder down.)

ARNOLD: Up here! Climb up! They're coming on stage!

(Mrs. Pope screams.)

MACREADY *(Pulling out his sword)*: Fight them off! Fight!

(Banging on the doors continues. Bridges begins to climb up the ladder.)

WEMYSS: The doors are breaking in.

BRADSHAW *(Grabbing others)*: Quick, through the house. Come on. Through the house. Take off your costumes!

(Actors start ripping off their costumes; one heads toward the stage.)

Not across the stage! That way! That way! There's a door! *(Grabbing an actor, who is taking off his costume)* There's no time! Go! Run!

(Actors run off. Ryder appears from the stage after having obviously battled his way there. He sees Macready.)

RYDER: Mr. Macready!

MACREADY *(Dazed)*: Stand back! Stand back! Or die!!!

RYDER: It's John. *(Beat)* John Ryder. *(Beat)* It's me.

(Macready finally lets Ryder near him. Ryder puts a coat over Macready's shoulders.)

BRADSHAW: Hurry!

(They all go off. The riot continues. Blackout.)

SCENE 7

11:30 P.M.

Forrest's dressing room; the Broadway Theatre. Forrest, half changed out of his Metamora *costume and Ryder and Macready, both disheveled and out of breath.*

Outside, in the distance, the occasional gunshot and whoops from a roving mob.

RYDER: There were some rocks thrown. Some boys, they— At first the soldiers fired into the air. But then one or two . . . *(Beat)* I suppose . . . *(Short pause)* I figured the last place anyone would think of looking for—

(He looks at Macready, who is very upset, trying desperately to get his breath.)

I need to find some horses. I need to contact friends. My guess is that they would kill him, it's a riot. No one's in control. *(Beat)* The soldiers are running through the streets firing. The police refused to leave the theatre. *(Laughs to himself)* We left with the audience. We just got out and ran. *(Beat)* Inside, I don't think there's . . . By now. The seats were being ripped apart. Someone set a fire under the balcony. *(Beat)* From the parquette. *(Beat)* They just suddenly were crawling over the seats, over people in the audience—from the parquette. How they got there . . . It could all be on fire now.

(Short pause.)

FORREST: Are people hurt? Someone must have been hurt.

(Ryder looks at Macready, who doesn't answer, then turns back.)

RYDER: We saw ourselves— What? *(Covers his eyes for a moment)* People are dead.
FORREST: I don't believe this.
RYDER: Who knows how many. Five, ten, at least. *(To Macready)* Right? *(Beat)* And a lot wounded. Seriously wounded. Twenty, thirty, fifty? I don't know.

(Pause.)

FORREST *(Suddenly turning to Macready)*: You goaded them! Why did you perform?!
RYDER: That's not fair.

(Short pause.)

MACREADY *(Quietly)*: I didn't *goad* anyone. Could I get a drink, please? The opposite is true.

(Forrest doesn't move.)

FORREST: Ten people dead, Mr. Macready!
RYDER: I don't know for sure how—
MACREADY: Could I get a drink, please?!

(Ryder looks at Forrest, then goes to a cabinet and pours the drink.)

FORREST: You should not have played.
MACREADY: They begged me. Irving promised me it'd be— He had a petition. Everyone said— *(Beat)* I wasn't to worry. I wasn't to . . .

(Macready starts to sob. Short pause. Ryder hands Macready his drink.)

FORREST *(To Ryder)*: People killed for what?
MACREADY *(Suddenly turning)*: They were shouting your name again!

(Forrest turns to Ryder, who nods.)

"Kill Macready! Three Cheers for Ned Forrest!"
FORREST: Why would they do that? That doesn't make sense.
MACREADY: "Ned Forrest—an American!"
FORREST: I have made it very clear that I —
MACREADY: I didn't want this! *(Beat)* After the other night, I . . .
FORREST: When you should have shouted them down. That's your mistake. You should have had the guts to shout them down! All of this could have been—!
RYDER: You don't know what you're talking about.

(Pause.)

MACREADY: I was told—if I didn't perform—I'd be hurting American . . . American what? They made it sound like I had to . . .
FORREST: For seventy-five percent of the house! I heard about this!

MACREADY: That had nothing to do with— *(Beat)* Money has noth-
ing to do with this. *(Beat; attacking)* "Three cheers for Ned
Forrest. Hurray for Forrest!" As they try to burn down a theatre!
FORREST: Those people have nothing to do with me! *(Walks away.
Pause. Finally to Ryder)* You want him to stay here?
RYDER: I shouldn't be too long. We can't go back to the hotel.
MACREADY: No.
RYDER: I'll take him to Boston. We have friends. *(Beat)* He can get
a boat home from there. *(Beat)* But if you don't want to . . .
FORREST: He can stay.

(Short pause.)

RYDER: He'll need some clothes.
FORREST: He can stay. Don't be long.

(Ryder hesitates, then hurries out. Pause.)

MACREADY: He didn't know where else to bring me. Could I have
another? *(Holds out his glass)*
FORREST: Listen.

*(Pause. From outside the noise of the mob. After a moment Forrest
goes and gets the bottle and pours Macready a drink.)*

Were they really shouting my name again?

(Macready nods.)

What the hell did they think they were doing?
MACREADY: You obviously—for them. For some of them. Repre-
sent— *(Shrugs)*
FORREST: I'm an actor!

(Macready shrugs again. Pause.)

MACREADY: Any money I do receive I shall give away. I did not perform for . . . *(Beat)* I'm not a greedy man. *(Beat)* The charities
I support, I should give you a list, I also give anonymously
to—

FORREST: Shut up. *(Short pause)* Please. Your generosity is well known.

MACREADY: Is it? *(Beat)* Good. *(Looks toward a clothes trunk, hesitates, then goes to look in it)*

FORREST: Take whatever you need. Whatever might fit. A cape maybe . . .

(Shrugs. Pause. Macready begins to look through the costume trunk. From outside, the gunshots and shouts come closer.)

(Suddenly he turns to the noise, screaming) Leave us alone in here!!!!!

(Pause.)

MACREADY *(Pulling something out of the trunk; quietly)*: Is this your Lear?

(Forrest nods.)

It's funny how we rarely get a chance to see each other's . . .

FORREST: I've seen your Lear. *(Beat)* I found the time to see your Lear.

(Short pause.)

MACREADY: Is that it? You've just seen it? You don't want to say——?

FORREST *(Quickly)*: I enjoyed it.

(Short pause.)

MACREADY: You've got an interesting costume.

FORREST: So did you.

MACREADY: Actually this sort of looks like mine. *(Short pause. Without looking up)* How was *your* play tonight?

FORREST: Fine. *(Laughs to himself)* There was no riot. A large section of my audience did not try to murder me. The theatre is not burning. Not a bad night. *(Beat)* They love *Metamora*, the noble savage. *(Beat)* Who has the decency to die. *(Smiles)* So they cheered as always. I was not very good tonight, I thought. *(Shrugs)*

MACREADY: As we get older . . . It's funny, isn't it? When we begin—when I began—I thought always about what they would think about me. *(Beat)* You want so much to please them. *(Beat)* But you get older—and that's still there—but . . . Well, it's us who start to judge them, isn't it?

FORREST: I'm not that old yet.

(Short pause.)

MACREADY *(Choosing to ignore him)*: Sometimes you stand on that stage and know you are achieving a level of excellence few before you have ever achieved. And you watch an audience watching you as if on some riverbank staring at the natural flow of water. *(Beat)* And then on other nights—probably like you felt tonight—you hate what you've done, perhaps even embarrassed—

FORREST: I didn't say I was—

MACREADY: And your audience receives you with rapturous attention and applause. *(Beat)* There seems to be no rhyme or reason. *(Beat)* The older you get, the more confusing it all becomes. The reaction. Like tonight, what you were telling me about your performance. Where's the logic.

(Forrest looks at him.)

And I'll tell you what makes it all even worse. It's going to see another perform—especially a part that you know like your own soul—and then witnessing grotesque exaggeration, which one could forgive perhaps in a novice, but when it's an actor of some note, some ambition. And then when the crowd—the mob, one should call them in this case—greets this fraud with its misplaced adulation, I find myself in an almost state of total fevered despair.

(Short pause.)

FORREST: I enjoy watching other actors—

MACREADY: When they are excellent! Which is so rare, as we both know so well.

(Short pause.)

FORREST: I enjoy watching other actors even when they're bad, even when they're silly.

MACREADY: But then when an audience praises—

FORREST: I enjoyed your Hamlet a great deal. *(Beat)* When I was in London. I enjoyed it. *(Short pause)* That dance you did— Hamlet's little dance before the Gertrude scene. I'd never seen anything like it. I will never forget it.

MACREADY: You're not the first to—

FORREST: A fancy dance? I asked myself. Where does this come from in the play? I knew no reference to it. I had never before seen an actor—

MACREADY: An expression of his madness. A color. A texture of the performance.

FORREST: And a costume for this dance which, if I remember correctly, had a dress with a waist up to about the armpits, huge overlarge black gloves—

MACREADY: True, I—

FORREST: A great big hat with a gigantic plume—

MACREADY: The character is mad!

FORREST: Is this Hamlet or Malvolio, I remember saying to myself. But still, I enjoyed it. *(Suddenly turns to Macready)* It's true, Hamlet is mad. And in preparation for my own performance I became a student of the mind's disease, visiting asylums and talking not only with the doctors, but also with the ill. And the result of this study, Mr. Macready, was the knowledge that true madness is expressed through the heart, not the costume. Madness is not funny clothes, but a funny soul.

MACREADY: We are different actors

FORREST: This is very true.

MACREADY: You study asylums and I study the play.

FORREST: That's not—

MACREADY: Perhaps I am old-fashioned, but I continue to believe that all one needs is to be found in the play. Mr. Shakespeare knew what—

FORREST: I don't disagree.

(Beat.)

MACREADY: Then perhaps all I am saying is—from one actor to another—a little more time with the text and a little less in asylums might do a world of good.

FORREST: You haven't even seen—

MACREADY: One hears, Mr. Forrest, one hears! It is a small business we're in.

FORREST: In that case, as we are talking text, perhaps—as one actor to another—I can make a suggestion as I have also seen your Othello.

MACREADY: You *are* a fan, I'm flattered.

FORREST: As I've said, I enjoy watching other actors—whatever they do. Anyway, *Othello. (Begins to recite)*

> Rude am I in my speech,
> And little blessed with the soft phrase of peace;
> For since these arms of mine had seven years' pith

(Macready joins in:)

FORREST AND MACREADY:
> Till now some nine moons wasted, they have used
> Their dearest action in the tented field;
> And little of this great world can I speak
> More than pertains to feats of broil and battle;

(Forrest drops out.)

MACREADY:
> And therefore little shall I grace my cause
> In speaking for *myself.*

FORREST: "For *myself*"! That's just how you said it when I saw you.

MACREADY: And that is the line.

FORREST: That's not the meaning though. *(Laughs)* Othello starts by saying he is rude in speech, how there is little he can speak about except battles. So what he is saying here is that he's bad at *speaking*, not that he doesn't want to talk or have people talk about him. He's not being humble, for Christ's sake, he's saying that he's awkward and out of place where he is! So the line should be:

And there little shall I grace my cause
In *speaking* for myself.

(Beat.)

MACREADY: That's a different reading. It's interesting. But it's just a different reading.

FORREST: It's the right reading!

MACREADY: That's your opinion.

FORREST: And when I go and see your Othello again that's how you'll be saying the line, I'm sure. *(Smiles)* Here, you want another one! The same scene:

> Which I observing,
> Took once a pliant hour, and found *good* means
> To draw from her a prayer of earnest heart
> That I would all my pilgrimage dilate . . .

And so on. *(Beat)* ". . . *good* means"! Not: ". . . good *means*"!

MACREADY: I don't hear the difference.

FORREST: He was after a *good* reason, a *good* way, a just way to get his promise. As opposed to a successful means to—

(From outside, sudden gunshots are even closer. Short pause.)

MACREADY: The other reading maybe. But not this . . .

FORREST: Fine. Fine. At least I got you to agree about one. *(Short pause)* I only brought it up because— What you said, about reading the . . .

(Crowd noise is heard from off. Macready looks through the trunk. Long pause. Macready pulls out a costume.)

MACREADY: Richard?

(Forrest nods. Macready pulls out an identical costume.)

Why two?

FORREST: I started with the hump on my left, and my left hand curled—then I broke my right wrist, so I had to change, put the hump on the right.

(Macready nods.)

Now I keep them both. I've found that if I've got three or four Richards close together, I switch back and forth. It helps the back.

MACREADY: Kean I think did that, too.

FORREST: Did he?

(Pause.)

MACREADY: Kemble too. I think. *(Beat)* Ever see Kemble's . . .

(He mimics Kemble's walk as Richard III. Forrest laughs.)

I don't know what it was about him. Every time he tried— Hamlet. Richard. Macbeth. *(Beat)* But did you see his Cassio?

FORREST: No, I— No.

MACREADY: Brilliant. *(Beat)* He was a first-rate actor, but only in a second-rate parts.

FORREST: I've known other—

MACREADY: An incomparable Cassio. *(Beat)* You've never played—

FORREST: No.

MACREADY: Neither have I. *(Pause)* There are so many great supporting parts in Shakespeare. When I was young we'd fight for them.

FORREST: They still—

MACREADY: Not in England anymore. You used to have to constantly look over your shoulder. People had ambition! Now no one wants to work. No one wants to begin. But they work in my productions. *(Laughs)* And so they hate me. *(Laughs)* You want to know what it's like in London today? I tried to correct this actor. He works for me. And he's a nothing. All I say to him is, "Please do not speak your speech in that drawling way, sir." I'm very polite. "Here," I tell him, "speak it like this: 'To ransom home revolted Mortimer!' That's how you speak it!" *(Beat)* He turns to me, in front of the whole company, and says, "I know that sir—that is the way, but you'll please remember you get one hundred pounds a week for speaking it in your way, and I only get thirty shillings for mine! Give me one hundred pounds and I'll speak it your way; but I'm not going to do for thirty shillings what you get paid one hundred pounds for."

(Macready laughs, Forrest smiles.)

Actors. *(Shakes his head. Short pause)*
FORREST: What I hate is when they come late for rehearsal.
MACREADY: Which happens more and—
FORREST: Once, a rehearsal of mine was being delayed by this actor; he only had a small part, but it was quite an important part in the first scene. So we were all waiting. *(Beat)* I became visibly upset. Everyone knew enough to stay away from me. And when finally the truant—a quiet gentlemanly man, who had never before been late for one second—once he arrived I knew I needed to make an example of him. *(Beat. Smiles)* So I said, "Sir, you have kept these ladies and gentlemen waiting for a full half hour."

(Macready nods and smiles.)

"You cannot be ignorant, sir, of the importance of a rehearsal in which every member of the company is to take part!" *(Beat)* At that moment, this actor looked at me. I could see there were tears now in his eyes.

(Macready smiles and shakes his head.)

And then he spoke. "Mr. Forrest, sir," he said, "I beg your pardon. I could not come sooner."

(Forrest looks at Macready, who snickers.)

"My son—my only son—died last night. I hurried here as soon as I could."

(Macready suddenly stops smiling. Short pause. Forrest looks at Macready and shakes his head.)

Actors.

*(Long pause. Macready goes back and looks into the costume trunk.
   Slow fade to blackout.*
   *The bare stage of the Broadway Theatre. Macready and Forrest
enter—each having thrown on pieces of different costumes. As they
enter, they are giggling and carrying swords.)*

Who taught you fencing?
MACREADY: Angelo?

(Forrest shakes his head.)

You haven't heard of him? He's wonderful. He's dead now.
But he was wonderful when I was young.

(They are center stage looking out at the house.)

FORREST: It's paradise. Even without an audience.
MACREADY: Especially without an—
FORREST AND MACREADY: Audience.

*(Forrest tips Macready's sword, he smiles and they begin to fence.
After some time:)*

FORREST: Come for a third, Laertes.
MACREADY: I thought *I* was Hamlet.
FORREST: You should have spoken sooner.

(They fence.)

You but dally.
I pray you pass with your best violence;
I am afeard you make a wanton of me.

MACREADY: I don't know his lines.
FORREST *(Stopping)*: You don't know Laertes . . .
MACREADY: I'm never listening at this point. *(Beat)* What is it?

(Forrest thought he heard something, but now shakes his head.)

FORREST: Should we go back into my—? Ryder shouldn't be much
longer.

MACREADY: I don't care.

FORREST: I suppose he will find us here.

MACREADY *(looking out)*: How many seats?

FORREST: Nine hundred and seventy-eight. *(Beat)* I added those seats over there.

MACREADY: Can they see—?

FORREST: No one's complained. I've been waiting for someone to complain, but . . . *(Shrugs)*

MACREADY: I wouldn't want to sit there.

FORREST: No.

(Macready walks to the apron to get a closer look, then turns to see the particular sight line. He shakes his head.)

MACREADY: No, I wouldn't.

FORREST: I do play to them at times. I try to. *(Beat)* I try to remember to, but they are way over there. Added fifty-three seats.

(Macready suddenly turns, thinks he hears something.)

It's outside.

(Macready nods.)

I have it for another five weeks. The sound is very good. Much better than a lot of . . . I hate your theatre.

MACREADY: It's not my . . .

FORREST: They should tear the Astor Place down, if you want my opinion.

MACREADY: That may in fact be being done.

(Forrest walks to the apron and speaks into the house, at first to show off the acoustics.)

FORREST *(As he speaks Othello he gains in passion)*:
It is the cause, it is the cause, my soul.
Let me not name it to you, you chaste stars!
It is the cause. Yet I'll not shed her blood,
Nor scar that whiter skin of hers than snow,
And smooth as monumental alabaster.

Yet she must die, else she'll betray more men.
Put out the light, and then put out the light.

(He chokes up.)

If I quench thee, thou flaming minister,
I can again thy former light restore,
Should I repent me; but once put out thy light,
Thou cunning'st pattern of excelling nature,
I know not where is that Promethean heat
That can thy light relume. When I have plucked the rose,
I cannot give it vital growth again;
It needs must wither. I'll smell thee on the tree . . .

(He cannot go on. He covers his face, hiding his tears. Pause.)

MACREADY *(Without looking at him)*: You should add a few *Othello*s
next week. *(Beat)* I'm sorry about your wife leaving.

(Forrest turns to him. Short pause.)

Play it out. *(Beat)* You are certainly right about the sound.
FORREST: Go ahead and . . . *(Tries to get a hold of himself)* Really,
go ahead . . .

(Short pause. Macready walks to the apron.)

MACREADY: You'll be hard to follow.
FORREST: Modesty? You're acting already, Mr. Macready. And acting well.

(Forrest smiles, Macready turns to the house.)

MACREADY:
Rumble thy bellyful. Spit, fire. Spout, rain.
Nor rain, wind, thunder, fire are my daughters.
I tax not you, you elements—

(From outside, quite near, gunfire and shouts.)

FORREST *(Screaming)*: I told you before, to just leave us alone!!!!!

(Pause.)

MACREADY *(Continuing)*:
... you elements, with unkindness.
I never gave you kingdom, called you children;
You owe me no subscription. Then let fall
Your horrible pleasure. Here I stand your slave.
A poor, infirm, weak, and despised old man.

(He stops, continues to stare out. Ryder has entered upstage, he carries a cape. Pause.)

RYDER: Mr. Macready?
FORREST *(Turning without seeing who it is)*: Leave us in peace!!!

(Macready turns, Forrest sees who it is.)

RYDER: I have the horses. *(Beat)* We must go. Put this on. *(Goes to give him the cape)* Why are you dressed like ... ?

(Macready looks at Forrest.)

FORREST: We were rehearsing—
RYDER: Rehearsing—?
MACREADY: Give me the cape. What's it like out there?
RYDER: It's gotten worse. *(Beat)* Reports are that there are nearly thirty-five people now dead. And hundreds seriously ... *(Beat)* Hundreds wounded. *(Beat)* We should hurry. There are people who are running through the streets looking for that English actor "Macreilly or whatever his name is." *(Beat)* Buses have been stopped, turned on their side and set afire, on just the rumor that you were aboard. *(Beat)* Our hotel—I had to go past. That too has been torched.
FORREST: Go.
RYDER: Put up the hood.

(Ryder pulls up the hood of the cape on Macready.)

We have a safe house for tonight in New Rochelle. We'll go to Boston in the morning. Come on.

(As they start to leave, Macready stops and looks back at the theatre.)

There's talk that they'll close the theatres.

(Pause.)

MACREADY: You should come to England again, Mr. Forrest. *(Beat)* And get away from all these troubles.

(Short pause.)

FORREST: I'm away from all these troubles here.

(Macready nods and leaves with Ryder. Pause. Forrest starts to go, stops and comes back. He looks around the theatre. With sword in hand, he stands, not knowing where else on earth he wants to go.)

END OF PLAY

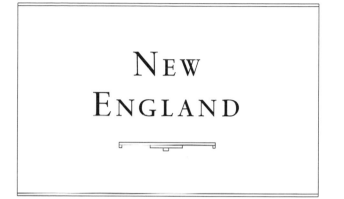

NEW ENGLAND

For Patricia Macnaughton and Peter Franklin

Production History

New England was commissioned by The Royal Shakespeare Company and was first performed by them on November 23, 1994, at the Pit in the Barbican, London. It was directed by Peter Gill; the design was by Hayden Griffen, the music was directed by Terry Davis; it was produced by Lynda Farran, the stage manager was Jane Pole, the deputy stage manager was Caroline Beale and the assistant stage manager was Lynda Snowden. The cast was as follows:

ALFRED/HARRY BAKER	David Burke
GEMMA BAKER	Diana Hardcastle
ELIZABETH BAKER	Selina Cadell
PAUL BAKER	Duncan Bell
SOPHIE BAKER	Annie Corbier
ALICE BERRY	Angela Thorne
TOM BERRY	Mick Ford

New England was subsequently produced by The Manhattan Theatre Club (Lynne Meadow, Artistic Director; Barry Grove, Executive Director) in New York City, on October 17, 1995. It was directed by Howard Davies; the set design was by Santo Loquasto, the costume design was by Jennifer von Mayrhauser, the lighting design was by Richard Nelson, the sound design was by Mark Bennett and the stage manager was Franklin Keysar. The cast was as follows:

ALFRED/HARRY BAKER	Larry Bryggman
GEMMA BAKER	Allison Janney
ELIZABETH BAKER	Mia Dillon

PAUL BAKER	T. Scott Cunningham
SOPHIE BAKER	Margaret Whitton
ALICE BERRY	Penny Fuller
TOM BERRY	Tom Irwin

CHARACTERS

HARRY BAKER, professor of music at
Dutchess Community College, New York State, sixties

ALFRED BAKER, Harry's brother, sixties

GEMMA BAKER, Harry's oldest child, thirty-nine

ELIZABETH BAKER, Harry's other daughter, thirty-seven

PAUL BAKER, Harry's son, thirty-two

SOPHIE, Paul's wife, forty-one

ALICE BERRY, Harry's girlfriend, fifty-four

TOM BERRY, Alice's ex-brother-in-law, forty

All the characters are English except for Sophie,
who was born in France.

SETTING

The present, a farmhouse in Western Connecticut,
just across the border from New York State.

SCENE 1

A small room on the ground floor, which serves as a study. Late afternoon; a Friday.

Harry Baker, sixties, sits at a desk. On the desk is a CD player and a row of CDs — all classical; Harry is a professor of music at the local community college. He reads or looks through a book as he listens to music—Debussy's The Girl with the Flaxen Hair *(played on the violin) begins with the scene.*

After a moment, Alice Berry, fifty-four, enters from the hall; she is Harry's girlfriend and she shares the house with him. She stops, looks at Harry for a moment; he is absorbed in thought or in the book or the music, and does not at first see her.

Harry suddenly lets out a large sigh.

ALICE: Harry?

(Harry turns, startled.)

How's the—headache? I'm sorry, I didn't mean to—you had a headache. You took some asprin?

(It has taken him this long to realize who has startled him. Finally, he nods and turns back to his book. The Debussy continues.)

Tom's here.

(No response.)

I just picked him up. His bus was even on time, if you can believe that. A miracle! *(Tries to smile)* He's very excited. A weekend out of New York . . .

HARRY *(Without picking his head up from his book)*: Who's Tom?

ALICE: Harry, I told you about— You said it was— We talked about!!—

HARRY *(Over this)*: It's fine, Alice, I just forget who Tom is!

(Short pause.)

ALICE: He's my—Bill's brother. He was my brother-in-law. So he's my ex—

HARRY *(Over the last part of this, turning to Alice)*: He was good to you, wasn't he? During your divorce. He was very helpful to you.

ALICE: He was, Harry. If you didn't want—

HARRY: I think that is wonderful! That Tom's here. Someone you like. Someone who has been—helpful.

ALICE: I hadn't seen him for—

HARRY *(Over this)*: Someone like that doesn't change. Someone— helpful. Good.

(He turns back to his desk. She looks at him, confused. He pushes a button on the CD and the Debussy begins again. Alice turns to leave and there in the door, having just arrived, is Tom Berry, forty. Alice is startled.)

TOM *(Smiling)*: Sorry. I couldn't find the— In the bathroom— which towels should I . . . ?

ALICE: Tom—this is Harry.

(Tom goes to Harry with his hand out to shake.)

TOM: How do you do? I can't thank you enough for— Sometimes the city— It gets so depressing. Most times! *(Laughs)*

HARRY *(At the same time, shaking hands)*: Welcome, to our humble— Alice has told me all about you— She's been looking forward to—

ALICE *(Over this)*: Tom said the bus ride up—

TOM: It was beautiful!

HARRY: It's supposed to be a nice weekend. Weather-wise.

ALICE: I heard it might rain, but—

TOM: Whatever. It's—great to be in the country.

(He smiles. No one knows what to say.)

ALICE *(Finally)*: I'll show you where we keep the towels, so if you need . . .

TOM *(To Harry)*: Thank you for inviting me. I'll see you later.

(Alice and Tom leave. Pause.

Harry pushes the button on the CD player and the Debussy begins again.

He opens the drawer of the desk and takes out a revolver. Without hesitation he cocks it, sets it on the desk, takes off his glasses. He notices that they are dirty, and with a handkerchief begins to clean them, then realizes what he is doing, laughs to himself and stops. He puts down the glasses, picks up the gun and puts the barrel to his head.)

ALICE *(Entering from the hallway)*: Tom's so happy to be— *(Sees what Harry is doing. Screams)* Nooooooo!!!!!!!!!!!

(He pulls the trigger, gunshot. He is dead.)

SCENE 2

Much later that evening.

   Part of the kitchen of the house. There is large rustic wooden table, which has been used both for eating and as a sort of desk. Piles of papers, bills, catalogs, etc.; a phone, whose cord extends to the wall, making a kind of obstacle for anyone going around the table. There is a transistor radio on the table.

The Debussy continues from the last scene, though over the theatre's speakers now.

Tom enters from the pantry; he carries a bowl, a spoon, a box of cereal. He does not hear the music. He sets his things down on the table and goes off again. From off, we hear the opening and closing of a refrigerator. Tom returns with a carton of milk. He sits, pours the cereal, the milk; he reaches across the table for the sugar. He spoons on the sugar and begins to eat. He stops and turns on the transistor radio. The Debussy is gone and from the radio we first hear a pop tune with a lot of static. Tom fiddles with the knob, tries another station, then another. He hits upon a religious program. He listens for a moment to the minister on the program as he eats.

The phone rings. Tom doesn't know what to do. He looks in the direction of the door. It rings again. And again. He puts down his spoon, begins to reach for the phone, when the ring stops—someone has picked up the phone on another extension.

Tom changes the channel again, then again, then again—everything is junk: pop tunes, commercials. After about the twelfth station, he turns off the radio.

In silence he eats.

Alice enters from the living room. She has a drink in her hand. At first she says nothing; Tom just eats. Then finally:

ALICE: That was Elizabeth on the phone. She'll be here in a minute. She's just down the road at the gas station. She couldn't remember the turnoff.

TOM *(Eating)*: Which one is—?

ALICE: She's the middle child. She lives in the city, too. *(Smiles)* She's in publishing.

TOM: In the same—?

ALICE: She's with a different house. *(Notices that he is eating)*

TOM: I found some cereal, I hope that wasn't—

ALICE: You haven't eaten anything, have you?

TOM: I didn't expect—

ALICE: You come out for the weekend and—and you don't even get fed! What could I have been thinking—

TOM: Alice, I'm—

ALICE *(Looking for food)*: I'm not normally like—

TOM: I am fine, Alice! Please.

(Beat. She stops looking around.)

I don't expect anything. Not now.

(Pause. Tom eats. Alice sips her drink.)

ALICE: You want a drink? I . . .
TOM: If I do, I'll find it.

(Neither knows what to say. Alice sighs.)

ALICE: I've been in his study—cleaning up.
TOM: I thought that's what that woman—
ALICE *(Over this)*: She missed some places. Look at this. *(Holds out the small photo album she's been carrying)* They're already in the album. I didn't even know he'd got the photos back yet. And they're already in his . . .
TOM: And that is unlike him?
ALICE: Very. *(Looks at the photos)* From Bermuda. We were there in— Last month.

(Pause. They look at the photos, saying nothing.)

(Hearing something) Was that a car? *(Listens)* No.
TOM: It looks like you had a really nice time.
ALICE *(Not hearing him)*: He's got papers . . . It'll take weeks to go through everything. I thought the priority seemed to be the cleaning. I didn't think his family should see— *(To herself, running through a list)* I called the school. I did that.
TOM: What school?
ALICE: Harry teaches at Dutchess— I didn't tell you this?
TOM: Maybe you did.
ALICE *(Over this)*: How could I not tell you this?! What could I have been thinking?!
TOM: Alice!
ALICE: You're staying, right?
TOM: If that's what you want.
ALICE *(Sighing)*: I can't face his family.

TOM *(Taking her hand)*: If I'm not in the way.

(He pats her hand. Alice, not listening to Tom, turns again toward the door, as if hearing something.)

ALICE: She doesn't like me. We've only met five, six times— Harry kept us apart. I asked him to. She's also in publishing.

TOM: So you said.

ALICE: So we know a lot of the same people. *(Hearing Tom)* Did I? *(Beat)* She's going to walk into here and start telling us all what to do. In my own home. There's her car.

(Sound of car in the driveway.)

I think I've done everything. I like that man at the funeral home. I thought funeral home people were supposed to be— I don't know.

TOM: I guess not all of them are. There are exceptions.

ALICE *(Smiling)*: And he is one.

TOM: I guess so.

ALICE: So—we're lucky. *(Sighs)* I feel like I haven't stopped.

TOM: You haven't.

(Elizabeth Baker, one of Harry's three children, enters. She is thirty-seven.)

ELIZABETH: Alice!

ALICE: Elizabeth!

(They hug.)

ELIZABETH: I don't know what to say. I don't know what to say.

(Alice begins to cry. Elizabeth hugs her. Tom tries to be inconspicuous.)

ALICE *(Crying)*: So—you couldn't remember the turnoff.

ELIZABETH: I knew it was— I should have just followed my instinct. Anyway.

(Alice gets ahold of herself and they part. Elizabeth looks at Tom; Alice sees this.)

ALICE: This is Tom. Berry. He was my ex-husband's brother.

TOM: I still am. *(Tries to laugh)*

ALICE: Right. That's true.

TOM: I always liked Alice. And when she left my brother I liked her even more. *(Smiles at his joke; no one else does. To Elizabeth)* How do you do?

ALICE *(To Elizabeth)*: Do you want something to eat? To drink?

ELIZABETH *(Shaking her head)*: There was no traffic.

ALICE: It's late.

ELIZABETH: That's why then. *(Looks at Tom again)*

TOM: I came up on the bus. This afternoon. I also live in the city.

ELIZABETH *(To Alice)*: This afternoon? I thought, it only happened—

ALICE: It did. I called you right away, Liz. Tom—happened to be here for the weekend.

(Beat.)

TOM: I needed to get out of the city and Alice was nice enough to . . .

(Pause.)

ELIZABETH: Do you have a Coke or something?

ALICE: I have some seltzer.

ELIZABETH: Seltzer's fine.

(Alice hurries off into the pantry. Tom and Elizabeth are left alone. Short pause.)

TOM: I'm sorry about your—

ELIZABETH *(Interrupting)*: I have a bag in the car. Excuse me.

TOM: Let me—

ELIZABETH: It's not heavy, please. *(Goes out)*

(Alone, Tom doesn't know what to do, he sits again, begins to take another bite of cereal, notices the photo album open on the table and begins to look at the open page.)

ALICE *(Entering with the seltzer and a glass)*: Where's—?

TOM: She's getting her bag.

(Alice sees that Tom has been looking at the album and she goes and looks over his shoulder.)

ALICE *(Pointing to a photo)*: Harry bought that bathing suit for me in Hamilton. That was so unlike him. He was scared to buy me anything. Afraid, he said, I'd just take it back. *(Smiles)* It took me about two days to get the nerve to wear it in public. Finally—I did. *(Short pause)* After your brother—

(Tom looks at her.)

I'd convinced myself I'd never meet another man. You see other women, my age and— You see yourself in their shoes. I expected nothing. Then I met Harry.

(Elizabeth enters with her bag. Pause. For a moment no one knows what to say. Finally:)

Here's your seltzer.

(Elizabeth finally takes it and drinks it.)

ELIZABETH *(As she drinks)*: I had lunch with Dick Riley last week. Your name came up, Alice. He said you were the best managing editor they'd ever had. *(Finishes drinking)* What a shame it was when you left. *(Beat)* So—know that even after a couple of years, you're still missed.

ALICE *(To Tom)*: I was cheap. I didn't know any better. That's all he means. *(Turns to Elizabeth)* The man at the funeral home— he's not bad. He's not what you'd expect.

ELIZABETH: Good.

(Beat.)

ALICE: Gemma and Alfred have made it as far as Denver. They have to wait till morning for the next flight. They called.

ELIZABETH: Good. *(Beat)* I mean good that they called, not that they have to wait—

ALICE: I understood. And Paul and Sophie—they'll get a flight in the morning as well. *(Turns to Tom)* From L.A.

TOM *(To Elizabeth)*: I was amazed when she told me everyone lives in the States.

ELIZABETH: Why?

TOM: That's rare, isn't it?

ELIZABETH *(To Alice)*: He wouldn't say that if he worked in publishing—

ALICE *(Over this)*: You wouldn't.

ELIZABETH *(To Alice)*: Have you worked out where everyone will sleep? It isn't a very big house.

TOM: I can move—

ALICE *(To Tom)*: There's the pullout couch—

TOM: The floor is fine—

ALICE: I meant for Paul and Sophie—

ELIZABETH *(Picking up her suitcase)*: Let's figure it all out.

ALICE: I think I have. Harry's brother can have my room. It'll work out. I'm going to the grocery store in the morning—

ELIZABETH: You're not going to cook! There are too many people! I won't let you, Alice. Gemma and I can share a bed. We shared a room as kids.

ALICE: That's what I thought.

ELIZABETH: What about Chinese?

ALICE: There's a terrific Chinese— Just in our village. Harry loves their dumplings. *(Stops and corrects herself)* He loved them. *(Short pause. Tries not to cry; turns to Elizabeth)* He did it in front of me. I think that's what I can't forgive him for. *(Beat)* But I don't think he meant to hurt me.

ELIZABETH: No—

ALICE: Because, he loved me. *(Takes Elizabeth's hand)* Your father was a very—tired man.

ELIZABETH: I know. And he'd been tired for years—long before he met you, Alice.

ALICE *(Looking up at her)*: Thank you

(Beat.)

ELIZABETH: This isn't a surprise. *(Then to change the subject)* So— it's Chinese! *(Turns to Tom)* Do you like Chinese?

TOM: Anything is fine with—

ELIZABETH *(Not listening to him, turning to Alice)*: I knew I'd have at least one good idea. I think Father once even mentioned the restaurant—

ALICE: Usually the Chinese food you get up here in the sticks, but this place—

ELIZABETH: I know what you mean. But I'll bet this place is great. Father always had good taste.

(Alice takes Elizabeth's hand.)

ALICE: Thank you.
ELIZABETH *(Realizing that Alice has taken this as a compliment)*: I didn't mean . . . But—of course that too. With you too. That's obvious. Father had impeccable taste.
ALICE: He was a refined and cultured man.
ELIZABETH: I always thought so. Come on. *(Helps Alice up)* Let's you and I figure out where to put everyone.

(They go. Pause. Tom is alone. He takes another spoonful of cereal and—)

SCENE 3

The kitchen, early evening of the next day.
  A few hours ago, Paul (the son) and his wife, Sophie, arrived by rental car from Kennedy Airport. Just a few minutes ago, Gemma (the oldest daughter) and Alfred (Harry's brother) arrived also by rental car from the same airport.
  Paul, thirty-two, sits at the kitchen table, surrounded by his two sisters, Gemma, thirty-nine, and Elizabeth. Alice is taking silverware out of a drawer in the table, to set the table for dinner. As the scene begins, Tom has just entered with bags of Chinese food.

PAUL *(To Gemma)*: If we'd known you were arriving at Kennedy—
GEMMA *(Over this)*: We didn't know ourselves. We had tickets to Bradley—
PAUL *(Over this)*: We'd have waited—
ELIZABETH *(Over this)*: You could have shared the car rental.
PAUL: Still it'll be useful to have another car up here.
GEMMA: The drive was wonderful. Very relaxing—
PAUL *(Over the end of this)*: This is my first autumn in three years. You forget what it's like—
ALICE *(Over this)*: Someone said it was supposed to rain.

GEMMA: How's L.A.?

PAUL: Warm and sunny.

ALICE *(To Gemma)*: And Albuquerque?

GEMMA: Sunny and warm!

(They laugh.)

TOM *(Who has been holding up the Chinese food, trying to get some-one's attention)*: I have the . . . !

ALICE: Let me help, Tom. That was quick. We're all here! Alfred and Gemma just arrived—

GEMMA *(To Elizabeth, over this)*: I love New England. You're lucky to be so close.

(The phone rings.)

ALICE *(Same time)*: Excuse me. *(Goes to pick up the phone)*

ELIZABETH *(Same time, to Gemma)*: I never get up here. Father had me up twice, maybe three times. I hardly could remember the way.

ALICE *(With her hand on the receiver, as it rings)*: I've told everyone it's the best Chinese I've ever had! Even in the city. And of all places— *(Picks up the phone.)* Hello?

TOM *(To the others)*: Actually, the place she sent me to   It appears to have closed. They'd gone out of business, I suspect. *(Beat)* There was another place. Just down the road. *(Holds up the bag of food)* There was hardly a wait. I don't know how they cook it so fast.

(The others look at Tom.)

ALICE *(Into the phone)*: Yes. At eleven. Here in the garden. Yes. Harry would have liked that. *(Beat)* Thank you so much. See you tomorrow. *(Hangs up)*

(Pause.)

TOM: I hope it's good. The food! *(Smells a bag)* It smells good.

ALICE: It's always good at that place. "Harry's Place" was what we called it. Because Harry . . .

ELIZABETH *(Getting up)*: We'll need some serving spoons.

ALICE *(Pointing to the drawer in the table)*: In that drawer. Elizabeth.

GEMMA *(To Tom)*: We haven't met.

ALICE: This is Tom. He's my— A relative of mine. Gemma. Harry's eldest.

TOM: How do you do?

(They shake hands.)

My sympathies. To all of you.

GEMMA: Uncle Alfred will be down in a—

ALICE: Harry's brother.

GEMMA *(To Tom)*: Were you very close to our father?

(Beat.)

TOM: Close? To tell the truth, I only just met him—

ALICE *(Interrupting)*: Where are we going to eat? There's the dining room.

ELIZABETH: Won't that be too formal? It's just Chinese—

GEMMA: And we're a family.

ELIZABETH: The kitchen's fine.

GEMMA: Let's eat here. I always eat in my kitchen.

ELIZABETH: Move a few things out of the way— *(Begins to pick up the papers on the table)*

ALICE: Smell how good that smells.

GEMMA *(Over this)*: We'll need large bowls or do we just serve it out of the boxes? At home I just serve it out of the boxes.

ELIZABETH *(To Alice, over this)*: Is it OK if I just pile these papers together?—

PAUL *(Interrupting)*: Sophie's still taking a nap! Shouldn't we wait for her?

(Beat.)

GEMMA *(To Elizabeth)*: I forgot she was here. I hadn't seen her so—

ELIZABETH: She's taking a nap.

PAUL: I just think she might feel— I don't know—to come down and find us all eating dinner . . .

(Beat.)

ELIZABETH: Couldn't you wake her up, Paul? I wouldn't want people waiting to eat because of me.

GEMMA: The food'll get cold.

PAUL: She didn't sleep at all last night. Or on the plane.

(Beat.)

ELIZABETH: We can reheat it for her later then.

ALICE: Maybe she's reading, I'll go and see if— *(Starts to go)*

PAUL: Let her sleep! Please. I want her to get some sleep.

(Beat.)

GEMMA: So we're to—what? The food's here. This makes no sense.

PAUL: I told her we wouldn't be eating for a while. That's what Alice told me—

ALICE: Because I thought there'd be a wait—

TOM: There wasn't any wait at the restaurant.

ALICE: On a Saturday night?! That's incredible. It's such a popular place.

(Short pause.)

GEMMA: So what are we going to—?

ELIZABETH *(Over this)*: What if we don't sit down? What if we say, put out the food and whenever anyone wants to— Buffet style. So no one's missing anything. How's that, Paul? We can keep reheating it, so it's always ready.

GEMMA: Sophie can't get upset about that

PAUL: It wasn't because she'd get upset—

GEMMA: I mean, it sounds fair.

PAUL *(Continuing)*: she's not the one upset, I am. I told her— She doesn't care. Why should she care? Whatever we want to do is fine with—

ELIZABETH: Fine! Then we'll need some plates—

ALICE: I'll get them.

PAUL: How would you feel if you walked in on— And there was your husband surrounded by his sisters, having dinner and you'd been told—

ELIZABETH: We understand, Paul. Forget it.

(Alice starts to leave, stops, notices the drink in her hand.)

ALICE: Who else wants a drink? I forgot to ask. I'll open one of Harry's good bottles of wine. I think he'd have liked that.

(Beat.)

GEMMA *(After looking at her brother and sister)*: I don't think any of us drink.

(The others shake their heads.)

I suppose we'd seen enough of what that can do—growing up. But please . . . Don't let us stop you, Alice.

(Beat.)

ALICE: Tom? What about you?
TOM: A— Small glass. Very small.
ALICE *(To herself as she leaves)*: More for me. *(Goes)*

(Pause. Tom begins to take the food out of the bags. Elizabeth and Gemma straighten up the table.)

GEMMA *(To Paul)*: You were right to stick up for your wife.
PAUL: I wasn't sticking up for—
GEMMA: That was a good thing to do, Paul.

(Short pause. They continue to get the table straightened.)

(To Elizabeth) Where's the body?
PAUL: Gemma, please!
GEMMA: Don't stop us from talking!
ELIZABETH: Some funeral home. Alice says he ought to be cremated.
PAUL: Oh God.
ELIZABETH: What do you think?
GEMMA: What did Father want?
PAUL: Does it matter?

ELIZABETH: Alice has this idea which— I don't know, it's not what I'd have expected from her. She seems so—matter-of-fact. That's her reputation in the city—very matter-of-fact.

(She looks at Tom, who smiles.)

TOM: I'll find some glasses. *(Goes)*
ELIZABETH: Alice has this idea in her head about standing in the garden and throwing his ashes into the air.
GEMMA: That's what she meant on the phone. Is that legal?
PAUL: What harm could—?
GEMMA: When mother died, she was buried.
ELIZABETH: I know that. But I do not think Father would have wanted to be buried next to mother.
GEMMA: Or vice versa.
ELIZABETH *(Shrugging)*: I don't know that. Do we know that? *(Short pause)* What did you feel when you heard, Gemma?

(Paul sighs.)

Ignore him. *(Turns to Gemma, then quickly, suddenly back to Paul to shut him up)* I wish to talk to my sister!

(Short pause.)

GEMMA: I—was angry. I don't think I have ever been so angry with anyone—ever. *(Beat)* I'd told Father—if he ever did do it— I'd hate him for the rest of my life.
ELIZABETH: You were angry, but you weren't shocked? I wasn't shocked. Was anyone shocked?

(No one says anything.
    Alice enters with the plates; Tom is behind her with a bottle of wine, a bottle of seltzer, glasses and a corkscrew.
    There is silence for a long time. Tom opens the wine bottle; Alice sets out the plates. When she finishes:)

ALICE: Since we're eating in the kitchen, I thought we wouldn't use our fancy plates. These aren't our good plates. We have much nicer plates than these. *(Short pause)* Do any of you smoke?

(Paul, Gemma and Elizabeth look incredulously at her.)

I didn't think so. *(Picks up her purse and takes out a pack of cigarettes. Taps one out, then lights it)*

GEMMA: Neither did Father. He hated smoke.

ALICE: Which is why he made me smoke outside. Even in the rain. The snow. *(Beat)* But from today—I can smoke where I please. As they say, every cloud has its silver lining.

ELIZABETH: Oh my God!

ALICE: I'm joking, Elizabeth! That was a joke! *(Beat)* Not the smoking—the silver lining. *(Beat)* I'm terribly sorry if it wasn't funny.

(She exhales, then takes a sip of her drink—the ice cubes clanking against the glass. Awkward pause.)

TOM: I'll just dish out the rice into a bowl.

ALICE *(As she exhales)*: Look at that rice. I told you the place was good.

PAUL: I think I heard a creak— Maybe Sophie's . . . *(Gets up)* I'll go see if she's awake. I'll tell her we're waiting for her.

GEMMA: I thought we weren't waiting for Sophie.

(Alfred, Harry's twin brother, enters. Tom sees him and nearly cries out in shock, irrationally thinking this is Harry's ghost. He nearly knocks over the wine bottle, glasses tip over, rice spills. The others cry out: "Careful!" "Watch out!" "Catch it!" as they scramble to save the glasses, bottle, etc.)

ALICE *(To Alfred)*: Are you unpacked?

ALFRED: Alice, I feel awful kicking you out of your room—

ALICE: That's silly. Did you look through Harry's clothes?

ALFRED: I haven't had—

ALICE: If there's anything that—

ALFRED: Later, Alice.

ALICE: Of course.

PAUL *(Explaining the table)*: We're waiting for Sophie. When she's awake—

ELIZABETH: I thought we were setting out the plates—

ALFRED: She's in the bathroom. She's using the bathroom.

PAUL *(To everyone)*: Sophie's in the bathroom.

(Tom has been staring at Alfred; Alfred now stares back at him.)

ALICE: This is Tom. You haven't met him. He was out getting the food when you arrived. *(Introducing)* Tom—Alfred, Harry's brother. Alfred—Tom. He's a relative of mine. Sort of.

ALFRED: And obviously a good friend of Harry's. Thank you for coming.

PAUL. If Sophie's awake—

ALFRED: She's in the bathroom—

PAUL *(Over this)*: Then we can set the table. Go ahead and set the table. We'll eat together at the table. *(Goes out)*

GEMMA *(To Elizabeth)*: What happened to buffet style?

ALICE *(Half whispering to Tom)*: They were twins.

TOM *(Still in some shock)*: When I saw him I thought—

ALICE: I know. It's odd for me, too.

ALFRED: Could I have a glass of that? I haven't had a drink for months.

GEMMA: You had two on the plane.

ALFRED *(Taking the bottle, ignoring Gemma; to Alice)*: I've been taking care of myself, Alice.

ALICE: It shows, Alfred.

ELIZABETH: Are we setting the table or not?

ALFRED: Is that the famous Chinese Harry was always going on about?

TOM: I'm not sure it's exactly the same—

ALFRED: He used to say, Alfred, we have the best Chinese takeout in this hick village than anywhere in New York City, San Francisco, Seattle. You name it. In this village, for Christ sake.

TOM: Actually, I don't think it's from the place he—

ALFRED: It smells good. Harry always loved food.

TOM: Did he?

ALFRED: Loved it. Talked about nothing else.

ALICE: That's not true, Alfred. He rarely—

ALFRED: Who cares? Now we can say anything we want about the bastard.

(Short pause. Alfred stands at the table; and suddenly he nearly collapses. Everyone hurries to him, to grab him, as they do they

shout: "What's wrong?" "Sit down!" "Get him some water!" "Are you all right?" etc.)

ALICE *(With a glass of seltzer water)*: Here, drink this.

(Alfred drinks. He holds up his hands—to show that he will be fine. He drinks some more, then finally:)

ALFRED: You said—in the study? Down the hall. *(Beat)* That's where it was?

(Alice nods.)

I just looked in. I didn't see anything. Have you been cleaning, Alice? *(Beat)* Get someone in. Do yourself a favor. *(Sips, then)* I threw up—in the study. I couldn't get anything to clean it up with. Sophie was in the bathroom.

(Beat.)

GEMMA: We'll clean it up, Uncle Alfred.

(Pause. No one knows what to say.)

ALFRED: We're eating in here?
ELIZABETH: Maybe you'd like get some air. The air on airplanes—
ALFRED: I'm hungry. I want to try some of my brother's famous Chinese takeout.
GEMMA: Give Alfred a plate—
ELIZABETH *(At the same time)*: Are we sitting down? I'm confused.
ALFRED: Pull up some chairs. *(Realizing)* I'm at the head. I suppose that is where I should be now.
ELIZABETH: We thought it'd be nicer—less formal in the kitchen.
ALFRED: I don't care where I eat.
ELIZABETH: I like it in here. We were all saying—how relaxed it is in here. Let's set out plates.

(Paul enters with Sophie, forty-one; she is French, though has lived in the States for many years.)

PAUL: Look who's awake!

(Everyone greets her: "Sophie!" "How was your nap?" "Sit down."
Gemma and Sophie hug, since they have not greeted each other
yet.)

ALICE *(Pointing to Tom)*: Tom you've met.

(During this, the phone rings and Alice picks it up.)

SOPHIE *(Over this)*: Why are you eating in here when there's such a
lovely dining room?!

PAUL: She's right. We could eat in the dining room. It'll be much
nicer there.

ELIZABETH: You agreed that the kitchen—

SOPHIE: Alfred?

ALFRED: I don't care.

ELIZABETH: We're all set up in— Gemma?

GEMMA: It is a nice dining room.

ELIZABETH: It's just so much less formal in here.

PAUL *(Over this)*: Everyone grab something. I'll take the glasses.

ELIZABETH: I like it in here.

SOPHIE: I didn't mean— *(To everyone)* If Elizabeth wants us to eat
in the kitchen—

PAUL: Of course, if Elizabeth insists . . .

ELIZABETH: I'm not insisting.

PAUL: Then Tom, could you bring the rice? You be in charge of the
rice.

ELIZABETH *(Over this)*: It just seems silly. We're already in the
kitchen—

ALICE *(Putting her hand over the receiver; to the others)*: They want to
know—should they send flowers or is there some charity . . . ?

(Beat.)

SOPHIE: Flowers are such a waste. Don't you think? They just die.

PAUL: A charity then. Did Father have a charity—?

GEMMA: Maybe the school—

ALICE: He hated the school.

PAUL: Was there anything he . . . ? *(Looks at the others)* I don't know.

(Beat.)

GEMMA: Who'd father want to give money to??

(Pause.)

ELIZABETH: I think flowers would be nice, myself.
ALICE: Then we'll have them send flowers!

(She returns to the phone, relays that flowers would be fine.
Everyone is standing, carrying something on their way to the
dining room.)

SOPHIE *(To Paul)*: I hope this isn't just because I said—
PAUL: Of course it isn't. It's just a good idea.
ALFRED *(To Gemma)*: What about the study? Who's going to
clean—?
GEMMA: There's probably a sponge under the sink in the bathroom.
Don't worry about it.
ELIZABETH *(To Gemma)*: Don't you think flowers will be nice?

(Alice puts down the phone.)

ALICE *(To Tom, who is balancing a few things)*: There's a tray in the
pantry. *(Calls out to everyone as they head off toward the dining*
room) Why are we moving? Why can't we stay where we are?
(Gets up and follows them out)

SCENE 4

The kitchen, a short time later.
    Alice, Tom, Alfred, Gemma, Elizabeth, Paul and Sophie sit
around the table, halfway through their Chinese meal. The papers,
phone, etc., have been pushed to one side, giving the table a very clut-
tered look.

PAUL *(As he eats)*: I think we actually like L.A. And I know that
sounds crazy.

ALICE: No one's eating the moo-shoo.

GEMMA: I tried it.

PAUL *(Continuing, over some of this)*: And I don't mean the weather. I like the people. I like my work.

ELIZABETH: Isn't it nicer in here than in that stuffy old dining room?

ALICE: It's not stuffy.

ELIZABETH: Don't you agree, Sophie?

SOPHIE: I didn't mean it to become a thing. I'm sorry.

ELIZABETH: It hasn't become a—"thing" as you call it. *(Smiles and eats)*

TOM *(To Paul, changing the subject)*: What work do you—?

PAUL: I read. I'm a reader.

ALFRED: Is that now a professional position in Los Angeles? *(Laughs)*

PAUL: For films. I read scripts and . . .

SOPHIE: Tell him.

PAUL: I give my opinions. About how to develop those scripts.

(Beat.)

ALFRED *(Sipping his drink)*: And what is your opinion?

GEMMA: We've had this conversation before. *(To Alfred)* You know what Paul does—

PAUL *(Over this)*: Depends on the script, of course.

ALFRED: I would have thought they'd all be rubbish.

PAUL: Some are and some—

ALFRED *(Interrupting)*: I can understand liking the weather. Even some of the people. But even you can't keep a straight face when you talk about their movies—

PAUL *(Over this)*: My face is completely straight!

SOPHIE: It is!

ALFRED: My mind would go to mush if I had to—!

SOPHIE: It's a good job! A way to learn the business!

PAUL *(Over this)*: I'm learning what people want!

ALFRED *(Yelling back)*: They don't know what people want!

PAUL: And in England they do?! *(Beat)* In London today there aren't three people who know how to make a successful movie. That's my opinion.

(Short pause. No one knows what to say.)

SOPHIE: And if Paul hadn't moved to L.A., we never would have met.

(Short pause, as Paul's family bites their tongues.)

ELIZABETH: Uncle Alfred, you're here. I wouldn't criticize.
ALFRED: They pay me twice what I got at Hull. Full stop. *I* didn't come for the culture.
TOM *(To Alice, referring to Alfred)*: What does he do?—
ALICE: He teaches English. *(Short pause. To everyone)* Tom *teaches*—acting.

(Everyone politely nods or mumbles, "Oh really.")

(To Paul) So he's in the performing arts as well.
TOM: Not in L.A. In New York.
PAUL: For theatre?
TOM: Some.
PAUL: I'd have thought you couldn't make a living from the theatre—
TOM: Students of mine—they do television, films, plays. I mostly do accents. *(Beat)* For Americans trying to be— *(Shrugs)* English? As well as the other way around.
ELIZABETH: There's a lot of need for—?
TOM: I survive. *(Beat)* I do the best I can. It's a living. *(To Paul)* I like Los Angeles, too.
GEMMA: For me—New Mexico is paradise. Isn't it, Uncle Alfred? I sit on my porch, brush in hand, and paint and before me— I don't even have to put on shoes! Before me is a landscape that is not only the most extraordinary I've ever seen, but it also *changes*. Totally, completely remakes itself, I don't know, five hundred times a day! Because of the light, the clouds, even the density of the air. I don't mean just shadows, I mean one minute it's yellow and the next it's blue! *(Smiles and shakes her head)* It's so different from England. Or the Alps or Provence where everything's fixed. Some mornings what gets me out of bed is the thought that if I weren't out there to paint it all, it'd be lost for good.

(Beat.)

ALFRED *(To Tom)*: She came to visit and she stayed. Every day, I blame myself.

GEMMA: An amazingly beautiful place. Even you say that sometimes. I can't imagine living anywhere else now.

ALICE *(To Tom)*: Gemma's a painter.

TOM: I'd guessed that.

GEMMA: I've wondered what Turner would have made of it. Where instead of just a sea or sky or horizon, there was a landscape that was constantly changing, that was all—movement. *(Beat. Smiles)* I try. But I'm no Turner, am I?

(She turns to Elizabeth, who says nothing.)

Elizabeth's bought four of my paintings. She said she bought them as an investment, but I think she just wanted to give me some money.

(She laughs to herself; Elizabeth does not correct her. No one is really eating the Chinese food, which is awful; they sort of move it around their plates.)

PAUL: Could you pass me the seltzer?

ALICE *(At the same time)*: New England's very beautiful as well.

SOPHIE: The drive up —

PAUL: I haven't seen autumn for years.

GEMMA *(To Alice)*: There must be— You must have all sorts of special places where you go. Natural—I don't know, you tell me.

ALICE: There's a waterfall that's supposed to be— I haven't seen it. I haven't actually driven around very much. Mostly it's just been to and from the city.

PAUL: It's a nice drive.

ALICE: I've wanted to see more, but . . .

(Beat)

TOM *(To Alice)*: How long have you lived here? Maybe you told me . . .

ALICE: Harry's had the place for

ALFRED: Years and years.

ELIZABETH *(At the same time)*: Fifteen, twenty years.

ALICE: I moved in two years ago, next month. The six months before that, I came up every weekend. *(Beat. Smiles)* First it was: "Come on, Alice, stay over Sunday night, take the early bus back." Then I was taking Fridays off. Then I quit my job. Sublet my apartment—then sold it.

(Silence. No one has anything to say.)

ELIZABETH *(Finally)*: Two years? It was that long ago? I hadn't even heard about you until . . . *(To her siblings)* When did Father tell about Alice?

(No response.)

GEMMA *(To Tom)*: And New York is nice as well.
TOM *(To Elizabeth)*: You're in the city—
ELIZABETH: East 81st.
TOM: I'm on the West Side. At 103rd.
ELIZABETH: It's gotten better there.
TOM: It has.
ELIZABETH: I love New York. I wouldn't want to live anywhere else. Nothing closes. You can stay out all night.

(Sophie sighs, wipes her forehead with her napkin.)

PAUL: What is it?
SOPHIE: I'm fine, I just—
PAUL: She's sweating.
GEMMA: Maybe the food, it does taste sort of—
ELIZABETH: I stopped eating it—
PAUL: She's hot.
SOPHIE: I'll be OK. It feels stuffy in here.
ELIZABETH: It would have been a lot stuffier in the dining room.
ALICE: The stove is on. We can turn that off; I don't think we need to keep reheating the—
SOPHIE *(Standing)*: Maybe I'm just tired. Would it be impolite if I— Maybe if I just lie down.

(Everyone adds: "Of course." "Please." "Get some rest." "Relax.")

GEMMA *(Over this)*: It's been an exhausting day for all of us.

SOPHIE: I'll come back down later. Maybe if I read. *(Touches her head)* There's aspirin or something in the bathroom?

(Alice nods. Sophie turns to go, then turns back:)

Paul, can you help me look for the aspirin?
PAUL *(Standing)*: I'm sure it's in the—
SOPHIE: Paul. Help me look.

(She goes. Paul hesitates, then hurries after her. Short pause.)

ELIZABETH: The dining room is stuffier. She always seems sick, doesn't she?
GEMMA: I hadn't noticed. Paul's never said—
ELIZABETH: Every time we're together, she's sick. *(To Tom)* She's nine years older than Paul. And I say that to flatter her—she looks great. When she's not sick. *(Beat)* She's even older than Gemma.
ALICE: Is anyone going to eat any more? . . .

(No response.)

ALFRED: How long has she been away from France? I don't think I know that.
ELIZABETH: Sophie hasn't lived anywhere but West Hollywood since she was eight. She puts that accent on.
TOM: It's a good accent.
ELIZABETH: Remember her mother? We met her at their wedding last December—she now sounds like she comes from Texas.
ALFRED: Isn't that where she lives?—
ELIZABETH: Sophie's no more French any more than I am!
ALICE: Maybe she puts the accent on to please Paul.

(Beat.)

ELIZABETH: How do you mean?

(Alice says nothing; Elizabeth considers this, then:)

I'll bet you're right. *(Laughs at the thought)*

ALFRED: She's a nice girl.

TOM *(Changing the subject)*: Funny, isn't it, all of us—we're living all over *America*. What does that say?

ALFRED: What?

TOM: It's strange. How did it happen? How did *you*—?

ELIZABETH: I think we all came for different reasons.

ALFRED: Harry was first. He led us all here. Blame him! *(Laughs)*

ELIZABETH *(Continuing)*: You can't generalize, I think. For me. London had become so . . . *(Makes a face)*

GEMMA *(Over this)*: I followed Alfred. He kept sending postcards of the desert.

ALICE *(Half over this)*: I was brought over years ago by my publishing company.

(This question has definitely animated the table—they talk almost at the same time.)

ALFRED *(Continuing)*: Harry left about—twenty years ago was it?

GEMMA: We were kids.

ELIZABETH: I was seventeen. Exactly.

GEMMA *(To Tom)*: What about you? You asked the question.

TOM: I was offered a job. As a stage manager. I started as a stage manager. I guess you're right, we shouldn't generalize.

ALICE *(Over this)*: And as for why Harry—Harry's wife, right? She'd just died. Their mother.

(Everyone is now listening to this.)

You children were all in schools. He wanted to . . . *(Shrugs)* Get away from some memories, I suppose. Clear his head. That's how I've always . . . *(Beat)* He didn't plan on staying. I don't know how many times he told me that.

ALFRED: His wife died? Twenty years ago?

ALICE: You must have known that.

(Alfred looks at his nieces.)

He came for—?! I don't know. A semester. That's all he said he was hired for. Then one thing led to another. And he stayed. *(Beat)* And one by one—you came. *(Beat)* What's wrong?

ELIZABETH: Mother died—two months ago.

(Pause.)

ALICE: What do you mean?

ELIZABETH: We were all at the funeral. Father was there. *(Beat)* He said you'd felt it wasn't appropriate for you to come. We understood, didn't we?

(She looks to Gemma who nods.)

ALICE: Two months ago? Where was the—?

GEMMA: Brighton. Where Mother lived.

ALICE: Harry was in England two months ago?? *(Then suddenly)* Oh that's right. Now I remember. Yes, I couldn't come. I hope Harry sent my condolences. I think I sent flowers.

(Pause. Paul enters.)

PAUL: A delicate flower! That is what I tell her she is. Sorry. Sophie'll be fine; she's tucked in, reading a magazine. *(Noticing the faces)* What's . . . ?

ALFRED: We were telling Tom how Harry came to the States.

PAUL: You've told him that Mother just threw him out?

ALICE: Did she?

PAUL: She'd had enough of him. She used to say that marrying Father was like buying a boat; your happiest times are when you get it, and when you get rid of it.

(He laughs, no one else does.)

ALICE: What exactly had your father done for your mother to throw him out?

(Beat.)

ELIZABETH *(After checking with her siblings)*: She never said. I don't think we ever asked.

GEMMA: There's a lot we don't know. Why didn't they ever divorce— *(She is about to continue a list)*

ALICE *(Interrupting)*: Harry was still married to your mother?
GEMMA: Didn't you know that?

(Pause.)

TOM *(To Paul)*: So your wife is just tired.
ELIZABETH: She looked tired.
TOM: I gather you've only been married—
PAUL: Not even a year. It's made a big difference in my life.
TOM: Something like—
ALICE *(Standing)*: Excuse me. *(Takes the bottle of wine and fills up Alfred's glass)* I should get more.
TOM: I can go if—
ALICE: I know where Harry's best stuff is hidden. *(Goes)*

(Beat.)

ELIZABETH: Father never told her he was still married.
GEMMA *(Picking up plates)*: Is anyone still eating?
TOM *(Taking a last bite)*: I've had a lot worse in New York.
ELIZABETH: Father didn't tell her. What does that say?
ALFRED: Harry once talked to me—about Alice.

(Beat.)

ELIZABETH: And . . . ?
ALFRED: He said he'd met this woman. Alice. And, I think he said, that their relationship was—the word he used was—"comfortable." *(Looks to Tom)*
TOM: She's a nice woman. I'm not going to repeat anything that could hurt her.
ELIZABETH: "Comfortable." *(Beat)* What are we going to do about this cremating idea? Alice said she thought that's what Harry would have—
PAUL: Alice said.

(Beat.)

GEMMA: Do we know what Father—
PAUL: Mother was buried.

GEMMA: And he certainly would not have wanted to be buried
with—
PAUL: Do we know that for sure?!!

*(Beat. Phone rings. In the middle of the second ring, it stops.
Someone has picked it up.)*

I'm still hungry. Maybe there's some peanut butter or something.
ELIZABETH: What are we going to do? Don't you think it's a mistake? I think we tell Alice that we want our father buried. If she
gives us any flack we tell her that's what he'd told us he wanted.
GEMMA: We should tell her now.
PAUL: What about the service tomorrow in the garden—
ELIZABETH: We'll make it a memorial. People can still come, whatever. *(Beat)* Is it agreed?

(The others nod.)

Then we'll tell her.
ALFRED *(Turning to Tom)*: How well *did* you know my brother?
TOM: I didn't know him at—
ALFRED: I think that's how most of his friends felt. Let me tell you
the truth. Harry wasn't a very nice man. He wasn't very nice
to me and I wasn't alone. And I got a job at the University of
New Mexico and he was working in a bloody community col-
lege! And he said this country would eat me alive! *(Laughs)*
You know what they say about twins? That there's always a
good one and a bad one.
TOM: I can't believe that's—
ALFRED: Guess which he was. *(Beat)* Go ahead and guess.

(Beat.)

TOM: The bad one?
ALFRED: You knew him well! Still, I think his friends—like yourself—were too hard on him. He used to say that to me. He had
a lot of sides to him— Harry. Be fair, Tom. Don't be too quick
to judge.
TOM *(Confused)*: I wasn't—

ALFRED: Give the man the benefit of the doubt, for Christ sake.

(Alice enters with a bottle of wine. The others look to Elizabeth to begin a conversation, but before she can begin:)

ALICE *(Opening the wine)*: That was the funeral home—we can pick up the ashes anytime now.

(She pours herself a glass of wine, sits down and opens the photograph album. No one says anything for a moment, then, holding up the album:)

Our photo album. *(Pointing to a picture)* Bermuda. *(To Elizabeth)* Harry bought me the bathing suit.

(Pause. She continues to look. No one knows what to say, when finally:)

TOM *(To Paul)*: Read any good film scripts lately?

ALFRED *(Almost chokes on his wine, laughing)*: Right!

PAUL: The funny thing about living in America as a foreigner is the way you see other foreigners act.

GEMMA *(Trying to stop him)*: Paul.

PAUL: They love to criticize. Everything's—what? Rubbish, Uncle Alfred? Some things are and some things aren't. That's how I see things, but . . . I had a friend from London visiting—to him everything was either stupid or plastic or barbaric. Then you couldn't get him out of the damn sun. At night you couldn't get him away from the damn TV. *(Sips his water)* But I know why this is. I've thought about this a lot. It's all so—threatening. It's too much for some people to handle. The size of everything. The importance of everything. So they're actually being defensive. They're scared. *(Beat)* I try to avoid people from home now. They're so predictable. *(To Tom)* To answer your question: I have read a couple of nice scripts this week. We'll see. I've been reading long enough to know that you can never know. You do your best. And try to have an impact where you can. *(Sips his water)* The other day, I had a thought. You get these kinds of thoughts reading scripts. Let's say there are maybe ten thousand film scripts in circulation in L.A. on any given day.

ELIZABETH: That many—?
PAUL: I think I'm being conservative. And each script will have at
least twenty copies. Probably more, but let's say twenty. And
each script—the rule is about a hundred and ten pages.
That's— I did the maths before, something like twenty-two
million pages of film script just—on any given day. *(Beat)*
Now if each writer were to say just decrease the margins—
both left and right—by say three spaces. Three spaces—no
more. It would mean each script would be about five pages
shorter—or a total savings of about one million pages, which
I'm told roughly equals two hundred trees. *(Short pause)*
I wrote a memo. *(Shrugs)* Who knows?

(Pause.)

ALICE: I did—know about Harry being married. *(Short pause. Goes
back to looking at the album)*
ALFRED *(Looking at Alice, then)*: He talked to me about you, Alice.
Harry.

(Alice looks up.)

He said the nicest things. He told me how much he loved you.
This new "gal" he called you. He said—you were everything
to him.

(Alice nods and goes back to the album.)

ELIZABETH *(To Paul)*: There are so many Brits in publishing here.
I have friends—Americans who say the only way to advance
is to go first to England—or fake a British accent. *(Laughs)*
GEMMA *(To Tom)*: Work for you!

(Laughter.)

TOM *(Over this)*: So that's why they take my classes!

(More laugher. Short pause.)

GEMMA: All my English friends—such as they are in New Mexico—
make fun. It's an easy place to make fun. On the one hand

I suppose Paul is right—they're scared. We are. But on the other, you can't help yourself—there's so much that's crazy.

ELIZABETH: Father used to make fun—lest we forget.

PAUL: Father was scared, too.

GEMMA: He didn't make fun, he hated. The last time I called him— he just started ranting.

PAUL: About?

GEMMA: He hated this country and everything it tries to be. Or doesn't try to be.

PAUL: He loved looking down his nose—

ELIZABETH: I never took him seriously when he talked like that. It was just talk. I laughed at him, Paul.

PAUL: You encouraged him.

ELIZABETH: He made me laugh, as I've just said. And he wasn't scared, Paul—he was angry.

PAUL *(Erupting)*: If the man wasn't scared then why the hell are we here?!! And he hated all right! But the only thing he really hated was himself!! *(Beat)* Isn't that now obvious?

(Pause.)

ALICE *(Holding up the album)*: You all might be interested in this. The photos go back years. You're all in here.

ELIZABETH: Pass it around.

ALICE: In a minute, when I'm done. *(Continues to look through the album as she lights a cigarette)*

ALFRED: I'm all in favor of keeping your sense of humor about things. Sometimes I think it's the only thing of any value that we have left. And if Americans wish to make fools of themselves in front of us—day after day after day after day—what are we supposed to do, cover our eyes? Well I don't. *(Shrugs)* So shoot me, Paul.

GEMMA *(To Paul)*: And I don't know what you're talking about. *(To Elizabeth)* Have you heard him do his American accent?

TOM: American accent—??

PAUL *(At the same time)*: Once. I did it once!

GEMMA *(Over this)*: Get off! Let's hear it, Paul!

ELIZABETH: When did he—?

GEMMA: At his wedding!

PAUL: I only do it in England!

ALFRED: Come on, Paul.

GEMMA *(Over this)*: Tom here can help you improve it!

(Elizabeth, Gemma, Alfred and Tom are now all shouting to Paul to do his American accent. He is resisting—all in good humor with a lot of sisterly pushing and nudging: "Please, Paul!" "We want to hear, Paul!" "I'll bet you can't do one!" etc.

As the noise reaches its peak, with people banging on the table and hitting glasses with knives, urging Paul to do his "American"—Sophie enters in a nightgown and robe.)

SOPHIE: What's . . . ?

(They see her and stop. Short pause.)

I'm sorry. I didn't mean to . . . You were making so much noise, I didn't know what . . . I see—you were just having fun. *(Beat)* Good for you. I'm sure it's not easy to find much to laugh about on a day like today. I'm sorry if I interrupted. *(Turns to go)*

PAUL: Sophie, sit down if you—

SOPHIE *(Interrupting)*: I don't think I'm dressed for a party. *(Beat)* Come up when you feel like it, Paul. When you're ready. I'll wait up. *(Goes)*

(Pause. Paul stands, looks at his sisters, then picks up a knife, and says in his best "Brando" or "Pacino":)

PAUL: Hey woman, how come you just don't cut the whole thing off!

(He turns back to his sisters, smiles and they burst out laughing. Through the laughter they shout: "He's good!" "That was very good."

Alice continues to look through the album. As the sisters laugh, Sophie returns.)

SOPHIE: Perhaps I will join you. *(Goes and sits next to Paul)* I can't sleep anyway. I told Claire I'd call at seven— her time.

GEMMA: How is Claire, you haven't said a word—

ELIZABETH *(Over this)*: I meant to ask . . .

SOPHIE: She's very upset, of course. She adored Harry. Even though they'd only met the one time at the wedding. Still, we always put her on the phone when we called. She said, when we told her—of course we didn't say how—she said, "So how many grandparents do I have now?" *(Smiles)* She's going to write you each a note.

(Beat.)

ELIZABETH *(To Tom)*: Claire is Sophie's nine year old—
TOM: I guessed.
SOPHIE: She's devoted to Paul. Worships him, doesn't she? *(Beat)* I'm jealous. *(Smiles)*
GEMMA *(To Elizabeth)*: What time is it?
ELIZABETH: Too early to go to bed.

(Short pause, then:)

SCENE 5

The kitchen. An hour or so later.
Alice, Alfred and Elizabeth are out for a walk.
Sophie sits at the table, talking on the phone to her daughter in California: what they are saying cannot be heard. Gemma is beginning to clean up the table, piling dishes, scraping plates, etc., and carrying them off to the sink and garbage. Tom and Paul sit across from each other, talking.

TOM *(In the middle of a story)*: "What are you up for, dear?" I ask. *(In American)* "It's a play by Oscar Wilder. Do you know him?" *(Own voice)* "Not for years. Have you done English accents before on stage?" *(American)* "I was in a show by George Bernard Shaw once." "Funny, I hadn't realized he'd written—shows. And what part did you play?" *(American)* "I was one of those dancers, you know, in the ballroom scene."
PAUL: What ballroom—??
TOM: *My Fair Lady.*
PAUL: Of course!

TOM *(Over this)*: Last year in her prep school. *(American)* "I wore the pink dress?" "I should have guessed just by looking at you. What else could you have played?" *(Sips his drink)*

PAUL: Once—

TOM: Just a second. *(Continues)* I reply, after listening to her act— I use the term loosely—for a few moments: "I can see there is nothing I can teach you." *(American)* "Oh, but there must be!" She had your typical American sense of irony. Anyway, to make a long story short, I tried. Her mother paid me fifty bucks to go and see her Gwendolen or *(American)* "Gwendolen" is how her fellow actors—again the term is used with freedom bordering on abandonment—referred to her character on stage. In the end I would hazard to say she was the most authentic thing in the whole evening. *(Beat)* I met the director after the "show," which by the way is the appropriate term for what I saw; they, the Americans, have that right—he was, I would say, the most tired human being I have ever been exposed to. He literally fell asleep while *he* was talking to me. But then I'd learned that this was something like the ninth prep school production of *Importance of Being Earnest* he'd directed in—I think he said—the last three weeks. But maybe I didn't hear him right.

(Gemma returns from the sink and picks up more dishes.)

PAUL: Where in England was he from?

TOM: He was from England, you knew! Bristol, he said. But he may have only been mumbling that in his sleep—a memory? Of something else perhaps?

(Sophie suddenly laughs at something her daughter has told her on the phone. Paul looks at her then back at Tom, who pours himself more wine from the bottle.)

He perked up after a couple of drinks though. His "Gwendolen's" mum was paying. Then after we were in this bar for a while, the mum says, *(American)* "So what did you really think?" To me. I look at the director, and he says, could I wait a minute, he's really interested in what I have to say, but he has to go to the loo. He gets up, goes—and we never see him again.

(Sips his drinks) I suppose he had another show to direct. He did say, sometime during the evening, that the high point of a busy artistic year was being allowed—by someplace somewhere—to do a production of a Chekhov play. He couldn't recall which one.

(Gemma laughs at this.)

PAUL: My favorite—
TOM: I haven't quite—
PAUL *(At the same time)*: I'm sorry, I didn't mean—
TOM *(At the same time)*: But go ahead, please . . .

(Beat.)

PAUL: My favorite's . . .

(Gemma stops to listen.)

I'm in line at the grocery store. I obviously must have said something, because this fellow behind me, hearing the accent I suppose, says *(American)* "What the fuck is going on with that queen of yours? Why she letting 'em push her around! If I was queen I wouldn't let nobody push me around. That lady needs some balls!" *(Smiles)* They say whatever comes into their heads, I swear. There's no—editing.

(Beat.)

TOM: That's funny. *(Continues with his story)* So—the mum, she says, "I thought every penny I'd laid out for those lessons was worth it." *(Looks at Paul and shrugs)* I suppose I must have done some good. I don't know. *(Beat)* I can't work miracles. But sometimes I guess I do OK.

(Paul nods.)

PAUL: It can be a strange place.
GEMMA *(As she picks up dishes)*: Sometimes—I pretend, when I'm sitting out on my porch, painting—I look out across the land-

scape and I say: this is Africa. Like a hundred, hundred and fifty years ago. Africa. *(Starts to leave with the dishes)* Or India. It makes me feel better for some reason. *(Goes)*

(Sophie holds out the phone.)

SOPHIE: Paul, talk to Claire. I have to get a book to read to her.
PAUL: I'll get it for you—
SOPHIE *(Over this)*: It's in my bag. You'll never find it. And besides, Claire's dying to talk to you. *(Into the phone)* Here's Paul, dear. He's grabbing the phone from me, he wants that much to talk to you.

(He obviously has not been grabbing the phone; she now hands it to him. As she does, to Tom:)

I always read to Claire at night. *(Goes)*
PAUL *(Into the phone)*: Hi! What did you do today? I'm sure you already have, I'll ask her to tell me. What's the weather like?

(Gemma returns from the sink.)

TOM *(To Gemma)*: I had one student. This was when I'd only been here a few years. My wife couldn't believe this.
GEMMA *(Interrupting)*: Your wife? I didn't know you were—
TOM: We're divorced. *(Continues with the story)* He comes in. His shirt's unbuttoned down to— And it's goddamn winter. *(Laughs)*
GEMMA: Was she English?
TOM: My wife? Yes. She's back in London now *(Beat)* When we were breaking up, I used to say to her *(In American)* "What's the matter, can't you take it?" *(Smiles)* She couldn't.

(Beat.)

GEMMA: I didn't mean to be—
TOM: That's—
GEMMA: I just suddenly realized. I don't know anything about you. Here you are at . . .
TOM: Alice wanted me to stay—

GEMMA: I wasn't saying— Of course you're . . . *(Stops herself)*
Kids?
TOM: Six and nine. Boys. In London.

(Beat. Then, changing the subject before it becomes too personal:)

GEMMA: Anyway, you were saying about a student . . .
TOM: He comes into my class, this kid really, and he says to me, in
front of everyone, *(American)* "I want to try some of that
British bullshit acting, you know—with the funny voice."

(He laughs, then she laughs, not quite understanding.)

PAUL *(Covering the phone)*: I missed that.

(Tom pours himself more to drink.)

GEMMA *(To Paul)*: A student of Tom's—he wanted to learn the way
the British act.

(Paul doesn't understand.)

TOM: Another story! A young woman—she's been a model, now she
wants to act. So I've asked her to prepare something. Not that
I'm going to reject anyone. God forbid that we have standards.

(Paul sets the phone on the table.)

So she recites, *(American)* "Thus do I ever make my fool my
purse." I ask her if she knows what she's saying. She says that
for her it means—how she shouldn't spend so much money on
clothes. She says, *(American)* "That may not be what it means
to others, but that's what it means to me." *(Beat)* I ask her:
does she know what character she is acting? She says, *(American)* "Iago." Very good. I ask her: did she know that Iago was
a—man? She says, *(American)* "So what? My last drama
teacher—" "Drama. Drama." My favorite American word.
"My last drama teacher said there were no male or female parts
anymore—only people parts." I want to say, I think your
teacher could have chosen a better word than "parts," but I bite

my tongue. *(Opens his mouth)* See? Seven years in this country and there's permanent teeth marks there. *(Continues)* "Only people parts." Interesting. Why not? I say to myself, she's paid in advance. Then about a half hour later, for the hell of it or maybe I'm just wanting to get into the swing of this "people part" notion, I say, "Now that you've done your Iago, what about trying Othello?" *(Beat)* You'd have thought I'd hit her in the face. *(American)* "Othello," she says in her lovely American, "I couldn't do Othello." "Why is that, my dear?" "Othello is a black man." Or is it "African American" now? I don't know and I don't give a fuck. Anyway, "A black man. And only a black man can play a black man." *(Beat)* I asked if she felt that was in any way contradictory to what she'd said about "people parts?" And she said, she didn't see why it was. *(Pause)* They don't see themselves. They don't question themselves.

PAUL: And the things you can't say. Sometimes I think a decent English comic would be in prison in a wink in this country.

GEMMA *(Entering from the sink)*: I thought you loved America?

PAUL: You can love something and still find fault with it.

(Sophie enters with a book.)

SOPHIE: I'd put it in your bag for some reason. *(Notices the phone on the table)*

PAUL: We had a nice talk.

(Sophie picks up the phone and begins to read from Charlie and the Chocolate Factory *to her daughter.)*

TOM: If they weren't so thin-skinned. Sometimes you just want to scream: "RELAX!"

(Noise outside.)

GEMMA: They're back from their walk.

TOM: Anyway, why did you let me go on like that? It must have been very boring, you should have stopped me.

(Alfred, Alice and Elizabeth enter from their walk; Alice and Alfred wear Wellingtons.)

ALICE: What a beautiful night. You should have come with us, Gemma.

PAUL: You've been gone for ages. Where was there to walk? I thought Father only had a half acre.

ELIZABETH: We walked through other people's. They don't have fences.

(She looks to Gemma, who picks up more plates.)

GEMMA: I've been picking up.

ELIZABETH: You shouldn't have to do it all.

GEMMA: I was hoping I wouldn't have to.

SOPHIE *(To everyone)*: Would you mind—? Please. Sh-sh. *(Continues to read over the phone)*

PAUL: Sophie, I don't think you can ask everyone— It's the kitchen—

SOPHIE: Fine! I'm sorry I'm in the way.

PAUL: No one said—

SOPHIE: I'll go upstairs. If it isn't a big bother could someone hang up the receiver when I get to the phone upstairs? *(Goes, carrying her book)*

ELIZABETH: Is that the same call she was making—?

ALFRED *(Taking off his Wellingtons; reads the bottom of the boots. American)*: "Made with pride in the U.S. of A." *(To the others)* Are we still doing our American?

ALICE *(Over this, to Elizabeth)*: I'll look for that stomach medicine—

ELIZABETH: You said it was in the medicine chest. I'm not stupid.

GEMMA: Is something . . . ?

ALFRED: Her stomach.

ELIZABETH *(As she leaves the kitchen)*: And you could help Gemma, Paul. You're not home. *(Goes)*

TOM *(Standing)*: Let me, I—

GEMMA: You're a guest. *(Turns to Alice)* Her stomach?

ALICE: It's the emotion. She holds everything in.

ALFRED: She said it was the Chinese food. I better open another bottle. *(Starts to leave for the pantry. American)* "What should it be? Red or white—or blush?" *(Laughs to himself and goes)*

(Gemma and Paul start to head for the sink, carrying the glasses, plates, etc.)

GEMMA *(As they go)*: I can't believe Sophie wanted us to be quiet—
PAUL: She didn't mean— Sometimes she says things without thinking. Who doesn't?

(They are gone. Alice and Tom are alone. Alice suddenly sighs.)

TOM: Are you all—?
ALICE: It's late. *(Beat)* And no one wants to go to sleep.
TOM: Alice—

(She turns to him.)

Take care of yourself. This can't be easy.

(She smiles, takes his hand and pats it.)

ALICE: When we were walking— Elizabeth spent most of the time on a bench— So Alfred . . . *(Beat)* He asked me to go to bed with him.
TOM: He's drunk. He's been drinking all—
ALICE: Thank you.
TOM: I mean— I meant, don't be too angry with him. Harry's death . . . Everyone in this house. You can see how emotional it all is.
ALICE: Thank you, again.
TOM: What do you want me to say?
ALICE: "Do you want to go to bed with him, Alice?" *(Beat)* And the answer to that is . . . *(Shrugs. Beat)* It was very beautiful out tonight. I love the fall. There was nearly a full moon. Maybe by tomorrow night. I'm going to have a cigarette. I don't give a shit. *(Takes out a cigarette and lights it)*
GEMMA *(Off; calling)*: My God, Paul's washing a dish!
TOM: Don't do anything that . . . You might regret tomorrow, Alice.
ALICE: What a bullshit thing to say to me!
TOM *(Over this)*: Then don't ask me for my—!
ALICE: Who asked you?! *(Beat)* Don't worry, I'm not stupid. I'm not going to bed with him. It's nice being asked, though.

(Alfred enters with the wine. Short pause. He looks at both of them.)

ALFRED: Did I interrupt something? What were you talking about?

(Beat.)

ALICE: Harry. Of course.

(Elizabeth enters with the medicine.)

ELIZABETH *(Entering)*: None of this kind of stuff ever works for me. I don't know why I'm bothering. Could you hand me a spoon?

(Tom takes a spoon out of the drawer and hands it to her.)

GEMMA *(Off)*: Elizabeth, look what our brother's doing. Have you ever seen him wash a dish in his life?

ELIZABETH: I'll get a camera! *(To the others)* Who's paying for that phone call by the way? She's still on the phone. Is she going to read the whole book to her?

ALICE: I assumed it was a credit card call.

ELIZABETH: I think we better ask Paul. *(Goes off to the sink)*

ALFRED: So you were talking about Harry. There were times when we'd be together, Harry and me, and I'd look at him, sipping his Scotch, and it was like I didn't know that man at all. I had no idea what he was thinking. What he was feeling. Which is a weird feeling, when the guy looks just like you.

PAUL *(Entering and heading for the upstairs)*: I'll talk to her. I didn't realize it was bothering everyone!

ELIZABETH *(Following him in)*: Alice shouldn't be asked to pay—

PAUL *(Over this)* Get off my back!

(He goes. Gemma also enters from the sink, wiping her hands. Pause. Elizabeth pours the medicine and drinks it. Finally:)

GEMMA: You know we've hardly talked about the service.

ALICE: Alfred and I were talking about it on our walk. He was saying he thought Paul wanted—to sing something.

GEMMA: Paul said that?

ALFRED: He hinted to me, when we were—

ELIZABETH: What does he want to sing?

(Beat.)

GEMMA: Father hated Paul's singing. It offended him.

ALICE: Perhaps that is why Paul wants to sing. Maybe each of us—
something. Before we throw the ashes into the garden. I was
going to read a poem.

TOM: Maybe it's none of my business, but what I would suggest is
that you make a list. Put what you're going to do in the order
you plan to do it in. You can always change, of course, but . . .
It's a good thing to have written down. That's been my experience. In front of people. *(Looks at each one of them)* I can be
secretary if you'd like. If that'd make it easier. Is there a piece
of paper?

(Everyone ignores him. Short pause.)

ALFRED *(Sitting and leaning over, he takes Alice's hand)*: I wasn't
lying. He told me that he loved you.
ALICE: I know he did.

(Beat.)

ALFRED *(To everyone)*: I noticed a pile of jigsaws in the closet.
Anyone else like to do jigsaws? I'll choose one. *(Goes)*

*(No one has anything to say. Elizabeth turns on the radio for a
moment—pop music—she turns it right off again. Alfred enters
with a puzzle.)*

(Holding up the front of the box) The Grand Canyon!

(Elizabeth suddenly grabs stomach in pain, she cries out.)

GEMMA: Elizabeth!

*(Gemma and Alice go to her, as she doubles over and nearly col-
lapses to the floor.)*

ALICE: Oh my God!
ELIZABETH: I'll be fine. Give me some water. I'm fine.

*(Alice gives her some water. Elizabeth sits back in her chair,
breathing heavily now. She wipes the sweat from her brow.)*

(Faintly) Do the jigsaw. I like jigsaws.

(Alfred opens the box and pours out the pieces onto the table. Paul storms into the kitchen from upstairs. He is very upset.)

PAUL: I'll pay for the goddamn call!!! What do you want—a check?! Cash?!!! Whatever you want!! Just get off my back!! She's trying to talk to her daughter!! Is that so bad?! Can't you leave her alone?!!! She's up there crying now. She thinks you hate her! I can't stand it anymore!! Grow up!!!

(He suddenly becomes aware that Sophie is behind him. She has been crying.)

SOPHIE: Paul, your sisters meant well. You shouldn't talk to them like that. *(Beat)* Apologize. *(Beat)* You heard me. Apologize.

(Beat.)

PAUL: I'm sorry.

(Sophie tries to smile.)

SOPHIE: I'm going to bed now—everyone. Goodnight.

(Everyone except Paul says— "Goodnight," "Goodnight, Sophie." Sophie turns to go, then turns back.)

Paul, stay up as late as you want. And visit. *(Leaves)*
ALFRED *(Over the puzzle)*: Anyone else ever been to the Grand Canyon? I know you have, Gemma. Elizabeth?

(She nods. He looks at the others, and one by one they nod as well.)

Everyone?
GEMMA *(To Elizabeth)*: You should go to bed. I'll take you up. Come on. *(Helps Elizabeth up)* Goodnight. Say goodnight.
ELIZABETH *(To the others)*: Goodnight.

(The others say, "Goodnight.")

ALICE: Sleep well.

GEMMA: I'll come back down and help.

(They go.)

PAUL: I'll finish the dishes.

TOM: Why can't I—

PAUL: I'm used to it. It's my job at home. *(Goes to the sink)*

(Tom now sits between Alfred and Alice. Alfred continues to work on the puzzle, turning over pieces, occasionally matching two. He continues this throughout the rest of the scene. Tom begins to feel a little uncomfortable between these two.)

ALICE: About a year ago, Alfred   *(Ignores Tom)* Harry started going on and on about this new student of his. A young woman. Said she was— Amazing. I ran into the two of them one afternoon in the parking lot of the college, chatting. She's beautiful. *(Beat)* You may see her here tomorrow. I think she's invited herself. *(Beat)* After seeing her, I said to Harry, what the hell did he take me for? I didn't want any of that. My last husband— *(Turns to Tom and pats his hand)* Tom's brother. *(Turns back to Alfred)* I'd had it with that. I can live alone. I don't mind. *(Beat)* He smiled—the way he smiled. The way you smile. He was a handsome man.

(Alfred looks up.)

And he kissed me on the lips or tried to. And he said, I don't believe what I'm hearing, Alice. That girl is probably the best violin student I've ever had in America. Her potential is limitless. Finally I feel my talents as a teacher can be fulfilled. You can't know how lucky I feel. Though of course I'm trying to convince her to transfer to Julliard. *(Beat)* I felt like shit. *(Looks at Tom, then back at Alfred)* He spent a lot of time with her. He loved teaching. *(Short pause)* Then one day, I happened by his office door. It was opened a crack. There's also a little window. And there she was with him. She had her violin. I saw her put it under her chin. Raise her bow. And I don't know what I was prepared for, Alfred, but—she was the worst violinist I have ever heard. *(Smiles without looking up)* I mean it was painful. *(Beat)* He screwed around all the time. Though after hearing the girl play I realized that there was some suffering on his part as well. It wasn't all . . . *(Shrugs)* Maybe even more suffering than pleasure. *(Smiles)* We can hope. *(Short pause. Reaches over and takes a sip of Alfred's drink)* So—a few months ago Harry was in England? At his—wife's funeral? What did she die of? Do we know?

(Beat.)

ALFRED: Her liver. She was a drinker.

(Alice takes another sip of Alfred's drink.)

ALICE: It was a nice walk. Harry never wanted to take a walk with me after supper. Except—when we were courting. For that one week—he would.

(She looks at Alfred. He looks up. They look into each other's eyes. Tom turns away and tries to be invisible.)

SCENE 6

The kitchen. One o'clock in the morning.
    Tom and Paul sit at the table, working on the puzzle—the frame is now completed. From above, there is a banging/pounding sound.
    Beat.

PAUL *(Looking up, after listening for a moment)*: Unbelievable. Don't you find it—? *(Stops himself)* What were we talking about?
TOM *(Without looking up from the puzzle; American accent)*: "What you don't understand . . ."
PAUL *(Remembering where he was; American)*: "What you don't understand about America is . . ." Fill in the blank. I don't know how many times I have been told that. "You don't understand"— that there was—"all these different races." That America is— "soooo big." That "we actually vote for our leaders."

*(More banging from above interrupts him. He stops. Gemma enters
from the sink and stove area; she has just made herself a cup of tea.
She wears a nightgown and a robe.)*

GEMMA *(Listening to the noise above)*: I hope to God I have Uncle
Alfred's genes.

PAUL: It's been going on for like an hour now. *(Beat)* Am I the only
one offended by this? By our—recently deceased father's girlfriend and our recently deceased father's brother screwing like
a couple of bloody rabbits up there in his own goddamn bedroom?!!

(He looks at Gemma, who sips her tea.)

No one else is even a little troubled by this turn of events? No?
Fine. Then it must be me. *(Turns to Tom)* What were we talking about? I keep forgetting.

TOM: I heard this once *(American)* "I love England. It's my favorite
of those countries." *(Beat)* I should have said—by "those
countries" do you happen to mean *Europe?* Europe the home
for the past three millennia to what we humbly call—Western
Civilization?!! *(Smiles and shakes his head)*

GEMMA: Don't you two get tired of complaining?

*(More banging upstairs. Gemma sits down at the table and picks
up a puzzle piece.)*

PAUL *(Pushing her hand away from his pieces)*: I'm doing the sky.
(Turns to Tom) Alfred once was telling— This must have been
at my wedding. I'm not sure. He's teaching a class. *(Turns to
Gemma)* What's his field again?

GEMMA: The Romantics.

PAUL: So—say he was teaching—Shelley? Whatever. And a student stands up in the class and says *(American)* "What the hell
does any of this have to do with my life? Why do I even have
to listen to you? You worthless Englishman!! Don't you know
you are nothing now? That you count for nothing in this
world! This is our world! Get it?! So why don't you just shut
up and listen!!" *(Laughs to himself)*

TOM: He really—?

PAUL: Something like that. I don't remember the exact words.

TOM: What did Alfred do?

(Paul looks to Gemma who ignores him and continues to look over the puzzle.)

PAUL: He didn't do anything. The students here grade their teachers, so Alfred says—you just have to take it.

(The banging seems to have reached its climax upstairs. They listen, then it stops. Pause.)

(Looking up at the ceiling) Silence. Dare we hope. *(Standing, arms outstretched)* Thank you, God! Maybe someone's finally come!!

(Elizabeth enters from the hallway in her robe.)

ELIZABETH *(Entering)*: Have you been hearing what's been going on upstairs? You can hear everything!

PAUL: They've stopped.

GEMMA *(Under her breath)*: I wouldn't bet on it.

TOM *(To Elizabeth)*: How's the . . . *(Touches his stomach)*

ELIZABETH: The medicine helped. Also the sleep, I think. I didn't know how tired I was.

PAUL *(Looking at his watch)*: You only slept for—

ELIZABETH *(Interrupting, to Gemma)*: Is that tea?

GEMMA: The water's still—

ELIZABETH *(On her way to the stove)*: Anyone else? . . . *(She is gone)*

(Beat.)

GEMMA: Who can sleep?

PAUL *(Over the puzzle)*: As long as Sophie can—

GEMMA: The light was on in your room. When I came down.

(Beat.)

PAUL *(Without looking up from the puzzle)*: Then I better go. *(Doesn't move. Beat.)* I've got one *(American)* "The farther east you go—the more dead they are." I swear I heard this. In California.

(Silence. They work on the puzzle. Suddenly both Tom and Gemma speak at the same time.)

TOM *(To Paul)*: I hear that you—
GEMMA *(Same time, to Tom)*: I wanted to ask—

(They stop themselves.)

TOM: Go ahead, what were you—
GEMMA *(Over this)*: No, please. It was just— What were you going to say?

(Beat.)

TOM: Remember your thought. I was only going to say that I understand you're going to sing tomorrow, Paul.

(Paul looks up.)

What are you going to sing?
PAUL: Who said that?
TOM: Alfred thought—
PAUL: I haven't sung in front of people in years.
TOM: You were a professional singer—?
PAUL: I took classes. I wasn't bad. But it was clear I was destined for the chorus, so . . . I hadn't even thought of singing. *(Beat. To Gemma)* Think I should? What would father have thought— such a mediocre voice sending him off.
GEMMA: I think he's already gone. Do what you want.

(Elizabeth enters with her tea and a cookie that she has found and now eats.)

ELIZABETH *(Eating the cookie)*: I think it's sick. Up there. How do they get the nerve? And do they think we're deaf?
PAUL *(Over the puzzle)*: So I'm not alone.
TOM *(To Gemma)*: What were you going to say— Before—
GEMMA: Oh right. I wasn't . . . I was going to ask— *(Looks at her brother and sister)* Don't get angry with me. *(To Tom)* Since you were here—I'd like to know what happened yesterday.

ELIZABETH: Gemma, it's one in the morning!—

PAUL: You don't have to Tom, I apologize for my sister.

GEMMA *(Over this)*: I mean—after. I understand what he did. *(Beat)* Were there police? I feel like I'd like to know. Should know. But if you don't want to— It's not that important. *(Pause. Goes back to the puzzle)*

TOM *(Remembering)*: The police did come. An ambulance. An officer talked to me. To Alice. He was pretty nice. Younger than me.

(He smiles. No one is looking at him. They are doing the puzzle.)

Alice was able to say she wasn't all that surprised, he'd been depressed, and so . . . That made things—quicker. *(Beat. Trying to recall more)* Some people from the ambulance cleaned up the study a little bit. I don't know how much you want to know?

ELIZABETH *(Sitting down now, to get closer to the puzzle; to Gemma)*: Move over a little.

PAUL *(To Elizabeth)*: The sky is mine. Do all that pink rock. *(Beat)*

TOM: Before the police came, Alice and I just sat in the hall outside the study. I wouldn't allow her to go back in. Once I'd seen . . .
. . . *(Beat)* I helped her wash her face. She had some blood . . . She'd seen him do it—you knew that. So everything she does— I think we should remember that. *(Beat)* I came in and she was just sobbing. I pulled her into the hall. I called the police. They took out the body in a body bag; on a stretcher. I drove Alice in her car to the hospital behind the ambulance. I don't even have my license with me. *(Beat)* A funeral director was called. We met him in a room of the hospital. Alice liked him right away. He's about my age. Maybe a little younger. *(Beat)* I'm just trying to recall if there's anything . . .
. . . It was the funeral director who gave us the name of the woman who did most of the cleaning up. Alice—Elizabeth knows this—found a few places she'd missed. You couldn't stop her. I couldn't have done it. There was a stain on the floorboards she couldn't get out or she didn't have the stuff in the house to get out. So Elizabeth—

ELIZABETH *(Doing the puzzle)*: I moved the carpet from one of the bedrooms. It's in the study now.

TOM: Where I'm supposed to sleep. *(Laughs)*

PAUL *(Looking up)*: Tom shouldn't have to—

GEMMA *(At the same time)*: We can't let him sleep—

TOM *(Over this)*: I can't sleep anyway, please! *(Pats the puzzle)* I'll just stay up all night. I often do.

(More banging from upstairs.)

PAUL *(Looking up)*: Now—the other one has to come! Jesus Christ . . .

(They all look back at the puzzle.)

TOM *(To Gemma)*: Is that enough? Is there a specific thing . . . ?

ELIZABETH *(Changing the subject)*: Who is this Alice anyway?

GEMMA: I thought you knew her from publishing—

ELIZABETH: I'm asking Tom.

(Tom is surprised by this.)

He's her relative.

GEMMA: I think we've imposed upon Tom enough for—

TOM: I don't mind. Let's see. Alice was married to my brother. I knew her then. I always thought she was one of the more alive people that I knew.

(More banging from upstairs.)

They seemed happy. My brother and— One of those couples who seem to get along. Then he found someone else. I thought he acted in a real shitty way. I told her so. Is this the sort of thing—?

ELIZABETH: It'll do.

TOM: We hadn't seen each other for a few years. We ran into each other a couple of weeks ago on Fifth Avenue, agreed to have lunch, had lunch. I'd just broken up with a girl.

GEMMA: Your wife?

TOM *(Shaking his head)*: This was just a few weeks—

GEMMA: Right. American? The girl.

TOM: That's right. Anyway Alice took pity on me, invited me up here for a weekend in the country. *(Beat)* So I could relax.

(The noise from above has stopped.)

She's a good person. She's gone through a lot.
PAUL: Sh-sh!

(Everyone listens.)

Dare we hope that this unpleasant experience is now behind us?
ELIZABETH: I'd only met Alice a few times. I think it's the same with all of us. I don't know—there's my father's house. My father's funeral service. Calling my father's friends. She's everywhere, isn't she? That's what I was thinking about upstairs. That I don't know who she is. Or what she wants.
PAUL: What are you talking about?
ELIZABETH: Father has a lot of things in this house. That were his. Open your eyes, Paul. Just look at the situation we're in: she decides about the cremation. She tells us where to sleep.
GEMMA: I thought you helped with that.
ELIZABETH: I did my best. Look, I don't want to make a big deal about this. I don't mean it to be a big deal. It's just something I've been thinking about.
PAUL: What is? I don't understand.

(Elizabeth holds her stomach.)

What's wrong?
ELIZABETH: I'm sure it was the egg roll. That's what I've been burping up. Forget it, Paul. Do your jigsaw. That's what you're interested in.
PAUL: I'm not interested in the jigsaw!

(Sophie now enters from the hall. She wears a thin, translucent nightgown.)

SOPHIE: Is no one going to sleep in this house? What night owls you Bakers are.
ELIZABETH: We got woken up by—
SOPHIE: Me, too. *(Yawns)* What was that noise? Sounded like a tree limb banging on the roof. Must have gotten windy all of a sudden. Is that tea?

ELIZABETH: There's still water in the kettle.

SOPHIE *(Yawning)*: I'm half asleep. *(She puts her arms around Paul's neck)* How's the puzzle coming? I love puzzles. They're a complete waste of time. I like that. *(Kisses him on the head)* What are you going to do, make me sleep alone all night? Your sisters can't be that interesting. *(Laughs)* Just joking. I'll make myself some tea. Anyone else? *(As she leaves for the stove)* I'm upstairs thinking: what do I have to do to get my husband to go to bed? *(Smiles, then as if another thought—she fans herself for a second with her nightgown)* I put on a cooler nightgown. It was hot in the room. *(Goes)*

ELIZABETH: You're not going to shut me up, Paul.

PAUL *(Over this)*: Leave me alone. This is all I ask.

ELIZABETH *(Over this)*: You never change!

GEMMA *(Over this)*: I don't want to talk about this! I don't want to talk about this! I don't want to talk about this!

(Alice has entered in a robe and bare feet. She stands, startled to see everyone. Short pause.)

ALICE: What's everyone . . . ? Do you know what time it is? I think it's—

ELIZABETH: We're having tea.

(No one knows what to say. Sophie comes in, having put on the kettle.)

SOPHIE: The kettle's on.

ALICE: You, too? What's going on?

SOPHIE: I was just telling everyone—there was a tree limb, banging against the roof. Did you hear it? *(Beat)* You must have, Alice. It woke me up.

(Beat.)

ALICE: I did hear it. Thank you. *(Goes to the table and picks up a bottle)* Alfred wants a . . . drink. I ran into him—in the hall. I'd been asleep. And then I suppose the tree limb . . .

PAUL: Sounded like a very big limb.

(Alice yawns.)

ALICE: I promised to bring this . . . He's waiting. Goodnight. Remember, tomorrow is going to be a long day as well. *(Turns to leave)*

ELIZABETH: Alice, when do we decide who gets what?

PAUL: This is not the time—

GEMMA: It's the middle of the night, Elizabeth!

ELIZABETH: I want to know!!

(Beat.)

ALICE: What's there to get?

ELIZABETH: There are chairs. Silverware. Plates. Photographs and frames. Books. Table.

ALICE *(Turning away)*: Take what you want, Elizabeth.

ELIZABETH *(Irrational now)*: How dare you speak to me like that!

GEMMA: Stop it, Elizabeth!

PAUL *(Same time)*: Leave her alone!

ELIZABETH: I only want what is fair!! This was my father!! Do you understand that, woman?! So how are we going to divide his things?! What is so wrong with that question?! Do we divide into three? In four . . . ?

ALICE: Is that what you want to ask me?!! Is it?!!! Or do you want to know why I— Do you think I didn't know you could hear?! I've lived in this house for two years and I know what can be heard!! But I didn't care! Why? Because I don't give one fuck what you—kids—think of me!! Why should I?!

ELIZABETH *(Nearly in tears)*: I don't know why I'm listening to this. What have I done?

TOM: I think we should stop before—

ELIZABETH *(To Alice)*: What you don't understand is I'm not interested in you, Alice. My question had to do with chairs, tables, there are lamps, rugs . . .

ALICE: He was so disappointed in all of you!!

ELIZABETH *(Desperately trying to stay calm)*: Books, there's his car, garden equipment—

TOM *(Putting his hand on Elizabeth's arm)*: I think you should talk about all this in the morning.

ELIZABETH *(Suddenly all of her anger comes out, directed at Tom)*: Who the hell are you? You little son of a bitch, you don't even

belong here. This has nothing to do with you!! Shut up! Shut
up! Shut up! *(Starts to sob. No one knows what to do. Pause)*

TOM: I think I'll take a walk.

PAUL: Tom, she didn't mean—

TOM: I know. I didn't take it personally. But I could use some air.

(He goes out. Elizabeth cries.)

ALICE: I'm sorry. We'll discuss everything. The house—that was
your father's. It's yours. I have a few things . . . I'll make a list
of what they are. *(Sits and pours herself a drink)*

(Sophie goes to Elizabeth and puts her arms around her.)

SOPHIE: It's all right.

(She pats Elizabeth. Short pause.)

ELIZABETH: I'm sorry about . . . *(Gestures toward where Tom exited)*
But it really is none of his business. What is he doing here anyway? *(Blows her nose)*

(Tom returns, unseen by anyone.)

Alice said on our walk that she can't get rid of him. She doesn't
know why he stayed. He didn't even know Father. You'd think
he'd know he didn't belong.

ALICE: I put him in the study for Christ sake. You'd think he'd have
taken the hint.

*(She laughs, as does Elizabeth. Then slowly they realize Tom is
there and heard all this. No one knows what to say. Short pause.)*

TOM: It's—raining. Outside. Just started. *(Beat)* I think I'll go to
bed now. Goodnight. *(Goes)*

(Elizabeth sniffles. Alice takes a sip of her drink.)

ALICE: I'm drunk.

SCENE 7

The kitchen. An hour later.
Gemma sits at the table, staring into space. Elizabeth sits, going through Harry's photo album that Alice had left on the table. From upstairs, we hear Alice screaming; the realization of what Harry did has hit her and she sounds like a wounded animal.
Gemma and Elizabeth pretend to ignore the screams.
Alfred enters from the hallway, obviously upset. He wears only his underpants.

ALFRED *(Entering)*: Where's Alice's purse? Have you seen—?
(Grabs the purse) Is this it? *(Opens it, digs around and pulls out a bottle of prescription pills)*

(Alice screams again.)

ELIZABETH *(Looking through the album)*: Can't you do something?
ALFRED: It's all just hit her. She needs to sleep.

(He goes back into the hall with the pills. Alice screams again. Pause.)

ELIZABETH *(Holding the album)*: Look at this. I tell you there are pictures of us I've never even seen before. You must be no more than six.

(Gemma, distracted, nods.)

Here's one of Paul. *(Beat)* I'm thinking of keeping this. The whole thing.
GEMMA: Oh God, Liz—!
ELIZABETH: I want it. She can't know who half the people are.
GEMMA: She'll make you copies. It's Alice's! *(Reaches over the table for the album)*
ELIZABETH *(Pushing her off; over this)*: She can't appreciate it like we can!
GEMMA *(Over this)*: It's not yours to take!

(They struggle over the album.)

ELIZABETH *(Over this)*: Let go! I want to take it!
GEMMA *(Over this)*: Give it to me!!

(Finally Gemma gets the album. Tom has entered to see the end of this fight. He wears pajamas now. Elizabeth and Gemma breathe heavily for a moment.)

ELIZABETH *(To Gemma)*: I don't understand you.

(They notice Tom for the first time. Beat.)

TOM *(To Elizabeth)*: I'm still here. Sorry. There's no bus service at two o'clock in the morning.

(He crosses the room and goes off to the sink. Gemma sighs.)

GEMMA: What that man must think of us.
ELIZABETH: Who cares? *(Gets up and leaves)*

(Beat.)

GEMMA *(After her)*: Goodnight, Liz! Goodnight.

(Beat. Tom enters, on his way back to the hall. He carries a roll of paper towels.)

(As he passes her) So—you teach acting.

(He stops.)

That must be very interesting. I love the theatre. In London I used to go all the time. I remember when I first came to the States—
TOM: Gemma, I'm tired.
GEMMA *(Over this)*: Uncle Alfred had invited me— I grabbed at the chance. I needed to get away. Perhaps like you needed to get away from New York and come up here—
TOM *(Turning)*: Alice invited me for this weekend. I didn't ask to come.
GEMMA: I'm sure she did, I didn't mean—

TOM: I had to get out of quite a few other commitments. It wasn't easy.

GEMMA: No.

TOM: I had other places I could have gone to. And then when—your father . . . What the hell was I supposed to do? I would have felt like I was abandoning—

GEMMA *(Over this)*: You don't have to explain.

TOM *(Continuing)*: I couldn't even get to the bus station. Alice wasn't going to take me. How could I ask—? I told her I'd only be in the way. With all of you coming— I asked her to let me leave. You think I'd want to put myself through—?! *(Stops himself)*

(Short pause.)

GEMMA: Thank God you stayed. You've been such a help.

TOM: I'm not hurt. I'm fine. You don't have to say anything. *(Beat)* There's a bus at nine. I found a schedule in your father's desk.

(Pause.)

GEMMA: What were we—? The theatre.

TOM: Gemma.

GEMMA: Anyway, I arrived here and I saw a show in New York. And there was this actor, long hair down to—almost growling, spitting as he talked. I remember thinking, is this acting? The growling, I mean. Then after about a year of living in the States, I began to realize I could not imagine there was anything else. Why do you have all those paper towels?

TOM: Alfred got sick in the study. Remember?

GEMMA: And no one cleaned—?

TOM *(Over this)*: I don't mind!

(Beat.)

GEMMA: What you must think of us.

TOM *(What has been on his mind)*: About the cremation, Gemma. Alice said to me—before any of you got here, when she had no one else to talk to—she said that Harry probably would not have wanted to be cremated. But it was something she believed in, so—she went ahead and did it. *(Beat)* She asked me if

I thought that was OK. *(Beat)* I don't mean to criticize Alice. But someone should know, I thought. Not that there's anything you can do about it now. I'm only saying, that sometimes Alice can say one thing to you and another thing to me. I wanted you to know that. *(Beat)* For Christ sake go to bed. *(Turns to leave)*

GEMMA *(Desperate)*: So where in London do you come from, Tom?

(Beat. He stops. From upstairs Alice screams a few times, still like a wounded animal.)

Where did you live?

TOM: Chiswick.

GEMMA: That's not too far from— Do you know Eel Brook Common? In Fulham, off the King's—

TOM: A friend of mine and I used to play tennis there.

GEMMA: My God, he knows our common!

TOM: There's a court—

GEMMA: Two! And a playground. It's not a very big common. Not that many people know it, in London.

TOM: Why should they!

(Beat.)

GEMMA *(Half to herself)*: That common is so close to where we lived!

(He turns to go.)

Tom! Ever since we got here, I've been wanting to tell someone.

(He stops to listen.)

I've got good news! I've been looking for the chance too . . . *(Beat)* I'm engaged.

(He turns back to her. Short pause.)

TOM: Congratulations—

GEMMA: He's American!

TOM: Why are you telling me—?

GEMMA: Like your girlfriend!

(Beat.)

TOM: I'm sure your family would be very interested in—

GEMMA: He's from New Mexico. He's even part Mexican, but his family has been here— Years and years.

TOM *(Over this)*: Why do I care about your—?

(Alice screams in the distance. This stops them both.)

GEMMA *(Referring to the scream)*: What a night. She's realized what she's lost. She's scared. God, let her sleep. *(Turns back to Tom)* My fiancé. He's big, you think of them as small—the Mexicans—but not him. He's tall. *(Beat)* Can't read at all, I think. He's my gardener. Or works for the man who does my garden. He doesn't know shit about art, music . . . As thick as a brick shithouse, his expression. A big dumb American like you see at the beach. *(Beat)* I love the way he feels. His body. And he's a nice man. Warm. Open. *(Short pause)* When I told father—he went crazy. *(Laughs to herself)* He said—what the hell is wrong with me? *(Beat)* He said—he'd given me culture. He'd educated me. He'd taught me right from wrong. I don't know what that had to do with— But it's what he said. Good from evil. Beauty from ugliness. And now—I do this— terrible thing. I told him he wasn't being fair. At least he should meet— But he just kept screaming at me: "Where have we gone wrong?" "Where have we gone wrong?" *(Beat)* "How did we get here?" *(Beat)* I didn't understand. But I'd never heard him shout like that—not at me. *(Beat)* "The barbarians are sweeping over us and all we do is kiss their ass." His words. I don't know what they mean. *(Beat)* I tried to calm him down. Usually I could find a way, but this time it was impossible. It just kept coming out. The anger. At everything. At me . . . I warned him, Tom—if he did anything to himself, I'd hate him forever! *(Short pause)* This was yesterday—this conversation. When I called—he was in his study. He'd been reading he said and—I could hear—listening to music.

TOM: Yesterday afternoon?

(Short pause.)

GEMMA: At first, when Alice phoned with the news—I blamed myself. I even thought *I'd* killed him. *(Beat)* I know that's unfair to me. I did nothing wrong. I was one thing maybe—a final straw to someone's . . . problem. It's taken me until now—to accept that it really had nothing to do with me.

(A single scream from Alice in the distance.)

(To Tom) Did it?

TOM: No. I'm sure it didn't.

GEMMA *(Suddenly relieved)*: I've put myself through so much today. *(Stands)* He should have been happy, dammit! With my news! I tried to tell him, Tom—we change. You have to. *(Starts to leave)* Thank you. I'll try and go to sleep now. Goodnight. *(Goes)*

TOM: Goodnight.

(Short pause. Tom hesitates, then picks up the roll of paper towels he'd set on the table, and he too heads into the hall, as Alice screams again.)

SCENE 8

The kitchen. Morning.

Alice, Alfred, Gemma, Elizabeth and Sophie are sitting at the table. Alfred is in a black suit, the women in black dresses. Two or three are drinking coffee. The table has been cleared of the papers, etc., and is very neat. In the center of the table is an urn—Harry's ashes.

SOPHIE *(Telling a story)*: There's a man—he's American of course. And he's standing in line to get into Buckingham Palace.

ALFRED: For the tour?

SOPHIE *(Nodding)*: And he asks the guard. *(American)* "When will we see the queen?" The guard says she's in Scotland. The man

is beside himself, he says, "The queen should be here! When
I go to Disneyland Mickey's there!"

(She laughs loudly, the others smile politely.)

My daughter told me that.

ALFRED *(To no one)*: Speaking of Disneyland, at least we don't have
one stuck in the middle of our country. *(Laughs)*

ALICE: Anyone want more coffee?

(Paul enters, also in a black suit.)

PAUL *(Entering)*: He's going to stay.

ALICE: Thank heaven!

ALFRED *(Same time)*: I would think—

GEMMA *(Same time)*: To leave now.

ELIZABETH *(Same time)*: Who did he think was going to take him to
the station?

(Beat.)

ALICE: And Harry's suit?

ELIZABETH *(To Alice)*: What about Father's—?

ALICE *(Over this)*: He hadn't brought a suit, of course. He was coming for a weekend!

PAUL: I rolled up the cuffs. He'll be OK. *(Sits)*

SOPHIE *(To Paul)*: I told them about the queen and Mickey Mouse.
They found it very funny.

ALICE: Thank God, it's a beautiful day. Did anyone else see the sun-
rise this morning, or was I the only one up?

*(Tom enters, wearing one of Harry's black suits, which is a few
sizes too large. The others look at him.)*

TOM *(After a moment)*: I don't want to look foolish.

(No response.)

GEMMA: Sit down and have some coffee. Make room— Let Tom
sit . . .

TOM *(Sitting)*: I didn't even bring a tie.

ALFRED *(To Tom)*: I never got to hear all your accents. I hear you do a very funny Midwest. Our dean's from the Midwest. *(Laughs to himself)*

TOM: I don't think I feel like—

ALFRED: I had a student stand up in class once, and say, *(American)* "You're nothing. Shut up!" *(Laughs)*

TOM: Paul told me the story—

ALFRED: He had a Midwest accent.

ALICE: We were just saying   it's a beautiful day.

GEMMA: It's not going to rain.

TOM: It rained last night.

ALFRED: Did it? When we went for our walk—

TOM: Later. I stepped out for a moment. And it was raining. Then I came back in. The guests are due in . . . ? *(Looks at his watch)*

ALICE: If you see a young woman, blond, very attractive—Harry's star pupil, the violinist—snub her. *(Short pause)* I'm terrible with names. Everyone—if I don't introduce you . . .

(Pause. Tom notices the urn.)

TOM: Is that the . . . ?

ALICE: I picked it up this morning. It was waiting for me. Do you want to look inside?

TOM: I don't think I need—

ALICE *(To everyone)*: The man at the funeral home, not the funeral director, but the little man who sits by the guest book—I think he works there. Anyway, he said to be sure, that when we throw the ashes—to keep our mouths closed.

(The others turn away.)

It's good advice! *(Beat)* Obviously there'd been a bad experience . . .

SOPHIE *(Standing and collecting the cups)*: If we're not going to have anymore cof—

GEMMA: Tom never got—

TOM *(Over this)*: I'm fine.

(Short pause as Sophie carries the cups off to the sink.)

ELIZABETH *(To Gemma)*: Did you know that father called her— Fifi?

ALICE *(Nodding to the urn)*: They had a catalog. I had no idea what Harry'd want. I picked that one out. It's nice, isn't it?

(Everyone quickly agrees that the urn is nice.)

A couple were quite gaudy. *(Shrugs)*

(Gemma notices Elizabeth looking at something on her lap.)

GEMMA *(To Elizabeth)*: What are you looking at?

ELIZABETH *(Holding up the photo album)*: Has everyone seen these photos—?

(Gemma grabs the album and hands it to Alice.)

GEMMA: Maybe you could make a few copies for us.

ALICE: Just say which ones you want.

GEMMA: Thank you.

(Alice starts to look through the album. Sophie returns from the sink, and goes and stands behind Paul, putting her hands on his shoulders.)

PAUL *(To everyone)*: Excuse me, if we have a minute . . . Sophie and I'd like to clear something up. *(Beat)* Yesterday—and God it was only yesterday when we arrived, wasn't it? *(Shakes his head in amazement)* When Sophie and I arrived— Elizabeth. Well, Sophie felt that you— When she came up to you to hug you? To console you? She says you turned away from her and ran to hug me.

ELIZABETH: Oh God! I don't remember—

PAUL: I didn't exactly see this either, but she says—

SOPHIE *(To Elizabeth)*: You sort of pushed me away—to get to Paul.

PAUL: And this hurt Sophie. Correct? But Elizabeth, you didn't mean to hurt her. That too is correct?

ELIZABETH: No. Of course— Why would I—?

PAUL *(To Sophie)*: There. That has been addressed and dealt with.

(Beat.)

ELIZABETH *(Needing to explain)*: I saw my brother. I wanted to hug him.

SOPHIE *(Wanting help)*: Paul.

PAUL: My Sophie is your sister-in-law. She wanted to console you. She wanted to be consoled herself. You should have let her do that. She has feelings, too. Our father's death—upset her as well. Is that right, Sophie?

SOPHIE: Maybe this isn't the time to bring this up . . .

PAUL: You asked me—!

SOPHIE *(Interrupting)*: But I'm sure your sisters want to know these things.

(Beat.)

ALICE *(Quietly, showing Alfred a photo in the album)*: Harry bought me this bathing suit. *(Looks at Alfred, then at everyone else)* I hope I didn't keep anyone awake last night. Alfred thinks it must have been either the egg rolls or the moo-shoo pork. What do you think?

PAUL *(Putting his arm around Sophie)*: She had just a bite of the moo-shoo and—

GEMMA *(Over this)*: Elizabeth—

ELIZABETH *(Over this)*: The egg rolls definitely!

PAUL: If we were Americans we'd sue!

(He laughs, others laugh. Beat.)

ALFRED: None of you probably know this, but last night—Alice and I had the chance to spend some time together.

(The others look down.)

To talk.

ALICE: We'd hardly known each other before. We'd only met the—

ALFRED: One time. At Paul's wedding.

ALICE: Paul and Sophie's wedding.

ALFRED: Alice couldn't make your mother's funeral.

ALICE: I sent flowers.

ALFRED: The one time. *(Looks at her)* I have asked Alice to come to Albuquerque.

ALICE: To visit!

GEMMA *(Over this)*: That's wonderful! And maybe even stay—

ALICE: I don't think—

ALFRED: Wait until she sees the colors!

GEMMA: Uncle Alfred's right—it's the colors, they'll shock you— they're lunar, that's how I describe them. *(Beat)* Alfred says they're vaginal.

(All except Paul and Elizabeth laugh.)

PAUL *(To himself)*: I suppose we see what we want to see.

(Beat.)

ELIZABETH: And what will you do about the house?

GEMMA: Elizabeth, we said we'd talk—

ALICE: Close it? Sell it? *(Beat)* And go west! That's what Americans are always doing, isn't it? At least for a visit. *(Beat)* I assume you want me to sell it. No one wants to live here? . . .

(Beat.)

GEMMA: We'll talk this afternoon—about the things.

ELIZABETH: Or tomorrow. *(To Paul)* Are you still flying back tomorrow?

PAUL: We can't stay—

SOPHIE *(Over this)*: Claire—

GEMMA: I'm going back tonight.

ELIZABETH: Tonight! You didn't say—

GEMMA: Into New York. I'm seeing friends. I'm hardly ever east anymore.

PAUL *(To Gemma)*: Tom's on the bus this afternoon—

TOM: Alfred was going to drive me into town—

GEMMA *(To Tom)*: I can drive you all the way in if you don't mind waiting until—

TOM: The bus is fine. I have the ticket.

(Beat.)

ELIZABETH *(To Paul)*: You're still here tonight.

(Paul nods. Beat.)

PAUL: Thanksgiving's in a month. Do we celebrate Thanks—?
ALICE: Sh-sh!

(Everyone is silent. Alice gets up and looks outside.)

I thought I heard . . .
SOPHIE *(To Paul)*: Are they late?

(Alice, who has picked up a book, opens it. She looks up.)

ALICE: If anyone asks, don't say anything about the college. Or if
you do, say Harry loved teaching there. Don't say the truth.
(Beat. Looking at the book) I thought, this was . . . right. Do you
mind? You'll hear it twice.

*(Everyone: "No!" "Of course not!" "Please." Alice looks at the
urn.)*

Once, only for the family, Harry.

*(She turns the urn so it "faces" her. She reads from Keats's "Ode
on Melancholy":)*

> But when the melancholy fit shall fall
> Sudden from heaven like a weeping cloud,
> That fosters the droop-headed flowers all,
> And hides the green hill in an April shroud;
> Then glut thy sorrow on a morning rose,
> Or on the rainbow of the salt sand-wave,
> Or on the wealth of globed peonies;
> Or if thy mistress some rich anger shows,
> Emprison her soft hand, and let her rave,
> And feed deep, deep upon her peerless eyes.

She dwells with Beauty—Beauty that must die . . .

(Pause. She closes the book.)

GEMMA: Father.

(Short pause.)

ELIZABETH: Paul? For the family? What did you plan to sing?

(Paul hesitates.)

ALFRED: Come on, Paul.

(He slowly stands.)

PAUL: I didn't know what to choose.
GEMMA *(To Tom)*: Have you ever heard him sing?
TOM: No, I——?
GEMMA: Come on, break our hearts. I haven't started to cry yet. You
    might as well get me going.
PAUL: I haven't sung in front of people for——
ELIZABETH: Why is it we have to apologize for everything?!!

(Beat.)

PAUL: OK. "Those of us who knew my father well"—this is my
    introduction—"knew my father well, will always associate
    this piece . . . with him. For you—Father. May you now have
    the peace you sought." *(Beat. Begins to sing "The British
    Grenadiers":)*

> Some talk of Alexander,
> And some of Hercules,
> Of Hector and Lysander,
> And such great names as these . . .

(With the first line the family bursts out laughing.)

GEMMA *(Over the singing)*: Great choice!!
ELIZABETH *(Over this)*: He'd love it!!
GEMMA *(To Tom)*: Father used to sing this while he shaved! It drove
    us crazy!
ALICE: He still does! Did!!

PAUL *(Continuing)*:
> But of all the world's brave heroes,
> There's none that can compare
> With a tow, row, row, row, row,
> Row, to the British Grenadiers!

(All except Tom try to sing along, banging the table to the march beat.)

EVERYONE:
> Whene'er we are commanded
> To storm the Palisades,
> Our leaders march with fuses,
> And we with hand grenades.

ALICE *(To Tom)*: Don't you know it?
TOM. A little.
GEMMA: Then sing!

EVERYONE:
> We throw them from the glacis,
> About the enemies' ears,
> With a tow, row, row, row, row,
> Row, the—

SOPHIE *(Shouting out)*: French!!!

EVERYONE:
> British Grenadiers!!!

(The family suddenly sings in a whisper, obviously as Harry used to do it. Whispering:)

> And when the siege is over,
> We to the town repair,
> The townsmen cry—

(The family shouts:)

> Hurrah boys,
> Here comes a Grenadier;
> Here comes the—

ALICE: Sh-sh!!!

(They stop singing. Beat. Alice goes and looks out.)

It's a car. The guests are arriving.

(Pause. Alice takes out a cigarette, lights it; takes one puff and puts it out. Everyone is straightening their clothes. Tom tries to straighten his.)

SOPHIE *(To Tom)*: You look good.

ELIZABETH: Paul, you better direct traffic. Tell everyone where to park.

(He nods.)

GEMMA: I can take their coats.

ELIZABETH: Put them upstairs.

PAUL: I thought it was outside—

ELIZABETH: Until everyone comes.

(They are on their way out.)

ALICE: Just one thing I meant to tell you.

(They stop.)

You should know this. *(Beat)* When people called—I told them, it had just been an accident. That Harry was cleaning his gun.

(She heads down the hall. The others look at each other and follow; Gemma tries to straighten out Tom's suit as they go.
*   The urn is left alone on the table.*
*   Debussy's* The Girl with the Flaxen Hair *begins to play.*
*   Off, the sound of greetings, condolences, cars arriving, offers to take coats, car doors closing, directions where to park, etc.)*

END OF PLAY

GOODNIGHT
CHILDREN
EVERYWHERE

For Zoe and Jocelyn

PRODUCTION HISTORY

Goodnight Children Everywhere was first performed by the Royal Shakespeare Company at The Other Place, Stratford-upon-Avon, on December 4, 1997. It was directed by Ian Brown; the set design was by Tim Hatley, the costume design was by Lucy Roberts, the lighting design was by Peter Mumford, the sound design was by Martin Slavin; the composer was Richard Sisson, the music director was Michael Tubbs, the production manager was Benita Wakefield and the stage manager was Monica McCabe. The cast was as follows:

BETTY	Sara Markland
ANN	Cathryn Bradshaw
VI	Robin Weaver
MIKE	Colin McCormack
PETER	Simon Scardifield
HUGH	Malcolm Scates
ROSE	Aislinn Mangan

Goodnight Children Everywhere was subsequently performed by Playwrights Horizons (Tim Sanford, Artistic Director; Leslie Marcus, Managing Director) by special arrangement with Gregory Mosher and Arielle Tepper on May 7, 1999. It was directed by the author; the set design was by Thomas Lynch, the costume design was by Susan Hilferty, the lighting design was by James F. Ingalls, the sound design was Raymond D. Schilke; the production manager was Christopher Boll, the production stage manager was Marjorie Horne and the assistant stage manager was Richard Costabile. The cast was as follows:

BETTY	Robin Weigert
ANN	Kali Rocha
VI	Heather Goldenhersh
MIKE	Jon DeVries
PETER	Chris Stafford
HUGH	John Rothman
ROSE	Amy Whitehouse

Characters

PETER, seventeen
BETTY, twenty-one, his sister
ANN, twenty, his sister
VI, nineteen, his sister
MIKE, early fifties, married to Ann
HUGH, late forties
ROSE, nineteen, Hugh's daughter

Setting

The living room of a flat in Clapham, South London

Time

Late spring, 1945

SCENE I

A large flat, Clapham, South London. Late spring, 1945.

The living room: chairs, a sofa, two small tables, one with photographs in frames. Three doors: one to the outside hallway and stairs, one to a hall which leads to two bedrooms and the W.C., and one that leads to the kitchen and the third bedroom (Mike and Ann's).

Ann, twenty, five months pregnant, sits on the sofa, her feet tucked under her, reading a book, or pretending to. Betty, twenty-one, fusses with the table.

After a pause:

BETTY: I remember on Peter's eleventh birthday Father turning on the gramophone, setting up chairs in a line, telling us to keep walking, then—grab a chair when he stopped the music. We couldn't stop playing the game. It was hysterically funny, do you remember?

(No response.)

There was one less chair, so . . . *(Beat)* Then it seemed like the very next day Peter was gone.

281

(Vi, nineteen, bursts in from one of the bedrooms.)

VI: He's here! I just saw them out the window!

*(Betty begins to fuss harder, mumbling, "Oh God, oh my God."
Vi rushes to the door, opens it, listens, closes it.)*

They're coming up the stairs!

*(Vi turns back to the room. She and Betty share a look. Betty stops
fussing and goes to her, takes Vi's hand and holds it tightly in hers.
Silence. Footsteps. The door opens.
Mike, Ann's husband, fifty-three, enters with Peter, the girls'
seventeen-year-old brother. He carries his suitcase.
Ann stands at a distance, watching.)*

BETTY: Peter! Oh my God, look at him! Look at you!

*(Betty and Vi rush him, hug him, they can't take their hands off
him. Mike watches with a smile.)*

(Still hugging Peter with Vi; to Mike) Was the train late?
MIKE *(Shakes his head, then)*: We missed each other. This photo you
   gave me . . . *(Holds up snapshot)*
BETTY *(Pulling Peter)*: Come in, come in. I've made you something
   to eat.
PETER: I'm not—
BETTY: Mike has extraordinary connections. The things he finds.
   Look at these chocolate biscuits.

(She has pulled him to the table. Peter notices Ann.)

VI: She wouldn't let any of us touch them.
BETTY: Take off your coat.

(Peter stares at Ann.)

PETER *(Smiles)*: I didn't know— *("about the pregnancy")*
ANN: One more surprise.
PETER *(To Mike)*: Congratulations.

MIKE: I mentioned on the way here about work in the surgery. We could use another pair of—

ANN: Later, Mike. Later. He's just got here.

(Peter tries to stop Betty fussing.)

PETER: Betty . . .

(He touches her hand, looks her in the eyes. She suddenly turns away and begins to cry. For a moment no one knows what to do. Ann goes and holds her.)

MIKE: It's a small surgery. Just me and another doctor. You'd get to do a number of things. Check in patients. We need the help. It's not charity.

ANN: Mike . . .

PETER: Thank you.

(Betty continues to sob on Ann's shoulder.)

MIKE: Betty is our nurse.

PETER: I know.

VI: Sit down, please, Peter.

ANN: How was the journey?

PETER: I missed a connection in Toronto. But I caught up. I met two—"boys" my age, who I hadn't seen since the trip over. Strange.

MIKE: You were in—

VI *(Answering for him)*. Alberta. *(Beat)* That's the left-hand side part. *(Looking at Peter)* You look like Father.

(She turns to Betty, who is trying to calm down, and who nods in agreement, staring at Peter.)

PETER *(Still standing with suitcase)*: Should I put—??

BETTY *(Breathing deeply, wiping away her tears)*: Mike and Ann, of course, have Mother and Father's room. Vi's moved in with me. So you have your old room back.

PETER: I didn't need my old—

VI: Father's library and the bathroom we had to give up.

PETER *(Confused)*: When—? *(To Betty)* You never wrote—
VI *(Explaining)*: They're another flat now.
BETTY: What was there to write?
VI: Maybe in a while— Mike thinks—we might get them back. Put it all back together. We have the kitchen.
BETTY *(Still staring)*: I used to bathe you. *(Smiles)* Please sit down. *(To the others)* He's a man.

(After a beat, this makes the others laugh.)

VI: What did you expect?!

(The laughter dies down. Awkward pause—what to say after so many years.)

MIKE *(Finally)*: I'm looking forward to hearing about Canada. It's a place . . .
PETER: That you'd like to visit?
MIKE: Not particularly. *(Smiles)*
PETER *(To Ann and Vi)*: And I'm interested in hearing all about Wales.
ANN: What's to tell? *(Shrugs)*
PETER: And Vi, you're acting.
BETTY *(To Ann)*: Listen to his accent.
ANN: I know.

(Peter has an American/Canadian accent.)

BETTY *(Answering Peter)*: Did you ever think she'd do anything else?
PETER: Mother would be pleased.
BETTY: I don't think so.
PETER: Father?

(They react, shake heads, laugh—of course he wouldn't be pleased.)

VI: I had an audition this morning. Do you know *Autumn Fire?*—
ANN *(Over this)*: It was on at the Duchess—
BETTY *(Over this)*: We saw it— When did we see it?

PETER: I don't know anything! I've been in Canada!

(Laughter.)

BETTY: It's very good.
VI: The part's Peggy. She's—
BETTY *(Over this)*: Tell him who Peggy is.
VI: She—
ANN *(Before she can explain)*: Just do the bit. What you did for the audition.
VI: But he just got here.
PETER: No, I don't *("mind")*—
MIKE: Which one is Peggy?
BETTY: Sh-sh.
ANN: Show him.

(Vi walks out, then returns as "Peggy.")

VI/PEGGY: "Hen, dear. It's been ages." *(Pretends to kiss "Hen")* "And Howard darling. You don't look ill at all. Or aren't you?" *(Trying to figure it out)* "Or wasn't that you? Is that brandy we're drinking?" *(Takes a sip of "Howard's glass")* "Mmmmm. Thank you. I was nearly sober. And—who—is—that?" *(Points to an imaginary man)* Hen says: "Have you met my cousin, Peter?"
BETTY *(Making a connection where there isn't any, to Peter)*: The character's name is Peter.
VI/PEGGY: "And where, Hen, have you been hiding such a man? Under your bed?" *(Holds out her hand for the imaginary man to shake)* "You—I'll see later." *(Walks across the room, to the imaginary Hen)* "A family secret, I suppose. Or is it—treasure."
MIKE: I'm going to pour myself a drink. *(To Peter)* Anyone—?
BETTY: He's only—

(Vi/Peggy sinks into a chair.)

VI/PEGGY: "There wasn't a living thing in all of Paris. Only the French."
BETTY *(To Mike)*: He doesn't want a drink.

(Peter notices the photographs on the small table, though he continues to watch Vi's audition.

Vi/Peggy sits, smoothing her crossed legs with her hand, as she continues:)

VI/PEGGY: "What a simply horrid week abroad. Thank God for champagne, or I'd actually remember it."

(Mike laughs, then Betty does, looking at Mike. Ann watches Peter who has picked up a framed photo, as he continues to watch.)

"What possessed me? No, I shall never again stray. I make this my oath, upon pain of death, never again shall I venture forth off this great island of civility, of kindness and beauty, and into the filthy godforsaken seas which surround it."

ANN *(To Peter)*: Then one of the characters—

BETTY *(Over this, explaining)*: Howard.

ANN *(Continuing)*: —asks, "So you'll never leave England again?"

VI/PEGGY: "England?! Who said anything about England? I was talking about—the Savoy."

(Laughter, and the audition is over. Peter sets the photo back down and applauds.)

ANN *(Teasing)*: Maybe mother wouldn't be happy.

(Laughter.)

VI *(All shyness)*: Peggy's supposed to be in her thirties. I told them I thought I was too young.

BETTY: You should let them decide—

VI: The tour's Grimsby, Warrington, Liskeard, and somewhere else, I forget. *(Beat)* They'll let me know. Maybe this week. *(Suddenly feels terribly awkward, everyone looking at her. Embarrassed)* Why did I do that? Of all things to— He just got . . .

(She turns away, quickly turns back to see Peter smiling and looking at her.)

What? Why are you staring?

(He suddenly goes and hugs her. This makes Betty start to cry again.)

PETER: Betty, please . . .
BETTY: Listen to that accent!
PETER: I'm sorry, but . . .
BETTY: I didn't say that it was bad.

(Vi breaks away, being very much the child now:)

VI: As long as Mother and Father don't find out.

(She hurries to the photo of their parents that Peter was looking at and turns it face down. Again laughter. Mike hands Peter a drink.)

MIKE: Here.
BETTY: He's seventeen years old!
MIKE *(Sipping his drink)*: My point exactly.
PETER: What I'd love is a cup of tea.
VI: I'll put the kettle on—
BETTY *(At the same time)*: I'll get it— *(Turns to Vi)* You do the kettle. I'll take his bag into his room. And see if the bed's made.
VI: I made it.
BETTY: And see if the bed's made—correctly.

(Betty and Vi hurry off, leaving Peter with Ann and Mike. After another short, awkward pause:)

MIKE: I'm standing there outside the buffet, holding up this photo—he goes by me—what, two or three times? *(Laughs and ruffles Peter's hair as if he were a boy)*
ANN: As long as it worked out—in the end. That's all that counts. *(Looks at Peter, then)* Come here.
VI *(Off, shouting)*: I'm so happy!!
ANN *(To Peter)*: Come here.

(Peter goes to her and she holds him, strokes his hair.)

I don't know what to say.

(She turns back to Mike who now sits, smiling, sipping his drink.
She turns back to Peter, begins to kiss his cheeks, rub his hair,
hug him, repeating:)

Look at you. Look at you. Look at you.

SCENE 2

Later that evening.
    Peter sits, plate of food in his lap. The others have eaten, plates to
their side or on the floor, or they have chosen not to eat.

ANN: At first—they seemed really nice. I was treated like I was
    someone special.

PETER: It was the same with me. Then—

VI: I didn't have this problem.

ANN: That's not true.

VI: She talks about this and—

ANN: You got as upset as I did.

PETER *(To Betty)*: You started to feel like they were thinking, Is this
    kid ever going home?

ANN *(To Vi)*: I saw how they looked at you. And how they looked
    at me. *(To Peter)* They adored the little ones.

PETER: In Wales you had to work?

VI: Work! What else did we do? What else did I do. I practically
    took care of her.

ANN: That's completely untrue! I was like—the mother, for God's
    sake.

VI: I don't believe this.

ANN: From the moment at the station, standing there with our little
    luggage labels with our names on them around our necks.
    When Mother let go of my hand—she put it in yours. I knew
    what she was saying. I was fourteen years old! But I held on.
    When they tried to separate us—who screamed? *(Beat)* Who
    took her fist and began hitting the lady who was trying to push
    my sister away into another queue? We're a family, I said. You
    can't separate us. *(Beat)* We're all we have. *(Beat)* This big
    house—the school was in one side, we slept in the other. This

was for about a month. Then we billeted with a couple. We slept together. *(Beat)* Vi and me. *(Beat)* He was a miner. He'd have his bath—we'd get our "Uncle's" bath ready—by the fire, then—off we go. Get out. Into the winter, summer—outside. Off you go. And wait. Sometimes we went to the pictures. Until Mum and Dad . . . And we weren't being sent any more money.

BETTY: I sent you money.

ANN: That's true.

(Pause.)

VI: They had a dog. A really nice dog—at the school. We loved the dog. A bit of a Labrador. Black. He began to follow me around. *(To Ann)* Remember? *(Back to Peter)* I took care of him. He slept at the foot of our bed. *(Beat)* I went to school. Came back. He was gone. He'd been volunteered to the army. Sniffing land mines in Belgium. I cried more than when Mum and Dad died.

(Short pause.)

PETER: Just a couple of days after I got to my "Aunt and Uncle's"—their big black-and-white cat had kittens. Nine. I was so—happy. To see them. Some—things—that—knew, understood—even less than me. *(Smiles, takes a bite)*

VI *(To Betty)*: I know what he *("means")*—

PETER: So my "Auntie," I suppose, seeing my—pleasure? She says, "Choose one, Petey."

ANN: Petey?

(His sisters giggle.)

PETER: It happened. I don't know how—

BETTY: Petey!!!

PETER *(Over their giggling)*: "Choose one! We'll have to drown the rest."

(The girls stop giggling.)

I look at those kittens in the barn. Each one. I touch each—
one. And I couldn't choose. It wasn't right to choose, I felt.
Auntie got impatient with me, and she drowned them all.
(Pause) When they put me in the field to work? I was put with
some Negroes. I said to Uncle—I'm a white man, I'm not a
Negro. And he took the palm of his hand and rammed it into
my head. I think I was passed out for about ten minutes. *(Beat)*
For weeks I thought about why he did that.

BETTY: He was probably trying to tell you that Negroes were just as
good as white people. He thought you were—

PETER: I thought of that. Sometimes I thought that was the reason.

(Beat.)

VI: Maybe he just didn't like someone questioning him.

PETER: Maybe. *(Shrugs)* In school there a kid hit me because he said
I had an uppity accent.

BETTY: You don't have a—

PETER: Then. I lost it. So maybe Uncle heard . . . *(Shrugs again)*
I never knew. *(Beat)* I feel there's so much I don't know.

ANN *(Agreeing with his confusion)*: Were we supposed to work or
not? Were we sent—to work? Was that part of the plan?

VI: We were sent to be safe?—

ANN: Why did I have to work? Margaret Wells? She came with us.
We were on the same train. We were at the same school— She
didn't work. Her "Auntie" taught her things. She had, I think,
two beautiful dresses that her "Auntie" embroidered . . . *(Beat)*
I've often wondered—did they put us together for reasons?
How did they—match us? Did they know something about
us—me? Or was it all—? When we got off the train— No one
had bothered to tell me this. *(To Vi)* You didn't tell me this—

VI *(Over this)*: What??

ANN: I'd obviously touched some soot on the train, and touched my
face with my hand—I saw it later in a window—there was a
streak of soot across my head. *(Shakes her head and smiles)*
Maybe when we were standing in the queue? Being—picked?
If I hadn't had that soot on my face—would I have learned to
embroider like Margaret Wells? Would I have been picked earlier, by someone—else? *(Short pause. To Peter)* You're not
eating.

(He holds up his plate, she takes it, looks at him, strokes his hair.)

PETER: I should go and unpack. *(He doesn't move)*
BETTY *(To Mike)*: This must be boring for you.
MIKE: No, no. It's not. I'll get another drink. *(Gets up and goes to get a drink, stops)* But just don't start blaming all those people. They interrupted their lives for all of you. They were heroes, in my mind. *(Goes off into the kitchen)*
BETTY *(To Peter)*: He's a nice man. A good doctor.
VI: He pays for all *("this")*
BETTY: I work.
VI: He and Betty.
BETTY: He's been very good to us all. Hasn't he, Ann?

(No response. This catches Peter's interest.)

(To Peter) She's never satisfied.
ANN *(Suddenly upset)*: How dare you say that?!
BETTY: If I can't say it, then who—
ANN *(Over this)*: Shut up! I said, shut up, Betty—
PETER *(Over this to Vi)*: What's??

(Vi ignores the question. Just as suddenly as they erupted, there is silence.)

(To Ann) How did you and Mike —meet?
VI: He works with Betty.
BETTY *(Correcting)*: I work with him.
VI: Betty brought him home.
BETTY: To meet my sisters. I had a crush on him myself, then.

(She laughs, no one else does.)

Ann and he make a wonderful couple. You knew that right away. They'll have a wonderful baby.
ANN: He's a nice man. As she says.
BETTY: Mother would have liked him. She would have approved. She was trying to become a nurse, you know.
PETER: I didn't—
BETTY: First it was a schoolteacher, then after the three of you went away, it was a nurse. She hadn't got that far when . . . It's why

she was out that day. *(Beat)* Mike, it turns out—isn't the world strange? It turns out was there as well. So she could have been one of the people he helped pull out. He helped pull people out from under all the . . . *(Beat)* I have often wondered . . .

VI: Father is buried in France. You knew that?

(Peter nods.)

BETTY: They sent us a ring. We don't think it was Father's ring.

(Mike returns with a drink. For a moment no one says anything. As he passes, Mike strokes Ann's head; she doesn't respond.)

VI *(Finally)*: At school they had attached a bell to a tree. We were told that if we spotted any enemy parachutists to run and ring that bell. *(Beat)* I could see the tree from my seat in the classroom. I used to daydream that like large snowflakes suddenly the sky was filled with parachutes. And no one else saw them. Everyone else was too busy—learning things. I ran out of the classroom. Reached the tree and the bell and began ringing it with all my strength. Soldiers suddenly arrived and captured all the bad people. Dad was always one of the soldiers. *(Pause)*

PETER: *I* used to dream of you. *(All of them)*

(He stands and goes and hugs each one in turn.)

I should unpack.

(He starts to go, but is stopped by:)

ANN: Vi was in a nativity play—playing Joseph.

PETER: Joseph??

VI: "Uncle" drew with coal on my face to make the whiskers.

ANN: She didn't know who Joseph was—

VI *(Same time)*: I didn't know who Joseph—

ANN: Then she's told he's—Mary's husband. And I tell her like Dad is Mum's husband. So she's there in the nativity, and everyone is watching, and she says: "Mary, give me a drink."

(Peter and his sisters all say: "Just like Father!!" and laugh.

Still smiling, Peter goes down the hallway to his bedroom. The others stop laughing.
    The sisters start to pick up the plates, etc.)

BETTY: He's got—so old.
MIKE: He's a boy.
VI *(Ignoring Mike)*: I thought I'd faint when I saw him.
ANN: He looks like Father.
VI: I see Mother.
BETTY: He used to be— He'd never sit still—
ANN *(Over this)*: He's tired. Think about what we look like to him.
VI: And the flat.
ANN: It must be . . .
VI *(To Mike)*: God it must be a relief for you—to finally have another man around! *(Smiles)*
MIKE: He's a boy—
VI *(Over this)*: Some—reinforcements against all us women!
MIKE: I haven't minded. In fact, I've rather enjoyed it.

(He laughs, as do Betty and Vi. As Vi picks up a plate, he leans over and tries to "pinch" her and she "squeals"—all a game they've played before. Ann shows no reaction to the pinching. Vi starts to head for the kitchen, laughing. As she goes, we hear Peter calling her: "Vi!" She turns and hurries down the hallway to him.)

BETTY *(To Mike)*: So what do you think?
MIKE: He's a fine boy. I like him.
BETTY: I knew you would.
MIKE: And I think we should be able to find a place for him in the surgery.
ANN: And not just sweeping floors, he needs to learn—
MIKE: I'll supervise his duties myself.
BETTY: Thank you.

(Beat.)

ANN: I mean it, Mike. Don't make promises you can't keep.

(This stops the room for a moment, then Betty turns to Mike.)

BETTY: You've been so good to us.

MIKE *(Shrugs)*: Remember I had a son. Not much older than your Pete.

BETTY *(Suddenly smiling)*: Or Petey as we now must call him!

*(She laughs.
    Suddenly Peter comes out of the hall wearing a full cowboy costume—chaps, hat, vest, spurs.)*

PETER *(Bursting in)*: Howdy, English folk!

(Laughter.)

And this is how they really dress in Alberta! *(Carries a couple of packages under his arm)*

ANN: I don't believe—

PETER: Except on Sunday for church, then they wear their fancy clothes! Hats out to *("here")*—

(But he is interrupted by Vi who appears in Indian clothes—her present from Peter. She has taken off her dress and put on a little Indian vest over her slip, hoisted up her slip and put on the skirt—looking sexy and a bit indecent. The others react, laughing.)

And here is Viohantas, Indian Squaw!! *(Turns to Betty)* And this is for you, Betty. *(To Ann)* And for you. *(Hands out their presents. To Mike)* I'm sorry, but I didn't get—

MIKE: Please.

PETER: And I didn't know about the baby when—

BETTY *(Opening her package)*: Where did you get the money? *(Opens the box, takes out a blouse. Immediately turns away, takes off her blouse and puts on the new one)*

MIKE *(During this)*: I'm turning away.

(The new blouse is low cut, exposing her bra.)

BETTY: How's this?

PETER *(Goes and touches her bra strap)*: You can't wear that with it.

BETTY *(Stunned; to her sisters)*: Since when did our brother become a women's fashion expert—? *(She turns, glances at Mike)*

MIKE: I'm not looking!

(She turns, takes off the blouse, then her bra, then starts to put the blouse back on. As she does, Ann opens her present—a necklace.)

ANN: It's gorgeous, Peter! Where did you—?
PETER: It didn't cost much.

(Vi, getting into being an Indian:)

VI: Remember we used to ride on Betty? She used to give Pete and—
ANN: Petey!
VI *(Grabbing Betty)*: Come on! Around the room!
BETTY *(Adjusting her blouse, ignoring Vi)*: What do you think? I don't think I could wear this out—
VI: Get down.

(Betty gets down, but continues to "ignore" Vi.)

PETER *(To Betty)*: Perhaps it's not meant to wear out, but rather—at home. With—whomever?

(He smiles. She nods, smiles, catches a quick look at Mike, then turns away.)

BETTY: I'll wear it around the house then.
VI: Come on, horsy. Let's go. Come on!

(Vi is on the back of Betty, who is down on all fours, though still seemingly oblivious to Vi.)

ANN *(At the same time, holding her new necklace)*: Peter, help me put it on.

(He goes to help. Vi now rides Betty, who constantly fiddles with the new blouse as her breasts are nearly uncovered though no one seems to notice.)

VI *(On Betty)*: Faster! Let's attack those Germans!

PETER: I think she's mixing up her wars.

VI: Yahoo!!!

ANN *(To Peter)*: I love it. *(Kisses him on the cheek)*

VI: Petey! You're next! Come on! Give her a ride! Come on!

BETTY *(To Mike)*: He used to do this all the time—

ANN: Come on!

> *(She drags him to Betty. Vi gets off, Peter gets on reluctantly; though doesn't put his whole weight on her. Betty rides around, begins to buck, as she used to when he was a small child. The others laugh as he tries to hold on. The phone rings, calming everyone down. Mike takes the call, then:)*

MIKE *(To Vi)*: It's for you.

> *(Vi takes it. Betty "whinnies" quietly, Peter slaps her bottom as he would a horse.)*

BETTY: Oh really!

> *(She suddenly bucks and he nearly falls off. Vi hangs up.)*

VI: I didn't get the part. The director.

> *(Beat.)*

BETTY: I'm sorry . . .

ANN: I thought you wouldn't hear until—

VI: He says he thinks I'm talented enough. He wants to have lunch.

ANN: He's after you?

> *(Vi doesn't respond, then:)*

VI: And he's something like twenty years older than me. *(Realizes what she has just said in Mike's presence)*

MIKE: God, then he must have a foot in death's door.

> *(He smiles, the others laugh. The faux pas is forgotten, or forgiven.)*

ANN *(Suddenly to Vi)*: Do you remember that when we used to play hide-and-seek, on rainy days, there was always a place that Peter would hide—and we never found him.

BETTY: I remember that.

VI: I don't remember.

ANN: Maybe you were too young. Maybe she didn't play.

VI: I'm older than Peter.

ANN: He was a boy.

VI: What's that—?

ANN: Where was that place, Peter?

(They look at him, then:)

PETER: Start counting.

ANN: What—?

BETTY *(Over this)*: What are we—?

PETER: Count!

(Ann looks at the others, then covers her face and begins to count. Peter and Betty go off to hide. Betty hesitates, then goes in a different direction. Peter goes off toward the kitchen.)

MIKE *(To Vi)*: Hide!

VI *(Whispers)*: Where?!

MIKE *(Whispers)*: Anywhere?

(He suggests behind the sofa. She hurries there, just as Ann finishes her count.)

ANN: Coming, ready or not—

(Peter walks back in. The others look at him.)

PETER: It was behind the ironing board in the kitchen cupboard. There's a hole. It's still there. *(Beat)* But I don't fit.

SCENE 3

The next morning.

Peter, barefoot, sits, his legs over the arm of a chair, a book in his lap. (He had been reading and is interrupted by Vi.) Vi stands in front of a mirror, straightening her clothes, fixing her hair. She wears her best clothes. As she fixes she talks:

VI: First this girl says to her "family" that she can't take communion. Her "Auntie" is all upset—we have a heathen in the
house! We've taken in a heathen! Then she has to tell them,
well—it's because I'm a Catholic.

(Betty enters, dressed. She carries toast on a plate.)

So she can't take communion.

BETTY *(Who has heard the story)*: But then she does.

VI: That's right.

BETTY *(Beginning to eat the toast)*: And she writes to her mother and
obviously—

VI: You weren't even there. *(Turns back to Peter)* Writes to her
mother and her mother writes to the local Catholic priest and
he comes to the house. And the girl tells him that, yes, she's
taken communion in the Protestant church and—

BETTY: And she rather liked it.

VI: And so the priest, he says to her, "Child you will never again be
allowed to take communion in a Roman Catholic service."
(Beat) Ten years old and he excommunicated her.

*(She leans over and begins to draw a line down the back of her
leg—to look like a stocking seam.)*

Finally they had to find another family for her. She became—
nervous. *(Finishes the seam, and turns to Betty to explain her
clothes)* They're making a picture in Leicester Square. *(Reaches
for the newspaper, tosses it to Betty)* Looking for people to be
society. You have to bring your own clothes. Pays a guinea for
the day. And lunch. *(Turns back to Peter)* How did we get started talking about . . . ?

*(Suddenly, with newspaper still in hand, Betty goes to Vi and tries
to lift up her skirt.)*

(To Betty, pushing her hand away) What are you—? Stop it!

PETER: Betty?!!

VI: Get away from me!

(Beat.)

BETTY *(Explaining)*: I just wanted to—to make sure she was wearing her drawers.

VI: Why wouldn't I—??

BETTY *(To Peter)*: Her audition yesterday? She came home and told me—while you were waiting to go in, she was sitting next to a girl. Vi notices her lift up her skirt—to cross her legs—and nothing. *(Turns to Vi)* So—? What?

(Vi says nothing. Betty continues to explain:)

So what does she say to Vi? You're staring at her and what does this "actress" say?!

VI *(Quietly)*: "We'll see who gets the part."

PETER: That's disgusting.

BETTY: Isn't it.

VI: That's not what it's usually like. And you don't have to tell everyone—

BETTY: He's your brother! And he's a man. What do you think about that—as a man?

PETER: I said, I thought it was disgusting.

BETTY: He's disgusted, Vi.

VI: She didn't get the part!

BETTY: How do you know that? Did you get it?! *(Reaches to look again under Vi's skirt)*

VI: It's not even an audition. It's only an extra!!!

(Betty flips up the skirt. Vi has her drawers on. Betty lets the skirt fall. Vi is upset, nearly in tears. She moves away from her sister.)

I have to go. Excuse me. Where's my hat?

(Peter gestures.)

BETTY: Let me get the shopping money and I'll walk with you as far as the tube.

(She goes to the kitchen. Peter and Vi look at each other for a moment.)

PETER *(To say something)*: Betty doesn't have to work today?

VI: The surgery doesn't open until noon on Tuesdays.

PETER: But Mike left—

VI: He goes to the hospital on Tuesday mornings. *(Beat)* Betty does the shopping on Tuesdays. Ann used to do it but with . . .

(Betty has returned with coat and bag.)

BETTY *(More explanation)*: And I don't mind one bit either. Ann shouldn't be carrying heavy . . . anything. Mike wouldn't hear of it, for one. *(To Vi)* He's so—thoughtful. Mike. Isn't he?

(Vi nods.)

We think Ann's the luckiest woman in the world. Don't we?

(Vi hesitates, then nods. Short pause. Betty stands looking at Peter.)

PETER: What?

(Beat.)

BETTY: Seeing you there, like that—with a book. You know what I just remembered? What I just realized I miss? Sitting around—together—all reading together. To each other.

VI: When have we ever done that?

BETTY *(Staring at Peter)*: Not for years.

(Beat.)

VI: Did Mother used to read to us?

PETER *(Shakes his head)*: No, Father did. *(To Betty)* For what? About a month? He'd come home from the newspaper and he'd read to us. Religiously—for a month. Then it just stopped. *(Shrugs)* Why?

BETTY: I don't know.

VI: How do you remember and I don't?

PETER *(Over this)*: It's a good thought. We should do it.

BETTY: Now that we're all together.

PETER: Exactly.

(Beat.)

BETTY: I feel like I don't know anything.
PETER *(Holding up his book)*: I doubt if Zane Grey is going to make you feel—
BETTY: It's a start.

(She turns, notices something about Vi's collar that isn't right, so she straightens it as a mother might. Then without saying anything more, they leave.

Peter puts down his book, goes to the screen or clothes rack and tub that lean against a wall. Sets the tub upright, places the screen/rack around the tub, then heads off to the kitchen.

After a moment, Ann enters from her bedroom. She wears a dressing gown. She goes and sits on the sofa, stands, turns on the radio, quickly turns it off. Sees the leftover piece of toast, takes a bite.

Peter returns carrying two large buckets of water for his bath.)

ANN: God, are my sisters loud.
PETER: Did we wake you?
ANN: You didn't.
PETER: I'm going to take a bath. Is that all—?
ANN: You live here, Peter.

(He smiles, nods, goes behind the screen and begins to pour the water in. Ann watches, then:)

We had such a nice bath, remember? It had little feet and little claws. So you could pretend you were on some animal. Or flying bird.

(Peter pours the second bucket.)

PETER: I never pretended that. *(Beat)* But it was a nice big tub.

(Short pause.)

ANN: But now we have a telephone. *(Looks at the phone)* That's something good. Better. *(Explaining)* Because of Mike and the surgery—

PETER: I assumed.

ANN: So we mustn't assume that everything just gets worse.

(Peter looks at her. She looks away.)

I think I pee twenty times a night. Did *I* wake *you?*

PETER *(As he heads back to the kitchen with the buckets)*: I slept like a baby.

ANN: You're home.

(Peter's gone.)

PETER *(Off)*: What?!

ANN *(Calling)*: I said you're—

(She stops herself. Takes another bite of toast. Looks at Peter's book. He returns with another bucket.)

I said you're home.

(He looks at her. He's forgotten the conversation.)

Never mind. Where's . . . ?

PETER: Vi's gone to be in a picture. Betty's shopping. *(Goes to pour the water into the tub)*

ANN: I used to go shopping.

PETER: But now you have to be careful what you carry.

ANN: Do I? Is that warm?

PETER: I've been heating it on the stove. *(Goes again)*

ANN *(Continuing the shopping drift)*: The queues are forever! You need the patience of Job!

(Peter's gone, Ann continues but really to herself or no one.)

Or nothing else to do. And that is just the impression you get standing in some of those endless queues—that people now have nothing to do. *(Beat)* Or nothing they want to do.

(Peter returns with another bucket.)

PETER: So now Betty does the shopping. That must be great for you. *(Starts to go to the tub)*

ANN *(Holding up his book)*: You reading this?

PETER: Yes, I—

ANN *(Reading the inscription)*: "To Petey from your Auntie Fay."

PETER: She gave it to me as a going away—

ANN: *Riders of the Purple Sage.* Kids book?

PETER: Not necessarily.

ANN: Looks like a kids book.

PETER: It's—

ANN: Do you miss her?

(Beat.)

PETER: What??

ANN: Do you miss her? "Auntie Fay?" *(More adamant)* Do you miss being called "Petey"?!! When you left we called you Peter!!

(Short pause. Peter goes behind the screen and pours the water into the tub. He comes out—sets down the bucket.)

Full?

PETER: Enough.

ANN: What do you remember of Mother?

(Peter is stopped by this.)

Betty remembers—so much more than me. But then she was here. She wasn't sent away. She was the lucky one—right?

PETER *(After a beat)*: Yes.

ANN: Is that what you think?

PETER: Ann—

ANN *(Almost yelling)*: That she was the lucky one?! I'll tell you about your sister. Put this in your head. *(Beat)* When Mother took Vi and me to the station, Betty was with us of course. She's told me, walking home with Mother, Mother all of a sudden fell onto the pavement and started sobbing. She hit her fists against a wall. She crawled. Betty, who wasn't very large— isn't, but certainly wasn't then—tried to pick her up. *(Beat)* At sixteen she suddenly saw a lot. When mother died, Father was home on leave. So when the telegram came, Betty had to read it—to Father, who, because it was ever so slightly ambiguously written kept saying—"But there's still hope, isn't there? Isn't there? Please tell me that there is hope." *(Beat)* So she had to convince him. Convince those two sky blue watery eyes. Convince Father that Mother was—gone. *(Beat)* Lucky her.

PETER: I didn't—

ANN: Take your bath.

(Peter just looks at her.)

(To herself, rubbing her eyes): I need sleep. *(Reaches over and turns the radio back on—dance music plays)* Young man, there are things you don't know . . . *(Shrugs)* Come here.

(Peter comes to her.)

Raise your arms.

PETER: What? Why—?

ANN: I said, raise your arms.

(Peter is confused, but he raises his arms. She looks at him seriously, then suddenly tickles him hard in the armpits. He pulls away.)

(Laughing) You are such a sucker! You always were! Do you do everything anyone asks you to do?!

(Peter looks at her totally confused.)

Grow up. Take your bath. It's getting cold.

(Peter turns and heads for the screen.)

Not only does he sound like a Canadian. He's come back with the wits of one!

(Peter stops, thinks of what to say, says nothing, then goes behind the screen to take his clothes off and get into the bath.)

Do you mind if I stay . . . ?

(No response. She listens to the radio for a moment. Behind the screen Peter is undressed. We hear him get into the water.)

Did Betty tell you we're having company tonight?
PETER *(Off, behind the screen)*: Some doctor—
ANN: I tried to tell Mike—your first full day here, why do we need—
PETER *(Off)*: He's trying to help me, Ann.

(Beat.)

ANN: Hugh. That's the man's name. Hugh. *(Beat)* Betty's been trying to hook him.
PETER *(Off)*: That's not the impression—
ANN *(Over this)*: And God knows I hope she does. Maybe then she'd move those doe eyes of hers off my husband.
PETER *(Off)*: Ann, I don't want to—
ANN *(Over this)*: Not that he doesn't encourage her. Not that he doesn't encourage all of them. Wait till you see his other nurse—she looks like she's twelve. He likes them young, that should be clear. *(Beat)* Isn't it?

(No response.)

Peter?
PETER *(Off, behind the screen)*: This doctor, Betty said, was invited so I could meet him. Mike's trying to give me a choice. This man needs help, too.

(Beat.)

ANN: Oh. So that's the reason he's invited. I'm sorry—I got it all terribly wrong.
PETER *(Off)*: Ann, Betty said—
ANN: Oh—Betty said, Betty said! Let me tell you something—you believe everything your sisters tell you, Petey, and I fear for your future.

(Beat. Then Peter suddenly finds this funny and laughs. Ann smiles and laughs, too.)

PETER *(Off)*: I don't care why this Hugh is—
ANN: Sh-sh! I like this.

(A song has come on the radio she likes. It is "Goodnight Children Everywhere." Peter listens as well, so that for a moment we don't hear the water moving around.)

RADIO:

> Goodnight children, everywhere
> Your mummy thinks of you tonight.
> Lay your head upon your pillow,
> Don't be a kid or a weeping willow.
> Close your eyes and say a prayer
> And surely you can find a kiss to spare.
> Though you are far away
> She's with you night and day.
> Goodnight children, everywhere.

ANN *(Over this)*: Vi and I had a special signal when this came on. We'd snap our fingers . . . *(Snaps them once)* . . . and it meant "Mother." That I was thinking about Mother. And . . . *(Two snaps)* Father. No one else knew.

RADIO:

> Sleepy little eyes and sleepy little head
> Sleepy time is drawing near
> In a little while
> You'll be tucked up in your bed
> Here's a song for baby dear:
> Goodnight children, everywhere . . .

(The pain is nearly unbearable, finally Ann turns it off before it finishes.)

PETER *(Off)*: They played that in Alberta, too. Some American lady sang it.

(Pause. Then from behind the screen Peter snaps his fingers once. Ann nearly collapses when she hears. She then snaps once as well.)

(Off) When the letter arrived about—Mother—Auntie read it to me. They'd sent it to her, to open it. *(We hear him play with the water, slap it—to do something)* Auntie read it out loud over the kitchen table, then folded the letter very carefully, put it back into the envelope, then handed it all to me. *(Beat)* She kissed my head and said, "They are savages. In Europe, that's what they are. No better." And then she took me outside—into their garden—and pointed to the mountains. "There," Auntie said, "is a better world. Mountains don't lie. Mountains don't cheat. They don't murder. They don't make war." And then we both cried.

(Ann picks up the photo on the table and looks at her parents.)

That night, she brought out photos of Mother.

(Ann is amazed by the coincidence of picking up a photo and having Peter, who can't see her, mention photos.)

Not at all like those on the table there. Of Mother and Auntie dancing. *(Beat)* You knew that Mother had been a dancer—
ANN: I think maybe I forgot.
PETER *(Off)*: Really? So maybe that's where Vi gets her acting—
ANN: I don't know.

(Beat.)

PETER *(Off)*: In fur coats. With their arms around each other. Kicking out a leg. Auntie had spent two years in London. They looked like children. Mother and her. Younger even— than us. With big smiles on their faces. Auntie said they were best friends. For those two years. *(Beat)* It's how Mother met Father—dancing.
ANN: What??
PETER *(Off)*: According to Auntie. And she was there. *(Beat)* There was another photo—they're in some costume with feathers, black shoes with a strap across—
ANN: Mary Janes.
PETER *(Off)*: I kept asking Auntie—what's this? When was this? She said, she couldn't remember. She just had the photos.

(Beat) Then she pulled out one of us. Betty, Vi, you and me. I couldn't be more than two. *(Beat)* There we were sitting in a drawer, thousands of miles away from here. *(Beat)* I didn't even know Mother knew her. I thought she was a farmer's wife. Then she brought out the photos.

(Short pause.)

ANN: I had to look through Mother's clothes. There was a dress— like that. With feathers. I thought it was . . . for a party. It's still in the cupboard . . .

(She goes to talk to Peter behind the screen, we hear him splash as he tries to cover himself up.)

PETER *(Off)*: Ann! *(Short pause)* What are you staring at?
ANN: Nothing. Nothing. *(Comes back out)* I'll get that dress out. Wouldn't it be great if it is the one in the photograph you saw? *(Goes and looks in the mirror)* I could try it on . . . *(Short pause)* Mike thinks I'm going to stay fat.
PETER *(Off)*: You're not fat, you're pregnant! Did he say—?
ANN: It's what he thinks. His first wife was terribly skinny.
PETER *(Off)*: I didn't know he had a first—
ANN: She was young, too. Then she got older. Why did you give Betty and Vi those pretty clothes and me a necklace?
PETER *(Off)*: What?

(Again Ann goes behind the screen.)

ANN *(Off)*: Why did you do that, Peter?
PETER *(Off)*: Ann!!!

(Short pause.)

ANN *(Off, quietly)*: What's that?

(He has an erection.)

PETER *(Off)*: I'm sorry.
ANN *(Off)*: Don't be. Me?

PETER *(Off)*: Ann, I'm trying to take a—
ANN *(Still from behind the screen)*: The first erection I ever saw, he
was a miner, he was all black.
PETER *(Off)*: I don't want to know, Ann.

(Pause.)

ANN *(Off)*: You going to do something with that?
PETER *(Off)*: It'll—calm down.
ANN *(Off)*: Will it?
PETER *(Off)*: Not if you keep staring at it.
ANN *(Off)*: And if I touch it?
PETER *(Off)*: Ann, what are you . . . ?

*(From behind the screen we hear the water move around as Ann
touches Peter.)*

ANN *(Off)*: If you don't want me to . . . Say something.
PETER *(Off)*: Ann.
ANN *(Off)*: Something besides Ann.

*(She is masturbating him. The water sounds get quicker, as her
hand moves quicker, then splashing, then he comes.*
   Silence.
   *Ann comes out from behind the screen, trying to dry the arm she
has just had in the water. She is shaking.*
   *She sits, unable to say anything. From behind the screen no
sound whatsoever.)*

(Finally) Mind if I turn on the radio?

*(She does. Music. We hear Peter get out of the bath. He puts on his
trousers and comes out, holding his shirt. As he reaches Ann, she
grabs his shirt.)*

Look at that. Let me darn it.

*(He stands uncomfortably, not knowing what to do with himself,
with his hands, etc. Music continues on the radio.)*

(With the shirt) My God, was there no one looking after you?
*(Gets the sewing box and sits. After a moment she looks up, smiles
at him, then begins to darn. As she sews:)* At school in Wales,
there was this big sign—official poster from the government:
"What girls can do to win the war." What jobs— Like—
(Nods to her darning) "Study your sewing machine," it said.
"Snug slippers from old felt hats." But we didn't have any old
felt hats in Wales . . . things to fix—so you wouldn't depend
upon, I suppose, your father. Get used to him not . . . there??
"When a drawer sticks . . ." Vi and I used to pretend that our
"drawers" were stuck— *(Mimes underpants stuck. She looks at
Peter who smiles)* They can get a child to believe anything.

*(Peter comes up to her. He is still shirtless, sockless. He looks at her
from behind, holds her shoulders. She sighs and leans back.)*

I'm sorry.

(He touches her hair, then leans down and tries to kiss her.)

No!!

(She pushes him back and slaps his hand. He is very confused now.)

No. *(Rubs her eyes, then)* Some days I lie awake in bed and
I think—but I'm still a child myself. What the hell am I doing
having a baby? *(Beat)* But I'll be a good mother. Won't I?

(He hesitates, then nods.)

I think I'm ready. I was like a mother to Vi for so long. *(Beat)*
And before that, before you—left—to you.
PETER: I thought Betty mostly—
ANN: We shared. She dressed you. *(Beat)* I bathed you.

*(Suddenly the door bursts open and Vi enters. Ann and Peter nearly
jump, and move quickly and guiltily away from each other.)*

VI *(As she enters, noticing nothing)*: It's raining! They won't be
shooting outside. At least I didn't waste my money on the tube.
(She is off down the hall to her room)

ANN *(To Peter)*: Have you finished your bath?

(Beat. Peter goes and turns the tub over into a drain. As the water pours out, Vi returns, having taken off her blouse. She carries another shirt. She wears a bra but doesn't seem in the least bit self-conscious in front of her brother.)

VI: So what are you two doing today?

ANN: I have some cleaning and washing —

VI: Peter, what about you?—

ANN *(Over this)*: Mike's asked him to drop by the surgery this afternoon. See what he thinks.

PETER: I don't think I'm ready for that yet. I think I want to take my time before—

VI: Then come to the pictures with me!! *(Puts her arm in his, still both shirtless)* I hate going alone. A girl alone—they come out of the woodwork. *(To Ann)* Don't they?

ANN: I wouldn't—

VI *(To Peter)*: Come on, protect me! I'll put my arm around you and pretend you're my big boyfriend. *(Laughs. She goes to get the paper)* What's showing? It'll say in the . . . Where's—?

(She sees the paper. Ann heads off.)

PETER: Where are you—?

ANN: I have a headache. I'm going to lie down. *(Starts to leave, stops)* Vi?

(Vi turns to her.)

Peter's not a little boy anymore. I don't think we should walk around like that in front of him.

(She goes. Vi smiles, then looks at Peter and smiles, then as she looks through the paper, she rather self-consciously puts her blouse on and begins to button it.)

SCENE 4

That night.
    Vi sits at the upright, slightly out-of-tune piano, playing as the others sing. The others now include Hugh, late forties, and his daughter Rose, nineteen. Betty is in the kitchen.

ALL *(Singing)*:
        The Bells of St. Mary's
        I hear they are calling
        The young loves
        The true loves
        Who come from the sea.

        And so my beloved
        When red leaves are falling
        The love bells shall ring out
        Ring out for you and me.

    (They finish, but Hugh, who has been standing and singing enthusiastically, starts one more chorus—alone. Vi plays for him. He has an OK voice, though obviously thinks it is a very fine one.)

HUGH *(Singing)*:
        The Bells of St. Mary's
        I hear they are calling

    (He sits on the piano bench next to Vi. He looks at her and smiles as he sings.)

        The young loves

    (He puts a hand on Vi's shoulder.)

        The true loves
        Who come from the sea.

    (Vi, without missing a beat, pushes his hand off her shoulder.)

        And so my beloved
        When red leaves are falling

(He gestures for all to join in.)

ALL *(Singing)*:
    The love bells shall ring out

(Peter tries to catch Ann's eye, but she won't look at him.)

    Ring out for you and me!

(As they finish, Hugh laughs and applauds the others. They laugh and applaud as well.
Mike, who has been holding a tray of drinks, begins passing them out. When Hugh gets his, he raises it to Peter:)

HUGH: And Pete, my boy—welcome home to England!
PETER *(Under his breath, correcting)*: Peter.
ALL: Welcome home!

(Those who don't have glasses reach for one, and the "welcome home" sort of fades out around the spilling drinks, clinking glasses, etc.)

ANN: And how we've missed him.

(Peter suddenly turns to Ann, who turns away. Betty enters from the kitchen carrying a cake.)

BETTY: Did I hear "welcome home"?!

(Reactions from the others: "Look at this!" "Oh my God!" "It's beautiful!" "A cake!" etc.)

(Over this) Four eggs went into this!
VI *(Explaining)*: We pooled our coupons.
BETTY: It's just out of the oven.

(The others smell.)

PETER *(Touched)*: Thank you.
BETTY: It was Ann's idea.

(Peter turns to Ann, hesitates.)

VI: Go ahead and hug her. She's not going to bite.

(Peter gives Ann a gentle hug of thank you.)

(To the others) Why are men like that with pregnant women? They think they're going to break them?

(She laughs. Ann smiles, first at Peter, then at the others.)

MIKE *(About the cake)*: Why are you showing him now? We haven't eaten.

VI: As if he couldn't smell it.

MIKE: What happened to surprises?

BETTY: We've had enough surprises.

HUGH *(Over some of this)*: A cake! So now we start to have cakes again! Now there's a sign that it's all over.

MIKE: I think it's just a cake.

HUGH: I haven't even *seen* four eggs together since— Things are back the way they used to be!—

BETTY *(To Ann, over this)*: Is that what a cake means?

(Ann shrugs.)

I'd better take it back.

VI *(Standing)*: I can do that. Sit down, Betty.

BETTY: Supper will be ready—in ten minutes.

(Vi takes the cake from Betty.)

PETER *(To Betty)*: Beautiful cake. Really.

BETTY *(Pinching his cheek)*: For my baby.

HUGH *(To Vi as she starts for the kitchen)*: I'm sorry about—putting my arm on . . . I didn't mean . . . It must have been a—reflex?

(He smiles at her. This has got the attention of the room. Vi says nothing and leaves for the kitchen.)

MIKE: What did you do?

HUGH: At the piano, I touched her shoulder. She flinched— You'd think I'd . . . *(Laughs)* I didn't mean—

BETTY *(Suddenly grabs his hand and puts it on her shoulder)*: Here. You can put it here. *(Laughs)* All of us don't mind.

(The others laugh. She wears her new blouse—without a bra. Hugh catches a quick look down her blouse.)

HUGH: Nice blouse.

BETTY *(Turns to Peter and says a little too loud)*: See!

PETER *(To Ann, confused)*: See what?

ANN *(Ignoring Peter)*: All he gave me was a necklace.

(She is wearing it. Rose turns and looks at it and smiles. Beat. Then, as Vi is out of the room:)

HUGH: She's a charming girl, Vi.

MIKE: She is.

HUGH: Plays the piano—very nicely. *(Turns to Betty, whom he is still holding)* She's the youngest?

PETER: No, I am.

HUGH *(To Betty)*: An actress too? I can see that.

BETTY: Why are we talking about Vi?

ANN *(To Rose)*: What about you, Rose, any brothers or sisters?

(Rose shakes her head. Hugh grabs her and hugs her—she barely lets him.)

HUGH *(Hugging Rose)*: All alone in the world, poor baby. *(As he hugs her, he turns to Peter)* So you were gone   five years?

PETER: Nearly six.

HUGH *(Still hugging Rose)*: My God, will our children ever forgive us?

MIKE *(Sipping his drink)*: What choice was there? So what is there to forgive us for?

BETTY *(Looking at Peter)*: Still—look how well he's turned out. Except for the accent! *(Smiling, goes to Peter)* And we'll get rid of that!!! *(Starts tickling him)*

PETER *(Trying to get away)*: Betty, stop it! Stop! Ann!

(Ann doesn't move.)

ROSE: I think he sounds like a movie star.

BETTY: A movie star!! Oh that's even worse!! *(Tickles him even more)*
HUGH *(Over this, nodding to Rose)*: Her mother ran off with an American.

(This quiets Betty.)

(To Rose) When was this? *(Smiles)*
ROSE: You know very well.
HUGH *(Continues)*: August '43. A journalist. He comes to talk to me about the demands of surgery. At home. What we have to cope with. I told him—we work twelve-hour days. "Don't you even come home for tea?" he asks. "No, sir. Not these days." Then for some reason—I come home for tea—and guess who's in bed with her mother? *(Laughs)* So there he is, trying to put on his trousers and he's shouting at me: "You lied to me! You lied to the press!"

(Laughter. Perhaps Hugh laughs a little too hard.)

BETTY *(Laughing, still a little giddy)*: Father would have liked that. *(To Rose)* He was a journalist.
HUGH *(To Rose)*: She's where now? I always forget.
ROSE: No, you don't.
HUGH: Cleveland, Ohio. I found a magazine with some pictures. Looks like a godforsaken place. *(Shrugs)* But I'm sure she's right at home.

(Short pause.)

ROSE *(Quietly)*: That's not how it happened.

(Vi comes out of the kitchen, everyone turns to her.)

VI *(Confused)*: What??
ROSE *(Graciously)*: You're an actress, I understand. You sing and play wonderfully well.

(Vi smiles, but is still a little confused why she is the center of attention.)

BETTY: She was almost in *Autumn Fire*.

ROSE: Which one—?

HUGH *(Interrupting)*: Rose sings. *(Beat)* Sing.

ROSE: Father—

HUGH: Like a bird. And dances. *(Turns to Peter)* When she was a kid, she used to pull up her skirt and really kick like she'd seen in the pictures. It was the sweetest thing—and sexy. *(To Rose, smiling)* I can say that now.

ROSE: Father—

PETER: I'm sure—

HUGH *(Over this, continuing)*: Now she's going to be a teacher. And that's very clever, isn't it?

PETER *(Being polite)*: How interesting—

HUGH *(Over him, to Ann)*: You know you've got lots of company, don't you?

ANN *(Confused)*: Company? What . . . ?

HUGH *(To the room)*: I don't think a day goes by— *(Turns to Mike)* Does it?

MIKE: I don't know what you're—

HUGH *(Continuing)*: —without two, three, sometimes five, even six women coming in—pregnant.

ANN: I do know two or—

HUGH *(Not listening)*: It's like a—what's the word I'm looking for?

PETER: Plague?

(Others laugh, then Peter laughs.)

HUGH *(Laughing)*: No! Anyway, I figure, and I've talked about this with Rose—and I think she's listened—it's teachers that are really going to be needed now. Someone to take care of all these bloody babies. *(Beat)* It's the field right now.

BETTY: Sounds like it.

HUGH: And Rose has got it worked out so . . . Tell them.

ROSE *(Embarrassed)*: Tell them what, Father?

HUGH: That if—you—how it's not a waste . . .

ROSE *(Biting the bullet)*: If I study to be a teacher and—and I get married, then well, I haven't really wasted my time. I can put what I've learned into helping my own children.

HUGH *(Rubs her head)*: Clever, isn't she? And realistic. Did you know that there are nearly two girls for every boy right now? *(To Peter)* Maybe you shouldn't be hearing this. *(Laughs)* For every healthy boy. So you've got to be realistic. *(Beat)* Betty's realistic.

BETTY: Am I?

HUGH: I've seen you at Mike's side. He'd better be careful or I'll steal you away! *(Laughs)*

BETTY *(Over the laughter)*: Please, steal me away!

(More laughter. She catches Mike's eye.)

MIKE *(Joining in the "joking")*: You'll have to fight me first!

BETTY *(Smiling)*: Is that really true?

(The laughter subsides, then:)

MIKE: Seriously, Betty's a fine nurse. Any surgeon would be lucky to have her at his side. *(Looks at Betty, then "presents her")* And she cooks!

(Peter laughs, thinking this is still the joking, but no one else does. Suddenly the conversation has taken a more serious tone.)

HUGH: I'm looking forward to supper. *(Turns to Betty)* And that is a very handsome blouse.

BETTY: Thank you.

MIKE: She manages the whole household. Doesn't she?

(He turns to Ann and Vi, who say nothing.)

BETTY: And I keep the books.

PETER *(Confused)*: What is—?

ANN: Sh-sh. *(Hits him to be quiet)*

(Hugh stares at Betty, who stands perfectly still.)

HUGH *(Finally)*: And you're the oldest.

(Betty nods.)

Usually the oldest is the most responsible. Most trustworthy.

MIKE: When Ann and Vi returned from Wales—Betty was like their mother. She did everything. *(Looks Betty over again)*

HUGH: I can't believe you wouldn't miss her, Mike.
MIKE: I know I would.

(Short pause.)

BETTY *(Finally)*: Dinner should be ready. Excuse me. *(Goes off to the kitchen)*
PETER *(Half-whisper to Ann)*: Isn't he going to look at her teeth?
ANN: Sh-sh!
MIKE *(To Hugh, as he fills his glass)*: Always the responsible one. She runs the surgery for me, Hugh. There are days when I think why did I even bother to come in.

(Beat.)

ROSE: Are you looking for a nurse, Father?

(No response. Suddenly Hugh turns his attention to Vi:)

HUGH: But you—you are a wonderful singer. And I love—to sing. As you probably figured out.
VI *(Barely hiding the lie)*: And you sing very well.
HUGH: Thank you.
ROSE: If a little too loudly.

(They laugh. Hugh turns back to Vi.)

HUGH: You sing. You play. You act?
VI: Yes. *(Stands, feeling awkward, caught in his stare)*
ANN: When we were at school, Vi won third prize for her singing.
HUGH: Only third prize?
VI: This was in Wales.
HUGH: Of course. What sort of plays do you like to act in?

(Vi doesn't know how to answer.)

I've always thought that backstage in a theatre must be one of the most—I don't know—there must be a real kind of excitement. Of life. Actors rushing around, changing costumes— right off the stage, I'm told— Waiting. Anticipating. Then!

(Slaps his hands) I've had two patients who were actresses. I know something about acting.

(He stares at her, then she goes and sits. He turns to Ann.)

And you, Ann, we haven't said a word about you.
ANN: I don't think Mike will let you steal me away.

(Laughter.)

(To Mike) Will you?

(More laughter.)

HUGH *(Looking at her)*: I haven't delivered enough babies. I should deliver more. *(Beat)* They're inducing more and more now, aren't they, Mike? It's so much easier to schedule that way. You go from one to the next, I'm told. And it's even safer for the mother, isn't it?
MIKE: As soon as her waters break, we plan to induce.
VI *(To Ann)*: Do you know about this?
ANN: Mike's told me what to expect.
MIKE: Which isn't much. We'll put her under. She won't feel a thing. She won't even know what's happening to her.

(He takes Ann's hand and squeezes it. Hugh suddenly turns to Peter.)

HUGH: Rose here, Peter, is also a very good cook.
ROSE: Daddy!
PETER: That's— *("nice")*
HUGH: And smart as a whip.

(He points to her head. Betty suddenly bursts out of the kitchen, wearing Peter's cowboy hat, and announces:)

BETTY: Dinner is served!

(The others react to the hat: "What's that?" "Peter's!" "Take it off.")

HUGH *(As they are going; to Betty)*: That's what I imagine my wife wearing now.

ROSE: I don't think they wear cowboy hats in Cleveland, Ohio.

VI: Is that where she——?

(Hugh suddenly interrupts by putting his arm around Vi and whispering something.)

Go ahead, if you want.

MIKE *(Stopping Peter)*: Peter, can you help me collect the glasses?

(As the others head off, Hugh breaks into another chorus of "The Bells of St. Mary's." Only Betty joins in. They are off.
Peter starts to collect the glasses.)

Do you like Rose?

(This stops Peter.)

You don't mind that she's here.

PETER: Why would I mind?

MIKE: Good. She's just a little older than you, I think. But probably not nearly as——experienced?

(He tries to smile, Peter looks at him, is about to say something, when:)

(Biting his nail) Ann talked to me about this morning.

(Beat.)

PETER: What about this morning?

MIKE *(Seemingly changing the subject)*: Today in surgery there was Mrs. Jones. She was with her husband—Mr. Jones. *(Smiles at the obviousness of this and continues)* She's been fainting. Dizzy. You could see the disease in her eyes, Peter. They both looked at me, expecting. Hopeful. This man had served his country. *(Beat)* I knew she was dying. I could have told them this. *(Beat)* They could have spent the next—months? Building memories? I could have begun this for them. But instead,

I said—something like: "Your wife, Mr. Jones, has a thirty to forty percent chance of extending normalcy through this year." "Thirty to forty percent?" I heard him say. "Better than we had hoped." Translated, what I said meant—she might maybe live through the remainder of this year—these next seven months, but probably not. But they heard something different. I'm a coward, Peter. I can't . . . It's not in my nature, I think . . . Don't hate me for that. *(Smiles at his own exaggeration. Then, holding out his arm)* That's me! Now you know me!

(He smiles. The singing from the kitchen has stopped. Ann appears.)

ANN: Mike? Peter?
MIKE: In a minute.

(Peter looks at Ann, who returns to the kitchen, from where we start to hear "The White Cliffs of Dover." Mike sighs, this is obviously very difficult for him. He sighs again, then:)

She told me about seeing you in the bath and what that made her feel, Peter. *(Tries to smile)* And then you sent her back to her room. Thank you. A child's punishment for a child's . . . *(Beat)* Good for you. And that is what happened.
PETER: Are you telling me—?
MIKE: And that is what happened. *(Stares at Peter, then)* Women when they are pregnant, Peter—I speak as a doctor—well they don't always do the rational thing. That's an understatement. *(Smiles)* So it's up to us. To help them out. Not let their—emotions—get the best of them. *(Beat)* She was embarrassed when she told me. Even contrite. Now I suspect she's forgotten the whole thing. As should you. As will you. *(Suddenly a big smile)* Come here! Here. *(Grabs him and holds his head)* God, I know this can't be easy. But know that you have me. All right? Anytime you want to talk. Need an ear. *(Steps back, holds open his arms as he did before)* That's me!
VI *(Off)*: Mike!!
MIKE: Coming!! *(Slaps Peter's shoulder)* I'll get Rose to help you with those . . . *("the glasses")*
PETER: I don't need any—

MIKE: She's a good-looking girl.

(He winks and goes. Peter picks up a few glasses. Rose appears.)

ROSE: I'm supposed to help . . .

(From the kitchen we hear: "Are we eating?" "Start serving," etc.)

Are those all the glasses?

(He hands her one.)

Thanks. I suppose we should take them back in the kitchen. *(Beat)* Do you ever go to the pictures? I love the pictures. I never say no to anyone who asks me to go to the pictures.

(Peter hesitates, then, without saying a word, heads for the kitchen. Rose, a little hurt, follows.
    Off we hear their arrival: "At last!" "Now can we eat?" etc. And the scooting of chairs being moved around the table, the murmur of talk. Then the clinking of a glass as Mike tries to get everyone's attention for grace.)

MIKE *(Off)*: Dear God, Father of us all, we ask You to bless this our table and we, Your children . . .

SCENE 5

Later that night.
    Radio is on—the glow of the yellow dial is the only light visible. Ann sits alone, curled up in a chair, smoking.
    Noise off, footsteps, voices, etc. Door to the outside hallway opens—Vi, Betty, Peter and Mike enter talking.

VI *(Teasing)*: Come on. Come on, Betty! Say what you think of him!
    (To the others) She won't say. Why won't she say?
PETER *(To Ann)*: You're sitting in the dark.

(They start turning on lights.)

VI: Is he your type? Is he not your type?
BETTY: He's not my type.
VI: He's not her type.

(They are taking off their coats, etc.)

Well I thought he was sort of good looking.
BETTY: I know you did.
VI: What is that supposed to mean?

(No response.)

ANN *(To Mike)*: What happened?
VI *(Continuing)*: So—I think you're making a mistake.
BETTY: What sort of mistake am *I* making, Vi?
MIKE *(To Ann)*: About Hugh.
VI: A doctor. Not bad looking. Divorced. *(Still teasing, Vi winks at Peter)*
BETTY: You don't know anything.
VI *(Smiling)*: I think she fancies this man, that is exactly what I think.
BETTY *(Upset, but the others don't see this yet)*: He's looking for a nurse! *(Turns to Mike)* Did you know that? I couldn't just leave you.
MIKE *(Smiling)*: You do what you want. *(Turns to the others and smiles. Leans over and kisses Ann on the head)* How's the headache?
ANN: I'm all right.
BETTY *(Erupts)*: So I just do what I want?! I don't think I even know what that is anymore! I think I've forgotten even what that means!
ANN *(Concerned)*: Betty—
BETTY *(Very upset now)*: I think it's been beaten out of my skull! I think all I know now how to do is take care of people! Do what you want!!

(Vi suddenly smiles. Confused, she turns to Ann.)

(To Vi) Go ahead and laugh at me!
VI: I wasn't laughing at—

BETTY *(It comes out)*: He was all over you, Vi.

VI: What??

BETTY: And you encouraged him!!

VI: I did no such thing.

BETTY: You selfish little girl. You've always been so selfish!

ANN: Stop it, Betty! Stop it!—

BETTY *(Over this)*: I saw you crossing your legs. We're talking about something else and suddenly—it's legs. How he likes legs! *(Beat)* I hate my legs. I hate them.

(She starts to cry and runs off to her bedroom.
     The others are stunned, having had no idea how serious this was.)

ANN: What . . . ?

VI: I did nothing. Nothing!

ANN: Something must—

VI: I think the guy's a joke. A moron. Why would I try and pick him up? *(Beat)* She's insane. *(Shrugs)* She shouldn't drink.

PETER: She hardly drank anything.

VI *(Yelling)*: Then I don't know what her problem is. Don't blame me!

MIKE *(Quietly)*: She must have heard . . .

VI: What?

(Beat.)

MIKE: Hugh and I were talking— I told him to—sh-sh. And Betty was walking back from the ladies. He looked at her—he said he thought her ankles were thick. *(Beat)* I didn't think she heard . . .

ANN: He said that?

MIKE *(Making light of it)*: We were looking at all the girls. Not just Betty. This one's nose is too small. This one's . . . you know. *(Suddenly remembering)* He liked her breasts. He said—Betty's got nice breasts. But thick ankles. So it was sort of—balancing: this is good, this is not as good . . . *(Beat)* He didn't mean anything by it. In his defense, he . . . *(Shrugs. Pause)*

ANN: She must like him.

VI: Not necessarily.

ANN: True.

(Suddenly the phone rings. They look at each other, then Vi picks it up.)

VI *(Into the phone)*: Hello? Oh . . . I'll look. *(She covers the receiver)* It's the tactful—Hugh. He's lost his hat, he wonders if he left it here.

(They immediately see it on a table. All point. Vi starts to uncover the receiver, then has a better idea. She sets the phone down and goes to the hallway and calls.)

Betty! Telephone! Betty! Betty!!

(Betty appears, very hesitant.)

It's—Hugh.

(Betty starts to go back. Vi grabs her.)

He's lost his hat. It's right over there. Tell him.

(Betty tries to leave again, Vi holds her.)

Tell him!

(Suddenly her sister and brother see what Vi is doing and join in: "Tell him, Betty! Please, Betty! Tell him! Tell him!" Even Mike joins in, but without really knowing what is going on. Ann, Vi, and Peter plead: "Betty!"
Betty finally goes to the phone, picks it up.)

BETTY: Hello? . . . It's Betty. Your hat's here.

(She starts to hang up. But Hugh has said something.)

What? . . . Thank you. It was Mother's recipe actually . . . I'll write it down if you like and post it . . . What? *(Beat)* Tomorrow? . . . Let me think. *(To the others)* Am I free tomorrow night?

(The others just stare at her.)

Yes, I think I am free. That would be very nice indeed. Thank you so much. Goodnight. *(Hangs up. Short pause)* He asked me out. On a date. I think I'll do the washing up now. *(Turns and starts to go, then stops and speaks to Mike)* He's a nice man. I like him. *(Smiles, turns to the others and tries to make a joke. Patting Mike)* And if I can't have Father here, then I'll have to settle for Hugh. *(Realizes what she has just said)*

PETER *(Quietly)*: Father??

BETTY *(Embarrassed)*: I mean—Mike. Mike here. I'm just joking Ann. *(Tries to laugh. Then, to say something:)* He's taking me to dinner. Hugh.

(She goes. No one says anything for a moment, then:)

VI: I'll help Betty.

MIKE: What was that all about? Sometimes I walk into this house and I feel I don't have a clue about what's going on. *(Turns to Ann, and Peter near her)*

PETER: I should probably go to bed.

VI *(Goes to Peter)*: Funny, your sisters, aren't they? *(Kisses him on the cheek)* Thanks for taking me to the pictures.

PETER *(To Ann and Mike)*: I'm sorry to report I didn't have to fight anyone off! *(Smiles)*

VI: And thanks—for coming home. Goodnight. *(To Ann and Mike)* I'll help Betty do the washing up. 'Night.

ANN: Goodnight.

(Vi goes into the kitchen.)

VI *(Off, to Betty)*: So I'm a selfish little girl, am I?

BETTY *(Off)*: I'm sorry, I didn't mean—

VI: I'm joking, I know—

(Door closes and we don't hear any more.)

ANN *(To Mike)*: I won't be long.

MIKE: I'll get myself another—

ANN: You've had enough to drink. Go to bed. Peter can keep me company.

(Peter is surprised by this. Mike looks at him, nods, then:)

MIKE: I'll read. *(Goes)*
ANN: I think he has a girlfriend. His nurse. *(Beat)* What do you think?

(Peter shrugs and goes to the bottle on the tray.)

What are you doing?
PETER: I want a drink.
ANN: You're seventeen years old! And I don't know what Mike is doing taking you to a pub—

(She tries to take the bottle away, Peter holds it out of her reach.)

PETER: Father gave me my first drink years ago. Right in this room.
ANN: What are you talking about—?
PETER: I was ten, I think.

(Ann suddenly realizes.)

ANN: Oh my God, are you drunk?!
PETER *(Over this)*: He poured me a beer. Then another. Then a third and I threw up. He said, "Son—if you're going to drink, then I want you to learn to drink right here in your home." *(Beat)* Well, I'm home. *(Pours himself a drink. Beat. Points toward the kitchen)* Maybe I should help.

(No response. He sits.)

I want to go to bed. *(Sips his drink)* Why did you talk about this morning with Mike?
ANN: Because . . . *(Shrugs)* he's my husband? I don't know. *(Beat)* But I didn't tell him what happened. Because nothing happened, Peter. We have to face that. Accept that. *(Beat)* Mike was terribly interested—in my feelings. He was almost sweet about it. *(Beat)* I think it was the doctor in him.
PETER *(Interrupting)*: I could have stopped you, this morning, you know.

ANN: Stop what? What happened? You sent me to my room. A naughty, naughty girl. *(Suddenly)* It was a dream! I'm not a freak! I hate it that you're drinking by the way. I really hate it.

(He sets down his glass.)

So—how was little—what's-her-name?
PETER: Who?
ANN: Hugh's—
PETER: Rose.
ANN: I knew it was some—form of vegetation. *(Beat)* She was a late addition to the night, did you know? Mike asked Hugh to bring her along for you. *(Beat)* After our talk— His conclusion was that you needed a date. Did you know that she was your date?
PETER: Yes.
ANN: Oh. *(Beat)* I look at you and see a ten-year-old boy. I've got to get used to this. I thought she was dear. Sort of. Maybe you should ask her out. Or maybe you have? I've got a little pocket money, you could take her to the pictures. She obviously likes the pictures. Let me give it to you . . .

(She gets out of the chair and goes to get her purse. Peter stops her, holds her arm. She shakes him off.)

No.

(Peter suddenly erupts.)

PETER: What game are you playing with me?!

(Beat.)

ANN: No game. None. *(Stares at him)* I'm trying to be—good. I'm trying to close my eyes and say: "Mother, please tell me what to do?" *(Beat)* There is no one in the world I'd rather hold— than you. To hug. To touch. I want you pressed against me. Breathing each breath with me. *(Beat)* I see the boy. I see—the brother. I see the man. Like pages in a book flicking by—faster and faster. Never stopping. All blurring into the next, Peter. All—at the same time. *(Beat)* I love you so much.

(Short pause.)

PETER: And what does Mother say?

(Laugher from the kitchen. Ann looks at him, then shrugs. Peter leans over and kisses her on the cheek.)

ANN: Tell me—was that a brotherly kiss? Or . . . tell me, Peter, because otherwise I should hit you. Should I hit you? *(Suddenly turns away)* Remember having to line up in the kitchen, when we'd all done something wrong? Mother had that big wooden spoon. Where was Father?

PETER: Probably drunk.

ANN: Probably on business. *(Continuing)* You were the youngest. So you were the last. And by then Mother would always say, "Now I think I've made my point." She couldn't strike you. Her daughters—no problem.

PETER: I remember being hit—

ANN: By us! We hit you, Peter! We took you out into the garden and gave you a good beating!

(She laughs. Betty and Vi come out of the kitchen, laughing, the best of pals now.)

BETTY: We're leaving the rest till morning. And I don't care if that's a sin! *(Noticing Ann and Peter smiling)* What??

VI: They were always the closest.

BETTY: That is true, isn't it.

VI: I used to be jealous.

PETER *(Explaining)*: Ann was telling me how you'd take me out to the garden—

ANN *(Same time)*: When Mother wouldn't hit him! With his cricket bat!

PETER: Cricket bat?

VI: Betty held you down.

BETTY: I was the strongest!

VI: And I made a little mark with my fingernail on the bat. For every smack—

BETTY: You hated that so we kept doing it.

PETER: I don't remember the bat.

VI: I'm sure it's here somewhere. This family throws nothing away.
(To Betty) Do we?
BETTY *(To Ann)*: By the way, I'm sorry about earlier . . .
ANN: Please.
VI *(Going up to Peter as if to kiss him on the cheek)*: Goodnight.
(Suddenly tickles him)
BETTY: He was always a sucker. Goodnight little brother!
PETER: Goodnight.

(They are halfway down the hall.)

ANN *(Calling)*: I'm going to bed, too!

(Vi and Betty are gone. Peter and Ann are again alone. Pause.)

(Then, as if picking up the old conversation) Anyway, I'm ugly.
A handsome boy like you—why would you want me?

(Peter looks at her.)

PETER: You're the most beautiful woman I know.

(Short pause.)

ANN: Have you ever had a girlfriend?

(Peter hesitates, then shaking his head:)

PETER: No.

(Short pause.)

ANN: Not even—"Auntie Fay"?
PETER *(Seriously)*: Stop it.
ANN: Sorry. It was a joke. Come here. Come here.

(Peter approaches her. Stops.)

PETER: Are you going to tickle me?

(Ann smiles, and shakes her head. She takes his head and presses it against hers. She kisses his cheek, his ear, his neck, then looks at him.)

ANN: At least I have better legs than Betty.

(This suddenly makes them both laugh, and equally suddenly this laugh turns into a passionate kiss. They pull away, breathless.)

I'll come to your room with you.

PETER: But—

ANN: Mike's asleep. I'm sure he's asleep. *(Beat)* I'll just check.

(She hurries toward her bedroom, leaving Peter alone. He waits, touches his face, sighs, bites his nails. Then, after a long pause, Ann returns.)

(Without looking at Peter) Mike wants another drink.

(She pours a drink and exits.)

SCENE 6

The next morning.
Peter, barefoot, but dressed, sits on the sofa, pretending to read his book.

BETTY *(Off, from her bedroom)*: Vi!!! I hate this! I look like I don't know what! Vi!!!

(Vi comes out of the kitchen.)

VI: I'm coming . . .

(Mike is right behind her, he holds his teacup.)

MIKE: Will you tell her we have to go—?

BETTY *(Off)*: Vi, help me!

VI *(To Mike)*: Tell her yourself—

MIKE *(Over this)*: Betty!! We have to—!!

(Betty enters from the bedroom. She wears one of Vi's tight-fitting dresses.)

BETTY *(Entering)*: I can't even bend over in . . . *(Tries, stops)*
MIKE: I like it!
BETTY: I'm not going to believe a word you say.

(She smiles. Mike laughs.)

MIKE *("Innocently")*: Why not? *(Laughs and winks at Peter)*
BETTY *(Turns to Vi, about the dress)*: Look, you can actually see the crease in my bottom.

(Mike "leans over and looks" and winks at Peter.)

VI: Is that bad?—
BETTY *(Over this)*: I can't walk in it. What else have you got? *(Heads for the bedroom)*
MIKE: Betty, we have to go to work! Can't you do that—?
BETTY: When? I get off at six. *(Turns back to Vi)* In this he'll think I'm a bloody whore.
VI *(As she and Betty go)*: I very much doubt that.

(Vi and Betty are gone.)

MIKE *(To Peter)*: Extraordinary. In the surgery—she's like a rock.

(He looks at his watch. Ann has entered in her dressing gown.)

There she is! Sleeping Beauty awakens! *(To Peter)* There's something to be said for a house full of women, isn't there? *(Back to Ann)* She walks. She talks. Or does she?
ANN: Good morning. *(Kisses Mike on the cheek as she passes him. Goes to the sofa. To Peter)* Is there room there?

(Peter moves and she sits down.)

(To Peter) Morning.

MIKE: Cup of tea?

PETER *(Starting to stand)*: I'll get you one.

ANN *(Stopping him)*: No, no, please. I don't want anything.

(Peter sits back down. Ann pats his knee.)

How did you sleep?

(Betty and Vi burst back into the room. Betty is now in her underwear; she holds a blue dress in front of her. Vi holds another dress.)

BETTY: Ann, which do you think, the blue or the green?

MIKE: Betty, I'm leaving in two minutes.

PETER: Wasn't the blue one Mother's?

(This stops everyone for a moment.)

BETTY: Was it?

PETER: I'm pretty sure.

VI: I think it was, he's right.

(Beat.)

BETTY: Then it's the blue one. Mother would have liked that.

VI: The hem's too low though. *(Leans down and pulls up the hem, revealing more and more of Betty's leg)* How's this? *(Higher, teasing)* How's this?

BETTY: Stop it!

VI: He'd like it like that! We know he likes legs.

(The others laugh, Betty pretends she didn't hear it.)

BETTY *(To Peter)*: You really remember Mother in this?

PETER: I think so.

(Betty sighs, presses the dress against her chest and starts to head back to her bedroom. As she turns, Vi notices a hole in Betty's underpants.)

VI: Betty, you can't wear . . . *(Sticks her finger in the hole)*

BETTY *(Hitting her hand away)*: What are you doing?

VI *(Sticking her finger back in the hole)*: There's a hole. You can't wear these—

BETTY: He's not going to see my—

MIKE *(Over this, turning)*: I'm not watching!

VI *(Over this, to Betty)*: Are you so sure of that?!

(Betty hurries out of the room.)

(To Betty, out of the room) Really, it's like dressing a child. *(Follows Betty off)*

MIKE *(Calls)*: I'm going, Betty! *(To Ann and Peter)* Tell her I've gone.

(He goes to the sofa, leans down and kisses Ann on the head. She rubs his arm with her hand.)

(To Ann) I forgot to tell you, Hugh mentioned last night that there might be a flat available in his building. I'll try and find out more.

(Ann freezes.)

PETER: What?

MIKE: Ann and I have been looking for our own—

ANN: No we haven't. Not for months.

MIKE: We just didn't find any—

ANN: We decided to stop looking. We liked it here—

MIKE *(Over this)*: We need our own flat!

(Suddenly Ann and Mike are shouting at each other.)

ANN: My sisters are here and my brother!

MIKE: Your sisters could have their own rooms!

ANN: And when the baby's born—

MIKE: That's my point!

ANN:—to have aunts and an uncle—to help, Mike!

MIKE: I'm going to look at the flat!!

ANN *(Waving her arms, gesturing to this flat)*: And who'll pay for—!!?

MIKE: I will pay, dammit!!!

(Pause. Mike looks at Peter, who turns away.)

ANN: This is an important conversation, we just can't—
MIKE: I have to go.
ANN: You're always doing this—
MIKE: Good-bye.

(He goes. Short pause. Betty hurries out of the bedroom, now in her nurse's uniform.)

BETTY: Where's—? *(Looks around, realizes Mike is gone)* Bye. Good-bye. See you tonight.

(She quickly kisses Peter on the top of the head, touches Ann's shoulder and hurries out after Mike. We hear her footsteps down the steps.
Vi appears in the doorway.)

VI: She's like dressing a doll. She has that much knowledge of clothes.
ANN: Well, I'm sure you helped . . .
VI: I tried. I did my best. *(Starts to put on a sweater)*
ANN: Where are you going?
VI: Into town. They might be filming that picture in Leicester Square. It's not raining today. *(Beat)* You two going to be OK?
PETER: Yes. I think so.
VI: Don't wait on her, Peter. She's stronger than she looks. And she's more than capable of taking advantage. I can swear to that.
ANN *(Smiling)*: Be quiet.
PETER *(Smiling)*: I'll—be careful.

(Vi goes to the door, stops.)

VI: You don't feel I'm abandoning you, do you?
PETER: You have to work. And Ann's here. And we did go to the pictures yesterday.
VI: True. That's true.
ANN: Now it's my turn—to be with him.
VI: Right. Good. See you later then.

(She goes, leaving Peter and Ann alone on the sofa.)

ANN *(Quietly)*: Bye. *(Turns to Peter, then turns away and stands)* So
. . . I hate Mike.

(Peter looks at her.)

You heard him. Sometimes I hate him. And sometimes I say to
myself, You shouldn't stay with someone you hate. And
I believe that. *(Shrugs. Picks up Mike's teacup)* Tea?

*(Peter shakes his head. Ann starts to head off for the kitchen, then
returns right away.)*

Father used to do that to me. *(Beat)* I remember once, he had
a taxi waiting. I helped him down with his bag. He let me. He
helped me help him. And as he was getting in after a glance
at the ticking meter? He said, "Ann, I've decided which school
you're going to." Then taxi door slam, and he was gone. No
discussion. Nothing. *(Beat)* Like you're a—thing to be told.
Like you are nothing. *(Beat)* I'm going to clean today. You can
help me. Move the chairs around, that sort of thing. *(Short
pause)* It's because of you that Mike's looking for another flat.
Suddenly we're—"crowded." *(Beat)* All I ask is for the
opportunity to talk about things. Before decisions are made.
Before things are done, and can't be—reversed. *(Looks at
Peter)* You are so young. I can't believe how young you are.
(Beat) So what are we going to do today? Should we talk about
it? *(Short pause)* I love this flat. I must know every inch.
(Pointing to the sofa) I remember God knows how old
I was—certainly not old enough to "get it"—but I came
around that corner. And there was Mother and Father on that
sofa. Right there, Peter. Her blouse was—it was hanging off
her shoulder. She was sitting on Dad. *(Beat)* The upholstery is
the same as it was then. We haven't changed it. *(Beat)* I'm not
going to the pictures with you. I've stopped all that. You can
go yourself if you want. *(Short pause. Thinks, then)* You step
outside today—just one foot out of your home—and it all
makes no sense anymore. And it's been building up to this for
a while. *(Suddenly remembers)* About a month ago, I was out—

You know the shop—it used to be a greengrocer's near the
surgery on High Street? Of course you don't know it. Well it's
reopened. And do you know what they're selling—the only
thing they are selling as far as I could tell? Crows. Dead crows.
Rows and rows and rows of hanging black crows. They're selling them—to eat, I think. *(Beat)* Go and have a look if you
like. Quite a sight. *(Short pause. Comes and sits next to him,
takes his hand, puts it on her stomach)* It's kicking. *(Her mind
drifts away)* You try and make sense—You start to ask yourself—should I do this? Should I do that? *(Beat)* You have such
a wonderful smell about you. *(Takes his hand and holds it)*
We're all alone. *(Pause. Suddenly stands)* I need to go for a pee.
Excuse me.

(She goes off down the hallway to the W.C.
Peter is alone. He sits, nearly frozen.
Ann returns, tying her dressing gown.)

Walking past your room, I noticed you haven't made your bed,
Peter. *(Beat)* If you'd like, I could make it. *(Beat)* Could
I make it? *(Beat)* I'll go and make your bed, Peter.

*(She goes off down the hallway to his bedroom. Peter watches her
go, stands, and follows her out.)*

SCENE 7

Early evening.
   Peter sits on the sofa, his book in his lap.
   *There is a knock on the door. Peter does not respond. Another
knock.*

VI *(Off)*: Is that the door? Peter, will you get it?!

(Peter does not move. Another knock.)

Peter?!

(Another knock. Vi hurries on from her bedroom.)

Did you hear the door?!

(Suddenly it is like Peter "comes to"—he really hadn't heard it. Vi opens the door, and there is Hugh, flowers in hand.)

HUGH: May I come in?
VI: Please, of course. Betty will be— Shall I take those? *(The flowers)*
HUGH *(Joking)*: They're not for you.
VI *(Embarrassed)*: I know. I meant—

(Hugh laughs a little too loudly.)

HUGH: And where is that beautiful sister of yours?—
VI: She'll be out in—

(Ann appears in the kitchen doorway.)

HUGH *(Seeing Ann and pointing)*: There she is! *(Laughs)*
ANN: Peter, get Hugh a drink. He's a man in need of a drink. You remember Peter.
HUGH *(Over this)*: I'm teasing.
VI: I'll tell Betty you're here.

(She goes. Peter has got up and goes to the drinks.)

HUGH *(As if explaining, to Peter)*: I have four sisters. *(Smiles)*
PETER: Whisky?
HUGH *(Nods, then)* Where's Mike? Is he ?
ANN: Not home yet. Any minute, I suppose.
HUGH *(Looking at his watch)*: I'm impressed. He's working—
ANN: Let me get you something to have with your drink.

(She goes into the kitchen, leaving Peter and Hugh alone. Peter hands Hugh his drink.)

HUGH *(Sips, then nods toward where Ann exited)*: When's the baby—due?
PETER: I don't know. *(Short pause. Peter sits back on the sofa)*

HUGH: He'll be a wonderful father.

PETER: Good.

HUGH: With some men—you can't tell. Me—I did my best. You
saw my best. But it's a winnerless race raising a child. As I used
to tell my ex-wife—the goal seems to be—to cause the least
harm you can. *(Sips)* He's a good man. Mike. Much admired.
I understand he pays for all this—

PETER: I know.

HUGH: Everything. *(Beat)* And now you too. Ann's a lucky woman.

PETER: And you're a lucky man.

(This confuses Hugh. He half smiles.)

HUGH: How so?

PETER: Betty. She's the smartest of all us—

HUGH *(Seriously)*: It's a date. *(Shrugs)* Don't make too much out of
it. You understand, I'm sure.

(Beat.)

PETER *(Continuing)*: The smartest, cleverest. She was the only one
of us who was ever able to finish anything. She finished school.
I'm sure she's a great nurse—

HUGH: But what about those ankles? *(Smiles)*

PETER *(Erupting)*: For Christ sake—she's not a piece of meat!!

HUGH: I'm teasing. I'm teasing you, Peter. If we can't take a joke
anymore . . . I told you—four sisters. *(Beat)* Sorry.

(Ann comes out with a tray of biscuits.)

ANN: What were you two—?

PETER: Hugh has four sisters.

ANN: My condolences. And how is your lovely daughter? *(Turns to
Peter for help)*

PETER: Rose.

ANN: Rose. I love that name.

PETER *(To Hugh)*: She wasn't scarred by the divorce?

(Both Hugh and Ann are surprised by the question.)

By your wife leaving you—for that American? The one you
found in your wife's bed? *(Beat. Smiles)* I'm just teasing.
HUGH: Ask her. *(To Ann)* Boys love her, as you can guess.
PETER: Was your divorce difficult? I suppose what I'm really asking
is—was it expensive? *(Glances at Ann, then back to Hugh)*
HUGH: Not terribly. We decided most things before even talking to
a solicitor.
PETER: And that made it—less expensive?
HUGH: Yes.

(Peter again looks at Ann. Vi bursts in.)

VI: Hugh, here she comes!

*(Betty enters in her mother's blue dress, hem raised to the knee,
looking great. No one says anything for a moment, then.)*

HUGH: You look great.

(Nervous laughter.)

BETTY *(Seeing the flowers)*: Are those for me? *(Takes them, kisses
Hugh on the cheek)* Thank you. *(To Vi)* Would you put them in
water for me?

(Vi takes the flowers.)

(To Hugh) Where are you taking me?
HUGH *(Shrugs, then)*: A drink first at the corner at the King's Head?
Then—dinner?
BETTY *(Making a joke)*: At the King's Head?!
HUGH: No, no I didn't mean—
BETTY: Sounds like fun. And then—after—we'll see.

*(The sisters react to this boldness: "Ohhhhhh!" Hugh laughs ner-
vously. Peter just watches.)*

HUGH: I like this girl!
BETTY *(Holding up her sweater, to Hugh)*: Would you mind?

(Hugh helps her on with her sweater.)

Should we go? Or do you want to finish that? *(The drink)*

(Hugh swallows the rest.)

(To Vi) Goodnight. *(Kisses Vi)* Goodnight, Ann. And baby.
(Kisses Ann) Goodnight. *(Kisses Peter)*
HUGH: Don't worry, she's in good hands. *(Laughs)*
PETER: Is that a joke too?—
VI *(Over this, suddenly "serious")*: Betty!
BETTY: What?

> *(Vi quickly lifts up Betty's dress a bit. Betty, confused, pushes her hand away.)*

VI: Just making sure you're all dressed.

> *(She laughs. Betty smiles at the joke. Everyone is saying: "Goodnight," "Have a nice time," etc. The door is closed, they are gone, and immediately all the smiles disappear.)*

PETER: Am I mad or did she look just like Mother?
ANN: Just like her.

> *(Vi nods. Pause. No one knows what to do. Ann starts rubbing her hands together.)*

VI: Are you all right?
ANN: I'm fine—
VI: Your hands are freezing.
ANN: I'll just put another jumper on. *(Starts to go)*
PETER *(To Ann)*: That was interesting what he said about getting a divorce. It doesn't have to cost—everything.

> *(Ann goes. Vi is confused by this, then turns to Peter.)*

VI: What a woman goes through to have a baby.
PETER: Is that why she's—
VI: I watch Ann and I think—never me. What about you? You want children?

PETER: I haven't thought about it.
VI: Men don't, I find. Of course they have less reason to. Or need to—think about it. *(Beat)* I loaned Betty a couple of French letters. She's a virgin, did you know that? Why would you? A virgin. She just told me. I couldn't believe it. I had to show her how to put them on. *(Holds up her finger and demonstrates)* To make sure it was tight . . . you . . . *(Stops)* You don't want to know about this. *(Beat)* Twenty-one years old and still a . . . I asked her—why? There must be some reason she's had for waiting. Some—principle? Belief? No, she said. There was no reason.

(Beat.)

PETER: So—Hugh????
VI *(Shrugs)*: She said—she wondered if it was finally time to grow up.
PETER: Grow up? Is that growing up? Is—Hugh—??

(Ann enters with another sweater.)

ANN *(Entering)*: What are we doing for supper? Anything?
VI: Sh-sh!!! We're in the middle of a very interesting conversation. *(Turns to Peter)* Are you a virgin, Peter?
ANN: Vi, you can't just ask—
VI *(Over this)*: If he doesn't want to answer, he doesn't have to.

(Beat.)

PETER: No, no, I'm not a virgin
ANN: I think I'll go and begin a supper. *(Goes)*
VI: She has no curiosity. *(Calls)* If you need any help, just . . . *(Beat)* She can't hear me. What about a drink? I need a drink. *(Gets up and goes to the drinks, stops)* We should have asked if she *(Ann)* was a virgin.

(She laughs. Peter smiles.)

"Let me get you a drink, Father." *(As she makes drinks)* That's what Mother always said. "Let me get—" Explain something

to me, why would a woman call her husband "Father"? *(Beat)*
What did you do today?

PETER: Nothing.

VI *(Not listening, handing him his drink)*: "Father"! Cheers. You
spent all day here with Ann?

PETER: Yes.

VI: Then you deserve that drink. Betty didn't even know how to put
one on and she's a nurse! You look different today. Why do
you look different?

(No response.)

You must have got some sleep. *(Beat)* I got the part in *Autumn
Fire*. The director changed his mind.

PETER: Congratulations.—

VI *(Over this)*: That's good, isn't it? I'll have to be away for a while.
On my own. You're the first to know.

PETER: Vi, I love Ann.

VI: So do I. *(Beat)* We're your sisters. You have to! *(Smiles)* Not
that it's always been— *(Touching her forehead)* I was looking
in the mirror earlier, see this? *(Points to a spot on her forehead)*
See this little mark? You know how I got that? You, Petey—

PETER: Don't call me—

VI: You hit me with a stone. I was maybe—four? Do you remember this?

(Peter shakes his head.)

Why should you. *(Beat)* The scars we leave. *(Sits down)* The
first time I had sex— Does this embarrass you?

(Peter shakes his head.)

Good. I was fifteen. He was a boy. Also from London. He hadn't
seen his parents for—years, too. We hung around. We played.
When Ann wouldn't let me play with her friends. *(Beat)* We
did it outside. In the woods. I didn't have anything. No one
told me about French letters. At least not how to get one. We
both were pretty frightened. He was younger than me. Same
as you. You'd like him, I think. I don't know where he is now.

(Beat) Then that afternoon—when I got back to the house from the woods? A telegram was waiting for us. To tell us that Mother had died. *(Beat)* Guilty? Did I feel guilty, Peter? The scars we leave. *(Beat)* There is no greater curse on a child, I believe, than to tie together once and forever—sex and death.

(Pause.)

PETER: I mean—I love Ann as a woman.

(Vi turns to him.)

I love her body. I love to touch—

(Vi suddenly slaps him hard across the face. He nearly falls over.)

VI: Stop it! Stop it!! That's disgusting!!

(Ann enters from the kitchen.)

ANN: What —?!
VI *(Making a "joke")*: He got fresh. *(Tries to laugh)*
PETER *(Trying to lie)*: I hit my head against . . . *(Looks to find something he could have hit his head against)*
ANN: Against what?
PETER: The sofa. The side of the sofa.
ANN: How did you ?
PETER: I was leaning and I ?
ANN: Why were you leaning?
PETER: I just hit it. That's all. I'm not sure how it happened. It was one of those—things.

(Ann goes to him and looks at the bruise. She touches his face. Vi watches.)

VI: Is the supper . . . ?
ANN: It needs to cook. *(Continues to touch Peter's face)*
PETER: I'm all right. I really am.
VI: Leave him alone.
ANN: What?? *(Lets go of Peter)*

VI: Leave our brother alone. He's not a child. We don't have to keep fawning over him.

(They look at each other.)

(Turning away) Leave him alone. What were we talking about? The day Mother died. I was just talking about the day Mother died. I walk out of the woods, a little bloody, and Mum's dead. We're not the sisters you left. Are we, Ann? So much happened. There's so much Peter doesn't know about. So much he's missed. *(Beat)* There was that woman. Weeks? Months later? After Mother's death, Father comes to visit us—with a woman. What was her name?

(No response from Ann.)

We never wrote to you about any of this. And the most remarkable thing was that she looked like Mother. Like a rather blurry carbon copy of Mother. Wouldn't you agree?

ANN: Exactly.

(Peter looks at Ann.)

VI: We look at her—we didn't know what to say. Father's got his arm around her. They hold hands. What am I to feel? Do I love her? Do I hate her? She tried—to be nice. At supper that night she was very nice. Then we went for a walk in the morning. Just "us girls." *(Beat)* And we learned, didn't we, that she was obsessed with Mother. With things he'd heard—been told—

ANN: That Father was telling her—

VI: Lies. How Mother had been so mean with some things—

ANN: Books, he told her.

PETER: Mother was never mean with books—

VI *(Over this)*: And positively extravagant when it came to other things—for herself. Shoes. How many shoes?? That was not true! He was lying to her about Mother! Mother bought maybe three pairs of shoes at one time only because she had such narrow feet that when she found shoes that fitted her—which was rare!—she bought a few pairs! That makes sense. Doesn't it make sense?! That doesn't make her a spendthrift. That doesn't make her selfish for God's sake!! She kept every damn shoe she ever bought and dyed them over and over and over! This wasn't our mother, woman! I know it sounds petty, but I can still see that face, that almost-Mother's face, how I wanted to slap that face as she said, I remember every word, as she took my hand on that walk and said: "It seems your mother wasn't a very kind woman. How hard that must have been for you. Still, I'm sure she tried to love you in her own way." *(Short pause)* We're weak, Peter. We've become very weak.

(To Ann) Leave him alone.

(Ann looks at Peter.)

PETER: I told her. She knows.

(Ann nods. Peter turns to her, leans and kisses her on the mouth and fondles her breast. She lets him.)

VI *(Covering her ears and closing her eyes, shouts)*: No!!!!!!!

(Silence.)

ANN: What else has he missed about our family, Vi? There's the letters. *(To Peter)* Why didn't he burn them? He was off to war, for God's sake! Letters to Father from women. Over years and years *(Beat)* Mother must have known.
VI: We disagree about that.
ANN: I've read them. Vi's read them. Betty's so far refused. Just say when. *(Takes Peter's hand in hers)*
VI: This is wrong. I hurt so much *(Holds herself and whimpers)* No. No. No.

(Short pause.)

PETER *(To Ann)*: Vi got that part in that play. The director changed his mind.
ANN: Good for you, Vi.
VI: I went to see the director today. At his flat. And slept with him. *(Beat. As a second thought)* The girl without— *(Gestures)* And her legs crossed? She had had the role.

(Short pause.)

ANN: As Vi said—we're not the sisters you left.

(Short pause.)

PETER: So poor Vi will have to be away from home for a while.

(Short pause.)

ANN: Mike's looking at a new flat, Vi—for the baby. So I could be away from home, too.

(Door opens, Betty enters.)

(Letting go of Peter's hand) Betty, why are you—?
VI *(Same time)*: Where's Hugh?

(Betty looks at them and smiles. She is suddenly calm, not at all the flighty person she has been.)

BETTY: I don't know. I just—left. I don't know what happened—it was like someone spoke to me and said: "Look at this man, Betty. Have you looked at him?" *(Beat)* So I did. And I saw— a nose I disliked. Talk about thick ankles—look at his nose. And hands—with all those hairs. And I hate his laugh. I hate his teasing. So why am I here? *(Beat)* This isn't me. So I said I didn't feel well and came home. *(Turns to Ann)* Ann, could you put the kettle on, please?
VI: I'll do it—
BETTY: Let Ann. She's always telling us not to wait on her.
VI: When has she said—?
BETTY: Sh-sh.
ANN *(Getting up)*: I'll put the kettle on. *(Goes)*
BETTY: In the pub. Hugh got quite close to me and said, "I hope this isn't difficult for you, but I've asked Mike to join us for dinner. I think he's bringing his other nurse."

(Ann returns.)

ANN: Kettle's on. *(Beat)* We'll eat when Mike's home.

BETTY *(Picking up a framed photo)*: I think it was Mother who spoke to me. Her voice. That's what I'm going to believe. Now I'm going to get out of her dress and give it back to her.

(She goes down the hallway to her bedroom. Ann looks at Peter.)

VI: Leave him alone.

(Beat.)

ANN: I should keep an eye on the stew.

(She hesitates, goes to Peter, squeezes his shoulder, then leaves for the kitchen.
Vi picks up the photo Betty had held. She sets it back down.
Peter stands, begins to follow Ann, when:)

VI: Stay in here.

(Peter sits back down. Beat.)

The ship after yours—the next ship carrying boys and girls to Canada—was torpedoed by the Germans and sank.

PETER: I know that.

VI *(Ignoring him)*: They wouldn't let anyone—go after that. You were the last. *(Beat)* We waited a full week wondering what had happened. If it had been your ship. *(Beat)* We thought then we might have lost you. I even imagined, sitting in the bath, what it would have been like, felt like—to drown. And to float to the bottom of the sea. Like a leaf, I thought, as it falls. We cried ourselves to sleep. *(Beat)* The first newspaper accounts said that the little boys had stood in perfect lines, all straight, all calm. Some could get into boats, some couldn't. Calm. Betty said that surely meant you couldn't be on that ship, our little Peter couldn't ever stand still. *(Smiles at Peter)* For a week we held our breath. And then we heard. You were in Canada. You were lucky. How we celebrated! Mum and Dad and Betty and Ann and me. How happy we were that our Peter was safe. I'd never known a happier day. *(Picks up the photo again)* I began to dream you were coming home. *(Beat)* Then, finally, you really were coming home. *(Sets the photo back down)* Now you're home.

(Stands. Calls) Betty, I'll help you with that dress!

(She heads down the hallway. Peter sits alone on the sofa.
Suddenly, from far off, the distant cry of a baby.
The cry gets louder and louder, closer and closer. The baby is screaming now.
Peter doesn't move, doesn't flinch as the baby continues to scream.)

SCENE 8

Months later. Midnight.
The room is dark. Outside, in the hallway, a baby is crying.
Someone is trying to unlock the door. Finally it opens and Mike and Ann enter. She carries their crying infant.

ANN *(Rocking)*: Sh-sh. They're not up. They're asleep. Maybe we should—
MIKE: They won't be for long. *(Nods down the hall to the bedrooms)* Someone's turned on a light.
ANN *(Rocking)*: Sh-sh. Turn on a lamp.

(Mike turns on a lamp. There is a cup and saucer on a table.)

Look at this mess. These children need a mother.
MIKE: It's a cup and saucer.

(Betty, tying her dressing gown, enters from her bedroom.)

BETTY: Ann? Is that you? What are you—?
VI *(Right behind her)*: They brought Mary!

(The aunts go to the child.)

BETTY: What's wrong? Is something wrong?
ANN: Sh-sh. Sh-sh.

MIKE: Colic. I tell her it'll pass. She's worried—

ANN: I'm not worried.—

MIKE *(Over this)*: And I'm also her doctor! Give her to them. Give her— Look at your sisters, they're drooling to— They won't drop her—

(Ann begins handing over the baby to Betty.)

BETTY: Sh-sh. Sh-sh. She's so sweet.

VI: What time is it?

MIKE: Midnight.

VI: What are you doing—?

MIKE *(To Betty)*: We miss you at the surgery.

BETTY *(Just rocks the baby, ignoring Mike)*: God, I love her.

(Peter appears in the doorway of Mike and Ann's old bedroom, now his. He has thrown on trousers, and is buttoning his shirt. He is barefoot.)

PETER: What is—all this?

MIKE: Peter! *(To Ann)* He is here. You weren't sure—

PETER: Sure what?

VI: Ann's brought Mary.

MIKE: I'll wager he guessed that.

PETER *(About the crying)*: What's wrong?

ANN: It's nothing—colic. It goes away. It's a phase, Mike says.

BETTY: Maybe she needs to be changed.

ANN: You can try that, sometimes—

VI: Or she's hungry.

ANN: I just fed her.

MIKE: We brought nappies—

BETTY: Let's take her into our room and change her on the bed. *(To Ann)* Do you mind?

ANN: I'll have my chances. Please. I hold her enough.

VI *(To Betty)*: Why don't you let me—

ANN: Please, don't fight over her.

(Smiles. Vi takes the crying baby out of the room. Mike sits on the sofa and sighs:)

MIKE: The lungs on that child. I am so tired.

(Soon he will fall asleep sitting up. Ann and Peter look at each other.)

ANN: I thought you might want to see your niece. You can go—if you want—
PETER: She's beautiful. I'll see more of her later. She's very beautiful.

(Big yawn from Mike.)

MIKE: Children . . .
ANN: It's not too late—?
PETER: No.
ANN: You were up?
PETER: Yes.

(Beat.)

ANN: You didn't come to the hospital. I don't blame you, they're—
(Beat. Looks around) Our first time out. We just brought her home, you know. She was crying. We couldn't sleep. *(Looks at Mike who is falling asleep)* I couldn't sleep. *(Smiles)* So I thought to myself—where can we go? Who'd take us in? *(Smiles again)* And I knew you'd be anxious to see her. To meet your niece. I thought you'd been waiting— It's great to see you.

(They look at each other. He reaches for her hand. She resists.)

You deserve better than me. You're my brother.

(Young Rose, Hugh's daughter, comes out from Peter's bedroom, wearing Peter's dressing gown.)

ROSE: Peter?? What's going on? Why is that baby crying?

(Ann is stunned to see Rose.)

PETER: Go back to bed. They'll be gone soon.
ROSE: Is the baby all right? It's not sick—
ANN: She's fine. They're changing her.
ROSE: Could I watch? I love babies.

ANN: Put some clothes on first.

ROSE *(In disbelief)*: What??

ANN: I said, young lady, put some clothes on first.

(Rose looks at Peter, hesitates, then hurries back to put on clothes.)

Was that who I think it was?

PETER: Rose.

ANN: Thank you, I forgot the name. God you people keep secrets.

PETER: We just went out for the first time tonight.

ANN: I see. *(Beat)* Good for you. Good for you.

(She goes to hug Peter. He hesitates, then allows himself to be hugged.)

Though I hope you don't get serious about her. You can do better than that. After all, you're my brother.

(This makes Peter smile. Ann sits in a chair. Mike is sound asleep.)

It's breezy outside. She'll probably catch a cold. *(Beat)* What kind of mother am I? *(Turns to Peter for comfort or a compliment)*

PETER: I don't know

(Short pause.)

ANN: When I was in labor, when I was—out. Mike made sure I was out. I had a dream about the baby. I dreamed my baby and I were taking a trip together. Just us. Her and me. We were climbing mountains somewhere. Maybe Canada? Your mountains?

PETER: They're not my—

ANN: The sky was so blue. Her face young and happy. And then suddenly she slipped, Peter, and she started to fall. I reached down and grabbed her hand. I was the only thing keeping her from death. *(Beat)* She was dangling over the side of a cliff, my hand gripping her wrist. She was so heavy, Peter. I thought my whole arm would fall off. But I held on. *(Beat)* Then somehow I found the strength, the power inside me, a power that surprised me, that I never knew I possessed, and I pulled my baby

to safety. I saved her, Peter. *(Beat)* I saved her. *(Beat)* And then
there she was again—a baby in my arms. *(Beat)* You'll adore
her. And she'll worship you.

(The crying has stopped.)

She's stopped crying.

(Vi appears.)

VI *(In a loud whisper)*: If you sing to her, she stops crying!

*(Vi hurries back to the baby. Off we hear Vi and Betty singing.
Ann and Peter listen.)*

PETER: What are they singing?

*(They and we begin to make out the song, "Goodnight Children
Everywhere":)*

VI AND BETTY *(Off)*:
  She's with you night and day.
  Goodnight children, everywhere.

*(Mike snores.
  Peter and Ann don't move, can't move, they only listen.)*

  Sleepy little eyes and sleepy little head
  Sleepy time is drawing near
  In a little while
  You'll be tucked up in your bed
  Here's a song for baby dear . . .

*(Fighting back tears, and without looking at each other, Peter snaps
his fingers once, thinking of Mother. Ann snaps her fingers once.
  Then after a moment, Ann snaps her fingers twice, thinking of
Father. Peter snaps his fingers twice.
  The singing continues. Rose bursts in buttoning her blouse. She
crosses the room and exits to go and see the baby. Neither seems to
notice her.
  From off:)*

Goodnight children, everywhere
Your mummy thinks of you tonight.
Lay your head upon your pillow,
Don't be a kid or a weeping willow.
Close your eyes and say a prayer
And surely you can find a kiss to spare.
Though you are far away
She's with you night and day.
Goodnight children, everywhere.

END OF PLAY

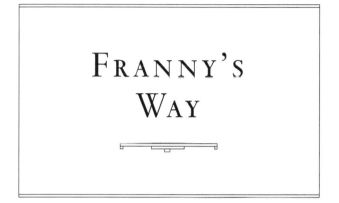

FRANNY'S
WAY

For Tim Sanford

PRODUCTION HISTORY

Franny's Way was first produced by Playwrights Horizons (Tim Sanford, Artistic Director; Leslie Marcus, Managing Director; William Russo, General Manager) on March 6, 2002. It was directed by the playwright; the set design was by Thomas Lynch, the costume design was by Susan Hilferty and Linda Ross, the lighting design was by Jennifer Tipton, the sound design was by Scott Lehrer and the stage managers were Jane Pole, Kevin Bertolacci and Clare Gardner. The cast was as follows:

FRANNY	Elisabeth Moss
DOLLY	Domenica Cameron-Scorsese
SALLY	Yvonne Woods
PHIL	Jesse Pennington
OLDER FRANNY / GRANDMA	Kathleen Widdoes

Franny's Way was subsequently produced by The Geffen Playhouse (Gilbert Cates, Producing Director; Randall Arney, Artistic Director; Stephen Eich, Managing Director) on June 28, 2003. It was directed by the playwright; the set design was by Thomas Lynch, the costume design was by Susan Hilferty, the lighting design was by David Weiner, the sound design was by Scott Lehrer and the stage managers were Elsbeth M. Collins and Andrea Iovino. The cast was as follows:

FRANNY	Elisabeth Moss
DOLLY	Domenica Cameron-Scorsese
SALLY	Susan May Pratt
PHIL	Jesse Pennington
OLDER FRANNY / GRANDMA	Penny Fuller

CHARACTERS

FRANNY, seventeen
DOLLY, her sister, fifteen
SALLY, their cousin, twenties
PHIL, Sally's husband, twenties
GRANDMA (Marjorie), Franny, Dolly and Sally's grandmother
OLDER FRANNY (she also plays Grandma)

SETTING

An apartment, Sullivan Street, Greenwich Village, 1957

I believe I essentially remain what I've almost always been—a narrator, but one with extremely pressing personal needs.

—J. D. SALINGER
from *Seymour: An Introduction*

PROLOGUE

Lights up on a tenement apartment, Sullivan Street, Greenwich Village. June 1957. Living room and kitchen are combined: chairs, kitchen table, refrigerator, counter, sofa, etc. Doors to two small bedrooms, one closed, one open. A door to the hallway. The bathroom is in the hallway and shared.

An open window through which we hear the sounds of Sullivan Street—traffic, voices, and those of Bleecker around the corner—distant jazz from a club (mostly horns, something like Miles Davis's Sketches of Spain*). Except for what comes from the window, the only light comes from the open bedroom and it is very dim.*

Late night. Late June. It is hot.

Slowly we begin to hear noises from the closed bedroom, a groan, a cry. A couple are making love. They reach a climax and the woman shouts out.

Pause.

Bedroom door opens. A young man, Phil, comes out. He is naked. In the bedroom, a young woman, Sally, sits on the edge of the bed, also naked. They are in their twenties and married.

Phil, wiping the sweat off his face, then onto some furniture as he passes, heads for the refrigerator. He opens the door—light—and takes out a bottle of beer. He opens it and drinks as he looks out the window; jazz in the distance.

He breathes heavily, catching his breath; he goes and turns on an electric fan. Sally comes into the room as Phil is turning on the fan.

PHIL *(Holding up his beer)*: You want a——? *(Sip)*
SALLY: Sh-sh. Sh-sh.

(She gestures toward the other bedroom. They listen for an instant, then relax, smile, even giggle as if they have gotten away with something. She nods, and goes to light a cigarette. He hands her the bottle, she takes a big sip, and they both end up looking out the window. He sits with her on the sofa and holds her, kisses her neck, she responds. Sips again, smokes. They listen to the music. She moves to it a bit.)

(After a deep sigh) God is it hot. There's no air out there. *(Looks at the fan)* Does that reach——? I can't feel anything.
PHIL: Let me try.

(As he stands, a metal object—a baby's rattle—falls on the floor. The noise makes the couple suddenly stop and turn to the open bedroom, expecting to hear something now. There is silence. This at first makes them smile, and Sally takes another sip or drag, but then she stops, looks concerned at Phil and heads for this bedroom.)

Sh-sh. Don't——
SALLY: I won't.

(She goes into the bedroom. Phil plays with the rattle.)

(In the bedroom) Phil? Phil? *(Louder)* Phil!! Come here!
PHIL *(Hurrying to the bedroom)*: Sally? What's——? *(Turns on the bedroom light—bright light)*
SALLY *(At the same time)*: Anna? Anna!!!! *(Nearly screaming. In the bedroom, holds up a baby. Screams)* Phil!!!!!!

(Sally begins to cry and scream. Phil tries to take Anna from her, but she pushes him away.)

What's wrong with Anna? Something's wrong. Phil!

PHIL: Don't shake her! Anna?
SALLY: Phil, she's blue!
PHIL: Wake up, wake up.
SALLY: Make her wake up! Please, help her, Phil. Help her!

(He runs out of the bedroom into their bedroom. He comes out try-ing to put on his pants. The jazz continues from Bleecker Street.)

PHIL: Oh God, Jesus, Anna, please, please.
SALLY: Sweetie. Wake up, dear. Open your eyes. Mommy's here.
Mommy's here. Wake up. Phil!
PHIL *(Screams)*: Sally!!!!

(Lights fade out.)

SCENE 1

The Older Franny speaks to the audience.

OLDER FRANNY: Cousin Sally's and her husband's baby was already dead when they found her in her bed. "Crib death" was what was written on the death certificate. Father said, "Who the hell knows why?" would have been just as appropriate.

I was seventeen. This death which swept as a tidal wave over the lives of Sally and Phil, was by the time it reached my distant shore—in Millbrook, New York—but a small almost unnoticed ripple. Perhaps I sent a condolence card. Or maybe I spoke to her briefly during one of her calls with Grandma. Or perhaps it was merely a "poor Sally" thought I had, which never even got expressed.

I had, after all, other things on my mind that summer. There was a boyfriend, with whom I had had my first sex, and he was now at NYU. And I loved him. Though his letters were begin-ning to get, if not less frequent, then less—interesting. Was this my fault? Or his? I was in the midst of my novel about the rivalries between five sisters in Victorian Yorkshire England, which consumed my summer afternoons. There was my new stepmother. I thought about her a lot. My mother I think I was adamantly choosing not to think about. So that took some time too. And then there was my name, my new, chosen, changed name. Changed from the matronly and phoney "Frances" to—Franny. My homage, I liked to call it, to the beautiful, frail, lost, fair-skinned, funny, faint-prone heroine of my life and J. D. Salinger's story. I saw myself navigating my way through life's sea of phonies. I was missing only her raccoon coat, but it was still summer—and my birthday was coming up. Anyway, as I said, I had a lot to think about.

So when Grandma offered to take my sister and me on a trip to New York City, it simply didn't occur to me that our purpose was to console my grieving cousin, but rather seemed the very understandable fulfullment of a seventeen-year-old's desire, if not need, to get the hell out of Millbrook and be hurtled headlong into that swirl of life called New York.

My little sister, too, had her own plans for this trip.

We took the two-hour train trip from Dover Plains to Grand Central, and climbed down into the subway and back up again downtown, up into the noise and music of the Village. We then walked down Bleecker with its clubs, doors left open because of the summer's heat, their sounds like breaths, puffs, exhaled into the street, into clouds of music we walked through, until we got here, on Sullivan, in the heart of Greenwich Village, which for my money and in my dreams was the very soul and center of the whole goddamn universe.

So it was on a Tuesday night, in August, 1957, barely six weeks after the baby—Anna's—tragic and inexplicable and, by me, nearly forgotten death, that my sister, age fifteen—

(Dolly enters from the hallway, small suitcase in hand.)

And me, age seventeen—

(Seventeen-year-old Franny enters, looking around excitedly. She too carries a small bag. Phil has come in with them, holding a larger suitcase.)

And our Grandma—she was about the same age then as I am now, so I'll be her—arrived, ready to spend two exciting and unforgettable days—of real life.

(Older Franny now plays Grandma throughout. August 1957. Eleven P.M. Jazz, though much more percussive than before, is now heard through the window, as well as the sound and noises of the street. Sally has come out of her bedroom and is greeting everyone. Everyone is speaking at once.)

SALLY *(To Dolly)*: Look at you. Who let you grow up?! *(Laughs)*

FRANNY: Where should we put——? *("my bag")*

PHIL: Anywhere.

SALLY *(Over this, continuing to Dolly)*: Does your father know how much you've grown up?

GRANDMA: He sees her every day.

SALLY: I'm kidding her, Grandma. *(To Dolly, not letting go of the subject)* I remember when you used to be——

PHIL: That's enough, Sally.

SALLY: Enough of what, I don't understand? What am I doing?

(Awkward moment, then)

GRANDMA *(To Sally)*: Oh dear, it's good to see you.

SALLY *(Pointing to Franny)*: And you, I knew you'd grow up.

FRANNY *(To Phil)*: What does that mean?

(He shrugs.)

DOLLY: Where's the bathroom?

SALLY: It's in the hall. We share——

GRANDMA *(Looking around now)*: What a nice apartment. *(It isn't.)* What's that music——?

SALLY *(Overexcited)*: There's a jazz club.
          (To Dolly as if to a child) You know what a jazz club is?

FRANNY *(To Grandma)*: We passed it, Grandma.

DOLLY *(To Phil)*: The bathroom's in the hall?

SALLY *(Hearing this)*: It's perfectly safe.

FRANNY: I'll go with you.

SALLY: Does she need someone to——?

PHIL: They just got here, Sally. I'll get you a towel—— *(Moves toward his and Sally's bedroom)*

SALLY: I put towels on their bed.

(Phil heads for the spare bedroom.)

GRANDMA: Are we staying in—? *("there")* How lovely. *(Barely concealing her disgust for the place)*
SALLY: You and Dolly will share— Is that all right with—
DOLLY: I heard. I've prepared myself.

(Laughter.)

SALLY *(To Franny)*: And you, it's either the couch, or we could put down a few cushions in the bedroom, if that would—
FRANNY: I'll think about it.
SALLY: Who's hungry? There's plenty of—
DOLLY: I have to use the—
SALLY *(To Phil who has a towel now)*: Phil, show her—
FRANNY: I'm going with her.

(Franny takes the towel and goes out into the hall with Dolly. Awkward moment. Franny appears again.)

Which door?
PHIL: The only one on the right.
FRANNY: Do we knock or—?
SALLY: No one's in there. I was just in there.

(Franny goes.)

I can't believe how the little one's grown. *(To Grandma)* Thank you for coming.

(They hug.)

PHIL: Yes, thank you, Marjorie. It's good to see you.
SALLY *(To say something)*: And Fran's a woman now—
GRANDMA: Franny. We must now call her—Franny. She'll tell you why. *(To Phil)* And how is work?

(He nods.)

You two are such a lovely couple.

(No one knows what to say.)

SALLY: Let me get you something to—
GRANDMA: We had sandwiches on the train. I brought sandwiches.
We hardly ate them. Are they excited. *(Beat)* You won't believe
what Dolly's done. You want to know what she and I are doing
tomorrow?

(Franny returns with Dolly behind her.)

FRANNY *(In the doorway)*: I think it's locked.
SALLY: No one was in there a minute ago. Philip, help them.
FRANNY: I didn't want to push too hard.
PHIL *(To Dolly, as they go out)*: God are you big!
FRANNY *(Teasing)*: What about me?
PHIL: You—you're still a kid and you always will be.

(Tickling her, laughter, the door closes behind them. Short pause.)

SALLY *(To Grandma)*: They're young women. *(Starts to light a cigarette)* I hope you'll be comfortable. It's not Millbrook.

(A siren goes by outside.)

You get used to the . . .

*(She looks around. Clearly Grandma does not know what to say.
Then pointing to the spare bedroom.)*

That was the baby's room. *(Suddenly changing the subject)*
What has Dolly ?
GRANDMA *(Confused)*: What?
SALLY: You were saying—Dolly's done some—
GRANDMA: You won't believe it. You know she's never been to New
York before—
SALLY: Really? I didn't know.
GRANDMA: You couldn't believe how excited— "Peel her off the
roof!" That's what her father was saying this morning. We're
seeing *My Fair Lady*.

(Sally is confused.)

That's what Dolly did. She organized—all by herself—tickets to . . . Her father paid for them of course—but she wrote off and— That's what we're doing tomorrow in the afternoon.

SALLY: That's exciting.

GRANDMA: Aren't you proud of her? I couldn't have done that at her age. She wrote away and everything.

(Phil returns.)

SALLY: What was—?

PHIL: It was stuck. The toilet door. Franny is staying with her.

GRANDMA: You remembered to call her Franny now—

PHIL: She told me.

GRANDMA: Do you know that short story—?

PHIL: I do. *(Beat)* And it's good. Marjorie, don't you want anything to—? *(Heads toward the kitchen area)*

SALLY: I offered. They've eaten sandwiches. No one is hungry.

PHIL: What about something to drink? You must be—

SALLY: She doesn't want anything. I asked.

GRANDMA: Actually, I am a little— *("thirsty")*

PHIL *(To Sally)*: Why didn't you offer—

SALLY: I did!

PHIL: You want a beer? There's Cokes, I'll bet the girls would like—

SALLY: I'll get them—

PHIL *(Over this)*: I'll get them!

(Pause as Phil goes to refrigerator and starts taking out Cokes.)

(The same safe subject) Dolly's gotten big, hasn't she?

SALLY: Like she all of a sudden sprang up. *(To Grandma)* You probably don't notice it as—

PHIL: She notices it. *(Takes out glasses for the drinks)*

SALLY: Maybe they don't want glasses. Kids like to drink from the bottle.

PHIL: We'll give them the choice then.

(Short pause.)

GRANDMA: Dolly didn't take a sheep to the Dutchess County Fair this summer. So I suppose that's over.

PHIL: She's growing up.

SALLY: I used to take my sheep. I used to sleep with my sheep overnight. A lot of kids did. *(Beat)* It was great.

PHIL: I'll bet.

SALLY: Bull. You hate the country. You hate animals. You hate—

PHIL: I don't hate animals.

SALLY: You think all farmers are—

PHIL: I do not.

SALLY *(To Grandma)*: He thinks our whole family are—

PHIL: I do not! *(Beat. To Grandma)* I don't.

SALLY *(Changing the subject)*: Dolly's never been to New York before. She and Grandma are seeing *My Fair Lady*.

PHIL *(To Sally)*: You wanted to see that.

SALLY: I'm jealous.

PHIL *(Moving toward the spare bedroom)*: Franny says she wants to sleep in there. I'll set up the cushions—

SALLY: I'll do that.

PHIL: I don't mind.

SALLY: Which sheets are you going to—?

PHIL: Which sheets do you want me to use?

SALLY *(Exasperated)*: I'll do it.

PHIL: I can make up a bed on a floor. I'm not that incompetent.

(They look at each other.)

SALLY: Go ahead then.

GRANDMA: I can help if . . .

(They ignore her. Phil goes into the bedroom. We see him through the open door as he makes up the bed. Sally goes to the refrigerator and starts taking a few things out.)

SALLY: I made a few things . . .

GRANDMA: Sally, it's after eleven. The kids should be going to bed. *(Pause)* What did you make? *(Goes and looks over the dishes, turns to listen to music)* Does that go on all night? The music.

SALLY: What music? *(Laughs a little too hard)* That's a joke Phil and I . . . Yeah. It does.

(Franny and Dolly return.)

371

DOLLY: What a neat bathroom. I can't wait to take a bath in that tub.

GRANDMA: Phil's making up your bed—

SALLY: So—*My Fair Lady*. Aren't you lucky. I'm jealous. *(Continues to set out food as she talks. To Dolly)* I have a friend who auditioned for a replacement in that show. She was in my acting class with me.

DOLLY: Really?

FRANNY *(Looking around)*: This is so neat. Look at this.

(She goes to the window. Dolly follows.)

SALLY: Don't get too close to that—

FRANNY: I'm not going to—

SALLY: I've told Phil a thousand times we need a bar, an iron bar, so no one . . . No child . . .

FRANNY: I'm not a child.

SALLY: I didn't mean— Doesn't anyone want something to eat?!
(Comes out almost as a cry, nearly in tears, trying not to cry)
I made things to eat.

(Phil comes to the doorway.)

PHIL *(Impatient)*: Sally.

SALLY *(Crying)*: I'm trying not to!

(Franny and Dolly are confused, they look at Grandma who begins to push them toward their bedroom.)

GRANDMA: You girls have a big day tomorrow—

DOLLY: Why is Sally—?

PHIL *(As they near him while heading for their bedroom; to Franny)*: So college! *(To the others)* Franny says she's looking at colleges!

GRANDMA *(To Sally)*: I didn't tell you, she's going to take a tour—

PHIL *(Teasing)*: NYU!

SALLY *(To Franny)*: I didn't know. No one tells me—

FRANNY: I have a friend who goes there. And—she wants me to look—

PHIL: And your father? Doesn't he know? He'd have a fit if you left Upstate— *(All three are in the bedroom now)* I can just hear him: "We have excellent colleges up here, young lady."

DOLLY: Sounds like Father.

FRANNY: Except for the "young lady" stuff. I've gotten him to stop that. I told him, "Another young lady, Dad, and this young lady is going to burn down one of your best barns." I meant it too.

(Phil, who obviously enjoys playing with these girls, goes: "Ohhh that scared him."
Grandma goes and hugs Sally.)

SALLY: I promised myself I wouldn't do that.

(Another hug, then:)

GRANDMA: Your father wants you home. Both of you. He's got his eye on a nice house. I've seen it. *(Beat)* Get away from here. And come home.

SALLY *(Wiping her tears)*: I'm an actress, Grandma. I've got a new teacher. I know he'll take me. He's going to help me with my singing. That's what I need.

(Phil comes out of the bedroom.)

PHIL: Is it all right if Franny borrows a robe? She forgot hers.

(Sally nods. Phil goes back into the bedroom. Sally gets a robe from their bedroom, returns.)

SALLY *(To Grandma)*: He won't touch me, Grandma. He doesn't want me, since . . .

(She tries not to cry. Grandma takes her hand, Sally pulls it away.)

He hates me. And I hate him.

(Grandma watches as Phil comes out of the bedroom to get the robe. Sally crosses and awkwardly hands him the robe. He goes back into the bedroom. Suddenly Franny and Dolly attack him— they were hiding behind the door. Screams, laughter, etc., from the overexcited young women. The night sounds/music and lights begin to fade. Grandma shouts: "Now get to bed. Phil, you're winding them up.")

SCENE 2

The middle of the night. The apartment is quiet, except for soft music coming from the radio in Phil and Sally's bedroom. No lights are on. A little street noise. No music from the club on Bleecker Street, it is too late. Franny comes out of the bedroom, now in Sally's robe. She is trying to make her way to the sink, though is having trouble seeing; she kicks the leg of a chair as she passes along the table.

At the sink, she turns on the tap and drinks. She notices the music coming from the bedroom. She slowly heads to the window where she looks out, lost in thought. A fire truck passes in the distance, voices from the street. Franny watches.

SCENE 3

Late the next morning. Light streams in from the window. The noise from the street is alive and present—people, crowds walking by, sirens, horns, etc.

Grandma is cleaning up after breakfast, still in her nightgown, and Dolly, dressed but a bit disheveled—she hasn't combed her hair yet, tucked in her blouse, etc.—stands at the window. Sally, in a robe, sits at the table.

DOLLY *(Looking out)*: It's so interesting.

GRANDMA *(To Dolly)*: It's not as much fun as it looks out there.

DOLLY: I didn't say it was fun. I said it was really really really interesting.

SALLY: It's that, Grandma. You can't argue with that.

GRANDMA: Look at that. Look at what he's wearing. Oh my God.

DOLLY: It's summer—

GRANDMA *(Going back to cleaning up, half to herself)*: On a public street.

(Pause. A church bell chimes in the distance.)

DOLLY: She's still in there?

GRANDMA *(Picks up the coffee pot)*: Should I throw it out—?

(Sally nods, then:)

SALLY: No, I'll take it. I could go and knock . . .

(Door to the hallway opens. Franny enters, dressed, combed, lost in her thoughts.)

Here she is.

(The others just look at Franny.)

FRANNY: What??? What's wrong? *(Starts to fix her hair)* Why are
   you looking at me?
SALLY: Nothing.
DOLLY: Phil had to shave in the kitchen sink.
FRANNY: What???? Why did he do that?
GRANDMA: He shaved in the——?
DOLLY: You were still in the bedroom, Grandma. *(To Franny)* He
   had to get to work. He works.
SALLY: Dolly——
FRANNY: What does that have to do with me?
DOLLY: You've been hogging the bathroom, Franny. How long was
   she in the——?
FRANNY: Why didn't he knock——?
DOLLY: *Everyone's* been waiting to use the bathroom——
FRANNY: Why didn't anyone knock?
GRANDMA: There's just the one bathroom——and it's not just for us,
   but for the whole floor. Isn't that right? It's not like home,
   Franny.
FRANNY. But why——?
SALLY: It's fine. Leave her alone. Philip didn't mind. *(To Grandma)*
   It'll give him something to talk about.
FRANNY: There's nothing for him to talk about! Jesus. What did
   I do? I don't understand.
DOLLY: She always hogs the bathroom. She doesn't think about
   anyone else needing to use the——
FRANNY *(To Dolly)*: Shut up.
GRANDMA: Girls——
DOLLY: I've been in there with her. She'll stare at herself in the mir-
   ror for——

FRANNY: Leave me alone! *(Looks at her sister)* What are you talking about? Do you know what you're talking about? Maybe if you took a bath a little more often, you wouldn't have to slap so much deodorant on.

GRANDMA: Franny—

FRANNY: You think no one can smell it? It's true. Smell her. Go ahead. *(To Sally)* You don't have to sleep in the same room as—

GRANDMA *(To Dolly)*: I didn't smell—

FRANNY: You can't smell anything, Grandma.

(Short pause. Dolly turns back and looks out the window.)

Bathroom's free.

(She turns to go into the bedroom. Dolly laughs under her breath, Franny turns back.)

Why don't you jump?

GRANDMA: Maybe I should get dressed.

FRANNY *(To Dolly)*: Or maybe you need a push—

(She hurries to Dolly; Sally grabs Franny.)

SALLY: Stop it! Stop.

FRANNY *(Same time)*: I wasn't going to—

SALLY: How old are you two anyway?!

(Dolly suddenly musses up Franny's hair and runs for cover.)

FRANNY: Damn you!

SALLY: Don't swear—

FRANNY *(Over this)*: What are you—? I just fixed . . . *(Tries to fix her hair)* I'll kill you.

GRANDMA: Who wants to use the bathroom next?

DOLLY *(Still all of her focus on Franny)*: Sorry to mess up your hair for your big—"appointment."

FRANNY: You shut up, Dolly.

GRANDMA *(Suddenly)*: What big appointment?

(Franny doesn't know what to say.)

FRANNY *(Under her breath to Dolly)*: You are in big trouble.

DOLLY: Me? Really?

GRANDMA: I thought you were just going to walk around the campus with your friend. Do you have an appointment at the college?

FRANNY: No, Grandma. I don't know what my little sister is talking about. But that is usually the case, isn't it? We must all be used to that by now. I should go. Betty's probably waiting for me.

DOLLY: "Betty"???

FRANNY *(To Sally)*: Betty's a friend from home. She goes to NYU. She promised to show me around. *(Trying hard)* Of course Father says there's a million good schools upstate or in New England, why in the world would a girl want to live in New York City when . . . When there's all that there, I suppose. *(Looks at Sally)* Betty's two years older. Very responsible. I'll be fine, don't worry. Is my hair—?

DOLLY: Oh God don't let her go back into the bathroom!!

FRANNY *(Suddenly turns on Dolly)*: And—Dolly what are your "big" plans for today?

(This stops Dolly, she looks at her sister, then:)

DOLLY: We're seeing the play. She *(Sally)* knows that.

SALLY: I'm so proud of you for sending off and getting tickets all by yourself.

FRANNY: She's not five years old, Sally. Far from it. *(Starts for the bedroom, then stops)* Oh, you're just "seeing the play." I see. Careful, sister. Now you leave me alone. *(Goes into their bedroom)*

SALLY *(Suddenly standing)*: We should all get dressed.

DOLLY *(At the same time)*: Grandma, we should go

GRANDMA: Mind if I use the . . . bathroom.

SALLY *(To Dolly)*: You've got loads of time. A matinee's not until two-thirty—

DOLLY: We're going to Gimbel's first.

GRANDMA: She wants to go to Gimbel's.

DOLLY: Get ready, Grandma.

GRANDMA: There's something there she's been looking for. At Gimbel's. She won't tell me what it is. It's a big secret.

(Smiles, even winks at Dolly, and picking up the pile of clothes she is going to wear, heads into the hallway to the bathroom. Pause.

*Dolly goes back to looking out the window. Sally looks at Dolly.
Then, to say something:)*

SALLY: So—you like shows, too.

(Dolly nods.)

I love them.

(Dolly smiles.)

How's your father? Surviving okay?
DOLLY: Sure.

(Sally doesn't know whether to say more, then:)

SALLY: I really like your father. A shame about what your mother
  did to him—
DOLLY *(Interrupting, she doesn't want to talk about it)*: He's just fine.
  Really.
SALLY: My dad thinks the world of him. Of his "little brother."
  Funny to think about it that way, isn't it? His little . . . Dad says
  your father's going through a lot, but who'd know? That's
  what he says. *(Beat)* You should have seen the letter your
  father wrote me after our baby . . . After what happened—

(Dolly suddenly turns from the window.)

DOLLY: Oh my God, Sally, I'm so sorry, I haven't said how sorry
  I am for what—
SALLY: I wasn't asking for—
DOLLY *(Same time)*: No, I know, but—
SALLY: I didn't mean to— I know your feelings. You don't have to
  . . . It's probably better that you haven't said anything. Let it
  all—heal.

(Dolly is still kicking herself for not saying anything.)

You don't want to just keep—picking at it. Then it'll never get
better. So . . . don't worry, I wasn't expecting . . .

DOLLY: I am sorry—

SALLY: And you guys are just kids.

FRANNY *(Entering, all dressed, carrying her purse)*: Who's a kid? Don't include me in—

DOLLY *(As soon as she sees Franny)*: Sally was just talking about her baby.

(It hits Franny, too.)

FRANNY: Oh God. Sally, I'm so sorry—

DOLLY *(Over this)*: She doesn't want— She isn't asking—

FRANNY: I wrote you, didn't I? I was planning to write you and Phil a long letter— I didn't know if I should say anything—

DOLLY *(Overlapping)*: She wants us *not* to talk about it.

FRANNY: That's what I would have thought—

DOLLY: So it'll heal, she says.

FRANNY: That's why I didn't—

DOLLY: Right, Sal?

(Sally looks at them and nods.)

SALLY: Whatever you think is best. I don't know.

(She smiles at her younger cousins, then:)

So—Grandma's looking good, I think. Don't you?

FRANNY: We see her all the time, so—I'm glad you think so.

DOLLY *(Laughing)*: Father's finally got her off her little tractor.

SALLY: She wasn't still—?

FRANNY: Just for the lawn.

SALLY: Still.

DOLLY: Yeah.

SALLY: I'm sure that wasn't easy.

FRANNY: What?

SALLY: Getting Grandma off the tractor.

FRANNY: No. It wasn't.

(No one knows what to say.)

SALLY *(Nods to the bedroom)*: I'm sorry if it's a bit messy in there.

FRANNY: No, it's—

DOLLY: No.

SALLY: The—cradle, we've been trying to—give away, but . . .
 (Looks at herself) I'm the only one *not* getting dressed. I better
 . . . *(Moves toward her bedroom)*

FRANNY: I should go. I'm meeting—Betty in—

SALLY *(Suddenly)*: Not yet! Stay another minute. I want to show you
 both something! *(Runs off into her bedroom. Off)* It won't take
 long.

DOLLY: What's she . . . ?

(Franny shrugs.)

FRANNY: I have to go.

DOLLY: Any message you want passed along?

(Franny ignores her.)

Just thought I had to ask. She'll want to know.

FRANNY: *If* she shows up, Dolly. Have you thought about that? If
 Mother *deigns* to turn up.

(Sally returns with her guitar.)

SALLY *(Tuning it)*: I'm supposed to play for this— There's a class.
 He's a fantastic singing teacher. I think he'll take me. But
 I have to sing . . . *(Tunes, then to Dolly)* I told you one of my
 friends auditioned for—the show you're seeing. *My Fair Lady.*
 And I've got a better voice than she does. *(Strums; to a worried
 Franny)* If you have to go.

FRANNY: No, I'm . . . I have time. How long do you—?

SALLY: You really want to hear it? Both of you? Really?

("Sure," "Yeah," etc., from the girls.)

I didn't know what to choose, then I thought a kind of jazzy—
 *(Starts to strum chords and begins to play and sing a slightly jazzy
 version of* Hernando's Hideaway *from* The Pajama Game.
 Sings:)

I know a dark secluded place
A place where no one knows your face
A glass of wine a fast embrace
It's called Hernando's Hideaway
Olé!

(The girls listen politely, without criticism. Sally smiles, strums louder as she gets more and more into it, even making castanet sounds on the face of her guitar with her fingernails.)

All you see are silhouettes
And all you hear are castanets
And no one cares how late it gets
Not at Hernando's Hideaway.
At the Golden Finger Bowl or any place you . . .

(She stops, feeling self-conscious. During the song, Grandma appears in the doorway, mostly dressed now. When Sally stops playing:)

GRANDMA: That's so good, Sally.
FRANNY: Terrific, Sal. Really. I'm sure that teacher's going to love it.
SALLY: You're just saying—
FRANNY: No. I mean it. I do. Ask Dolly. I have to go.
DOLLY: It was great.
FRANNY: I'll see you tonight. I'll be back tonight. *(Hurries out)*
GRANDMA: Where is she meeting . . . ?
DOLLY: Betty. I don't know. But she knows.

(Sally continues to pluck the guitar.)

SALLY *(To no one in particular)*: I love that song. It's so much fun.

(Franny bursts back in.)

FRANNY: Sal, the phone's ringing out there.

(We hear it in the hallway.)

What should I . . . ?

SALLY *(Handing Grandma the guitar)*: I'll get it.

(She follows Franny out into the hallway, leaving the door open. Franny goes.)

DOLLY: We have to go soon, Grandma.

(Sally picks it up, the phone stops ringing.)

You should get dressed, come on.

GRANDMA: I'm almost ready. *(Hands Dolly the guitar and heads for the bedroom. Stops)* I only heard the end, but that sounded . . . good. Did it to you?

DOLLY: It did. Grandma.

GRANDMA: It's nice to hear her sing.

(She goes into the bedroom. Outside a siren goes by. Sally hurries back in and runs to the window and shouts:)

SALLY: Franny!!! Franny!!!

GRANDMA *(From the bedroom)*: Is anything—?

SALLY: It's fine, Grandma. *(To Dolly)* She heard me. I know Franny heard me. She just didn't want to hear me. It was your father.

DOLLY: Father? What's wrong? Is something?

(Sally suddenly sees Dolly holding the guitar.)

SALLY: Don't touch that! Put that down! I just tuned it!

(Dolly, stunned, puts the guitar down.)

(Suddenly guilty) I didn't mean it that way. I didn't mean you couldn't touch it. I'll teach you to play a few chords, if you want. It's just that when someone doesn't know how to . . .

DOLLY: Sure. I'm not going to touch it.

SALLY: I didn't mean—!! *(Stops herself. Trying to be calm. She turns back to Dolly)* Do *you* know where she's meeting this guy? You know about the guy? Of course you do. Is he her boyfriend?

(No response.)

Grandma's going to have a fit. She's my responsibility. If you
come and stay with me, I think it's only fair . . .

DOLLY: How did Father find out about the guy?

(Sally looks at her.)

SALLY: Your stepmother found a letter in Franny's bureau.

DOLLY: What was she doing in Franny's bureau?!

SALLY *(Overlapping)*: I don't think that makes any difference now!

DOLLY: She shouldn't be in our rooms!

SALLY: He read me part of this letter! How this guy has a friend with
an off-campus apartment. How this friend is away this afternoon. How he's got the key, everything but the size of the bed!
Your father's so upset. She doesn't know what she's doing.
She's a kid.

DOLLY: I hate her. Not my sister.

SALLY: I don't know what to tell . . . *(Looks toward the bedroom)* Your
father's ready to get on a train.

DOLLY: He won't. He just says things like that. Maybe now they'll
stay out of our rooms.

SALLY: She's only seventeen. When I was seventeen—

DOLLY: You going to tell Grandma?

SALLY: Won't your father tell her when you get home?

DOLLY: I don't think anyone tells Grandma too much anymore.
(Short pause) My stepmother was looking for Franny's
diaphragm.

(Sally turns, confused, when she hears this.)

Last week she accused Franny of owning one. Franny denied
it of course.

(Sally suddenly laughs.)

SALLY: Where would Franny get a dia—?

DOLLY: But she brought it with her. So that's why she didn't find it.

(Grandma comes out with a sweater.)

GRANDMA: Will I need a sweater? Is it going to be like yesterday?

SALLY: It's going to be warm, Grandma.

(Grandma goes back into the bedroom to return the sweater.)

(To Dolly) So this—"guy." It's nothing special. Something she does all the time. Since she's got the diaphragm . . .

(Dolly shrugs.)

I'm sick. Just don't tell Phil. He's a real prude when it comes to certain things. It's the Midwest in him. And he still thinks of you girls—as kids.

(Grandma comes out, straightening herself.)

GRANDMA: You've got the tickets?

DOLLY: Yes, Grandma.

GRANDMA *(Not listening, to Sally)*: Phil gave us four tokens before he left for work this morning.

SALLY: He told me he was going to do that. You sure don't want to take a—? *("cab")*

GRANDMA *(To Dolly)*: What is so important about Gimbel's? Look at the mess we've left. We shouldn't leave you with—

SALLY: There is no mess. Please. Go. And have a wonderful time. I hear it's a terrific show.

GRANDMA *(To Sally)*: You think I look sophisticated enough for a Broadway show?

DOLLY: Good luck with the audition.

SALLY: What???

GRANDMA *(To Dolly)*: I don't want to look like I come from the boondocks.

DOLLY: The singing audition. To get into that—

SALLY: Oh right. Thanks! Bye!

GRANDMA *(To Dolly)*: You'd tell me if I didn't look right. Your Grandfather wouldn't, he'd let me—

(Door closes. They are gone. Silence. Street noise. Sally does not know what to do with herself. She fiddles with the guitar, starts to play, stops. She takes the guitar into her bedroom. She returns and begins picking up the apartment. Outside the window she hears children play-

ing. She goes into her bedroom and turns on the radio. Music plays.
She returns to get her cigarettes. Hears the children and goes to the
window to watch. As she sits on the sofa, Older Franny, still
dressed as Grandma, enters and speaks to the audience:)

OLDER FRANNY: I hadn't heard Sally call after me; or I if had, it hadn't
registered as anything more than one more sound among the
millions and millions of sounds which make up Sullivan Street.

(Sally lies back on the sofa and curls up.)

At the corner I waded into Bleecker, as one wades into any
fast-moving river, cautiously, but with pleasure, and hurried—if you can be said to hurry when you are watching
everything—toward the Riviera Café.

(Sally has fallen asleep.)

Our meeting spot. My boyfriend had sent me the address.
I expected to find him waiting, impatient, with a "why-are-
you-always-late" look upon his face. The kind that I could
only wash away—with a kiss. But he wasn't there, waiting for
me. *(Beat)* I took a table outside and ordered coffee. I think it
was the first time I ever ordered coffee in a restaurant.
I watched the people go by. The couples. The attractive young
men in their sleeveless summer shirts. I felt like you feel on a
beach with the waves breaking across your ankles, legs, thighs,
and then running away. That's how the people outside the
Riviera came and went. Like waves. I could sit here all day,
I said to myself. *(Beat)* There was a phone booth on the corner and the first two times I tried my boyfriend, his line was
busy. The third time he picked up. I've been waiting at the
Riviera, I said. Did I get the time wrong? *(Short pause)* You
see, he said in a rather—happy—voice, he'd met this girl, just
the weekend before, and he really wished he could tell me in
another way—I deserved that—and by the way, there's lots of
fun things I could do in New York by myself, did I want a list?
And hey, would I like to meet his new girl, she's real real nice,
and the two of us would really really get along, and to this day
I remember not so much what he said, but the smell in that

phone booth, a mixture of stale cigarette smoke, some half-eaten thing that had sat in the sun too long, and urine. Anyway, I hung up on my boyfriend, and threw up in the booth. Now if a teenage girl throws up in a phone booth in the middle of Millbrook, half of the town would be there to find out what was wrong and to tell your parents. Suffice it to say that in New York, or at least Greenwich Village, people are more respectful of your privacy. At least that's how I like to think of it.

I went back to my table and paid for my three coffees. I felt a little faint and found the bathroom—a tiny, dirty room with a hook to lock the door. I sat on the toilet seat, rubbed a wet towel across my face and tried to stop crying.

I think I did faint. But I guess I didn't hurt myself when I fell. Someone shouted through the door to see if I was all right. I suppose they'd heard this thud or something or maybe just my sobbing.

I left the Riviera intent on spending the rest of my one day in New York walking and seeing firsthand what I'd imagined a million times. But instead, I found myself walking the few blocks back to Sullivan Street, staring for who knows how long at the fire escape on the front of the building, which for all the world now looked like an insect climbing up, then walking up the three echoey flights of cold stairs, until I was back here.

(Door opens, Franny comes in, her clothes messy, her eyes red from crying. She stands in the doorway.)

Where I'd convinced myself I'd first change my tear- and vomit-stained clothes, but where I also knew, in my heart of hearts, I'd never leave for the rest of the day.

(Sally does not stir. She is asleep on the couch. Franny now notices her.)

I'd expected to find the apartment empty, which is why Sally'd given me my own key.

(She sets the key on the table.)

But it wasn't. Sally was still there, still in her nightclothes, curled up on the sofa, asleep.

(Franny hears music playing from a radio in the other room. She watches Sally for a moment.)

What I didn't know then, and wouldn't know for years, was that Sally had had no intention of going out that day. Just as she'd had no intention of going out the day before or the day before that. Just as she'd no intention of ever leaving her apartment again.

(She watches Sally.)

And this is how she'd spent every day, since the death of her baby. *(Beat)* At the time though, I knew none of this. At the time, I thought only about how much I hurt. And how much I needed a bed to cry on.

(Franny goes into the bedroom, closing the door.)

SCENE 4

Middle of the afternoon.
   The radio is still on in the bedroom, though a different song is heard. The street noise has a different quality—slower, easier than in the morning. Hallway door opens, Phil enters carrying a couple bags of groceries. (He does all the shopping, chores, etc., since Sally no longer leaves the apartment.)
   Sally is still asleep, curled up on the sofa. She stirs when he closes the door, but does not wake up. Phil takes the bags to the kitchen table and begins to unpack. Throughout the entire scene the music plays on the radio in the bedroom.

SALLY *(Waking up)*: What's . . . ? *(Sees Phil)* What time is it?
PHIL *(Putting groceries away)*: About four in the afternoon.
SALLY: Anyone . . . ? *("else here")*

(Phil shakes his head, then:)

PHIL: I see you haven't even gotten dressed.

(Short pause.)

SALLY *(Smiling)*: Come here. Come here. Sit with me.

(He ignores her.)

PHIL *(Unpacking)*: I got some nice chops for tonight. He trimmed
the fat off for me. I'm getting good at this. Look at these.
(Holds one up. She looks at the chop)
    (Finally): Have you even washed? Your grandmother's
here. Your cousins. What are you doing?!
SALLY *(Suddenly smiling, changing the subject)*: You want to hear
something about my little cousin—?

(He turns away.)

I was going to my audition!
PHIL: No you weren't.
SALLY: I was!! Don't you talk to me like that, you creep! *(Beat)* I was
going.

(He unpacks. She smokes.)

I don't sleep at night. I fell asleep. I must look a mess. *(Looks
at him)* You could say something. "No, honey, you don't look
a mess. You look sweet." "I love it when you just wake up."
"I love that little girl look you have then, I—" I remember,
Phil. Word for word. *(Looks at him)* He's even stopped listening. *(Big sigh. Then)* What was I—? My little cousin, Franny.
You know what she's doing right now? Little Franny's out
fucking some boyfriend. That's what all this was about. Her
wanting to come down here. See a college? Lies. *(Explaining)*
The stepmother up there—what's her name?—found a letter.
What the hell she was doing going through her stuff, I don't
know, but . . . Right now, in some crappy student apartment,
she's fucking him. Maybe even next door. *(Pretends to listen)*
Shh. *(Laughs)*

*(The door to Franny's bedroom has slowly opened a little. Neither
Phil nor Sally notices.)*

PHIL: Let her fuck, so what? What's wrong with that?

SALLY *(Suddenly)*: What's wrong with fucking? I don't know, Phil. You tell me.

(She looks at him. She gets up and looks at him across the kitchen table. She leans, nearly exposes her breasts.)

What is wrong with it?

(She tries to touch him, but it is clear he can't even touch her.)

What else besides the chops are we having for dinner?

PHIL: Mashed potatoes. String beans. I thought we'd go get Italian ices for dessert. The kids I thought would like that—

SALLY: What kids? Have you heard a word I said? I wouldn't call running off with   And she's got tits like—bigger than mine I suppose you like that. And she knows what she's got too. *(Beat)* So do you think she's attractive?

PHIL: Sally, what are you talking about?

SALLY: Is she the type you'd fuck?

(No response.)

You've got to be fucking someone, and it certainly isn't me.

PHIL: Don't be pathetic.

SALLY: A little late for that.

(He tries to ignore her.)

I should get dressed. After all, we have guests. *(Beat)* I was dreaming of our baby. That's the dream you woke me from. *(Trying to make a joke)* You should apologize for that. *(Then:)* That's why I woke up smiling. She was all right, you'd be happy to know. She was maybe three. She was running. And smiling. She could talk. I loved her little voice. When Dolly was three I used to babysit her, so maybe that's why . . . The spark. *(Beat)* Anna running through the park. Or maybe it was in the country. Grandma says Dad would help us get the house. Back home. I told her—I'm going to be an actress. I am an actress! I need to live here. I need all the city has to—

PHIL: So get out of the house.

(This stops her, then she tries to stay calm.)

SALLY: I will. *(Heads to the bedroom, stops in the doorway)* I'd expect
you to be a little more—understanding. We all have our
crutches . . . *(Beat)* Look at you, Phil. Sometimes I think we
need to look at you. You used to say going to church was for
your parents and other hypocrites and phonies. Remember
saying that?

PHIL: You've done this already, Sally.

SALLY *(Continuing)*: That you didn't need that crap. Real *thinking*
people saw through all—

PHIL: I went once! I shouldn't have told you.

SALLY: But you did. *(Forces a smile)* And now who's the hypocrite,
Phil? Who's the phony just like your parents? Who got on his
little knees and prayed: "Oh dear God, help me! Help me! Take
away these evil thoughts I have about doing harm to myself!"

PHIL *(Erupts)*: I shouldn't have told you!!

(Short pause.)

SALLY: That—was a reaction. Thank you.

*(She goes into the bedroom. Phil takes out a beer and opens it. In
the bedroom, Sally takes off her nightgown and puts on a skirt. She
comes back out, straightening the skirt. She is naked from the waist
up. She comes up to Phil, pretending to fix her skirt.)*

PHIL: Don't walk around like that in front of the window.

SALLY: Why? It's our home. *(Walks in front of the window)* Actually,
I seem to recall *you* saying something like that—to me. *(Half
to herself)* "Sal, it's our home. We can walk around any way
we want." *(To him)* I think this was right after your suggesting
I take off all my clothes. *(Teasing, trying to be seductive)* "You
mean, I don't have to wear . . . ?" And you put your finger to
my lips, and whispered: "You're home. You don't have to wear
anything." *(Beat)* "You don't have to wear that." And you
touched me. "Or that." "That." *(Looks at him, smiling)*
Remember? And we didn't close the shades either. *(Goes up to
him)* And *I* said: "You don't have to wear—"

PHIL: Get dressed, Sally. You want your grandmother to come home and find you like this?

SALLY: You mean, like I am? Like we are?

(He turns away. Sally approaches him from behind. She presses up against his back. She rubs her breasts against him, trying desperately to interest him. She reaches around to try and hold him. He is shaking his head. Gently he pushes her hands away. She reaches down and tries to touch his groin, he pushes her harder away. And she erupts. Suddenly she starts hitting him on the head and back, while at the same time trying to press her breasts against him, as if two contradictory impulses were happening to her—her anger and her need. Neither says anything or makes a sound. Sally just continues to hit—Phil makes little effort to protect himself—and press herself on him, touch him, get him to touch her: a grotesque moment of self-abasement. The door to Franny's bedroom suddenly closes. Phil and Sally stop when they hear the noise. Phil goes to the door and knocks. Nothing. As he reaches for the knob, the door opens—Franny is there.)

(To Franny) What are you doing here?!! *(Turns to Phil)* Did you know she was—? *(Covers her chest)*

PHIL: No.

FRANNY: I was—writing in my journal . . . *(Holds up her journal that she has been clutching)*

SALLY: How long have you been here?

FRANNY: I just got in.

(They stare at her.)

I was writing. In my journal. I just started. Excuse me.

SCENE 5

Early evening. In the dark, Grandma's voice calls out:

GRANDMA: Franny! Dinner!

(Franny opens the bedroom door. Grandma, Sally, Phil and Dolly are finishing setting the small kitchen table for dinner. They are talking as they finish up, taking their seats at the crowded table. Street noise from the window.)

(To Sally) Your father's even picked out one house.
SALLY: Which one? Do I know it? *(A glance at Phil)*
GRANDMA: On Chestnut. The white one with the gables?
SALLY: What happened to the couple who—?
GRANDMA: He's retired. And the stairs are too much.
SALLY *(To Phil)*: Remember that house? I drove you by it—
GRANDMA *(At the same time)*: And they have a son in Baltimore, so they're thinking—
SALLY: How did Father know it'd—?
GRANDMA: Did you ever talk to him about it?
SALLY *(To Phil)*: I didn't. I swear. Anyway, we're staying here.

(Franny has slowly moved to the table.)

FRANNY: Where am I supposed to—
SALLY: Get a chair and push in. This isn't formal. *(Laughs to herself. To Franny)* You didn't hear us setting the table?
FRANNY: I—

(Everyone is digging in, passing the food, commenting: "Dig in." "Looks great." "These chops are so lean." "Phil had them cut off the fat. He's a good shopper," etc., while Franny drags out a chair to the table and sits, squeezing in. Out of this innocuous table conversation comes:)

SALLY: Phil was saying when we were making dinner— Tell them.
  (Reaches over and touches his hand)
PHIL: About?
SALLY *(Smiles to everyone)*: Work today. Your guest.
GRANDMA: What??
PHIL: An important writer came to the office today. It's a publishing office so how strange is that? *(Laughs. No one else does)*
GRANDMA: Who was the writer?
PHIL: I don't think you'd—
SALLY: Tell them.

PHIL: Edmund Wilson. Do you know . . . ? *(No one does)* He's . . . fat. *(Laughs)* Mr. Farrar and Mr. Cudahy were showing him around. We had to almost stand at attention. The three of us in publicity. He won't give interviews. He won't promote his books at all. He even showed us a little card he hands out that says: "I won't give interviews. I don't give autographs. I don't—whatever." He seemed to think that was clever. *(Beat)* And I suppose maybe it is—to anyone except the some-one whose job it is to promote his damn books. *(Takes a bite of food)* He's a good writer though. Worth the trouble. That's what I'm told.

(Pause. They eat. No one is interested in Phil's story, but he continues.)

He'd sold his new book to another publishing house— Doubleday. So they were trying to woo him back. That's what it was all about. I learned this . . . *(Short pause)* Anyone want to know any more about it?

(No response.)

GRANDMA *(Turns to Franny)*: How was your tour of the college?
SALLY: Yes, let's hear about that.
GRANDMA: Did you like it?
FRANNY: Sure.
GRANDMA: You met up with your friend all right?

(Sally looks at Franny.)

FRANNY: I did.
GRANDMA: She was helpful?
FRANNY: She was.
SALLY: Tell us what you liked most about the college.

(Franny looks at the others, then:)

FRANNY: The library's neat. I liked that.
SALLY: You liked the library. Spend much time in the library with your friend?

FRANNY: Enough. But she has a lot of studying to do, so that's why—as you both know—I came back early. *(Takes a bite)* So how was *My Fair Lady?* I haven't heard a—

GRANDMA: We've talked about that. Dolly will tell you later—

SALLY: Tell her now. She should know just what a little conniving sister—

PHIL: Stop it.

SALLY *(To Franny)*: Your sister planned, it appears, a little more than a trip to a show. They're in Gimbel's, she and Grandma and . . . *(Turns to Grandma who says nothing)* They're looking at sweaters? It was sweaters, right?

GRANDMA: Yes.

SALLY: And suddenly Dolly looks at her watch. Oh my God, she says, let's go to the perfume counter. Why? says Grandma. You want to look at sweaters, don't you? But Dolly nearly drags Grandma to the perfume counter. The clock strikes twelve and guess who is waiting there?

FRANNY: Mom.

(Reaction from the others.)

SALLY: She knew. She's a part of this. *(To Grandma)* I told you this.

FRANNY *(Over this, to Dolly)*: Was she alone or did she—

DOLLY: Alone.

SALLY: She wouldn't have the guts to bring him. Isn't it enough to— And what's Grandma supposed to do?

GRANDMA: She was made up like a—

DOLLY: She looked beautiful.

FRANNY: I'm sure she did. How long were you with her at the perfume counter, Dolly?

GRANDMA: A couple of minutes.

FRANNY: Oh.

SALLY: Then they had lunch.

FRANNY *(Amazed)*: Together? I didn't know you were going to have—

DOLLY: Mom bought us lunch.

FRANNY *(To Grandma)*: Yours, too, Grandma?

(Grandma shrugs as if to say: "What could I do?" Franny starts laughing.)

SALLY: What's funny?

PHIL *(To join in)*: Where'd you eat?

DOLLY *(Looking at Franny)*: Some place called—Dempsey's??—

SALLY *(Over this, to Franny)*: And she went to the show, too. Little
miss arranger had worked everything out.

(This gets Franny laughing again.)

She'd sent away—

FRANNY: Who paid for—?

DOLLY: Dad.

(A burst of laughter from Franny.)

But Mom's paying him back.

SALLY: He won't take money from her.

DOLLY *(To her sister)*: We had seats together. Mom sat next to me.
She misses us so much, Franny.

(Franny stops laughing.)

SALLY *(After a quick glance at Phil; to Franny and Dolly)*: What that
woman did to your father. You don't treat a husband like that.

PHIL: She fell in love.

GRANDMA: I think it's best if we don't say a word about this to their
father.

(Short pause. Franny stands, taking her plate to the counter.)

PHIL: You're done? You haven't eaten—

FRANNY: I'm not hungry. *(Looks to Dolly)*

SALLY *(Eating)*: Your first time in New York. And you arrange tick-
ets, lunch, a meeting with— We're going to have to watch her,
Franny. She's sneaky. *(To Phil)* Think of the position she put
Grandma in. What could she be thinking?

PHIL *(Eating)*: That she wants to see her mother. That's all she's—

SALLY: That woman's a whore.

(Dolly gets up and takes her plate to the counter, joining her sister.)

(To Grandma) And I'm serious, you're really going to have to keep an eye on Dolly. If this is how— Lying to us. Stealing—

PHIL: What did she—? *("steal")*

SALLY: Money for the theatre tickets, from her father . . .

DOLLY *(To Sally)*: Mom's paying that back.

SALLY *(Continuing)*: . . . money for a trip that was supposed to be about—something else. I know we're not that much older than those two, Grandma, but that only means we *(Phil and I)* remember what it's like. At their age. So there are problems, but you have to control yourself. That's what growing up means, girls. *(Back to Grandma)* Aren't I right? *(Grandma hesitates, then nods)* This is for your benefit, girls, please. I'm not trying to be mean. *(To Phil)* Am I?

PHIL: No.

(Sally reaches over and touches Phil's hand. He eats. To Grandma:)

I remember sitting with their *(Franny and Dolly's)* father—he took me into his study—after their mother had left. I felt sort of flattered that he chose me, though maybe he was talking to anyone. *(Laughs)* But I was flattered. And all he talked about was how much he loved those two girls.

(Grandma nods.)

How they're his life. His two daughters.

SALLY *(To Phil)*: I don't think he talked to everyone. I think he chose you. Just like *my* father chooses to confide in you. *(To Grandma, explaining)* When we visit? You raised two great sons, Grandma. How did you do it?

GRANDMA: Luck, I suppose— *(Laughs to herself)*

SALLY: What?! *(Looks to Phil, then back to Grandma)* Tell us what's funny.

GRANDMA: Those two boys always weren't so good.

SALLY *(A little too excited)*: My father?!! Oh!!

(She laughs, then suddenly turns to Franny and Dolly at the counter:)

Listen to this, girls. Grandma's going to tell us about our fathers—when they were boys.

(Franny and Dolly don't move.)

GRANDMA: They were—wild boys.

(Big whooping laugh and clap of the hands from Sally. Smile from Phil.)

Now they're—the two most straightlaced men you'd find—anywhere.

(Franny and Dolly certainly agree with this.)

But—
SALLY: Didn't they fight a lot as boys?

(Clearly Sally has heard these stories before.)

GRANDMA: Fight? They were at each other's throats.

(Laughter from Sally.)

I remember—
SALLY *(Excited, to Phil)*: Here comes a Grandma story. *(Touches Phil's hand again)*
GRANDMA *(To Phil and Sally, sincerely)*: You are such a wonderful couple. *(Quickly continuing)* When Edward won that red bicycle in the grocery store contest. Robert was beside himself.

(Sally looks back to the girls on "Robert." Clearly Robert is the girls' father.)

"Thou shalt not covet thy brother's bike." Isn't that one of the ten commandments?

(Laughter. Grandma obviously isn't that funny, but she's getting a great response from Sally. Lights begin to fade. Franny and Dolly remain at a distance, stone-faced.)

Anyway—he "borrowed" it— And there he is riding his brother's bike, coming down a gravel hill, and he tries to turn— I can still see Edward's face. I've never seen something *that* red . . .

(Franny and Dolly watch from a distance.)

SCENE 6

Later that night. Jazz music is heard coming from the window. It will play throughout the scene. The room is mostly dark, only a single light is on. Franny and Dolly are alone together. Dolly is holding a letter. Franny sips a beer.

DOLLY: She's so beautiful. I guess I forgot that. After two years you forget. When I was nearly at the perfume counter—
FRANNY: Dragging Grandma.
DOLLY *(Smiles)*: Yeah. And she came around—
FRANNY *(Trying not to sound interested)*: What was she wearing?
DOLLY: Dark blue dress, with a white print. With straps, little cape. The dress went right below the knee. A funny, wonderful little hat, she wore angled. Mom can wear things that other people . . . Gloves.
FRANNY: White?

(Beat. Dolly shakes her head.)

Dark blue?

(Dolly nods.)

DOLLY: You going to open it? *(The letter)*

(Franny ignores her.)

She didn't seem—
FRANNY *(Interrupting)*: What?
DOLLY: I mean after what we'd been told— She seemed to— She started crying, Franny. *She* started . . .

FRANNY: Mom cries easily.
DOLLY: Does she?

(Beat.)

FRANNY: Yeah. It means nothing.
DOLLY: I thought Grandma was going to have a heart attack.

(Franny smiles.)

I think it took her half an hour before she realized that I'd . . .
You know—
FRANNY: That you hadn't just run into—
DOLLY: Yeah.

(They both laugh, then silence.)

Open it. It's to you.

(Franny hesitates, then takes the letter and opens it. Finds a photo, looks, then has to close her eyes—the emotion is too great.)

How old are you there?
FRANNY *(Suddenly)*: You know I don't believe a word she says. And
you shouldn't either. She's only going to hurt you. If she had
wanted to see us—
DOLLY: She said she's tried. She's had a lawyer try. She's even called
Father and begged—
FRANNY: I can't imagine Mother begging for anything. Certainly
not for us. *(Starts to put the picture and the unread letter back in
the envelope)* This was a mistake Dolly—
DOLLY: She asked why we didn't answer any of *her* letters.
FRANNY: What letters?
DOLLY: She's written tons of letters—to both of us, she said.
FRANNY: And you believe her?! Oh Dolly!

(Short pause.)

DOLLY *(Picking up the Playbill of* My Fair Lady*)*: I can't even
remember the show. As soon as the lights went down, I guess

so Grandma couldn't see or do anything to stop us, Mom reached over and took my hand and held it in hers.

(She hands Franny the Playbill. *Franny looks through it.)*

Then she pulled it to her, and pressed it against her chest. Then she kissed it. I put my head against her shoulder. She stroked my head. She touched my cheek. I looked up at her. We cried through the whole play. *(Beat)* At the intermission, Mom went outside to smoke a cigarette. Grandma tried to buy me some candy, but I just followed Mom. Grandma said something about how: "You haven't given up that awful habit, have you, Jennifer?" The cigarettes.

(Franny nods. She understands.)

Grandma wanted me to go inside with her, but I wouldn't. Then Mom snapped open her purse—I remember the purse— with thin gold stripes and a gold band—

FRANNY: I don't remember the purses. *(Tries to laugh)*

DOLLY: And took out a photo. And said here, Dolly, this is "my man." *(Short pause)* That's what she said, called him—"my man." Grandma made this awful sound and sort of ran away— for an instant, 'cause she was back in a second, but not before I had a chance to look . . . Back inside, she slipped it into my hand, and I hid it in my program.

(Franny realizing, shoves the Playbill *back at her. Dolly opens it and takes out the photo of their mother's lover.)*

Here he is.

FRANNY: I don't want to see—

DOLLY: Look, Franny.

FRANNY *(Erupts)*: I don't want to see—"her man!" Get it away from me!

(She pushes the photo away. Hallway door opens and Sally enters, having used the bathroom.)

SALLY: I'm done. Thank God I sneaked in there before Franny, or— *(Smiles)* But I learned my lesson there.

(Franny ignores her, so she smiles at Dolly as if it was Dolly she'd been speaking to.)

DOLLY *(To say something)*: Think what I go through at home.

SALLY: You must have the patience of a saint.

DOLLY: Thank you. I think I do.

(Sally moves toward her bedroom.)

FRANNY *(To Sally)*: Can I go down to that— *("jazz")*

SALLY: No. The night's over for you, young lady. And for all of us as soon as Grandma and Phil get back from their walk. It's . . . *(Starts to look for the time, then:)* And besides, I'd have thought after your day, you'd be very very tired. *(Forces a smile. Then half to herself as she heads for the bedroom)* When I was seventeen, I didn't even know what a diaphragm was!

(Sally goes into her bedroom.)

DOLLY: She knows about— Father called—

FRANNY: I heard—

DOLLY *(Over this)*: They'd found a letter, about how you were going to meet—

FRANNY: So what? Does Grandma know—?

DOLLY: I don't think she told her—

FRANNY: I don't care what they think. They're idiots. They are complete phonies. *(Beat)* And so is Mom.

DOLLY: That's not true.

FRANNY: How did she know about my dia—? *(Seeing Dolly's guilty face)* Forget it. *(To herself, mumbling)* Father and his bitch. *(Suddenly, hits the chair or sofa)* Shit!

(Beat.)

DOLLY: And Mom is not a phony.

FRANNY: Believe what you want.

DOLLY: And by the way—she did say that she'd seen me in the play.

FRANNY: What??

DOLLY: The play I was in. She saw it.

FRANNY: No she didn't. She didn't even know about you being in the—

DOLLY: I told her about it. I called her and—

FRANNY: You called her? Mom? When? You didn't have her number—

DOLLY: I had gotten it out of Dad's desk. There's a—divorce file. You know Father, he's so— *("organized")*. I knew it was there. And I found it and I called her and I told her because I thought she'd really really want to know that I got the part of the young girl in *Our Hearts Were Young and Gay*. I thought she'd really want to know about my costume. Because she always made our costumes with us for Halloween. So . . .

(Franny just watches her sister, who is close to tears.)

And she couldn't wait to see me in the play, she said. I didn't ask her, I didn't make her, it's just what she said. *(Beat)* And then she wasn't there.

FRANNY *(Smiles)*: Yeah.

DOLLY: But she *did* come. And she asked me if I liked her flowers. I never got any flowers. Did I?

FRANNY: I don't remember any. What do you mean Mom was there?

DOLLY: Remember the little boy playing the steward on the ship? And how he came on stage all proud and was supposed to be saying: "All ashore who's going ashore!" but instead shouted: "All aboard who's going ashore." And then cried? *(Beat)* Mom said that was her favorite part. I hadn't said anything about it, she told me . . . Her favorite—except of course for me. *(Smiles. Short pause)* How could she have known—?

FRANNY: Father probably told—

DOLLY: They don't talk!

FRANNY: You believe her?

(Dolly nods.)

That she was there?

DOLLY: In the back, so Father—

FRANNY: So no one could see— *(Stops herself)* You never got any flowers. They were probably never sent—

DOLLY: When we left today—and we were hugging. Again I thought Grandma was going to die, but . . . We're hugging and she says how much she loves me. And you. And then she said . . .

(Franny waits and listens.)

—her last words today were— She said: "Don't trust your father."

(Pause. The jazz plays in the distance.)

How was *your* afternoon?
FRANNY: Great. We pretty much wore out my diaphragm.
DOLLY: Is that what happens? They wear out?

(Sally enters in a robe, and goes to the couch to read a magazine. She turns on a lamp, then suddenly realizes.)

SALLY: Oh I know what you two have been doing.
FRANNY: What?
SALLY: You little snoops.
DOLLY: What are you talking about?
SALLY: You've had the lights out.

(They look at her, confused.)

So you can spy on . . . *(Nods toward the window)*
FRANNY: At what?
SALLY: Aren't they there? *(Looks out the window)* Across the street. One floor higher. They often "forget" to close their shades. *(Looks at the girls. A statement)* You haven't seen them. So what have you been looking at?
DOLLY: We haven't been looking at—
FRANNY *(Same time)*: What is she talking about?
SALLY: A couple. About Phil's and my age. They walk around— without—anything. Right past the window. One, then the other. Sometimes one'll run past, then he'll hurry behind her. Then you don't see them for a while. *(Looking)* I figure off to the left—that's their bedroom. They have a bathroom, I think. And to get to that they must have to pass . . . *(Beat, looking out)* That's the—study or whatever. They've got a TV. You see the blue light sometimes. I've seen him sit—there's a chair. When he sits you can see his arm. Sometimes I think she sits with him or—on him. All you see is his arm, and her, like— *(Gestures)*.

You sort of imagine what they're doing. *(Beat)* Maybe they're just watching TV. Maybe they're talking politics. *(Smiles)* But that's not what it looks like—with the arms. Once his arm was like— *(Turns her back to them)*, and hers—turned the other way *(Facing the girls)*, and it's—lower, so she's, and at a certain moment, they held hands . . . *(Beat)* You two probably don't understand, but you will when—

FRANNY: You're imagining that she's sucking him off.

(Short pause.)

SALLY: That's correct. *(Looks at Franny)* Don't think you can shock me. You can shock your grandmother. You can shock your father, but I see right through you. I see who you are—*and* who you think you are. And there's a real big discrepancy, my dear. *(Pause. Looks out the window. Smiles to herself)* Sometimes, I think they look at us. We often—forget to close the curtain. And we walk around—Philip and me, like . . . I don't know when I've last worn pajamas or a nightgown. And Philip of course wears nothing. *(To Franny)* I'm sorry if this—

FRANNY: If this what??!!

SALLY: I mean—you two are just kids. *(Smiles. Notices the beer on the floor next to Franny)* Is that a beer you have? Did Philip give you that?

FRANNY: I took it myself.

(Sally nods, thinking.)

SALLY: I remember when I was your age, sneaking my first drink—

FRANNY: It's not my first—

SALLY *(Over this, to Dolly)*: Swallowing it really fast I thought I was so neat. So grown-up. I wasn't going to listen to what anyone said, I felt I could do what I wanted. Then the room started spinning, and then there was my father holding my head over the toilet bowl as I barfed up my guts. *(Laughs)* It's not easy growing up. I know. Believe me, Franny, I know all about it. I've been there. *(There is nothing to say. Finally she looks toward the door)* How long are Grandma and Phil going to be out?

(No response.)

I think I'll read in our bedroom. *(Picks up her magazine)* Goodnight, Dolly. *(Looks to Franny, but decides not to get too close)* Goodnight Fran. I mean—"Franny." That's so cute. *(Goes into her bedroom)*

FRANNY: What a cow.

DOLLY: She's OK. She's gone through a lot.

(Franny picks up her beer and takes a sip.)

FRANNY: Want some?

(Dolly nods. She takes a sip.)

Want your own?

(Dolly nods. Franny goes to the refrigerator, takes out another beer, opens it, hands it to Dolly and lights a cigarette. Then:)

I hate her guts.

DOLLY *(Picking up Franny's letter)*: You going to read this?

(Franny ignores her, then looks out the window.)

FRANNY: Someone's turned on the lights over there.

DOLLY: You know she *(Sally)* told Grandma and me this incredible dream she had. This morning when you were in the bathroom, she told us about what she dreamed last night?

(Franny just nods and continues to watch out the window, sipping her beer and smoking. Jazz plays off.)

She dreamed she'd just moved into a new town. Her family had moved— She was a kid, and they had a dog which they brought with them? And as soon as they moved in, the dog died. *(Beat)* And her father—I think he says something like, let's not take it to the vet, that's just a waste of money. So she's given the job to bury the dog. But then a neighbor, a new neighbor, because they just moved in and didn't know anybody yet, says that if she buries it, it'll only smell up the place, so he says she should cremate it. "What's cremate?" she asks.

FRANNY: She didn't know what—?
DOLLY: In her dream. She's that young.

(Franny nods.)

"Burn it," he tells her. So she pours gasoline over the dog and lights a match. *(Beat)* And as the dog goes up in flame—it starts to howl and scream something awful. She even mimicked what it sounded like. *(Tries to demonstrate)* I can't do it like she did.

(Franny now turns to Dolly, fascinated.)

So she runs inside and gets her dad's .22, hurries out and chases around this dog that's on fire and shoots it. Well all the neighbors are out now and watching, and everyone is horrified at what this girl's done—set a dog on fire and then shot it. And she knows that as long as she lives in this new town, that's what people will think of her. That's how she'll forever be known. *(Beat)* That's it. That was her dream. Amazing? You know the essay I have to write this summer about "a real interesting character"? Well . . . *(Gestures toward Sally)* It's going to write itself.
FRANNY: I think she's pathetic.
DOLLY: She lost her baby, Franny.
FRANNY *(Shrugs)*: So get over it.

(The hallway door opens: Grandma and Phil return from their walk. She is very tired, he holds her by the elbow. Franny and Dolly hide the drinks and cigarette.)

PHIL: Sit down. I'll get you a glass of water.
FRANNY: What's—? *("wrong with Grandma")*
GRANDMA: I'm fine.
DOLLY: Sit down, Grandma.
FRANNY: Sit down.
PHIL: Your grandma's a little tired. It was a bit longer walk than she thought. And it's been a long day.
GRANDMA: I'm just sleepy. Really. What time is it?
PHIL: Nearly eleven.

GRANDMA: I never stay up this late. Where's——?

FRANNY: She's gone to bed.

PHIL: Her light's still on——

GRANDMA: Don't bother her. *(Yawns)* I should just go to—— *(Taking the glass of water)* Thank you.

(She sips. Tries to catch her breath. The others watch and say nothing. Feeling she is being watched:)

I'm not used to stairs.

SALLY *(Off)*: Grandma! Is that you?

PHIL: We're back!

GRANDMA: I should go and say goodnight to that beautiful wife of yours. *(Goes into Sally's bedroom)*

PHIL *(To Dolly)*: You should be getting to bed too, shouldn't you?

DOLLY: I'm not tired.

PHIL: What's that? *(Notices the beer)* Have you been——?

DOLLY: Maybe I will go to bed. Goodnight. Night. Goodnight, Franny. *(Kisses her)* Phil.

(He bends to kiss her, she tickles him and runs away.)

PHIL *(To Franny)*: What about you?

(Franny shakes her head.)

Never going to bed?

(Franny smiles and shrugs as Grandma comes out of the bedroom.)

GRANDMA: Remind me to buy her a nice nightgown for Christmas. I'll use the bathroom if that's——

(But before she can head there, Dolly runs out of their bedroom, carrying her nightgown and hurries into the hallway to use the bathroom.)

PHIL *(As Dolly runs off)*: Let your grandma——

GRANDMA: Maybe I'll get ready for bed first. I'll say my goodnights in a minute. *(Tries to smile and heads off)*

FRANNY: She looks exhausted.

PHIL: She was fine. Then all of a sudden about four or five blocks away, I thought she was going to fall down. We had to stop every few feet. That's why we we're . . .

FRANNY: Dolly put her through a lot today. *(Beat)* I think she thought she'd never see my mother again. And of course she has to be polite. Even—or maybe especially—when she hates someone, she has to be polite. That must be hard. *(Beat)* Not that I would know.

(Phil is picking up the room.)

PHIL: I don't think a fifteen year old should be drinking beers. *(Noticing the ashtray)* And smoking cigarettes.

(Beat.)

FRANNY: Who cares what you think?

(He takes the beer, then turns toward his bedroom.)

PHIL *(Noticing)*: She's turned off her light.

FRANNY: Better go to bed then.

(He continues to pick up. She listens to the jazz.)

You want to take me to that club?

PHIL: No.

FRANNY: I'm old enough.

PHIL: I know.

FRANNY: Then why not? *(Takes her beer back from him. Sips)*

PHIL *(Incredulous)*: What are you doing?

FRANNY: I didn't finish that. I want to go there.

(He looks at her, sipping her beer, a flirty pout on her face. He approaches her, and suddenly dives at her and tickles her. She tickles back. Dolly enters from the hallway, now in her nightgown, sees what is happening and runs to join in: "Get him! Get him! Not me, him!" "Stop! Stop!" Then as Phil is pushed off the sofa onto the floor:)

PHIL: I give up! I give up!
SALLY *(Off)*: Phil? Philip?

(Pause. They stop and listen.)

Phil?

(He gets up and goes into their bedroom. Muffled voices from the bedroom: "What are you doing out there?" "Nothing." "Aren't you coming to bed?" "In a few minutes.")

DOLLY *(To Franny)*: Don't forget the letter.

(Phil comes out of the bedroom, stopping at the doorway.)

PHIL *(To Sally in the bedroom)*: Would you like the door closed?

(We don't hear the answer, but Phil doesn't close the door. Turning back to the girls:)

(To Dolly, pointing) You—to bed.
DOLLY: Night. What about—?
FRANNY: I'm coming. Let Grandma use the bathroom first.
PHIL: Goodnight.

(Dolly goes off to her bedroom. Pause. Jazz plays.)

FRANNY: So you don't wear anything to sleep in?
PHIL: What??

(He looks at her. She smiles. Then she turns and looks out the window.)

FRANNY: They just turned their lights off.
PHIL: What are you talking about?

(She stares at him.)

(Finally) What hasn't my wife told you about?

(Dolly comes back out.)

DOLLY: Grandma's asleep. She hasn't used the bathroom. Should I wake—?

PHIL: Let her sleep.

FRANNY: Is she still in her clothes—?

DOLLY: No, she changed.

FRANNY: Good.

(Dolly starts to go back, stops.)

DOLLY: Franny, you can use the—

FRANNY: Thanks. I know. Goodnight.

(Dolly goes into the bedroom. Phil sips from Franny's beer.)

PHIL: "Franny." I think that's really neat, by the way. I've been meaning to say that.

FRANNY: What?

PHIL: Changing your name. Because of the Salinger story. I think it's an incredible story.

FRANNY: Me, too.

PHIL: Obviously or you wouldn't have—

FRANNY: Do you think she's pregnant or having a nervous breakdown? In the story. *(Beat)* Franny.

PHIL: I know. I—maybe it's both.

FRANNY: That's good. I hadn't thought of that.

PHIL: That's—what a lot of people think now. Anyway, it's a neat thing to do. If only my name were Zachary, then I could—

FRANNY and PHIL: —be called Zooey!

(They laugh. Short pause. Phil looks toward his bedroom, then:)

PHIL: You've read "Zooey"?

FRANNY: In the town library. The school library doesn't get the *New Yorker*—

PHIL: I wouldn't think—

FRANNY: And Dad forgot to get it in Poughkeepsie, when he went . . .

PHIL: I have a copy. But it's the only one—

FRANNY: No, no I—

PHIL: And it sold out in like— *(Snaps his fingers)*

FRANNY: I heard. Though not in Poughkeepsie.

(He smiles. An awkward pause.)

PHIL *(Finally)*: Lying in your bathtub, smoking cigarettes, talking to your mother, who's sitting there, smoking cigarettes. And she's a vaudevillian. To me—that's New York. That became New York. You try and think, so what is the difference between Ann Arbor and New York? I think of Zooey in the bathtub. I don't know why really. *(Smiles at her)* It seems so— I don't know. Sometimes this place can seem so scary. New York. *(Franny nods)* And sometimes it's like it just sort of wraps its arms around you. The sounds, people . . . *(Drifts off in thought, then)* You think you'll come here to go to school?

(Franny shrugs.)

What does your boyfriend say?
FRANNY: He's—begging me to come.
PHIL: I'm sure.

(Another pause. The jazz plays. Franny plays with the letter.)

(Noticing the letter): What's—?
FRANNY: From my mother. I haven't read it yet. *(Short pause)* What do you think he's going to write next? Salinger. *(Phil shrugs)* Could be a million things. There's so much we don't know about—the twins. Waker? In the conscientious objectors' camp? What's that about? I think what Salinger's got to do is start putting things together. Show how the Glass family fits together. Right now it's just—bits, fragments—
PHIL: Fantastic bits—
FRANNY: True. But I think he's only begun something . . . Something that is going to define our time.
PHIL: Huh.
FRANNY: I can't wait.
PHIL: Me, too. *(Beat)* I'm going to bed when I finish this.
FRANNY: Don't drink too fast.
PHIL: I won't.
FRANNY: Sip and you'll remain standing. Father's advice.

(Phil sighs, wipes the sweat off his forehead.)

Earlier this summer I was in a show at home. I was a flapper.
In the chorus. In my high school gym. Something to keep the
kids out of trouble. *(Smiles)* God was it hot in that gym. My
dress stuck to my backside. *(Looks down at her backside)* Kept
having to pull it off. In the middle of a dance. *(Not thinking
about what she is saying)* I don't know if I want to be in theatre
or not. Dolly wants to, but . . . I like books. I think I'm pretty
enough though.

PHIL: You are.

FRANNY: How's Sally doing with her acting? She doesn't seem to be
doing much work right . . . now . . . *(Realizes this is the wrong
thing to bring up)* I should go to bed. Goodnight.

*(She stands. Looks at Phil, then leans over and kisses him on the
cheek. As she does, he turns to her. And they kiss on the mouth. She
sits next to him, and they look at each other. She touches his face.
He looks her over. He suddenly gets up and closes his bedroom door
and turns off the lamp. He comes up behind her, touches her on the
shoulder. She looks up at him, and as she watches him she reaches
under her skirt and takes off her underpants. She puts her head
against his hand. He kisses the top of her head. She suddenly turns
and they kiss passionately. She rubs her hand across his chest and
unhooks his pants belt. Still kissing, she unzips his fly. Her hand is
in his crotch, his hands are up her skirt, under her blouse. When at
the height of this heavy petting, Phil suddenly breaks away.)*

PHIL: No. I can't. Franny, this isn't right. This is wrong.

*(He tries to get ahold of himself, breathes deeply. She watches him.
He zips up his pants, hands her her underpants. She watches. He
then takes her hand and squeezes it, and goes into his bedroom,
closing the door. Franny cries. She tries to get ahold of herself. She
turns on the lamp, notices the letter from her mother. This makes
her sob. She hides the letter under magazines and continues to cry.
Lights fade. Music fades.
Immediately lights come up and new, wilder jazz music plays
from the club on Bleecker. It is two hours later. Franny is still on
the sofa. She is awake and listening. She is crying, and can't sit
still, can't settle.)*

*From Phil and Sally's bedroom: the sounds of the couple mak-
ing love. As they approach climax, the noises/sounds/cries become
more and more violent, animal-like, and profound, as if something deep, painful, uncontrollable is being touched and released.
Franny listens, then stands and goes into her bedroom and closes
the door.)*

SCENE 7

*The next morning. Street noise is heard out of the window. Dolly is
packing in the bedroom.*

*In Phil and Sally's bedroom doorway, Sally, still in her robe, is fin-
ishing up* Hernando's Hideaway *on the guitar for Phil and Grandma,
who is at the sink cleaning up. Phil is getting dressed.*

SALLY *(Singing)*:
At the Golden Finger Bowl or any place you go,
You'll meet your Uncle Max and everyone you know.
But if you go to the spot that I am thinking of
You will be free
To gaze at me
And talk of love!

*(Franny enters from the hallway and goes into her bedroom to fin-
ish packing)*

Just knock three times and whisper low
That you and I were sent by Joe.

(Dolly enters with her suitcase.)

Then strike a match and you will know
You're in Hernando's Hideaway
Olé!

(Appreciative reaction from Phil and Grandma.)

He's a fantastic teacher. I think he'll take me.

GRANDMA: Of course he will . . .

SALLY *(To Phil)*: What do you think?

PHIL: I think you're good. I always have. He'd be a fool not to take you.

GRANDMA: I can't believe she hasn't played that for you, Phil.

(Franny comes out with her suitcase.)

SALLY: I didn't think he wanted to hear it.

GRANDMA: Of course he did. Phil loves to hear you sing. Did you hear what he said? What time is it?

SALLY: Oh God, the time!

PHIL: We're fine. There's—

SALLY: What time's their train?

GRANDMA: I better strip the bed.

(Grandma heads for her bedroom.)

SALLY: You don't have to do that. Phil?

PHIL *(Following Grandma)*: I'll do that, Marjorie.

(Phil sees Franny.)

FRANNY: We're packed.

GRANDMA *(As she enters the other bedroom)*: I love Sally's singing, don't you, Phil?

(Grandma begins stripping the bed.)

SALLY *(To the girls)*: Everyone slept so late. We slept so late. *(Smiles to herself)* There's no time for breakfast. I'm sorry—

FRANNY: Oh we're not hungry. Are we, Dolly?

(Dolly is hungry, but says nothing.)

She's fine.

SALLY: There's some bread from last night—

DOLLY: I don't want to miss the train. Dad's meeting the train.

SALLY *(Smiles at them, then)*: I wish you could stay longer. I really do. It's been really good having you here. And next time, *(To Franny)* we'll have that boyfriend of yours over for dinner, too.

(Phil brings out Grandma's suitcases.)

Phil was saying how he'd like to meet him.

(Phil hurries back into the bedroom.)

Grandma should tell you two about the house she went to see last night with Phil. He was telling me about it.

FRANNY: What house?

SALLY: It's just a few blocks away. Where she lived.

FRANNY: Where who lived?

SALLY: Our grandma.

PHIL *(Off)*: Sal, Marjorie's making the bed!

SALLY *(Heading for the bedroom)*: Grandma, I told you I'd make it!

DOLLY: In Greenwich Village? Grandma lived in Greenwich Village?

FRANNY: When was this?

(Sally has disappeared into the bedroom. Voices are heard off.)

DOLLY: I don't understand.

FRANNY: Me, too. I don't understand anything.

(Sally suddenly appears in the bedroom doorway.)

SALLY *(Back to Grandma)*: You think I should? Phil? Maybe I will. Maybe I'll come. *(Heads for her bedroom)* Is there time? I have to get dressed.

GRANDMA *(Coming out of the bedroom; to the girls)*: Sally's coming with us to the train station.

PHIL *(To Grandma)*: She's coming with us. She's getting dressed.

FRANNY: When did you live in Greenwich Village, Grandma?

GRANDMA: A million years ago.

FRANNY: You lived in New York City??

GRANDMA: I must have told you that. I don't want to be one of those old ladies who is always repeating themselves.

PHIL: They don't know. Tell them. They're interested.

SALLY *(Coming out of the bedroom, getting dressed)*: There's probably a lot you don't know about your grandma. Did you go inside? I meant to ask you that.

PHIL: I wanted to ring the bell.

GRANDMA *(To the girls)*: I remember leaning out the second-floor window of that house and watching the soldiers march down Fifth Avenue, on their way to war.

FRANNY: What war??

GRANDMA: Us girls waving our scarves. *(Winks at the confused Dolly)* Accidentally letting one go. Float down past the boys, to see if they would look up. And they did. *(Laughs)*

(Sally, listening, laughs maybe a little too hard from the other room. She is keyed-up.)

People were screaming. My husband, your grandfather was one of them. He says he probably marched right past me. But I never picked him out. There were so many boys.

DOLLY: How long did you live in New York City, Grandma?

GRANDMA: A whole year. Maybe a little more. While Grandpa was at war.

PHIL *(To Franny)*: The First World War.

GRANDMA: It's all changed now. It's all different.

(Short pause. Everyone is a little confused, then, explaining:)

The house. Where I used to live. I told you why I was sent to the city?

PHIL: You told me, Marjorie.

GRANDMA: It's incredible now that you think about it.

SALLY *(Off)*: I haven't heard this—

GRANDMA *(Continuing)*: But at the start of the war, your great-grandfather had to hire all these day workers for the farm. All these—men. There was a lot of pressure to grow things for the war effort. So he needed a lot of men? Whatever kind of men he could get. *(Smiles)* But he worried that maybe it wouldn't be right for me . . . So he sent me here! Sent me to New York.

(The girls look at her, incredulous.)

FRANNY: He sent you to New York City to be safe from men????

(Grandma nods.)

Incredible.

(They burst out laughing.)

GRANDMA *(Over the laughter)*: And it took my father a whole year
to figure out what he'd done! And did I have fun!

*(More laughter. Then Sally, now dressed to go out, comes out. Phil
and Grandma are nearly overcome with emotion.)*

SALLY: I'm ready, we should go.
GRANDMA: We have everything? We haven't forgotten anything?
FRANNY: I don't know.
GRANDMA: Let me just check . . . *(Heads back to the bedroom)*
SALLY *(Following her)*: If you did, we can always mail it—

(Phil hands a magazine to Franny.)

FRANNY: What's this?
DOLLY: What is it?
PHIL: An old copy of the *New Yorker*. With a wonderful story in it.
FRANNY: I can't take this. It's your only copy—
DOLLY: Let me see—
FRANNY: No, you'll rip it. *(Takes it)*
SALLY *(Coming back out with Grandma)*: What's that?
PHIL: Nothing.
FRANNY: The Salinger story—
DOLLY *(To Phil)*: Why are you giving *her* presents?
FRANNY: Because he likes me better!
DOLLY: He does, does he?

(Dolly grabs Phil and tickles him, he fights back, tickling.)

SALLY *(To anyone who will listen)*: I can't believe I'm taking you to
the train!
GRANDMA: Come on, girls. We're going to be late. Leave Phil alone.
Come. Pick up your bags.

(Sally suddenly joins in the tickling.)

We have to go. Phil, why don't you walk with your wife.

(They all continue to tickle as she pushes them out.)

Let's go. Girls, let's go. Girls!

(They go out into the hallway, still trying to tickle each other. Grandma stays behind, and again becomes Older Franny. She speaks to us:)

OLDER FRANNY: And so I went home that summer. And tried to finish my Victorian Yorkshire novel—with no success. And tried to forget a boy—with a good bit more success. And tried to find a much better hiding place for my diaphragm.

Nine months later, my cousin Sally and Phil had a new baby. They came up to show her off. Uncle Edward took them to see the house on Chestnut, and they never left.

I did read Mom's letter—a few billion times. Dolly, my clever little sister, organized an unescorted "shopping trip" that Christmas to New York City. We were to meet Mother in front of Saks. She appeared down Fifth Avenue, through a light snow, amidst the haze of the streetlamps, her fur collar framing—that beautiful face. Like a vision—that is how she appeared to me; and that is just about how real, sadly, she proved, to be. Dolly disagrees, and says I just should have spent time with her—like she did. *(Shrugs)* Grandma lived only another five years. Women, it has recently dawned on me, die young in my family.

And little Annie? The baby? She's buried in Queens. For a while there was talk of moving her to Millbrook. But that stopped years ago. I think she's been forgotten.

(Short pause. Street noise continues from out the window.)

As we get old, we start to see the— *(Searches for the word, then)* fragility of . . . well everything. *(Short pause)* But when we're young, thank God, we are oblivious.

(Suddenly Franny charges back into the room. From down the hall cries of: "Franny!" "We're going to miss the train!" "We can send it to you!" etc.)

FRANNY *(Shouting back)*: I'll just be a second!

(She looks around, then hurries to the sofa, desperately searching for something she's forgotten. The Older Franny watches. Young Franny flips over magazines and finds what she is looking for—her mother's letter. She sighs, folds it. Then she suddenly notices something else. Sticking out between the cushions in the couch: her underpants from the night before. She grabs them, looks around, doesn't know what to do. She tries to hide them on her body, then slides them inside the pages of the New Yorker she is carrying, smoothing down the pages, as she hurries out shouting:)

I'm coming!!!

(Older Franny looks out the window, as the street sounds continue: they are alive, music in the distance from Washington Square, cars, laughter, church bells, siren, and so forth.)

END OF PLAY

RICHARD NELSON's plays include (besides the five in this volume) *Rodney's Wife*, *Madame Melville*, *The General from America*, *Misha's Party* (with Alexander Gelman), *Columbus and the Discovery of Japan*, *Left*, *Principia Scriptoriae*, *Life Sentences*, *Between East and West* and *The Vienna Notes*. His adaptations include *Tynan* (with Colin Chambers, based on *The Diaries of Kenneth Tynan*); Jean-Claude Carrière's *The Controversy*; Strindberg's *Miss Julie* and *The Father*; Chekhov's *Three Sisters*, *The Seagull* and *The Wood Demon*; Pirandello's *Enrico IV*; Fo's *Accidental Death of an Anarchist* and Beaumarchais's *The Marriage of Figaro*. He has written three musicals—*James Joyce's The Dead* (with Shaun Davey), *My Life with Albertine* (with Ricky Ian Gordon) and *The House of Bernarda Alba* (with Michael John LaChiusa)—the screenplay for the film *Ethan Frome*, and the book *Making Plays* (with David Jones).

He has received numerous awards both in America and abroad, including a Tony Award (Best Book of a Musical for *James Joyce's The Dead*), an Olivier Award (Best Play for *Goodnight Children Everywhere*), Tony nominations (Best Play for *Two Shakespearean Actors*; Best Score as co-lyricist for *James Joyce's The Dead*), an Olivier nomination (Best Comedy for *Some Americans Abroad*), two Obies, a Lortel Award, a New York Drama Critics Circle Award, a Guggenheim Fellowship and a Lila Wallace-Reader's Digest Writers Award. He is an Honorary Associate Artist of The Royal Shakespeare Company, and lives in upstate New York.